JEFFREY B. FERGUSON

The Sage
of Sugar Hill

GEORGE S. SCHUYLER AND THE HARLEM

RENAISSANCE

YALE UNIVERSITY PRESS   NEW HAVEN & LONDON

Dedicated to the memory of my father
Theodore Watson
who was

Set in Scala and Scala Sans type by Duke & Company, Devon, Pennsylvania.
Printed in the United States of America.

Library of Congress Cataloging-in-Publication Data
Ferguson, Jeffrey B., 1964–
    The sage of Sugar Hill : George S. Schuyler and the Harlem Renaissance / Jeffrey B. Ferguson.
        p.   cm.
    Includes bibliographical references and index.
    ISBN 0-300-10901-6 (alk. paper)
    1. Schuyler, George Samuel, 1895– 2. Harlem (New York, N.Y.)—Intellectual life—
20th century. 3. African Americans—Intellectual life—20th century. 4. Novelists, American—
20th century—Biography. 5. Conservatives—United States—Biography. 6. Journalists—
United States—Biography. 7. African American journalists—Biography. 8. African American
novelists—Biography. 9. Harlem Renaissance. I. Title.
    PS3537.C76Z66 2005
    813'.52—dc22

                                        2005005779

A catalogue record for this book is available from the British Library.

10 9 8 7 6 5 4 3 2 1

CONTENTS

FEW CONCEPTS APPEAR MORE deserving of satirical treatment than race. Yet very few American writers have devoted themselves to the task. Mark Twain, Herman Melville, H. L. Mencken, and Sinclair Lewis stand out on this account among white canonical authors. Among black writers, from whom one might expect great enthusiasm for derisive ridicule of racist thought, Wallace Thurman, Rudolph Fisher, Ralph Ellison, Ishmael Reed, and Charles Johnson provide the best-known examples. One might quibble a bit with this particular selection of authors, but adding or subtracting a few would do little to alter the main point. For the most part the American discourse on race has provided a stronghold for sincerity, melodrama, sentimentalism, and deep seriousness, but it has admitted the spirit of irony and humor only with the greatest discomfort and trepidation.

For George S. Schuyler, who devoted a large portion of his career as a black journalist and novelist from the early 1920s to the late 1970s to a thoroughgoing satire of the race concept, this discomfort indicated a telling weakness. In his view the facts of American race relations reduced to a dynamic of wholesale cultural and biological intermixture made even more powerful in some ways by repression and denial. According to Schuyler, this granted the ironist clear advantages of insight over the moralist, who tended to ground his or her antiracist appeal in stale rules and regulations that every racist enjoyed violating. Schuyler also rejected the gradualist and the conformist, both of whom believed that blacks had to become more like whites to demonstrate their qualification for the fruits of American democracy. He believed that black and white Americans shared the same fundamental values and the same cultural shortcomings. Although he protested mightily against unjust racial practices, Schuyler also challenged the protester, whose need to cast blacks as victims had both utility and debilitating effects when taken to extremes.

Schuyler's keen challenge to the moralist, the gradualist, the conformist, and the protester—combined with his fifty-five-year career as a prominent black journalist—would in itself make him a good subject for a critical book about American race relations. But his use of the satirical mode as a means to this end really sets him apart among American intellectuals in general and among black American intellectuals in particular. Rather than simply advocate open intellectual, cultural, social, and biological mixture of the races, Schuyler fashioned a satirical style that employed racial transgression as an inherent feature of intellectual practice. His social and cultural ideal, which conflicted in every way with the sentimental dreams of those who desired uninterrupted harmony at the table of interracial brotherhood, involved a confrontational and sometimes violent process of interchange among individuals, groups, and the ideas that they represented. In the process of advancing his turbulent and in many ways contradictory alternative solution to the "Negro problem," Schuyler criticized, cajoled, and dismissed almost everyone in his era—white and black, conservative and radical, racist and antiracist—who had anything of significance to say about the race question. He did this mainly for the black audience of the *Pittsburgh Courier,* whose assumptions about race he challenged, almost always with a laugh, for four decades. This fact alone speaks volumes concerning the diversity of discussion among blacks, which our treatment of American intellectual history has only begun to recognize. In his most becoming guise, Schuyler symbolizes this diversity even as he challenges the liberal values that stand behind the celebration of diversity for its own sake.

I first encountered George Schuyler's unique approach to the race question in an introductory black literature course in the early 1980s. At the time Schuyler's raucous satire *Black No More* (1931)—which told the story of a treatment that allowed blacks to turn white—was something of an experimental choice. Although more than fifty years had passed since its publication, the brilliant absurdist humor of Schuyler's satire still seemed somewhat ahead of the pace of Black Studies, then a young and embattled field still more in need of heroes than iconoclasts. Also, Schuyler's reputation as a prominent archconservative and anticommunist, established during the second half of his career, from the late 1940s until the 1970s, contributed further to his exclusion. In fact, for the few people in the field who knew about him, he seemed the closest approximation of a black poster child for all the wrong causes. In this spirit the introduction to the 1971 edition of *Black No More* that we used for class (written by Charles R. Larson) sincerely discouraged the reader from contaminating her mind with Schuyler's caustic sacrilege.

In the context of the early 1980s, with most Black Studies professors involved in one way or another with a long series of struggles—from South African divestment to affirmative action to multiculturalism to the civil rights backlash of the so-called Reagan Revolution—the field had something of a "circled wagons" character, even as it struggled to expand its theoretical, ideological, and substantive range. The prevailing perception of threat, rooted in the fear that earlier gains might be lost, made talk of loyalty and disloyalty so prominent in the field that even as a student I found it palpable. I also found such talk, and the battles that formed around it, a bit confusing. A threatened and embattled area of study required some loyalty, I thought, but I could not make up my mind concerning what this meant. I also worried that excessive constraints on intellectual freedom might render the study of black Americans static and stale when thriving meant propagating in all directions, even in the ones that appeared dangerous at the time. My reservations notwithstanding, this last thought granted creative disloyalty a decidedly positive valence in my emerging list of intellectual values—and this made *Black No More* a fantastically liberating and cathartic reading experience.

Among the several books I had read at the time from the Harlem Renaissance, nothing came close to the irreverent force of Schuyler's satire. Unlike the authors of these other books, I thought, Schuyler could genuinely laugh—and make me laugh—at the many ridiculous dilemmas of race in America. While I had known something of this comic ability to exist among ordinary blacks, I had never encountered it in a black intellectual. Although I would not have articulated it this way then, I was in my own way reacting against the overwhelming weight of representativeness that made black thinkers adopt styles of self-representation that would confer a kind of standardized dignity on the group. This imperative severely narrowed the field for independent forms of self-fashioning among black thinkers. As an aspiring black intellectual, and as a college junior addicted to independence, I considered this a negative constraint that did not bode well for my own hopes and dreams. Therefore the example Schuyler offered as a black intellectual who had rejected the prevailing mood of seriousness and sincerity among his peers struck me as something of a revelation. It seemed significant not because Schuyler always laughed at the ideas or people that I would have imagined myself laughing at; indeed, I regarded some of his targets as mistakes. Still, the sheer fact that he laughed, and did so with such consistency and self-possession, made him a unique figure in my mind, one of those rare people who did not sound or act like anyone else.

Years of subsequent research in graduate school and beyond have added a great deal of detail to the basic picture of Schuyler that I formed as an undergraduate, but the main theme remains essentially the same. This book presents Schuyler as a centrally important twentieth-century black intellectual and as an essentially liberating figure for his unique application of satire to the race question. Although it does not shy away from pointing out the satirist's most flamboyant moments of nearsightedness, farsightedness, and outright blindness, the book's central concern remains the complex intellectual and political commitments that make Schuyler irreducible to such one-word descriptions as socialist, conservative, amalgamationist, integrationist, or antiessentialist. In his effort to fashion and project a unique black American identity, he took pleasure in playfully pitting such typical categories against one another. At different points in his career he embraced almost all of them, especially the ones he found useful in disputing what he regarded as the narrow racially motivated standard of his average reader.

In its fundamentals this book stands as an act of recovery. As such it reveals many previously unknown facets of Schuyler's life and works. Still, it does not aspire to the work of a full biography. Instead, the volume explores the most important strain in Schuyler's thought and focuses most heavily on the years in which that strain received the broadest and deepest expression in his published works. In the following pages, readers will find ample commentary on the entire span of Schuyler's career, but the main trajectory of the book extends from his first days as a writer in the early 1920s to the publication of *Black No More* in 1931. These years, which corresponded with creative explosions in American and black American literature, set the mold for the rest of Schuyler's career. Beyond the concern of explaining Schuyler's trajectory of personal development, a focus on the 1920s also provides an opportunity to explore a larger set of questions: What good can it possibly do to write satire about race? How can irony, nay-saying, and fun-poking dismissal lead to a worthwhile racial politics? Does satire offer an alternative to the predominant norms of the race discourse? Can it have a healing effect in this context? Questions like these force us to consider the broader range of tendencies that constitute the American discourse on race at the same time that they compel close attention to the specifics of what Schuyler satirized and why.

As a whole, *The Sage of Sugar Hill* provides a detailed portrait of an important black intellectual in a formative period of his development. Yet, as it analyzes Schuyler's intellectual mission in the 1920s, it remains concerned with issues of contemporary relevance. In the post–civil rights era we have become increasingly aware of the many complicated issues that have made race in America much more than a simple matter of black and white. Class, gender, globalism, and multiracial identities have all exerted their complicating influence in recent decades. Schuyler's ironic, open approach to the race question anticipates in many ways this new historical circumstance, where the invention of multiple racial identities has begun to supersede accounts of group distinctiveness based on narrow assumptions of biological essence or static notions of tradition. Schuyler struck an early blow for audacious independence on racial issues. This book attempts to bring this challenge to the reader in a way that does the satirist's mission some justice. If I am successful, the reader may well find, to borrow from Ralph Ellison's protagonist in *Invisible Man,* that on lower frequencies, George Schuyler does indeed speak for you!

ACKNOWLEDGMENTS

AT TIMES WRITING A BOOK seems like the loneliest of tasks. Yet no one truly writes alone. Convention dictates that an author place his own name and no other at the head of his work, but an honest glance at the page reveals innumerable words and sentences that he simply could not have made his own if someone had not given them to him first. Looking up from the page, and all around at the entire shape of his life, every self-conscious author recognizes the countless individuals who listened and read, who provided commentary, information, inspiration, encourage-ment, patience, strength, and love. He realizes that they were there when he wrote, even when he felt most alone.

As I look up from the page, I find that many people were there with me as I wrote this book. In a spirit of caring and generosity, they gave me words. They also gave me a long list of intangibles that I cannot ade-quately describe. Of course, my mistakes are wholly my own. Without the able assistance of the following individuals, I would have surely made many more. My former dissertation adviser, Werner Sollors of Harvard University, helped me a great deal during the earliest phases of this proj-ect. Even more than that, his faith in my ability has always provided a source of strength. Henry Louis Gates Jr. provided the original idea of writing seriously about Schuyler. For this, and for his continuing sup-port, I am grateful. For innumerable impromptu conversations about

Schuyler at Au Bon Pain and on the streets of Cambridge during my years in graduate school, I must give a special thanks to Gerald Gill. For giving me a research assistant's job to study Schuyler's role in the Liberian Labor Crisis during my years as an undergraduate, I am grateful to Glen Loury. I must also thank John Stauffer, of Harvard University, who read several chapters of this book at a late stage of its development and provided valuable counsel and encouragement.

Among my colleagues at Amherst College, Uday Mehta and David Blight read large portions of this manuscript and offered great advice and friendship. Rhonda Cobham-Sander provided intellectual support in the form of an ongoing dialogue during summer walks down the Amherst bike trail during early stages of the project. This not only clarified my thinking but also made my summers more pleasant than they would have otherwise been. Other members of the Amherst faculty read parts of this manuscript, talked with me about specific issues, or offered encouragement at various stages. They are Rowland Abiodun, Andrea Rushing, David Wills, Hilary Moss, Rosalina De La Carrera, Dale Peterson, Hugh Hawkins, Gordie Levin, Marissa Parham, Martha Sandweiss, Barry O'Connel, and Allen Guttmann. I have also benefited from the advice of former members of the Amherst faculty: Bob Gooding-Williams, Patrick Johnson, and Eddie Glaude. I would also like to thank Amherst College for a well-timed Trustee Faculty Fellowship, which afforded me the much-needed time to write large portions of this book.

In a more personal connection I would like to thank my mother and best friend, Virginia Jones Porée, for lending her skills as a typist, for offering her reflections on my writing, and for a much longer list of more intangible contributions. My friends Jay Bland, Joe Cooper, Herbert Watkins, Noel Ignatiev, John Farrell, Brenda Coughlin, Bhamathi Viswanathan, and Julie Lee all read parts of my work and played a role in improving its quality. Philip Cooper and Blanford Parker went far above and beyond the call of friendship by listening to me read large portions of this book out loud and giving me immediate and crucial feedback. This played a special role in getting me through my worst moments of doubt.

Lastly, I would like to thank research assistants Ben Beckman and Seoha Kim, and the special collections staffs at the following libraries: the New York Public Library, the Schomburg Center for Research in Black Culture, the George Arents Research Library at Syracuse University, the Beinecke Rare Book and Manuscript Library at Yale University, the Moorland-Spingarn Collection at Howard University, and the Amherst College Library. Without the generous assistance of librarians at these institutions, my research for this book would have surely suffered.

CHAPTER ONE

The Problem of George S. Schuyler

FOR MOST READERS THE problem of George Samuel Schuyler seems simple. Specialists in African American literature or twentieth-century American intellectual history may know a few facts about him. Otherwise, very few people are familiar with him at all. Although Schuyler did much to earn this obscurity, we might still wonder whether he deserves it. If measures of sheer public exposure and numbers of pages written in a lifetime determined the amount of scholarly attention given to a thinker, he would already be the subject of extensive study.

During Schuyler's years at the *Pittsburgh Courier,* from the mid-1920s to the mid-1960s, the newspaper grew from a small weekly circulation of thirty thousand copies to black America's most popular newspaper.[1] In this span Schuyler's column "Views and Reviews" appeared almost every week, covering every issue of importance to black Americans. In addition, during the same period Schuyler penned all the unsigned editorials for the *Courier.* Because he rarely received instructions from the ownership about how to treat individual issues, it is fair to say that he was a one-man editorial policy for black America's most popular newspaper for nearly forty years. In addition to editorials Schuyler contributed innumerable feature articles, short stories, anonymous articles, and reviews to the *Courier,* all in a distinctive writing style that made him the country's leading black journalist for much of his career.

The *Courier*'s circulation figures provide only the most conservative estimate of how many people read Schuyler's work. Each copy of the newspaper probably had at least two or three readers who found it lying around barber shops, restaurants, and on kitchen tables all over black America. In addition to his efforts for the *Courier,* Schuyler also contributed to such other black publications as the *Messenger,* the *Crisis, Phylon,* and *Negro Digest.* Because of this wide exposure, amplified by yearly lecture tours and occasional radio appearances, Schuyler received a hearing among blacks equal to that of any thinker of his time.

Schuyler's work also appeared often in mainstream journals. During the 1920s and 1930s he was the most frequent contributor of any race to the *American Mercury.* He also published articles in the *Nation* and *Modern Quarterly.* Because of this, he reached white readers with more regularity than almost any black intellectual of the period between the wars. From a literary standpoint his novel *Black No More* (1931) remains noteworthy as the first full-length satire written by a black American, and his journalistic writing, especially the satirical column he cowrote with Theophilus Lewis, "Shafts and Darts," presents a lasting example of literary technique employed for political ends.[2]

In *The American Language,* H. L. Mencken—the thinker with whom Schuyler has most often been compared—praised him in the highest terms: "Mr. Schuyler is the most competent journalist that his race has produced in America. There are few white columnists, in fact, who can match him for information, intelligence, independence and courage." In a 1937 letter to publisher Blanche Knopf, Mencken extended his good opinion of Schuyler beyond the realm of journalism: "Schuyler is the best writer the Negroes have ever produced, and moreover, he is a highly intelligent man. . . . He loves to tell the truth, and the truth in this case is full of surprises. . . . I really believe that he could give you something extraordinary."[3]

In a 1933 letter to the *American Mercury* the poet Melvin Tolson declared Schuyler not only a notable writer but a remarkable person as well. Introducing Schuyler "both as a writer and a man," Tolson described him as one of the most "civilized" personalities on the American scene: "He stimulates more differences of opinion than any other Negro writer. His column 'Views and Reviews' . . . is the most discussed column in Negro America." Tolson claimed to have heard Schuyler's opinions "attacked and defended in barber-shops, Jim Crow cars, pool rooms, class rooms, churches, and drawing rooms." Further supporting his characterization of Schuyler as a sophisticated personality and outstanding provocateur, Tolson praised the columnist for inspiring criticisms running from the sublime to the ridiculous and for enjoying with particular relish the most adverse statements of his detractors. "One evening in his apartment on Sugar Hill," Tolson revealed, "he showed me a scrapbook full of them, and I had many a hearty laugh myself." Again emphasizing Schuyler's popularity, Tolson wondered what would happen if the editor could say his own funeral sermon. He speculated playfully that the event would solve the railroad depression because "Aframerica" would send "her hundreds of thousands." They would come for a multitude of reasons, Tolson imagined, but they would all enjoy themselves.[4]

In the early 1990s historian Robert Hill discovered more than seventy stories, some of them novel length, that Schuyler produced under eight pseudonyms during the 1930s. Although many of these stories seem on the surface somewhat formulaic attempts at newspaper fiction, a closer look reveals a much deeper complexity. Not only do they represent a major contribution to the fiction appearing in black newspapers during the period, but they also alter the interpretive challenge involved in understanding the intellectual and political breadth of Schuyler's omnivorous mind.[5]

Considering the evidence for Schuyler's importance as an intellectual figure, we might wonder why his story has not received more detailed academic attention. The answer to this question may well be reduced to a single incident when Schuyler said the wrong thing, in the wrong tone, about the wrong man, at the wrong time: "Dr. King's principal contribution to world peace has been to roam the country like some sable Typhoid Mary infecting the mentally disturbed with perversion of Christian doctrine and grabbing fat lecture fees from the shallow-pated." Schuyler wrote this one month before Martin Luther King Jr. accepted the 1964 Nobel Peace Prize. Continuing this line of thought, he asserted that King, like most of those receiving the prize awarded yearly to "pious frauds for the purposes of political propaganda," had done nothing to promote peace. In fact, Schuyler said, King's achievements had been closer to the opposite, considering his success in spreading mayhem all over the South by packing jails "with negroes and some whites, getting them beaten, bitten and firehosed, thereby raising bail and fines to the vast enrichment of Southern law 'n' order."[6]

Although Schuyler's editorial appeared in the ultraconservative *Manchester Union Leader,* readers of the *Pittsburgh Courier* still heard about it. Predictably, many sent letters requesting the writer's dismissal. Anger and concern about the *Courier's* declining readership gave Schuyler's boss, P. L. Prattis, good reasons to dismiss him, but deference to Schuyler's many years of service would delay this until 1966, when a new owner purchased what little was left of the once great newspaper.[7] Perhaps more amazing than Schuyler's 1966 dismissal from the *Courier* after forty-four years was the fact that the ownership tolerated him for so long. The King incident provided only one in a series of statements made by Schuyler that seemed almost calculated to make the vast majority of black people hate him. In this respect 1964 was a big year. Six months before the infamous King editorial, Schuyler ran for Congress for the Conservative Party of New York against Adam Clayton Powell Jr.[8] During the campaign he claimed that Harlem was suffering the ravages of welfare colonialism begun during the Roosevelt era. Not surprisingly, he lost badly.

In July of the same year riots broke out in Harlem, Newark and Elizabeth, New Jersey, Philadelphia, and other northeastern cities. Ignoring the pleas of Prattis and other *Courier* editors, Schuyler seized the moment to extend his case against civil rights leaders. In a letter to the *New York Times* he placed the entire blame for the rioting on King, Bayard Rustin, James Farmer, and James Foreman. Not long after his letter appeared, Schuyler said on a radio show in Missouri that he intended to vote for Barry Goldwater, a powerful congressional enemy of civil rights, in the upcoming presidential election. Naturally, controversy ensued. Prattis wrote a letter to Schuyler emphasizing the "incalculable harm" he had done. True to form, the iconoclast had few regrets. In a letter to Eleanor Lofton, the acting publisher of the *Courier,* Schuyler suggested that the situation might present an opportunity for "full-fledged debate" on the merits of civil rights and on "all other controversial matters." Neither Lofton nor Prattis shared Schuyler's enthusiasm for debate. Prattis sent him a terse note: "Don't send any more editorials."[9]

As extreme as they seemed to Schuyler's superiors, the events of 1964 did not surprise anyone who had been following his column regularly.

The King editorial provided only the most notable episode in a long series of editorial stabs aimed at the Civil Rights Movement dating back to the 1950s. Although he had many reasons for making such attacks, Schuyler's most outlandish accusations centered on the suspicion of communist influence on such men as King and Farmer. Where others saw black, Schuyler saw red. Some thought that he derived a perverse pleasure from accusing as many people as possible of working for the communist menace, especially if they fought for civil rights. These accusations punctuated an anticommunist career that also included enthusiastic support of Joseph McCarthy and vitriolic denunciation of such confirmed black communist leaders as W. E. B. Du Bois and Paul Robeson in the 1950s.[10]

Although Schuyler denounced communism earlier in his career, he did not make a crusade of it until after World War II. In the late 1940s alone he devoted more than fifty articles in his *Pittsburgh Courier* column "Views and Reviews" to this cause. He also became a powerful promoter of American government propaganda. His most widely read essay of the period, "The Phantom American Negro," argues that the suffering black person so common in novels like Richard Wright's *Native Son* and in the minds of uninformed Europeans was a myth. He used a series of tendentiously selected statistics to show that not only had blacks made a tremendous amount of progress in America since the turn of the twentieth century, but they also enjoyed a higher standard of living than either their brethren in Africa or many of those who were "crying over them" in Europe. That an educated and informed black man would venture such an argument proved as important in making the article excellent propaganda as the argument itself, which downplayed the effects of racism. "The Phantom American Negro" began as an address to the Congress for Cultural Freedom in Berlin with an almost unbelievable title: "The American Negro Question without Propaganda." Later it was inserted into the *Congressional Record* and reprinted in the *Freeman*, the *Christian Science Monitor, Reader's Digest,* and sixteen other publications.[11]

No one really knows exactly why Schuyler, who claimed to be a socialist well into the 1930s, shifted during the 1940s from a leading voice on the left to one whose words would make a red-baiter like Westbrook Pegler urge whites to "read this Negro." Certainly Schuyler drifted rightward along with many former leftist intellectuals between the Great Depression and the age of "liberal consensus." The cruelties of fascism in Germany and Spain along with the moral disaster of Stalinism in Russia combined to convince such men as John Dos Passos, Max Eastman, and many others to abandon Marx only to turn to an opposing philosophy. No doubt, some of the circumstances affecting their attitudes and decisions had a similar impact on Schuyler; but his case also had its own special features. Becoming a conservative—especially an outspoken archconservative—allowed him to play his favorite game: flirting with the status of "race traitor." Schuyler's success in earning this label has markedly affected scholarly interpretations of his work. His positive critics have sought to avoid guilt by association, while his detractors have had to face the difficulty of explaining how they could find Schuyler odious but still interesting enough to write about. Most of Schuyler's positive critics have circumvented this problem by focusing almost exclusively on his literary works or on a part of his career that does not carry the same taint as the 1950s and the 1960s. His more hostile critics have inclined toward the opposite, tending to interpret his early works as part of the entire complex that brought him to what they see as the wrongheadedness of his later years.[12]

This state of affairs exists in part because of how forcefully the Civil Rights Movement has affected the way Americans think about race. Among their many achievements—which include the passage of civil rights legislation, the inauguration of affirmative action policies, and the alteration of the consciousness of the average American about what constitutes racism—civil rights leaders as well as their interpreters have succeeded in associating The Movement with the very essence of black identity. Before the protests of the 1960s identification with disruptive political tactics formed one option among several. Afterward, however, it became something of an obligation as historians reconceived the black experience in terms of resistance and protest. The irony of Schuyler's case resides in how vehemently he resisted the resisters; how he saw in their radicalism a constraining orthodoxy covered over with mere symbols of assertion. In other words Schuyler saw in the civil rights activists fundamentally what they saw in him—and he did not like it. This is what remains so compelling about him. He provides one of the greatest examples of resistance black America has ever produced. Does it stretch irony too far to call him a representative man?

Schuyler always detested apology. Therefore, without mitigating the sheer ugliness of his 1964 editorial on King, we might recognize in it a series of targets that transcend mere personal attack. Among these targets racial orthodoxy stands out as the most obvious. Should blacks conform to a strict code of beliefs as a sign of race loyalty? Should they censure members of the group who do not conform? Schuyler also targets hero worship in his remarks on King. Should such a diverse group as black Americans line up behind a single charismatic leader? How much of the desire to do so should we attribute to the slavish need for a black messiah or, to put it in more secular terms, a benign black master exchanged for a white one? Although Schuyler questioned the political and psychological efficacy of applying a master narrative of individual heroism to black leaders, he also contradicted the tendency to glorify the folk. Do the black masses really have greater insight into matters of justice and freedom than other Americans? Should we think that they know exactly how to fight racism simply because they have suffered from it? Such tough questions challenge fundamental narratives that frame the activities of those most closely associated with positive social change on the race question. The mere willingness to bring such questions forward would have been enough to anger Schuyler's audience in 1964, but he went much farther than that.

We risk some distortion in stating Schuyler's deeper concerns as questions. Accusation, irony, provocation, and invective were his stock in trade. For Schuyler, King did not simply believe the wrong ideas; rather, he spread disease and perversion like a "sable Typhoid Mary." In calling for the editor's head, the readers of the *Pittsburgh Courier* reacted as much to the satirical form of Schuyler's editorial as they did to its substance. The majority of *Courier* readers had few doubts about the relevant narrative for King. He represented for them the best qualities of the black American struggle for justice and freedom. Through love and nonviolence, methods seemingly ordained by God himself, King exemplified dignity in the face of oppression. His acceptance of the Nobel Prize underscored for this audience, as it does for many Americans today, the universal quality of King's struggle: its linkage to the larger human struggle against oppression all over the world. In response to this compelling story, Schuyler cast King as a monster and a fool, as a diseased and arrogant man capitalizing on the worst tendencies of the mob. Rather than portraying King as an apostle of love, Schuyler depicted him as a man filled with self-hatred, a craven fool bent on revenge. To top off his point-for-point reversal of what most blacks believed about the civil rights leader, Schuyler published his attack in a white conservative newspaper for readers who had anything but black people's best interests in mind.

In the face of this, what choice did Schuyler's *Courier* audience have except to see Schuyler himself as he had portrayed King: as a monster, a fool, a dangerous agent of destruction spreading his disease to those with low intellectual resistance? Given these conclusions about the editor, the choice to punish him by the most available means would seem the most reasonable path. The promotion of love and reconciliation could not have been the most important matters on the minds of King's defenders as they wielded their own acid pens to accomplish this end. What else could Schuyler have gathered from this but confirmation of his contention that the Civil Rights Movement only added to the general circus atmosphere of American race relations, one in which impotence impersonated power, revenge posed as justice, hatred masqueraded as love, and small men became icons of the people?

From one angle the episode surrounding Schuyler's 1964 statement on King might appear the worst place to look for a representative moment in the editor's career. By this time Schuyler's political views had changed drastically from those he entertained before World War II. Also, as a satirical statement, the King editorial failed to balance its destructive anger with humor in the manner of Schuyler's best efforts in the 1920s and 1930s. Still, compelling continuities remain. Schuyler's list of implicit targets in his statement on King—the dangers of black orthodoxy, hero worship, and the glorification of the folk—had not changed from the beginning of his career; nor had his attack on religious belief, dishonesty, gullibility, and excessive pride. The controversy around the King editorial also proved typical of Schuyler. In both his younger and his older days Schuyler constantly fashioned himself an enemy of convention and established power. In the 1920s this posture took the form of leftist agitation against capitalism, and in the 1960s it appeared as opposition to the state and all of those threatening to expand its dominion. Perhaps Schuyler's conviction concerning the power of his enemies inclined him to the unfair attack. He seemed to glory in the confused swirl of accusations that followed a well-timed act of rhetorical violence. Although studying the battles of Schuyler's late career might provide some of the more dramatic examples of this posture, we must inquire into Schuyler's formative influences and early career to understand better its personal and intellectual roots.

Not long after Schuyler's dismissal from the *Courier* in 1966, his somewhat distorted autobiography, *Black and Conservative,* made its appearance. In this book Schuyler presents himself as a lifelong conservative, a patriot, and a constant enemy of communism. Skillfully combining solid facts from his life with an entirely doubtful narrative, he emphasizes his origins as a member of a northern black working-class aristocracy of talent going back to the American Revolution. He idealizes his closest relatives, almost all of whom apparently understood how to balance a certain highbrow sense of cultivation with strong working-class identity and race pride. The title of his book, *Black and Conservative,* extends this polemic. It represents a belated attempt to refute the black nationalist leader Marcus Garvey, who said in the 1920s that blacks could not be conservative because they had nothing to conserve. Against this Schuyler points to his own career as an attempt to conserve the black American ability to adjust and survive in a rapidly changing modern society. Thus, in defining himself as a conservative, he implicitly calls on the pragmatic trickster tradition even as he evokes decency, patriotism, order, and other "traditional" values that he shared with Richard Nixon, Barry Goldwater, and other Republican allies.[13] Despite its skew, *Black and Conservative* remains the best source concerning the facts of Schuyler's life and career. For all of its distortion and omission it still manages to tell the unique story of a singular career. Correcting the book's more obvious omissions does not change this. Schuyler remains important, but for reasons that his public persona of 1966 could never contain.

Although he spent his boyhood in Syracuse, New York, Schuyler's birthplace remains hard to verify. So does the identity of his biological parents. Although he always claimed to have been born in Providence, Rhode Island, little proof exists to verify the claim. Schuyler may also have been adopted. While he lived with his widowed mother, Eliza Jane Schuyler, young George was probably the ward of his grandmother Helen Fischer, in whose Syracuse home both he and his mother stayed. Despite these complexities, there seems little reason to doubt Schuyler's birth date—25 February 1895. He relates this date in his autobiography with the same confidence that he reports his blood relation to his parents. Family legend held that Schuyler's grandfather fought with General Philip Schuyler in the American Revolution, but the name could have easily come from elsewhere. In *Black and Conservative,* Schuyler describes his father, the head chef at a local hotel, as a stately man who dressed well and insisted on "baronial" living. Yet it appears suspect that Schuyler remembered him so well, as he was only three when his father died. The story grows more suspicious when Schuyler claims not to remember his father's funeral very well, saying that it had no meaning for him.[14]

Two years after his father's death Schuyler's mother married an ambitious migrant from Georgia named Joseph Eugene Brown. Schuyler describes his stepfather in *Black and Conservative* disdainfully as a stocky, light-colored man with "a false eye [that] . . . he kept in a glass of water over night." Schuyler seems almost willing to forgive Brown for this, and for his membership in more than one black fraternal organization, in light of his ability to move the family into a beautiful home in the suburbs. He admits that his family shared the general northern black prejudice against southern migrants, regarding them as uncouth and uncultured. For his ability to defy this stereotype, Schuyler grants Brown a begrudging measure of esteem.[15]

Schuyler's description of his mother leaves little doubt that she also liked Brown for his ability to provide. An instinctive rationalist who rejected her own mother's belief in magic, she provided young George with early training in reading, writing, and proper pronunciation. Schuyler also attributes his race pride to his mother's bookshelf, which contained volumes on such black heroes as Frederick Douglass and Harriet Tubman. In addition to books on black leaders, his mother possessed among her one hundred titles an illustrated text on blacks in the military called *The Black Phalanx.* As a little boy sitting on the floor paging through this volume, Schuyler first became fascinated with the black men who fought "in all of America's wars." With his self-esteem buttressed by early exposure to reading and race pride, Schuyler found the trials of grammar school and high school in racist Syracuse well within his capabilities. Although integrated, the schools of that city reflected the racial tensions of the larger society. No doubt, these tensions—along with Schuyler's unstable family situation and his instinctive love/hate relationship with authority—contributed to his attraction for satire. His earliest experiments with the form mocked the pretense of his teachers and questioned the wisdom of his high-school lessons.[16]

Schuyler had all of the ambitions one would expect of a boy with strong capabilities. As he grew older, he became increasingly aware of the limited career opportunities for blacks in Syracuse. This made military service seem like an attractive option. As a fourteen-year-old, he experienced something of an epiphany when black soldiers camped for maneuvers on the Syracuse circus grounds. The sight of these soldiers with "their superb order and discipline, their haughty and immaculate noncommissioned officers, and their obvious authority" opened his eyes to a vision of possibility. His only previous experience with black men in uniform came from watching his friends' fathers in ludicrous fraternity outfits that "represented nothing." To this the black soldiers of the Ninth Cavalry bore a striking contrast: "They represented the power and authority of the United States. They were clean, upstanding, orderly, and polite. . . . How they contrasted with our uninviting lot in Syracuse!"[17]

Indeed, Schuyler could not wait to leave that uninviting lot behind. When he turned seventeen, in 1912, one year before his legal eligibility, he convinced his mother to lie about his age so that he could become a member of the Twenty-Fifth Infantry. Schuyler's army years, between 1912 and 1918, set the direction of his later thoughts and activities in crucial ways. His mother allowed him to go into the service because she thought it would "make a man of him." She probably did not anticipate that it would also help to solidify his affection for satire. In conformity with his mother's wishes the army broadened Schuyler's base of experience. As a soldier, he first encountered large numbers of black Southerners and learned somewhat begrudgingly to appreciate them. The army would also show him the importance of organization, a value that significantly aided Schuyler's career as a journalist. In addition, he traveled while in the army, being stationed in both Seattle and Hawaii. While in Hawaii, he encountered for the first time a society where racial mixture constituted the norm. This theme figured prominently in his later writings. Schuyler's experiments with satire continued and matured between 1912 and 1918, as he published fledgling efforts in the *Honolulu Commercial Advertiser* and in a typewritten sheet called *The Daily Dope. The Service,* a weekly civilian-edited magazine for soldiers in Honolulu, also published such early works as "The Fable of the Self-Opinionated Chieftain," "The 16th Decisive Battle of the World," and "Waiane Waftings."[18]

In addition to the positive lessons of army life, Schuyler also learned of loss. Soon after he arrived at Fort Lawton, Washington, the seventeen-year-old private received news of his mother's death. Stationed three thousand miles from home, Schuyler had to face the starkest of facts. Having lost his father, grandmother, aunt, and now his mother, he could count on no one but himself. This sense of loss, loneliness, and desperation may have made him invest more heavily in becoming an excellent soldier. In the years that followed, he compiled an exceptional military record. Eventually Schuyler rose to the level of drill instructor at the historic black officers training camp at Fort Des Moines, Iowa, in 1917. At Fort Des Moines, Schuyler found himself among a large group of college-educated blacks for the first time. The experience of being a drill instructor but not being regarded by his charges as "good enough" to join their exclusive clubs probably heightened his sense of irony and his disdain for the black upper class, and intensified his negative feelings about leadership. These themes reappear throughout Schuyler's later writings. His promotion to first lieutenant in 1917 probably strengthened his ironic attitude toward leadership and the pursuit of status. For Schuyler, Fort Des Moines epitomized the foul odor of empty victory. Although the black officers training camp represented an advance to some black political leaders, Schuyler could see from firsthand experience that the government intended to use its graduates only for propaganda. This increased his frustration with the army immeasurably.[19]

These feelings reached a climax one morning in the summer of 1918 when Schuyler approached a Greek bootblack at the Philadelphia train station. The Greek, whose accent revealed his immigrant status, loudly refused to shine a "nigger's" shoes. This prompted in Schuyler a torrent of anger. He muttered aloud: "I'm a son-of-a-bitch if I serve this goddamn country any longer!" At that moment he decided to desert. The fact that an officer of the U.S. Army could not get a shoeshine from a recent immigrant proved too much for the twenty-three-year-old lieutenant. He rashly removed his uniform and attempted an escape to Chicago. Police stood waiting for him when he disembarked, however. Because he brought his uniform along, he was able to convince the authorities that he only wanted to change into something more comfortable. The lie secured his release. On the road again Schuyler continued to San Diego, where he worked for three months as a dishwasher. Fearing inevitable arrest, he turned himself in just before he would have been declared AWOL. A military court sentenced him to five years on Governor's Island, New York. Eventually the term became one year and was then further reduced to nine months for good behavior.[20]

Schuyler took this story to his grave. He mentioned it neither in his autobiography nor in his 1960 interview for the Columbia Oral History Project. In place of the painful truth, he explained in *Black and Conservative* that after a few months at Fort Dix he went to Camp Meade in Maryland, where he trained new recruits. When the war ended in November 1918, he said, the army almost immediately discharged him. After leaving the army, he claimed to have taken a civil service job processing war prisoners on Governor's Island. This reveals the less important part of the truth but neglects the crucial matter: he was one of the prisoners. Indeed, Schuyler did work for an officer under whom he served in the Twenty-Fifth Infantry, and he did serve as a clerk, but he did not return to a "sunny two-room apartment in Harlem" after a hard day's work. Rather, he returned to a gloomy cell. Schuyler wrote in his autobiography that life went well for him at this time—he had a job, a wonderful apartment, and a beautiful girlfriend.[21] The truth appears closer to the opposite, however. After completing his prison term, Schuyler continued on the staff at Governor's Island. As a free man, he took an apartment and started seeing a girlfriend. This blissful period ended when postwar budget cuts eliminated his job after only three months.

During his prison term, which probably began in the fall of 1918 and lasted through the spring of 1919, Schuyler had plenty of time to formulate his thoughts on the meaning of the war. Given the evidence of his subsequent career, his disillusioning experience in the military probably had a radicalizing effect on him. The postwar depression only intensified this feeling. After leaving prison, Schuyler floated from one menial and tenuous form of employment to another. The title of the essay he published about this period, "From Job to Job: A Personal Narrative," summarized the main theme well: he started as a porter for a drugstore, moved on to a similar job with a printing press, then to a brass factory, and finally to two different jobs as a dishwasher. He later wrote about his experience washing dishes in a 1931 *American Mercury* article called "Memoirs of a Pearl Diver."[22]

Schuyler attempts a delicate balancing act in *Black and Conservative* relating his increasing interest in socialism during this period. He claims that as he floated from job to job in the early 1920s, he also pored over such publications as the *Call,* the *Nation,* and the *New Republic,* as well as the works of Marx and Engels, and hundreds of socialist tracts and newspapers. Although none of these writings interested him, he wrote, intellectual curiosity kept him awake long enough to wade through them.[23] Could it be that during this part of his life Schuyler had deep intellectual interest in thinkers he did not like? This seems unlikely, but in his zeal to remake his past in *Black and Conservative,* Schuyler gives this impression.

Beaten down by the experience of going from one bad job to another in New York City, Schuyler decided in 1921 to go home and start all over again. The strategic retreat served him well because soon after his return to Syracuse, he secured a good-paying union job at a construction site. Not long after this, in November 1921, he joined the Socialist Party. Although in his autobiography Schuyler attributed his membership in the party to the intellectual barrenness of Syracuse, the context of his decision suggests a broader set of motivations. In light of his desertion from the army and his increasingly entrenched working-class existence, it seems logical that Schuyler would find the socialists attractive, both for their stance in favor of unions and for their strong position on the war. No doubt, intellectual curiosity also played a role, as the socialist critique of capitalism granted their politics a distinctly intellectual flavor.

Despite Schuyler's attraction to reading and thinking, personal and developmental reasons probably weighed most heavily in his decision to join the Socialist Party. The party provided Schuyler with a way to reconcile his love of letters with his working-class identity. It also helped him to make sense of his anger at the military and at racism, and made it possible once again for him to "be somebody." As the educational director of the Socialist Party in Syracuse, Schuyler wrote speeches and such pamphlets as "An Intelligent Program for Intelligent Negro Workers." He also organized a community forum held in the assembly hall at St. Philip's Episcopal Church and spent time on a street corner addressing "the indifferent populace in the downtown area."[24] All of this helped to make Schuyler's return to his hometown a great personal success. Nevertheless, his basic opinion of Syracuse remained the same. Riding his wave of newfound success, he soon returned with his savings to the excitement and opportunity of New York City.

This time, with pockets full, he pledged to enjoy New York and to meet a different class of black people than he could in his days of bouncing from job to job. Upon arrival he went straight to Harlem, where he took a room at the Phyllis Wheatley Hotel on 135th Street, which was owned and operated by the Universal Negro Improvement Association (UNIA). Curious about the excitement surrounding the Garvey movement, Schuyler attended the packed meetings at Liberty Hall and read the UNIA weekly, *Negro World*. Although in later years he would express vehement disdain for Garvey in numerous editorials, he always acknowledged the wisdom of the leader's critique of black intragroup racism.[25] Schuyler himself had very dark skin, which he suffered for as much among blacks as whites. Therefore the ironies of black self-hatred never ceased to fascinate him and always occupied a central place in his criticism of the black mentality. No doubt, attending the Liberty Hall meetings helped to focus feelings that he always had. In this sense Schuyler owed Garvey a debt that gives his continuous and sometimes ugly excoriation of the leader in his writings all of the markings of the anxiety of influence.

Before he ran out of money, Schuyler enjoyed a wide array of intellectual and cultural offerings in Harlem. He attended the literary evenings at the 135th Street branch of the New York Public Library, the meetings and forums at the Harlem branch of the YMCA, and the meetings of the socialist Friends of Negro Freedom in the Lafayette Theater Building on 131st Street. He also frequented the People's Institute in Cooper Union, where he heard such thinkers as Norman Angell, Will Durant, and Everett Dean Martin. In addition, he took classes at the Rand School from John Watson, Thorstein Veblen, and others. References to these thinkers appear frequently in his later writings.[26] Given the choice, Schuyler would have continued this period of intellectual immersion, but his money dwindled after only a month. On the threshold of poverty once again, he began eating on the cheap in the Bowery and looking for employment.

After a couple of botched experiments with railroad jobs in New Jersey and Pennsylvania, Schuyler took up residence with a group of hobos in the basement of a church on Avenue A called Saint Marks-in-the-Bouwerie. This church also served as a school for him. Not only did he enjoy the lectures on highbrow matters given there by Old Bill, the hobo intellectual, but he also learned of a world unknown to the "respectable" people in his past. This marginal world, which seemed to Schuyler more democratic than the one occupied by the pious and moralistic members of the so-called higher orders, made him think differently about his own desire to "be somebody."[27] Although he never left this value behind, he learned increasingly as the years passed how to achieve distinction by calling it radically into question.

While living downtown as a hobo, Schuyler continued to attend the forum given by the Friends of Negro Freedom every Sunday in Harlem. As a result, he came to know A. Philip Randolph and Chandler Owen, the editors of the *Messenger*. When Owen went on the road in early 1923 to seek advertising for the magazine, Randolph hired Schuyler as office manager. Realizing that his home in the church basement could not last, Schuyler gave up his colorful but impecunious life as a hobo, taking what possessions he had to a cheap room in Harlem.[28] Schuyler's presence immediately benefited the *Messenger* because he brought a strong sense of order from his experience in the military. On his first day Schuyler began arranging the files and establishing better organization around the magazine's messy offices. Soon after, he also began to write.[29] Between 1923 and 1928, Schuyler published plays, short stories, and feature articles in the *Messenger*. He also contributed a weekly satirical column called "Shafts and Darts," which would do more than any of his other writings to display his unique talents.

The column employed a wide array of satirical devices in addressing the race question, including farce, parody, reductio ad absurdum, irony, and biting colloquial language. In opposition to the heavy and serious tone of sustained intellectual argument, Schuyler organized his column around a series of short comical strikes. Sometimes these strikes featured a remarkable compactness of allusion, requiring wide knowledge of current events, the black intellectual and social scene, history, social theory, literature, and a good sense of humor for full appreciation and enjoyment. Although "Shafts and Darts" maintained a wide range of reference, it focused most centrally on the race question. Through an eclectic juxtaposition of monthly darts, Schuyler used the column to open up the range of critical viewpoints that his readers would bring to the problem of blacks in America.

While "Shafts and Darts" stands as Schuyler's most notable achievement with the *Messenger*, his other contributions to the socialist journal also merit attention. As editor of the *Messenger*, Schuyler recruited his friend J. A. Rogers to write a column on black historical figures and Eugene Gordon to write a monthly feature on the best editorials in black newspapers. He also published some of the early work of Langston Hughes and Zora Neale Hurston. Before Schuyler became editor, the *Messenger* never involved itself much in the publication or evaluation of literature. Schuyler brought this dimension to the magazine. In addition, he achieved the more dubious distinction of helping to make the *Messenger* more congenial to black capitalism.[30]

While making his mark at the *Messenger,* Schuyler also gained exposure in Harlem intellectual circles. In connection with his duties at the magazine, he worked with Rogers, Theophilus Lewis, Robert W. Bagnall, William Pickens, W. A. Domingo, Gwendolyn Bennett, Bruce Nugent, and Wallace Thurman. Of these, Rogers and Lewis became special friends. Schuyler lunched with Rogers almost daily in the YWCA cafeteria in Harlem and bunked at Lewis's apartment with Nugent and Thurman. The Sunday roundtable discussions at A. Philip Randolph's apartment widened Schuyler's circle of associations even further. There he met the heiress A'Lelia Walker, the venerable newspaperman T. Thomas Fortune, and the *Negro World* editor William H. Ferris.[31]

Although it contributed to Schuyler's notoriety, the *Messenger* could not pay him more than ten dollars a week. Even for well-known black writers opportunities to publish in mainstream magazines proved rare. Relative unknowns like Schuyler had almost no chance to make a decent living through writing. For this reason the offer by Ira Lewis, general editor of the *Pittsburgh Courier,* to write a column for three dollars a week came as a godsend.[32] Although small, this initial salary provided an important supplement for the impecunious editor. A job with the *Courier* also meant opportunity. Schuyler knew that with hustle he could make yet more. Ever sensible and businesslike, Schuyler attempted to build his new column on the success of "Shafts and Darts," which he continued to write with Theophilus Lewis. Initially he named his new venture "This Simian World," but only three weeks later he changed the title to "Thrusts and Lunges," probably to place more emphasis on the broad-ranging quality of his critical wit. In October 1925 he changed the name of the column yet again, to the relatively more dignified "Views and Reviews," the same title that James Weldon Johnson used for his column in the *New York Age.* Schuyler probably appropriated Johnson's title to indicate that he had arrived. His column retained this name until he left the *Courier* in 1966.

In 1927, in the midst of Schuyler's rise to prominence, an opportunity came along to extend his public identity into his personal life in a unique way. During a particularly busy day at the *Messenger* office, a white woman named Josephine Cogdell, an occasional contributor to the magazine, arrived at Schuyler's door wearing her sexiest dress. Suddenly, Schuyler's deadlines disappeared. Transfixed, he talked with Josephine the rest of the day, and that night he took her dancing at the Savoy. As one night of dancing led to another, the unlikely pair fell in love, and in 1928 they inaugurated the first interracial celebrity marriage in Harlem since the boxer Jack Johnson carried his challenge to American racism beyond the ring in 1911.[33]

Today we might underestimate how radical a gesture an interracial marriage was in the 1920s. At that time twenty-six states had declared the practice illegal. Beyond this, a rising tide of racist sentiment in the country posed a real threat to anyone willing to violate publicly the prevailing notion of racial order. Some blacks, especially nationalists, agreed with these sentiments, albeit for different reasons and to milder effect than white racists. They thought it a violation of group pride to marry outside of the race. This probably made Schuyler cherish his bond with Josephine even more. Writing provided one effective outlet for his antiracist views, but having the white daughter of a Texas banker as his wife granted his politics a highly tangible application. This became even more the case with the birth of his precocious daughter, Philippa, in 1931. Becoming a concert pianist of world renown by her teenage years, Philippa performed so well on measures of intelligence that her parents regarded her as a case of "hybrid vigor."[34] Through her they envisioned the potential rise of a new and superior American racial type, a mulatto master race of instinctive democrats.

Although Josephine made most of the sacrifices required to raise Philippa, George did his duty in at least one sense. Even during the Depression he provided well for his family. Throughout the difficult 1930s they maintained their residence in the Lincoln Apartments on Sugar Hill, the Harlem home of the black elite. Their neighbors included such luminaries as Walter White, Aaron Douglas, Elmer Carter, Jack Johnson, and W. E. B. Du Bois. Maintaining his family in its upper-middle-class circumstance on a black journalist's salary in the 1930s required Schuyler to work almost incessantly. National speaking tours, investigative reporting assignments, and an almost unbelievable output of stories and articles provided the necessary funds, but the cost to the family proved great. Geographical distance ultimately turned into emotional distance. Love letters from such remote places as Liberia and Mississippi did little to convince his wife of his faithfulness.[35] For more reasons than money Schuyler found it impossible to settle into the quiet domestic middle-class life that he constantly criticized in his columns. Ambition, addiction to work, and sheer energy pushed him incessantly to the next assignment. In a sense Schuyler never left behind the essential emotion of that little boy in Syracuse who idolized the black soldiers of the Ninth Cavalry. Surely he wanted to claim for himself the benefits of the private life and of the domestic sphere, but ultimately they held a distant second place behind the seductions of mobility, intellectual status, and notoriety.

Although Schuyler's many journeys away from home harmed his personal life, they did produce extraordinary journalism. By 1926, a year before he met Josephine, Schuyler had already secured a reputation as a remarkable investigative reporter. Eleven months after starting his column for the *Pittsburgh Courier*, he volunteered to go on a tour of the South. This resulted in the classic series "Aframerica Today." For each installment in this series Schuyler reported on the number and condition of black-owned homes, black businesses, schools, interracial relations, intraracial relations, and the state of black political power in towns and cities like Memphis, Tennessee; Muskogee, Oklahoma; and Louisville, Kentucky. While he took note of the ravages of white racism in all of the cities he covered, Schuyler focused mainly on what black Southerners had done to improve their lot within the limitations of segregation. Against the expectations of those who thought of the South as a monolith, he found a wide diversity of political and economic situations. Surprisingly, even in the Deep South he discovered cities where black advancement surpassed that in the North. Nevertheless, Schuyler visited few cities where he thought blacks had taken full advantage of their opportunities. His disappointment with this constituted the main theme of the series.[36]

In 1931, at the behest of publisher George Palmer Putnam, Schuyler embarked on another investigative reporting tour, this time as a special correspondent for the *New York Evening Post* investigating conditions in Liberia. Putnam was disturbed at a League of Nations report claiming that the Liberian government had sold "boys" to Spanish plantations on the island of Fernando Po, off the coast of Nigeria. From January to May 1931, Schuyler gathered evidence corroborating these findings. In June and July of that year he published a series appearing in the *New York Evening Post,* the *Buffalo Express,* the *Philadelphia Public Ledger,* the *Washington Post,* and other mainstream papers condemning the conditions in Liberia. This series established Schuyler as an investigative reporter of international reputation. In addition to his newspaper articles on Liberia, he published a novel in 1931, *Slaves Today: A Story of Liberia,* which dramatized the conditions in the African nation through a melodramatic love story.[37]

Many black intellectuals, especially nationalists, including the increasingly nationalistic Du Bois, thought that Schuyler's unrelenting criticism of the Monrovia regime played into the hands of white racists intent on using the Liberian labor crisis as an example of black people's inability to govern themselves. From this standpoint Schuyler's advocacy of the continued presence of the Firestone Tire and Rubber plantation in the troubled nation seemed like the work of a traitor. For Schuyler, however, the presence of the American company seemed necessary for development. Unless the natives of the country learned economically viable modern skills, he thought, their independence could not last. Sustainable sovereignty required an up-to-date economy. This kind of thinking made Schuyler's enemies accuse him of working for Harvey Firestone. No evidence exists that Schuyler accepted money from the rubber tycoon.[38]

If one knew Schuyler only through his articles on the Liberian labor crisis and the voices of his detractors, his subsequent writings denouncing imperialism in Africa might come as a surprise. Yet the basic thought behind all of Schuyler's articles on Africa remained the same. The situation in Liberia provided Schuyler with the opportunity to denounce black-on-black exploitation. More commonly, African politics featured the crimes of European oppressors, whom Schuyler also castigated whenever he could. Three years after his series on Liberia, Schuyler turned his attention to the Italian invasion of Ethiopia. Here, sounding very much like the black nationalists who criticized him in 1931, he announced that only a "Negro with . . . ice water trickling through his arteries" could avoid the desire to strike a blow at imperialism by helping the Ethiopians in their hour of need. The majority of blacks felt this way, he wrote, and for once he agreed with them. Although Schuyler expressed skepticism in other places concerning the wisdom of wasting energy fighting foreign racism instead of concentrating on the same problem at home, he found special meaning in the Ethiopian crisis. By appealing to the rising tide of black nationalist feeling in the 1930s, he thought that he could rally the black American masses against fascism and imperialism at the same time. Because he saw all of the Western powers, including the United States, going in the direction of centralization and dictatorship, he thought that the darker nations of the world might provide hope for all of humanity by opposing them.[39] Simultaneously, and some would say "paradoxically," he hoped that by asserting themselves as a group, both nationally and internationally, blacks would make themselves more attractive to whites as political allies and as potential marriage partners. Shuffling subordinates stood no better hope than truculent separatists of achieving the delicate balance necessary to maximize group success. Thus where many thinkers have viewed the relationship between black pride and race-mixing dichotomously, Schuyler understood it dialectically. Although his thinking sometimes veered dramatically in the direction of race pride in the 1930s, especially in response to the Ethiopian crisis, Schuyler always maintained a strategic two-sidedness, as he had from the beginning of his career.

Historian Robert Hill emphasizes this important point in his introduction to *Ethiopian Stories,* a book featuring two of Schuyler's stories about Africa that appeared in the *Pittsburgh Courier,* one written under his own name and the other under the pseudonym Rachel Call. Although Hill's introduction highlights the basic continuity between Schuyler's editorials in his own name and his stories written under pseudonyms, his afterword to the compilation *Black Empire* complicates matters by arguing that Schuyler used his serials "Black Empire" and "Black Internationale"—which together relate the rise of an African Empire under an evil scientist who uses biological terrorism and technologically advanced weaponry to vanquish the combined military might of Europe—to articulate a radical nationalism that he could not utter fully in his own name. To support his position, Hill cites a letter Schuyler wrote in 1937 saying that the popular "Black Internationale," which he wrote under the pen name Samuel I. Brooks, "is hokum and hack work of the purest vein" and had nothing to do with his personal beliefs. Rather than taking this letter at its word, and counting "Black Internationale" as a hoax entirely in keeping with Schuyler's earlier writings and with the venerable practices of satirists throughout the ages,

Hill uses it to invent an alternate political identity for the *Courier* editor. In doing this, he makes the same interpretive mistake that Schuyler mercilessly exploits in his audience, whose enthusiastic response to the "race chauvinism and sheer improbability" that the satirist "crowded" into the story confirmed his "low opinion of the human race." Therefore, by taking "Black Internationale" and "Black Empire" too seriously, Hill fails to account for their actual political and literary value.[40]

As mentioned earlier, the stories published by Hill represent only part of a much larger literary outpouring by Schuyler during the 1930s, a decade when he produced essays, fiction, and editorials at an unbelievable pace. In addition to working as publicity editor for the *Crisis* in these years, he wrote all of the unsigned editorials for the *Courier*, produced installments of his weekly column "Views and Reviews," participated in various investigative reporting ventures, and invented a chapter or two of serialized fiction every week. If all of the material he published in the *Courier* during this period had had a byline after it, the paper would have seemed largely his own creation. He used pseudonyms in part to avoid the monotony of putting his own name on everything he wrote.[41] Also, he probably wanted to give the impression that the *Courier* had a stable of talented writers on its staff.

As Schuyler extended himself into new territory in the 1930s, he continued to comment with his characteristic intellectual independence on every question of public importance facing black Americans. Of these none caused more controversy than his opinions on the Scottsboro trial. Of all the commentators in the black press, Schuyler criticized most vocally the communist effort to defend the nine boys accused of rape in Alabama. Convinced that the communists cared nothing about racial justice, or about the boys, but only manipulated the case for their own political interests, he rebuked them at every opportunity. Schuyler's virulent anticommunism of the 1950s and 1960s stems directly from this debate with the communists and their supporters in the black press over this controversial trial. At one point his rivalry with the communists became so heated that during the Angelo Herndon trial in 1932, another hotly debated episode in the black press, Schuyler kept a gun next to his typewriter while he wrote.[42]

Another controversy emerged over his opposition to the "Don't Buy Where You Can't Work" boycotts of white businesses in the 1930s. Schuyler generally tended to support black economic activism because he thought it indicated a turn toward political realism. Therefore, for the most part, he encouraged the idea of boycotts during the late 1920s. But he started to reconsider this position when the idea of boycotting became popular. By the 1930s Schuyler had become the active promoter of black economic cooperatives through the Young Negroes' Cooperative League. He envisioned this organization helping working-class blacks to start nonprofit companies specializing in the production of low-cost food, clothing, and other items of necessity. Because Schuyler did not have much faith in white goodwill during these hard economic times, he thought that blacks should focus on what they could do for themselves. This inclined him further against boycotting, which promised little, he felt, beyond symbolic victory over individual whites who did business in black communities. Because most blacks did not work in black communities, he reasoned that protests there might prevent them from getting jobs where most of them did work—in white areas. He argued that this bad effect would outweigh any good the protests might do.[43] If blacks wanted to have a greater effect on the overall situation, Schuyler thought, they should ignore symbolism and use cooperatives to create more jobs for themselves.

Schuyler's views on electoral politics during the 1930s caused no less controversy than did his ideas about economics. Throughout the 1920s he emphasized in numerous satirical sketches and editorials the foolishness of the American political system, the dishonesty of politicians, and the ignorance of the average American voter. Although he believed that the average citizen could make a difference in local elections, Schuyler thought of national politics as an orchestrated show for the benefit of the ruling class. Throughout the 1920s and 1930s he accused every candidate running for national office of inordinate greed, deception, and criminal neglect of the people. On the race question he suspected them even more. Schuyler knew that any candidate hoping to win a national election had to appeal to large groups of racist voters all over the country, especially in the South, where segregationists held power out of proportion to their numbers.

As a minority group, Schuyler thought, blacks had to use intelligently what little power they possessed to realize any benefit from national elections. Because Republican presidents after Reconstruction had shown more interest in winning the traditionally Democratic southern white vote than in granting loyal black voters the smallest measure of fairness, Schuyler wondered why blacks did not try harder to play the national parties off against each other. For this reason he reserved some of his harshest criticism for black Republican Party functionaries who continued to show party loyalty for meager patronage jobs and other scraps at the cost of their people.

Although he expressed his opinion in a more conservative style than Schuyler, Robert Vann, the owner of the *Pittsburgh Courier,* agreed with the fundamentals of the editor's position. By the late 1920s Vann had decided to lead the push for political realignment. In 1932 he put the entire weight of his increasingly influential newspaper behind Democrat Franklin Roosevelt. For his efforts Vann received an appointment as assistant attorney general in Roosevelt's New Deal bureaucracy. This pressured Schuyler, then the *Courier's* head editorial writer, to emphasize the positive prospects of the New Deal in his unsigned editorials.[44] Although Schuyler had for years encouraged blacks to show independence from the Republican Party, he turned his guns on Roosevelt almost immediately after the Democrat took office. Vann never forced Schuyler to follow a company line on Roosevelt but probably would have done so if Schuyler had not understood so well when to ignore or soften his personal opinions in writing the *Courier's* official editorials. Schuyler loved to take controversial positions, but he also knew how to hold a job. Later, after Vann became disaffected with isolation and powerlessness in Washington, the difference between Schuyler's statements about national politics in "Views and Reviews" and in these unsigned editorials diminished.[45] After Vann's flirtation with national power ended, Schuyler gave full vent to his highly negative opinions on Roosevelt in both of his columns.

Although many blacks remained suspicious of Roosevelt in 1932, the reputation he established for sensitivity to black causes made him a favorite by 1936. Fearing that black voters would fall for Roosevelt as foolishly as they had fallen for the Republicans in earlier years, Schuyler criticized him vigorously. He asserted that Roosevelt earned his popularity among blacks by public relations gestures rather than legislative action. While he stopped short of calling Roosevelt a racist, he did accuse him of serving the forces of racism in his party. Rampant discrimination in such New Deal agencies as the Civilian Conservation Corps (CCC) and the Agricultural Adjustment Administration (AAA) provided enough proof, he argued, that when it came to dollars and cents, Roosevelt knew whom to serve. Schuyler regarded Roosevelt's main achievement during the Depression as the cheap purchase of working-class loyalty for the ruling class.[46] Although he derided black communists in this era, he did not mind sounding a similar note in the case of the president.

The rise of fascism had a tremendous effect on Schuyler's assessment of the New Deal. He thought that Roosevelt's expensive scheme of bureaucratic expansion and make-work would render the national debt unmanageable. As this debt mounted, New Deal programs would deliver fewer jobs to white American workers. Using past economic crises as models, especially the economic downturn after World War I, Schuyler thought that black people would become scapegoats as poverty-stricken white workers searched for sacrificial victims to ease their pain. He also thought that under difficult economic circumstances American workers would, like their German and Italian counterparts, crave a centralized state power under a fatherlike leader who would impose on them the intoxicating combination of discipline, romantic mission, military domination, and bureaucratic control. As a result, Schuyler saw the key ingredients of fascism in what most others regarded as hopeful public policy.[47] He also recognized these elements in communism, especially in the Soviet Union. As time passed, he even concluded that socialism shared a deep affinity with fascism. He reasoned that any state system with high levels of bureaucratic centralization required a tiny circle of elites to control increasingly large domains of the society. Once Schuyler made this leap, regarding state control as an inherently antidemocratic slippery slope, he began to slide down his own slope toward the conservatism of his later years.

With the potential for increasing debt and the decreasing contentment of the average citizen looming over the American economy, Schuyler saw Roosevelt making choices similar to those of Hitler and Stalin. He concluded that the president, like his European counterparts, would have to solve the problem of the Depression through war. In this he followed the logic of the most conservative arguments against the Roosevelt administration. During the early stages of World War II, Schuyler constantly accused the president of a warmongering hunger to enter the fight on the side of the imperialist British. From Schuyler's perspective, above all else World War II was an imperialist war pitting American and

British fascism against that of the Germans and the Japanese. At times he even questioned whether it mattered which side won: "Whether the Anglo-American plutocratic allies or the Nazi-Fascists survive, the important states of the future will be totalitarian because machine civilization can only survive where the economy is planned. . . . [T]he progressive enlargement and strengthening of . . . controlled economy in the British and American empires indicates the direction we are going regardless of the outcome of the war. In such an economy the four freedoms will be as dead as they are in Axis Europe. . . . [U]nder the circumstances the lot of black people will certainly be no worse and probably no better regardless of which gang wins."[48]

Although he opposed German fascism, Schuyler also hoped that the Axis powers would fight well enough to exhaust the Allies. This would help to weaken American and British domination of the darker peoples of the world. Therefore Schuyler did not weep at Allied losses, especially to the Japanese, whom he considered a good example of "the chickens coming home to roost" for the imperialists. Consistent with this stance, Schuyler combined his warmongering tendencies with a strategic isolationism. He urged Americans to stay home and work on their own problems and encouraged blacks not to enter the armed forces until segregation ended. He had little use for the double "V" campaign—victory abroad and victory at home—promoted by both of his employers, the National Association for the Advancement of Colored People (NAACP) and the *Pittsburgh Courier.* Because he stated his views in an uncompromising fashion, and sometimes with a definite pro-Japanese slant, Schuyler stood out as the most radical voice in the black press on the issue of the war.[49]

Of all the aspects of World War II that Schuyler protested in his column, the internment of the Japanese inspired his most urgent and indignant rhetoric. Long before Pearl Harbor, Schuyler wrote that the racist logic of Western imperialism would overdetermine a clash between emerging Japan and the United States. Because he recognized race as a central element of this conflict, he easily predicted the internment of the Japanese the day after the historic surprise attack. With the element of race figuring so heavily in the struggle, he did not find it difficult to discern which side deserved his sympathies. Besides racism, Schuyler asked, what could justify placing innocent American citizens into camps? The idea seemed to him strikingly similar to what the Germans did to the Jews for similar reasons. Neither German nor Italian Americans had to suffer the same treatment. Given the dark/light logic of these events, Schuyler wondered if blacks might suffer a similar fate. Therefore he urged his readers to think of the Japanese American struggle as their own.[50]

Such ideas did not sit well with the Federal Bureau of Investigation (FBI). Fearing black disloyalty, it conducted a thorough investigation of the black press during the early stages of American involvement in the war. In their search for evidence of pro-Japanese and pro-German sentiment, federal investigators gave Schuyler's column special attention. Several reports by the FBI cited his editorials for their pro-Japanese views.[51] Although Schuyler never went to trial for his outspoken opposition to the war effort, his willingness to state his unvarnished views in the face of government harassment speaks volumes concerning his courage, dedication, and gritty determination to make a difference.

After the war Schuyler made the turn toward conservatism described earlier in this chapter. His earlier anticommunism and his fears concerning the implications of Japanese internment provide part of the explanation for this shift. Also, the rise of fascism altered Schuyler's views concerning the potential of centralized government while simultaneously undermining his already shaky faith in people's ability to govern themselves. Moreover, fascism reinforced Schuyler's awareness of worldwide racism and buttressed his already existing doubts that any grand scheme could change its course. Even taking all of this into account, the intensity of Schuyler's anticommunist paranoia in the 1950s remains hard to explain. It may well be that having found himself a conservative for the first time in a career marked by constant opposition to the status quo, Schuyler had to become a "radical" conservative to preserve important parts of his self-identity and public image. Regardless, it appears that his political approach during this era involved an emerging acceptance of the relative permanence of race as a primary factor in American and international politics. During the 1920s and 1930s he harbored more hope that the salience of race would decrease over time. In the early 1940s he worried that as blacks became more educated, they would become more militant and more inclined to build fortresses of race pride and exclusivity.[52] The combination of unrelenting white racism and decreasing black tolerance for injustice seemed to him a formula for disaster, especially in the presence of an increasingly centralized federal government. Truculent blacks played dangerously with murderous white hatred, the destructive potential of which became more total as the state penetrated almost every aspect of American life. Because the white majority controlled the coercive forces of the state, Schuyler thought that blacks had to conduct their freedom movement with extreme care.

With hindsight, the flaws in Schuyler's post–World War II analysis seem clear. He underestimated how much the liberal consensus after the war needed blacks for legitimation. Having emerged from a war against German racism, the United States could less afford the appearance of intolerance. In addition, as blacks moved north after the war in unprecedented numbers, they became a force in electoral politics that no presidential candidate could afford to ignore. Although Schuyler feared the increasing centralization of the government, he miscalculated how important such a force could be if it took up the cause of integration or enforcement of voting rights. Moreover, he misjudged what a profound moral force such as that brought by Martin Luther King Jr., the Freedom Rides, or the indefatigable efforts of his former ally A. Philip Randolph could accomplish in the new political atmosphere after the war. He also overestimated the white willingness to commit genocide.

Whatever the faults of Schuyler's postwar analysis, it does contain a fascinating juxtaposition. His conservative turn came about as his trust in whites decreased. When one considers that visions of genocide and race war dominated his imagination of race relations during this period, it may seem that Schuyler entertained something much more like an ironically inverted black power position than a garden-variety American conservatism. Of course, such ironies did not fascinate the multitude of enemies he made among liberals and on the left during the 1950s, 1960s, and 1970s.

If this short sketch of Schuyler's life shows nothing else, it demonstrates clearly his talent for making enemies. From his controversial column "Shafts and Darts" to his interracial marriage to the archconservatism of his later years, Schuyler fashioned himself as a useful irritant. Although he sometimes stated his opinions on issues in seductive terms, he never expected his audience to follow him. Instead, he flung himself into the cultural fray, always attempting to inspire the reexamination of important beliefs. His use of provocation, invective, name-calling, and other forms of rhetorical violence flowed directly from this ideal. So did his constant embrace of contradiction, both in his thinking and in his politics.

Schuyler brought uncompromising skepticism to the race debate of his day. This remains his greatest achievement. As much as any other figure in American intellectual history, he resisted the degradation of the race discourse into its characteristic vices: sentimentalism, reification, condescension, and hatred. Schuyler's ability to oppose these through a conscious method of controlled violence grants him a unique place in American and African American letters. To understand his method more fully, and to appreciate its unique contribution to American and African American modernism, we must return to Schuyler's early career. In the 1920s he established himself as the premier satirist of the Harlem Renaissance in an era when satire had its greatest hold on the American imagination. By examining the aims of satirists in this period, and by considering some of the more general goals and methods of their literary forebears, we may find a way to value his prodigious career without granting him the embrace that he would have despised anyway.

CHAPTER TWO

The Ten Commandments

"PERSONALLY, I AM ONLY interested in getting our folks thinking all around the problems confronting them rather than following blindly our two-by-four leaders. Get people to thinking and they will work out their own salvation."[1] This was George Schuyler's answer in 1926 to readers who wanted more from him than the satirical name-calling and negative critique that had, up until that time, made his reputation. Recognizing Schuyler's status as a leading voice in the black press, and secretly hoping that he might open himself up to ridicule, his readers wanted to hear him express his solution to the "Negro Problem" directly and fully in programmatic form. Detecting the hook in the bait, the satirist chided his readers for their slavish desire for big answers from big men. In the process he challenged the whole idea of a so-called Negro Problem and questioned the adequacy of problem/solution thinking in approaching issues of social justice. Mocking his readers' expectation of a definite program for the Negro, he offered them a list of ten "suggestions," in a form reminiscent of the Ten Commandments, for what people who find themselves incapable of independent thought should do in the coming year.

Before reviewing Schuyler's list, it is important to recognize the author's general attitude toward the question it purports to answer because it is the history of that question, and its framing in the American public discourse of the 1920s, that he wanted to challenge. At the turn of the twentieth century the debate surrounding the New South provided the most common frame of reference for the rhetoric of problems and solutions for the Negro. Within this discourse the "Negro Problem" was something for white men to solve. The title of Thomas Nelson Page's 1904 contribution to the debate, *The Negro: The Southerner's Problem,* sums up this sentiment very well. As far as authors like Page were concerned, the "Negro Problem" reduced to an issue of social control. How could whites keep a new generation of Negroes, born after the Civil War with no knowledge of slavery's disciplining lash, in the subservient place that their natural endowments demanded? How could they keep this New Negro from insisting on rights and privileges incompatible with the God-given order of things?[2] Answering these questions required strategic proposals for keeping blacks economically productive, poor, and quiescent at the same time. Perhaps more difficult than making such proposals, for writers like Page, was reconciling the backward-looking aspects of their "peculiar" racial order with the idea of a New South: an emerging modern industrial force, reconciled with the main currency of the nation but nonetheless maintaining its distinctive regional culture.

Understood this way, as a problem of white southern adjustment, the "Negro Problem" inspired many solutions, ranging from extermination to expatriation to separation. Strangely enough, it required a black leader, Booker T. Washington, to propose the most popular "solution" to the dilemma of the white South. Through his industrial education scheme, so slyly articulated in the Atlanta Exposition Address of 1895, Washington assured whites all over the country that blacks would remain economically useful and politically docile, that they would provide the backbone of a mobile and modernistic New South while reminding whites in every possible way of the comforts of the past.[3]

In response to Washington's accommodating solution to the "Negro Problem," and in opposition to those who thought of the Negro as a white man's problem, W. E. B. Du Bois explained to his readers in *The Souls of Black Folk* just what it felt like to "be a problem." In doing so, he claimed the Negro question as black intellectual property. Although he did not hesitate to point out how whites suffered morally and spiritually from the American racial divide, Du Bois placed his greatest emphasis on the problem of black "double-consciousness," a condition of the heart and mind stemming from the duality of black and American identity under conditions of segregation and racial oppression.

To the doubleness permeating every aspect of black existence, Du Bois offered a double solution. On one side he advocated radical protest aimed at breaking down the social, political, economic, and cultural barriers between the races. On the other he supported a program of cultural recovery rooted in the intellectual exploration of such profound creations of the black inner world as the "Sorrow Songs," which he regarded as both uniquely black and uniquely American at the same time. Beyond this the "Sorrow Songs" represented for Du Bois the fruits of black American "second sight," a keen perception of the fundamental tragedy of existence derived from the bitter lessons of slavery and its aftermath. Du Bois hoped that these two "solutions"—protest and cultural recovery—would prove mutually reinforcing. He wanted the recognition of black beauty in tragedy to inspire the sense of dignity required to continue the political struggle against racism. At the same time he hoped that the pride derived from actively opposing oppression could deepen the desire to recover profundity from the most unlikely sources.[4]

In one sense we might derive Schuyler's ironic approach to the "Negro Problem" from Du Bois, who served as a seminal influence for most black thinkers of the 1920s. As he shows clearly in challenging his readers to think "all around the problems confronting them," Schuyler followed Du Bois in placing a heavy emphasis on black people addressing the chaos in their own minds at the same time that he encouraged a radical posture toward white racism. Schuyler also joined Du Bois in viewing the "Negro Problem" ironically. Yet where Du Bois invoked the passion and pain of tragedy to characterize the American race complex, Schuyler employed the disfiguring energies of satire. Where Du Bois found inspiration and wisdom in such moving black cultural creations as the Sorrow Songs, Schuyler invoked the tradition of black humor, the wisdom of which resided in its sharp recognition of the ludicrous and outlandish in American race relations. As a humorist and a satirist, Schuyler also implicitly challenged Du Bois's high-toned and sentimental register of feeling. For him the "Negro Problem" required a rougher treatment more appropriate to its origin in the raw willingness of one group to dominate another and the requirement on the part of the oppressed to see the oppressor with tough-minded realism.

In submitting the "Negro Problem" to satirical humor, Schuyler challenged Du Bois's approach in at least one other way. By not trying to solve the "Problem" for his readers, he implicitly rejected the idea of the black intellectual as someone who should stand above the black masses as a race expert. Instead, Schuyler conceived of the black intellectual as an agent provocateur. Although he shared with Du Bois the desire for a black intellectual class, he exchanged the elitist notion of a middle-class "Talented Tenth" for a wider distribution of intellectual values among all classes of blacks. While Du Bois wanted the "Talented Tenth" to move the race forward by embracing a benevolent and altruistic ethic of service, Schuyler wanted intellectually motivated and practically informed black individuals of all classes to move themselves forward first and to serve the race when it made rational sense.

In taking this angle on the issues facing black Americans in the 1920s, Schuyler had many race experts in mind besides Du Bois. Kelly Miller, Marcus Garvey, Eugene Kinkle Jones, Robert Russa Moton, and many other black public figures joined a long list of white race experts in the 1920s in placing their solutions to the "Negro Problem" before expectant audiences. This made Schuyler wonder if the great rush to provide answers did not itself reinforce the problem. In his view the very expectation of a single large answer to the race question brought with it a totalizing assumption of basic differences between the races. The fantasy that such an answer would require deep social analysis by a penetrating intellect or a great political genius seemed to him no less rooted in this belief. Because of this he found the tendency to celebrate such figures suspicious at best.

Against the expectation that a great man would come along and provide a permanent solution to the race question, Schuyler insisted that the so-called Negro Problem did not exist at all. Instead, there were only Negroes who had problems that were themselves complexly intertwined with issues of class, international politics, and region. Any worthwhile form of black political unity would therefore have to come out of a sophisticated public discussion of these issues. Schuyler did everything he could to keep this discussion going on a broad basis. Provocation and biting humor provided his best weapons in achieving this end. The refusal to answer important questions, especially false questions, flowed directly from the use of these rhetorical methods.

*

Now, with Schuyler's objections to the question set before him by his readers established, let us turn to his "Ten Commandments" of 1926, keeping
in mind that the very form of his response to the request that he offer
a "program for the Negro" ridicules the person who would put him in
the position of playing God and Moses at the same time. In Schuyler's
words:

1. Support Negro business and spend as much as you can
with them—and do it because they are Negro businesses.
White businesses employ white clerks and skilled help because
they are white.

2. Help to promote, organize and support new Negro en-
terprises based on sound business principles. Assume that
all the officers handling money are likely to "Go South" with
the funds; so have them bonded, and let the security company
worry.

3. Help to lower the Negro death rate by spreading the
Gospel of sanitation, hygiene and early medical attention, es-
pecially in regard to venereal diseases, the greatest menace to
Negro health.

4. Buy at least one piece of ground in 1926—preferably in
the North, East or West—even if it is only half an acre in the
suburbs of your town; but don't buy "a pig in a sack"—see
what you are getting.

5. Join a labor union and bargain collectively for wages,
conditions of work and hours of labor. If you cannot join a
white union, form a Negro union; but belong to some union.
This goes for so-called professional workers as well as the
bozo swinging a pick. If you must ape the white man, ape
some of his virtues occasionally.

6. Don't ask more or less of the Negro business man than
you actually do of the white merchants you have been trading
with. Negro businesses should concentrate on service, clean-
liness, modernity and neatness, and attempt to excel their
white competitors in these things.

7. Stop dealing in faith and face the facts. This is the age of
materialism, not mysticism. Practice enlightened self-interest

and develop intelligent skepticism. Examine all sides of every question. Be "from Missouri."

8. Spend more time and money on the inside of your head than on the outside.

9. Give less time, energy and money to getting ready to die, and more to the business of living.

10. Read Frederick [sic] Nietzsche, Max Stirner, Ralph Waldo Emerson, Anatole France, Thomas Paine, Thoreau, Bernard Shaw, Oscar Wilde, Ibsen, Tolstoy, Boccacio, Balzac, Rabelais, Zola, Flaubert, Havelock Ellis, Swift, Mark Twain, and Samuel Butler. Use your public library for a change. Get some real culture. You can be relieved of your money but not of your culture.[5]

With the ironic quality of Schuyler's 1920s writing in mind, we might observe that this list of "commandments," with all of its playful vagueness and generality, is the closest he ever came in this period to articulating systematically a program for black people. For this reason it provides a good point of reference for framing some of the important aspects of his thought. Because it offers his program in the form of a seemingly spontaneous inventory of elements, Schuyler's list represents well the form followed by most of his writing in the *Pittsburgh Courier* and the *Messenger*. The bulk of this corpus consists of occasional commentary addressing issues as they arise. Rarely do any of Schuyler's editorials or satirical commentaries even address the same topic in one space. Instead, his typical effort consists of a few paragraphs on one subject followed by a few observations on another and so on until his space for that week is filled. Although his magazine articles in such organs as the *American Mercury* presented his ideas in a more systematic form, they depended fundamentally on ideas originally expressed in dozens of editorials. Thus their relative length and systematic clarity do not make them better guides to Schuyler's thought than his more varied statements in the *Courier* and the *Messenger*.

Understanding Schuyler requires recognition of the crucial role that immersion in the moment plays in his writing, especially in his editorials. Admittedly these qualities are common in journalism. One can find inconsistencies of every sort in the writing of every journalist with a long career, even those who pride themselves on the pursuit of systematic intellectual positions. Such practices as writing on deadline do not lend themselves to the accomplishment of scholarly rigor. Still, Schuyler's self-conscious embrace of satire and irony grants to his inconsistencies something more than the normal effect of writing under pressure. The right to turn around and state with vehemence the opposite of what he had said yesterday was an important part of what he represented. Sometimes one of his readers would point out places where he contradicted himself or where he gave that impression. To this Schuyler would blithely respond that consistency indicated no "especial virtue." By this he meant that what one regarded as true at the moment deserved more weight than one's past utterances. This principle flowed like a corollary from Schuyler's pragmatic relativism: "No generalization is absolutely true," he once said, "not even that one!"[6]

Looking at Schuyler's "Ten Commandments" as a whole, one finds elements from almost all of the major political positions being debated at the time in the black press. Schuyler combined the Bookerite business boosterism of the National Negro Business League with the unionism of A. Philip Randolph's *Messenger* group. He joined a vaguely nationalistic call for group loyalty with an encouragement to experimental and individualist skepticism. Despite his willingness at times to criticize and sometimes even to lampoon individual positions, Schuyler recognized that all of the major "solutions" proposed by black leaders—whether Tuskegee-style accommodationist conservatism, Urban League bureaucratic liberalism, NAACP legalism, *Messenger* group socialism, or Garveyite nationalism—had some merit. They each provided essential ideological and practical tools for every black person's toolbox. He insisted that the effectiveness of these tools depended ultimately on individual imagination creatively engaged within concrete historical situations.

The general similarity between Schuyler's position in the "Ten Commandments" and philosophical pragmatism seems clear. In *The Harlem Renaissance in Black and White*, cultural historian George Hutchinson argues that pragmatism, along with the cultural anthropology of Franz Boas and cultural pluralism, constituted an important element in the intellectual matrix connecting black and white thinkers in the 1920s. From Charles Sanders Peirce to William James to John Dewey, philosophical pragmatists sought an alternative to both idealist and realist paradigms.

Their most distinctive contribution in this direction was a theory of truth that hinged on experience rather than on the correspondence of ideas with a final Truth or with an empirically known "real" world. Rather than a mental phenomenon occurring exclusively within an individual mind, pragmatists conceived of experience as an interaction between self and world. Truth is a product of this interaction rather than something that precedes it. Because they conceive of truths as results of human action, pragmatists judge them by their consequences. Instead of regarding truth as the end of a quest for the real, they think of it as a human invention deeply implicated in the kind of world it helps to create.[7] In asking his audience to "think," Schuyler had something like this in mind. He wanted his readers to trust their own experiences rather than depending on the word of authority. Moreover, he wanted them to engage their problems creatively, one might even say artistically, not simply to solve individual problems but to reinvent democracy in their own terms.

Despite these affinities, one can go too far in equating Schuyler's view with those of Peirce, James, and Dewey. He certainly read these thinkers, but his editorials reveal a greater familiarity with social scientists like Thorstein Veblen, Robert Park, and Charles S. Johnson, who applied pragmatist frameworks in sociology, economics, and political science. Still, it is important to acknowledge that Schuyler never called himself a pragmatist, nor did he ever discuss directly the elegant riddles that fill the pages of James and Dewey. Looking at his "Ten Commandments," one finds an important affinity with pragmatism, but one also encounters a tendency to evoke notions of realism that both James and Dewey would have regarded as unfortunate at best. Regardless, Schuyler's self-conscious embrace of satire as an artistic mode engaged in creating a more skeptical, pluralistic, and democratic audience did reflect much of what Dewey envisioned in his pragmatist aesthetics. At its heart Schuyler's "Ten Commandments" demands that readers try to imagine a preferable form of society in part by engaging familiar problems with the inventiveness of a great artist or, perhaps more precisely, with the corrosive wit of a great satirist.

Stated this way, Schuyler's mission might appear pragmatic without seeming all that practical. Taking his ten suggestions individually, one could question whether any of them would really help alleviate any black social, political, or economic problem of the 1920s. How many blacks in Schuyler's audience really had the money to purchase a piece of land in

1926? How many had the time or the requisite skills to visit the library or to make the tiniest dent in Schuyler's formidable reading list? Such practical objections to Schuyler's specific ideas are easy to devise because most of his suggestions reflect a certain jaunty optimism about the power of rationality, materialism, and cosmopolitanism to counterbalance the heavy weight of segregation, poverty, cruelty, and self-doubt. Schuyler generally agreed with most New Negroes of the 1920s that the movement of 1.2 million blacks to such northern urban centers as Chicago, Cleveland, Detroit, and New York presented new possibilities for positive change. Like the influential Harlem Renaissance art critic Alain Locke and many others, Schuyler recognized in this demographic shift unprecedented potential not only for economic and political progress but for spiritual change as well.[8]

In his famous introduction to *The New Negro*, Locke argued that the new urban locus of black American life had set the submissive, politically unconscious, and culturally retrograde Negro of the past on the road to extinction. In his place there appeared a more confident, assertive, and self-aware Negro who stood ready to make a distinctive contribution to the complex ethnic diversity of American culture. This New Negro could articulate a proud and complex relationship to his African and his American cultural past even as he took full responsibility for creating his world-historical present. He stood in relation to the Old Negro as Paul did to Saul, a thoroughly transformed being who hoped to convert others. Harlem, his race capital, would do for him what Dublin did for the New Ireland or Prague for the New Czechoslovakia. It would provide him with greater access to the latest intellectual and political movements, exposure to modern economic life, and greater familiarity with people from every corner of the globe.[9] Most important, it would allow him to speak finally and fully for himself and thereby offer the world a unique voice and message.

Whatever their differences, Schuyler, Alain Locke, Louise Thompson, Charles S. Johnson, Jessie Redmon Fauset, Marcus Garvey, Zora Neale Hurston, Langston Hughes, W. E. B. Du Bois, and nearly every other thinker and activist of the Harlem Renaissance agreed that the energy radiating from the emerging black urban scene provided a basis for new struggle and new hope. It offered a reason to believe that despite continuing difficulties, the Negro could play a key role in making for himself a glorious destiny. In his "Ten Commandments," Schuyler asserted his own version of this faith by insisting that no matter where they lived, blacks could make an immediate break with the past by adopting the skeptical intellectual orientation of modern urban life. He implied that this reorientation would make the greatest difference in changing political, economic, and social circumstances. However corrosive, his ironies and inconsistencies never fully obscured this faith. In fact, they were rooted in it.

Still, Schuyler's agreement with his peers only provided a backdrop for many disagreements. His version of the New Negro—at once an ironist, a socialist, a pragmatist, a humorist, a lover of women, an insistent antiracist, and a dedicated antiromantic—required above all else controversy and opposition. One of the most interesting features of Schuyler's 1920s editorials was the drama surrounding his battles with those who entertained other notions concerning what the modern black person should be. At different points he debated and derided Du Bois, Garvey, Robert Russa Moton, and Kelly Miller. He also fought with lesser known editors and leaders such as Gordon Hancock of the *Norfolk Journal and Guide,* Fred R. Moore of the *New York Age,* and Robert Abbot of the *Chicago Defender.* The way Schuyler performed in these debates made some of his readers think of him as a potential "leader of the race"; but, as noted earlier, he rejected such titles. During the 1920s Schuyler preferred to retain his independence and with that his ability to portray himself as a maverick, a voice in the wilderness advocating a cause all but lost.

What is a New Negro? What moral dilemmas must he reconcile? How does he act in the face of new challenges and new ideas? As one can tell from Schuyler's response to readers requesting a solution to the "Negro Problem," he answered these questions by setting an example of skepticism, rationality, realism, and critical thinking rather than offering blueprints or "two-by-four" schemes. Much more than a space where the author presented his favorite ideas, Schuyler's articles and editorials of the 1920s together constituted a site where the author invented himself as a character in the realm of public discourse. Following the fate of this character as he took on established race leaders, political figures, and the major thinkers of his time, observing him as he ventured to England, the ancestral home of the Anglo-Saxon, or as he rode the Jim Crow car through the racist South, provided a drama that transcended both the theoretical and the programmatic implications of his individual utterances. Reading the thoughts of this individual from week to week, witnessing him encountering new situations and new intellectual challenges, provided a black audience itself only recently introduced in large numbers to the world of industry, mass communications, and skyscrapers with one way to measure the possibilities of a new world.

Schuyler's editorials also provided an opportunity to contemplate further new limitations and disappointments. In the "Ten Commandments," Schuyler adopted an ironic and humorous tone in suggesting some of the realities that made a solution to the Negro question hard to imagine. Although he focuses narrowly on black shortcomings in this editorial, it is not hard to see how the general spirit of his wry response to foolish readers points to the larger political, economic, and cultural realities that mocked black aspiration in the 1920s. Looked at through one ideological lens, Harlem was a race capital. Viewed differently, perhaps more realistically, it was an overcrowded ghetto teaming with exploited laborers from the South. One could say something similar concerning all of the black sections of northern cities. Although Harlem's "nice" areas such as Sugar Hill and Seventh Avenue may have kept it from being a slum, they also represented a class divide that no talk of race unity could overcome. Like every ethnic elite, middle-class Harlemites often felt compromised, even threatened, by unsophisticated newcomers.[10] Working-class and poor blacks returned these resentments in kind. When they referred to the "better class" of blacks as "dicty," they made a one-word commentary on what they regarded as the worst kind of servility—that of the hypocrite who would rather imitate the oppressor than embrace his own kind.

External tensions complicated and exacerbated these internal problems. As black troops marched triumphantly up Fifth Avenue in 1919, few of them could have fully expected the convulsion of racist hysteria that led to the "Red Summer" of 1919, the return of the Ku Klux Klan, and the precipitous rise in the number of lynchings that would mar the 1920s. It is also unlikely that very many black soldiers returning to the South expected to find crowds of fearful and hysterical whites waiting at the train station to strip them of their uniforms and return them to an even harsher version of life as usual. Schuyler's prison cell on Governor's Island, New York, provided a unique vantage point from which to view the events of 1919.[11] As the proud members of the heroic 369th Infantry marched and then danced into the arms of friends and lovers, Schuyler, only a few miles away on Governor's Island, suffered the fate of a deserter, himself a prisoner cataloging prisoners of war. One can imagine that this condition may have provided him with second sight concerning the kind of America to which the black conquerors of the Rhine would return. From Hawaii to Fort Des Moines to that fateful day in the Philadelphia train station when the insult of a Greek bootblack convinced him to abandon life as a first lieutenant, Schuyler's military experience provided a harsh preparation for an era where hope and aspiration would often seem foolish next to what was really possible, and where genuine accomplishment would appear paltry compared with the noble dreams that inspired it. When he said seven years later that there was no solution to the "so-called Negro Problem," Schuyler spoke in part from the frustrations of his personal past, from experiences that must have made all of America appear to be a prison house of absurdity.

However bright the expectations of those who applauded the burgeoning black urban life of the 1920s, the overriding reality for most blacks in this period remained essentially the same as it was at the turn of the twentieth century. Large numbers of blacks moved to the North during and after World War I, but 80 percent of the population remained in the South, only to suffer the withering absurdities of segregation. For some observers over the years the injustices committed against blacks in the segregated South have provided justification for a tragic understanding of black history; but considering the ridiculous amount of effort southern whites put into separating the races in every way, one might do just as well in regarding it as something more like a cruel farce. The southern mania for race separation extended beyond schools, parks, conveyances, and residences to graveyards, mental institutions, and homes for the elderly. Courts even had white and black Bibles. After the automobile became popular, some localities protected whites from the humiliating experience of being passed by a black motorist by designating special times for blacks to drive on certain roads. In one city whites found it necessary to segregate the pet cemetery. In another they prevented blacks from using umbrellas for fear that they represented a display of pride too great for racial inferiors. Some of the most ridiculous efforts of the segregationists can be found in their attempts to codify in law just who was white and who was not or which races could get married and under what circumstances.[12]

Still, nothing matched the maniacal paranoia inspired by the very thought of white womanhood. In most southern towns black men would quake in terror if they mistakenly brushed against a white woman while walking down the street. To apologize, especially if it involved such normal courtesies as doffing the cap or smiling, would certainly lead to a lynching, as would any gesture that signified an assumption of dignity and equality. Under the system of segregation, whose precise rules varied from town to town, blacks felt themselves vulnerable to the desires of even the sickest whites. The courts, which were dedicated to preserving alongside the written law an unwritten "Negro law," offered blacks little protection from even the most outrageous assaults on human dignity.[13] One can only imagine the thoughts that crossed the mind of a black defendant as he faced a white judge and an all-white jury after swearing to tell the truth on the Jim Crow Bible.

If the effects of this system had not been so cruel and devastating, it might be less remarkable that blacks could sometimes laugh at their circumstances. Drawing on a long tradition going back to slavery, blacks in the Jim Crow South used humor to exploit the myriad opportunities segregation provided to point out the weakness that masqueraded as white superiority. One joke told the story of a black man brought into court for kicking a white man. The judge asked him why he did this. The black man answered, "Well, Capum, what would you do if someone called you a black son of a bitch?" The judge replied that this would be unlikely to happen. "Well, Capum," the defendant responded, "S'pose they call you the kind of son of a bitch you is?" Another joke focused on the almost unbelievable array of devices invented to keep blacks from voting. After answering all of the reasonable questions placed before him by the registrar, a black farmer was asked: "What is a writ of habeas corpus ad testificandum?" Exasperated, the farmer replied, "Yassir boss, I know 'zactly whut dat is, too: dat's jes' a special kinder 'rangement an' device to keep a Negro f'om votin'!" Another joke focused on the absurdities of southern racial etiquette: In referring to her black servant, a white woman told her son, "I and John will look for the chickens." Her son, a sixth-grader, said that she should say, "John and I . . ." The mother immediately responded, "Grammar or no grammar, boy, I won't put any Negro ahead of me."[14]

No humiliation of segregated society escaped the reach of black humor. Every stereotype—from black sexual prowess to body odor, intellectual incapacity, disunity, pretension to class status, drunkenness, and loudness—inspired a series of jokes that balanced self-deprecation with a larger awareness of the fundamental insanity that made these stereotypes possible. In *Black Culture and Black Consciousness* historian Lawrence Levine recites a copious sampling of this humor. One of his examples is a particularly devastating instance of self-directed black laughter: a monkey standing in the road begging receives a dime from a white traveler. Before he can get out of the way a black man speeding down the road runs him over. When the wagon stops, the monkey thinks to himself, "This brother isn't too bad. He's coming back to help me." The black man stoops over the monkey. Seeing the dime still clutched in the monkey's paw, he snatches it away and drives off. Sadly shaking his head, the monkey responds, "Our race just won't do."[15]

Although they were not themselves nearly as good as ordinary blacks at producing this kind of dark humor, such Harlem Renaissance intellectuals as Hughes, Fauset, Du Bois, and James Weldon Johnson acknowledged its unique power and insight. In his autobiography Johnson expressed his fascination with black laughter, even as he revealed an uncomfortable relationship to it: "The situation in which they were might have seemed hopeless, but they themselves were not without hope. The patent proof of this was their ability to sing and laugh. I know something about the philosophy of song; I wish I knew as much about the philosophy of laughter. Their deep, genuine laughter often puzzled and irritated me. Why *did* they laugh so? How could they laugh so? How *could* they laugh so? Was this rolling, pealing laughter merely echoes from a mental vacuity or did it spring from an innate power to rise above the ironies of life? Or were they, in the language of a line from the blues, 'Laughing to keep from crying'? Were they laughing because they were only thoughtless? Were they laughing at themselves? Were they laughing at the white man? I found no complete answers to these questions."[16]

Recognizing the comic tone of the "Ten Commandments" and the majority of Schuyler's writings in the 1920s, one might ask the same questions about him: At whom is he laughing, and why? Contemplating the multiple purposes of black humor from the trickster tales to the jokes and riddles of the Jim Crow and migration periods can help us to arrive at a partial answer. As almost all observers of black humor have pointed out, jokes like the ones cited earlier provide catharsis by inverting the position of the powerful and the powerless. In addition, they allow tellers and listeners to express anger while at the same time supplying intellectual and moral distance. For example, most jokes in this tradition that focus on whites show how efforts to maintain a social system predicated on racial superiority require oppressors to deny or ignore their own fallibility. Of course, this makes them perfect targets for laughter. Lofty claims to superior social station inevitably place a great strain on realism. As these claims expand, so does the comic distance between the imperfections and discontinuities of empirical human existence and the illusions of the man or woman on top. Despite her power, and in many ways because of it, the oppressor spins for herself a precarious web of circumstance. Those who thought carefully about jokes like these could hardly miss this joyful life lesson.

As the joke about the monkey in the road demonstrates in devastating fashion, the show of superiority among blacks provided another fertile field for humor. Like jokes focusing on whites, black-on-black laughter provided both catharsis and insight. Most centrally this kind of humor focused on how oppression could corrupt some blacks by making them want to imitate the oppressor, exploit their own people, invest in shallow materialism, revere fake symbols of exalted status, or, as in the case of the monkey, invest too heavily in an ideal of black peoplehood. The illusion of victimhood, also an element in the monkey joke, inspired just as much ridicule as fake superiority within the tradition of black laughter. Instead of acting like they were better than others, some blacks responded to oppression by contenting themselves with ignorance or sycophancy. Black humor focusing on the country rube or other fools served as a reminder that subordinate social status did not require blacks to succumb to stereotype. Even jokes that highlighted such racist favorites as black body odor, racial epithets, sexual prowess, or thievery had this effect because they repossessed and rearticulated terms that would always remain hurtful if left in the hands of the oppressor.

As Levine points out in *Black Culture and Black Consciousness*, the self-deprecating mode of black humor, along with the closely related method of telling jokes about painful but unavoidable experiences, might seem to those unfamiliar with its social and cultural context like acquiescence to self-loathing and self-deprecation when it serves the opposite purpose just as well.[17] This does not mean that no black person ever employed corrosive racial humor for less than admirable reasons, only that the subject of black humor is complex and covers a much wider range of causes and purposes than the concept of self-hatred can account for.

In explaining the purposes behind jokes concerning such painful realities of oppression as lynching, jail, whipping, and other denigrating ordeals, Levine borrows from Freud to outline a type of humor that reinforced the desire of the ego to survive even the worst circumstances. Among blacks of the Jim Crow period, jokes abounded concerning how much better the food was in jail than at home or how the chains were better crafted and more secure. This kind of wit underscored the will of the person who refused to allow the circumstance of her body to take over her mind, of the rebellious spirit that used laughter to deny an oppressor dominion over her soul.[18]

In addition to these counterintuitive qualities, Levine emphasizes that even the most devastating in-group humor could serve a community-building function by underscoring common group experiences.[19] At times individual jokes enforced group norms or standards of behavior; they also promoted an idiom for representing problems within the group that generally avoided the self-righteous tone of protest and group uplift rhetoric. Certainly some of the community-building effect of black humor also derived from its tendency to scapegoat. Whether the butt of a joke was a member of the black upper class, a black country rube, a cruel and ignorant white authority figure, poor white Southerners, or an Irish immigrant, those listening to it and laughing at it could feel themselves bonded with the teller and with each other in their common aggression toward a degraded and undermined other. This particular feature unites humor across cultures, but black American laughter gains its special character for its selection of specific targets, which represent engagement with the special historical circumstances and challenges presented by American racism over the years.

These reflections on black folk humor bear an important relation to Schuyler because of all the qualities of his 1920s journalism—stinging satirical invective, wide intellectual reference, brisk occasional commentary, the superior pose of the author—none creates a more striking impression than the sheer fact of persistent humor. As the "Ten Commandments" indicate, along with the many examples of Schuyler's wisecracks, jokes, witticisms, and caricatures in the *Messenger* and the *Pittsburgh Courier,* the author's distinctiveness consists not only in his ability to provoke laughter but in his capacity to do so while addressing topics that in conventional discussion are freighted with seriousness. As the jokes cited earlier indicate, Schuyler did not invent the idea of laughing about race and class oppression, nor was he the first to recognize the possibilities of employing this kind of humor as a weapon in the struggle against these evils. When he pointed out the foibles of white oppressors, he carried on a long and venerable black tradition. The same is true of his deflating remarks concerning blacks, especially preachers, doctors, and country bumpkins. Even when he recalled stereotypes—as in the tale of a black chicken thief who discovered the wonders of chloroform—Schuyler repeated stories that his readers would have recognized from jokes that they were telling every day on street corners and in barber shops.[20]

Although the "Ten Commandments" makes no direct reference to specific jokes or stories in the manner of Schuyler's other editorials and articles, it does allude to some of the major themes of black in-group humor. These are made clear by the references to thievery, for example, in the funds "Go[ing] South" in number two; black sexual activity, as in venereal disease being "the greatest menace to Negro health" in number three; pretension concerning class status, as in aping white virtues for "so-called professional workers" and "the bozo swinging a pick" in number five; and ignorance, as in the suggestion to spend more time "on the inside" of the head rather than "on the outside" in number eight. The general framing of the "Ten Commandments" as a list for fools who cannot think for themselves also serves the same end. By using irony and in-group humor, Schuyler reinforces his main message—that blacks have resources available to them to solve their problems—while avoiding the high horse of the self-righteous "race man." Thus he places a playful but serious question mark after the whole idea of the "Negro Problem" even as he suggests how blacks might make themselves more politically and economically effective. Still, to appreciate fully Schuyler's ability to criticize through laughter, we must go beyond his use of humor to the cutting and biting qualities of his rhetoric. In other words we must consider the cultural and intellectual forces that made satire a compelling choice for him. To locate the most important of these factors, we must, to borrow Schuyler's language in the "Ten Commandments," "Go South" by way of accounting for the general sensibility that undergirded the segregationist mind-set from the late nineteenth century through the 1920s.

Perhaps the system of segregation would seem a little less absurd in retrospect if it had not been buttressed by a veritable cult of sentimentalism, benevolence, and paternalism. This cult may well have reached its high point in 1922, when a proposal came before Congress to erect a monument in memory of the "faithful mammies of the South." In defending the bill, Congressman Charles Steadman of North Carolina spoke to the nobility of the gesture. Going back to antiquity, he declared that no one had thought to erect a monument to an inferior race to commemorate qualities that made it worthy of gratitude. His congressional colleagues were so moved by Steadman's speech that they gave him a standing ovation. Only black protest prevented the proposal from actually making it through the House of Representatives. Still, this protest did not prevent the same episode from recurring in 1939.[21]

The persistence of this proposal before Congress indicates the importance of sentimentalism as an ideological prop for racism just before and during the period that Schuyler made his reputation as a writer. "Remembering" loyal mammies who gladly nursed white children before their own, black slaves who refused to abandon their defeated masters after the Civil War, or old slave storytellers who passed away the free time on the old plantation spinning tales for children served to make an implicit case against the present. This case rationalized the plantation as the proper place for an inferior race. There, the myth had it, blacks could do the kind of work that best suited them, in the right climate, under the supervision of a white master/father who cared for them as members of an extended family. Emotional bonds rather than those of interest or duty held this social order together and granted to it a certain beautiful and idyllic quality.

To understand why this kind of society could seem so pristine and wonderful, one must take note of the basic tenets of sentimentalism, which Southerners found useful throughout the nineteenth and early twentieth centuries for justifying their peculiar way of life. At its root sentimentalism reduces to a basic proposition about the relationship between morality, society, and human nature. It holds that as part of their nature human beings have moral feelings that constitute the very core of the social impulse. Because these feelings comprise the essence of the moral life, they must be cultivated and treasured as inherently valuable, even sacred, counterbalances to the cold realities of modernity.[22] Originally conceived as a way to wrest from Enlightenment rationalism and instrumentalism a greater measure of human dignity, sentimentalism became almost synonymous with popular literature throughout the nineteenth century in every Western country. Broadly speaking, this literature, which varied in its specific expression across time and within different national contexts, provided readers with the occasion to experience their sacred emotions, to recognize within their most intimate feelings that which connected them to family and nation. Within the various subjects depicted by this literature, none provided a better opportunity for experiencing these feelings than the travails of social inferiors such as poverty-stricken children, helpless women, or ignorant blacks.

Because it encourages tender feelings toward the downtrodden and unfortunate, sentimentalism has played a positive role in many progressive social movements from the eighteenth century to the present. It has also played the opposite role at times because of the emphasis it places on moral feelings rather than actions. Also, sentimentalism tends to reinforce preexisting social hierarchies and can cohabitate quite happily with conservative ideas concerning social and cultural cohesion. The concept of inherently moral feelings, which constitutes the very core of sentimentalism, makes it possible to justify almost any feeling, even murderous hatred, as moral so long as it seems to reinforce a communal ideal. This unfortunate manifestation of sentimentalism figured prominently among the major ideological tendencies of the South in the late nineteenth and early twentieth centuries.

Southern whites invented this pristine and idyllic picture of slavery to state a case against everything they thought wrong with emancipation, which, according to them, placed blacks into social and moral circumstances that conflicted with their natural capacities. These whites vowed to defend themselves and humanity by any means necessary against the black primitives in their midst, whose very existence as free people threatened and offended moral sensibility.[23] From their standpoint segregation represented an effort to restore the conditions that once made benevolence and altruism toward blacks possible. In this view separating the races helped to prevent inevitable violent conflict arising from interracial contact. Disfranchisement "purified" the political system. Lynching provided a needed protection against dark forces that threatened white community. It also served to eliminate black troublemakers who might spread their disease to other blacks. And all of this occurred as racists throughout the South wept bitter tears over "Old Black Joe."

The system of segregation not only required a sentimental social imagination; it also fed off of a long list of melodramatic oppositions. As a theatrical and literary mode, melodrama specializes in placing undivided character types—the villain, the hero, the love interest—into stark and dramatic opposition within simple plot structures that end either in victory or defeat. Because it juxtaposes extremes, melodrama places great emphasis on the production of powerful sensations in the audience. Toward this end it employs a series of typical devices, including extreme situations and predicaments beyond the scope of everyday living, moving musical scores, dramatic depiction of events, graphic representation of bodily suffering, and heavy focus on destructive acts of nature. At the heart of all the excitement, a story of the suffering and redemption of a victim/hero provides the main dramatic adhesive. The audience derives its conviction of the hero's virtue from watching him suffer and obtains a feeling of moral closure and relief from his righteous revenge against the source of evil.

Quite often this victory results in the return of innocence and order, usually in a form similar to the one that the story started with. Although melodramas do not always end this way, unspoiled and simple goodness—whether in the form of a particular state or configuration of society, a beautiful love affair, or the heart and soul of an individual—always appears as the object that the hero must recover or preserve at all cost. Just as they glorify innocence and suffering, melodramas also privilege action over thought. Rather than the hero's reflections and perceptions, his actions matter most in illustrating his virtue and in bringing about the resolution of his suffering. For this reason many popular movies today succeed in focusing almost exclusively on action. Yet even without interesting dialogue or plotlines, these movies, and the action heroes at their center, can become quite popular with audiences for combining fantasies of unbound willfulness and power with virtue and morality. Given the emphasis it places on action, we might regard melodrama as the opposite of sentimentalism, which grants primacy to feeling over action.

Nevertheless, melodramas commonly make use of sentimental formulas to heighten emotional engagement with moral problems.

Although some critics claim to find the melodramatic mode in literary and theatrical works produced before the Enlightenment, it is during this period that melodrama began to take on the characteristics that we recognize today as indispensable to soap operas, movies, pulp fiction, and the news. Like sentimentalism, melodrama arose throughout the West in the late eighteenth and nineteenth centuries in response to such powerful destabilizing forces of modernity as rationalism, instrumentalism, and secularization. As a counterbalance to slackening church authority, it reinforced standards of conduct and conferred a sense of transcendent moral and ethical weight on everyday human affairs. Thus melodrama provided through its emphasis on music, gesture, inexpressible emotion, the mystery of desire, and the embodiment of pure good and evil in otherwise everyday figures powerful emotional release analogous to that accompanying religious ceremony.[24]

In the United States the melodramatic imagination has grown up in part as a response to democratic values, which place the hanging sword of negotiation over almost every cultural value of importance. In this context the feelings of moral certitude produced by melodrama provide a sense of relief, especially about those issues most threatening to a sense of order. One might even say that the condition of democratic uncertainty has made the melodramatic story of quintessential American "goodness," which still looms large in the legitimation of government action, attractive beyond all evidence to the contrary. The need to preserve this sense of "goodness" against such discreditable phenomena as slavery, lynching, segregation, ghettoization, peonage, and discrimination has contributed mightily to establishing melodrama as an obsessive gesture of the race discourse.

Returning for a moment to the late-nineteenth- and early-twentieth-century southern segregationist version of this obsession, we find a long list of stock characters—the Mammy, the Sambo, the pure white damsel, the black rapist, the chivalric white male—placed in dramatic opposition on a postemancipation social stage where victory and defeat were the only conceivable options. Sex, violence, and illogical and ungrounded justifications for extreme actions all played a major role in the segregationist racial imagination.[25] Because these aspects of the southern racial ideology are so well known, they provide a convenient way to illustrate some of the more widely shared aspects of American racial melodrama that span across time and region. In *Playing the Race Card* historian Linda Williams provides a detailed account of these conventions in her discussions of Harriet Beecher Stowe's *Uncle Tom's Cabin*, D. W. Griffith's *Birth of a Nation*, Alex Haley's *Roots*, the O. J. Simpson trial, and many other examples.

On one side of American race melodrama we find the image of the "bad" or angry and vengeful black. Quite often this character appears in American fantasy as a deranged male criminal or as a rapist with an insatiable primal hunger for virginal white flesh. This story has traditionally provided racists with a formula for transforming black degradation into a guilt-relieving and action-justifying tale of white victimization.[26] On the other side of race melodrama we find the black victim/hero, whose noble and undeserved suffering evokes compassion and respect. Harriet Beecher Stowe's Uncle Tom provides the most famous example of this type, which has served as a template of sorts for the creation of a wide range of characters, both male and female, real and fictional. Americans commonly gain a great deal of guilt relief through their compassion for such noble figures as Uncle Tom, but it is not necessary for the "Tom" character type to display nobility to inspire sympathy. He only has to suffer.

Although it has made some recent advances toward academic respectability, melodrama has long suffered from association with simplicity, self-indulgence, and bad art. Certainly, this is the most common association it held for such modernists as T. S. Eliot, Ezra Pound, Jean Toomer, and H. L. Mencken in the 1920s. Yet conceived of more broadly as an intellectual mode, one can find it in the most sophisticated writers and thinkers.[27] Freud, Henry James, and Du Bois all embrace it in one way or another. Nor should we think that sentimental and melodramatic modes of imagining society always lead to simpleminded or evil ways of conceiving race relations. Over the years, and to George Schuyler's consternation, melodrama has proven just as useful for blacks as it has for whites. The dramatization of undeserved black suffering at the hands of evil and ignorant whites or within the clutches of a biased and cruel "system" has provided one of the best weapons in the arsenal of the black freedom movement. When wielded correctly, this weapon has galvanized blacks into making righteous claims against the system. It has also led at times to genuine sympathy between the races and to the passage of laws, in both the nineteenth and twentieth centuries, which have undeniably advanced American democracy.

Schuyler never denied this. Nor did he fail to notice the good that melodramatic fantasies of race heroism could do in buttressing black collective self-confidence. Yet looking at the whole dynamic of racial melo-drama—which involved paranoid white claims to victimization, conde-scending sympathy toward black victims, agency-endangering black fan-tasies of overwhelming white power, black self-hatred, and black racism against whites—Schuyler questioned whether the losses stemming from this form of imagination did not outweigh the gains. More than most, he realized that whatever rewards race melodrama offered in sympathy and guilt relief, it always ended where it began, in racial bifurcation. At its ex-treme this bifurcation took the form of willful and destructive action aimed at eliminating the other. In its more benevolent guise, it appeared as a race-preserving rhetoric of cooperation. In the "Ten Commandments," Schuy-ler's call for black self-sufficiency and ironic realism takes explicit aim at the most melodramatic accounts of the black experience circulating in the 1920s. Rather than dwell on white people's actions, Schuyler addresses what blacks themselves can do to improve their circumstances. Instead of offering such romantic "solutions" as escape to Africa, race patriotism, or moralistic appeals to decency, Schuyler tells his readers to join the age of materialism and skepticism. In this way he attempts to counterbalance the most common gestures of the public conversation on race.

Given the centrality of sentimentalism and melodrama to the race dis-course from the nineteenth century through the 1920s, it is easy to see why Schuyler counted them as almost synonymous with the "Negro Prob-lem." By attacking these twin ideological buttresses of racist thought, he thought it possible to weaken and perhaps even topple the edifice. Therefore his choice of satire as an antiracist weapon seems almost per-fect. Nothing could oppose more perfectly the central tenets of these two modes of social and literary imagination. To counter the tendencies toward extreme and simple opposition, easy moral closure, and self-justifying emotional release within melodrama, Schuyler used satire to undermine uncomplicated polarities, to promote the recognition of moral ambigu-ity, and to encourage challenging self-reflection. In contrast to the moral optimism and tender emotions of sentimentalism, Schuyler's satire challenged his readers to reflect realistically on human imperfection, hypocrisy, and the agonistic aspects of discourse. Although melodrama and sentimentalism tend to reduce the mysteries of the unseen to what can be most literally felt and seen, satire, as Schuyler employed it, encouraged a balance of reason and play as the proper response to an empirical world much more complicated than any of the interpretations invented to explain it.

Admittedly, few generalizations apply exhaustively to the riotous array of poems, essays, folk tales, novels, jokes, sermons, and intellectual positions that one might call "satirical." Whether satirists have through the ages been predominantly moralists, as Pope and Dryden emphasized, angry and vicious misanthropes—as their enemies have often charged—or literary artists seeking the perfection of form remains an open issue among critics. The larger question of whether on balance satire elevates readers to moral or artistic contemplation or reduces them to their most base aggressive drives and petty interests also remains open. Some critics even question the value of elevation to moral and intellectual contemplation altogether, basing their sense of satire's value on how powerfully it frees readers from these limiting categories.[28]

At one time or another satire has served almost every political and class standpoint: the aristocrat has employed it in thumbing her nose at the crudity of the lower orders; the commoner has written it to castigate the powerful; and the frustrated social climber has used it to maul those above him while battering those below.[29] Sometimes satire has allowed the narrowminded to dismiss enemies with rhetoric rather than arguments. In the hands of broader and more humane souls, it has provided the occasion for healing catharsis, especially in historical situations where collective madness had made cool, rational response seem inadequate.

It adds considerably to the complexity of satire that no specific literary form corresponds to it. Because of this, Alistair Fowler, a most enthusiastic literary classifier, has called it "the most problematic mode to the taxonomist." Most commonly, satirists mock well-established and accepted literary forms by grafting their corrosive creations onto them. Therefore one can find satires in the form of travel books, epics, diaries, dictionaries, and newspaper articles. One could even broaden this list to include some modes of literary criticism, philosophy, history, and other areas of intellectual inquiry.[30]

The diversity of satire makes any attempt at exhaustive definition into a search for "fool's gold." Still, we might mention two elements that most satires have in common. The most noticeable of these elements is irony, which we might broadly define as a mode of rhetoric employing statements that mean something other than what they say. Of course, many literary forms employ irony, but it is the element of attack that sets satire apart from other ironic modes. Such rhetorical techniques as parody, reductio ad absurdum, and burlesque provide typical weapons for the rhetorical ambushes that typify this literary mode. The clearer the object and the heavier the attack, the more satire tends toward pure invective or denouncement, while more obscure or multiple objects and a more oblique style of address usually accompany open ironic play.[31] In many cases concern with morality, ethics, or artistic form may guide or temper a satiric attack, but this need not be the case. Satirists may fire their poison darts for reasons of political expedience, narrow prejudice, or to express the pettiest personal hatreds. For this reason one should not take the mere appearance of satire as an indication of laudable goals. To gain the most accurate measure of how and why a particular author employs satire, one must eschew general definitions and count on historical and intellectual context as the best guide.

For understanding Schuyler, no aspect of historical context carries greater weight than the general popularity of satire as a mode of social and cultural criticism in the 1920s. Led by Mencken, the dean of American letters in this period, writers like Sinclair Lewis, Don Marquis, and Ring Lardner made the 1920s into a golden age of American satire. In addition to biting humor, these debunkers held in common a list of typical targets, all of which served their general assault on American provincialism, moralism, sentimentalism, and cultural narrowness. These included the philistinism of the industrial bourgeoisie, the provincialism of small-town America, the greed of money-hungry politicians, the vapidity of popular culture, the blindness of unreflective patriotism, the tyrannical excesses of the reform impulse, the childlike ignorance of popular myth, the confusion of sexual relations, and the narrow pettiness of fundamentalist crusaders. This long list could be even longer because the debunkers devoted themselves to full-scale rhetorical terrorism against almost everything the average American in the 1920s held dear. Because of this, their descent from such corrosive precursors as Mark Twain and Ambrose Bierce seems both clear and well earned. Although less obvious, their intellectual ties to the muckraking journalists who exposed the evils of late-nineteenth-century capitalism, politics, and urban life are equally important.[32]

When muckraking lost its ability to shock audiences in the years around 1910, those who wished to carry on the spirit of this influential style of journalism shifted focus. They rejected the moral tone of late-nineteenth-century styles of muckraking for a morally ambiguous, ironic, and comic mode of presentation. They also abandoned the economic and social issues that dominated the writings of their predecessors for an almost exclusively cultural critique. Because most of them either received their initial training as fledgling writers with newspapers or continued as journalists throughout their career, the cultural muckrakers of the 1920s brought a hard-boiled and realistic spirit to even their most highbrow literary efforts.[33]

The debunkers of the 1920s represented only one wing of a more general intellectual and cultural rebellion in the United States that began in the decade or so before World War I and continued until the Depression. While the sheer multiplicity of intellectual positions and cultural movements that contributed to this rebellion defies reduction to a single idea or cause, we might take the opposition to the norms of the Victorian period, especially assumptions concerning the oneness of modernity and progress, as the general target. Whether they were modernists who employed experimentation with artistic form to undercut assumptions concerning the unity of art and easy moral formulas, pluralists who supported cultural multiplicity over Anglo-conformity, socialists who questioned the benevolence of the invisible hand, or antipuritans who challenged the efficacy of sexual repression, the rebels of the 1920s carried out a many-sided mission of destruction against values that they found constricting and unusable under new circumstances. Because it marked so forcefully the element of barbarity at the heart of modernity, World War I provided momentum for the skeptical spirit of these thinkers.[34] So did social and economic changes such as the rise of mass communications and the ascendancy for the first time of the city over the small town as the dominant locus of American life.

The pitched battle between the advocates of big-city values and those of the countryside and small town provided satirists of the 1920s with a specific focus. Throughout the ages satire has often thrived within the context of large fundamental debates over how to live and why. The first century in Rome, the Renaissance, and the Enlightenment all present examples of this sort, where large cultural cleavages made it tempting for one group of men to look at another as fundamentally different, and perhaps inferior or evil, for their radical departure from a formerly dominant set of values. In such contexts, satirists like Petronius, Rabelais, Erasmus, Pope, and Swift made their cultural mark as ironic advocates of the new values. By painting the opposition as foolish and laughable rather than absolutely evil, they sought to mitigate and even heal the rapacious desires released by epochal social change. Instead of opposing these desires directly, they attempted to deflect them through the ironic use of language. Although the changes in American culture in the 1920s fail to qualify as epochal on the scale of the Renaissance or the Enlightenment, they do represent a major shift, perhaps the only major shift, in the nation's fundamental way of life. As ironic advocates of the new social values of the period, the satirists of the 1920s attempted to achieve national healing through ridicule. In this they followed the most famous of their satirical forebears.

Given the attempt by satirists of the 1920s to talk across a gaping divide in American culture that had been developing since the eighteenth century, it did not require a gigantic leap of imagination for Schuyler to see the uses of militant irony in the context of race. Refracted through the regional divide of North and South, the race question had provided one of the great points of rupture in American life for more than a century. In the years surrounding World War I, the black migration effectively nationalized the Negro Problem and made race an important aspect of the big city/country divide then facing the nation.

Because of these trends, and given the general popularity of satire in the 1920s, we might well wonder why many more black writers besides Schuyler did not choose to devote themselves to it. The general idea of the New Negro—militant, modernistic, skeptical, audacious, worldly-wise, and aggressive—would seem to overdetermine the adoption of an assertive and aggressive ironic mode. Many black writers of the 1920s did try their hands at satire. Walter White, Theophilus Lewis, Wallace Thurman, Rudolph Fisher, J. A. Rogers, Eugene Gordon, Robert Bagnall, and many others occasionally dipped their pens in acid, but none (except perhaps

Thurman and Lewis) brought to their efforts the kind of aggression Schuyler would routinely apply to his various targets. Also, no black writer of the 1920s employed satire to address anywhere near the range of issues that Schuyler treated in his editorials, magazine articles, and stories and in his novel *Black No More*.

Recognizing the inherent difficulty of saying why a group of thinkers did not adopt a particular idea or mode of action as opposed to why they did, we may acknowledge a few ideological trends that militated against the development of black American satire in this period. Among these, none exerted a greater retarding influence than sentimentalism and melodrama, whose formative role in shaping American thought on race relations has already been outlined. Without these two ideological forces, and the cultural assumptions behind them, most modes of protest rhetoric in this period would have been impossible. This is especially true of progressive protest rhetoric rooted in the offended dignity of the cultivated victim of racism so evident, for example, in such Claude McKay poems as "If We Must Die" or in some of Du Bois's *Crisis* editorials. As many writers have noted in criticizing the elitism of the major voices of the Harlem Renaissance, this rhetoric generally assumed the goodwill of truly cultivated individuals who could presumably sympathize with the display of injured dignity of talented blacks and act according to these feelings. Such assumptions stood in opposition to the development of any kind of satire.

The same can be said of race loyalty rhetoric, which discouraged the use of aggressive irony toward other blacks, especially when this involved laughter. Because the New Negro, at least as articulated by Alain Locke, defined himself so radically against everything that signified the black American past in slavery, he had to suspect the motives of all racial humor. Minstrelsy had placed such a negative mark on the idea of laughing about black life that sincerity and earnestness became informal requirements of the new black voice. Although satire does not have to employ humor, these rhetorical restrictions certainly narrowed the terrain on which it could be applied.

Similar pressures also affected the previous generation of black writers. Still, one finds among them precedents on which their literary and intellectual heirs of the Harlem Renaissance might have built. Occasionally, one encounters in black magazines and in the black press around the turn of the twentieth century short satirical statements and stories focusing on the absurdity of race relations. Careful readers may also find light satirical moments in the stories of Charles Chesnutt and in the poetry of Paul Laurence Dunbar. J. A. Rogers's *Superman and Man* and James Weldon Johnson's *Autobiography of An Ex-Colored Man* also express a strong satirical tilt. Of the early experimenters with race satire, none explained his thoughts on the subject more eloquently or directly than Johnson, whose career helped to usher in and nurture the New Negro spirit of the 1920s. In a 1918 *New York Age* editorial on Mencken, he explained in direct terms the value of satire vis-à-vis the race question: "What could be more disconcerting and overwhelming to a man posing as everybody's superior than to find that everybody was laughing at his pretensions? Protest would only swell up his self importance. There is a lesson in Mr. Mencken's method for Negro writers. Take the subject of lynching, for example; when the average Negro writer tackles the subject he loudly and solemnly protests in the name of justice and righteousness. By this method he may reach every one, except the lyncher. As far as this method reaches the lyncher at all, it makes him take himself more seriously."[35]

This statement expresses well some of what Schuyler sought to accomplish in the use of satire and humor. Rather than address the racist as if her actions were reasoned and measured, Schuyler joined Mencken in exposing her as a Swiftian "yahoo." As Johnson implies, no mode of expression provides better weaponry for this kind of dismissal than satire. Although the angry protester stands earnest, upright, and indignant on the ground of morality, he succeeds only in exposing his weak and injured consciousness. More important, he makes the racist feel significant and powerful. He also gives the impression of a certain naiveté concerning the fundamentals of racism. If the racist cared about the moral judgments of his victims, he would not be a racist. As a creature formed from fear, he only hopes to inspire the same. Therefore the dismissive, corrosive, and audacious laughter of his most feared enemy, the black superior who refuses victimhood, would seem the perfect weapon against him.

Still, Johnson miscalculates a bit in regarding the transformation of the racist as the most appropriate goal for satire directed at the race question. Instead of changing the racist's mind, Schuyler hoped to crowd her out by making her an object of derision for black and white cosmopolitans who might otherwise take her too seriously. He also thought that the example of a fearless satirist would inspire blacks to oppose such racists with more vehemence and imagination without making demoralizing appeals for special favors from "good white folks." This rejection of "special pleading" and victimhood implied for him unrelenting criticism of other blacks. In this respect he went beyond Johnson's conception of the satirist as progressive race champion by satirizing his own people. As the "Ten Commandments" attests, in doing this he flirted with some of the same devices that racists used to malign blacks and that blacks used to denigrate each other. Rejecting the posture of the morally correct "race man," Schuyler attempted to use the destructive power of racist thought against itself. Rather than repressing this kind of thinking, or getting caught in the losing bargain of trying to prove to whites that it did not apply to gentlemen such as himself, he used it in an effort to liberate himself and his audience.

To understand Schuyler this way, one must appreciate how implicated he felt in the evils of the ridiculous world he depicted in his writings. In *Satiric Inheritance* literary critic Michael Seidel argues that moral implication constitutes the very heart of satire. In making this argument, he achieves a compromise between theories that equate satire with moral concern and those that emphasize its release of aggressive and antisocial tendencies. He asserts that the satirist makes himself a monster by exposing the monstrosity of accepted laws, norms, and moral formulas. Like the Nietzschian genealogist, Seidel's satirist demonstrates the lowly origin of the highest values, but she does not primarily employ historical data to accomplish her task. Instead, she is a close and suspicious observer of the present. While the satirist claims the distance necessary to see clearly what most people cannot see at all, the knowledge she expounds seems the product of the closest intimacy.[36] Thus the old question arises in the mind of the reader: Does it take one to know one?

As Seidel constructs him, the satirist derives a certain power and respect from his ability to reveal unsweet truths. At the same time he cannot avoid association with the ugliness that he describes. In other words he maintains a strong concern and association with moral reform, but he cannot control the cyclical process that this concern places in motion. Hiding behind a mask of literary artifice, he denies himself even as he heaps ridicule upon others. Like a diseased man, he infects his readers, who despise him for alienating them from their world, for making them ugly. They revere him for his ability simultaneously to reveal evil and, by doing so, to sweep it away. At its core this is the dynamic of Schuyler's career as a writer. The ugly truth was his province and irony was his vehicle. Although he maintained a basic concern with the immorality of racism, he could not avoid association with the ugliness that he employed to sweep away the evil he despised. His readers enjoyed and even admired his bad-boy identity even as they disliked him for it. That is, he played the role of scapegoat for a group whose identity remained inseparable from that very concept.[37]

While its conformity with every aspect of the satirical tradition from antiquity to the present seems doubtful, Seidel's model does shed light on some of the major themes in Schuyler's writing. Another important aspect of Seidel's theory posits a disjunction between satire and the very idea of tradition. As the ultimate product of alienated consciousness, satire parodies and derides the most legitimate literary forms and all claims to tradition as justification for action. In other words it embodies antiliterature and antigenealogy. As the ultimate voice of the disinherited, the satirist represents decline, death, decay, ugliness, and the grotesque even as she provides hope for new beginnings by rejecting established codes. Against the unproblematic subject who receives her dispensation through established and legitimate channels, the satirist is the trickster who exposes the discontinuities and distortions that make legitimating narratives possible.[38] Thus the satirist represents the eternal return of the thief who would steal what no one can own.

Because it portrays compellingly and unapologetically the victory of ugliness and disinheritance, of rejection and servitude, of tricksterism and play over narratives of tradition and legitimate birth, it would seem that satire, at least as Seidel presents it, should have had greater play among black writers in the 1920s. No group in the United States could claim a collective experience with greater thematic similarity to the basic motifs of this literary mode. As a group of former slaves in a nation regarding itself as the epitome of freedom, highly intermixed with their former masters but with nothing to show for it, who could make a greater claim to disinheritance than black Americans? Widely considered both physically ugly and sexually alluring, deeply familiar and hopelessly alien, highly creative and culturally underdeveloped, elaborately expressive and helplessly inarticulate, distinctly separate and genetically dangerous, black Americans, it would seem, lived more perfectly and more consciously the contradictions and falsehoods of their own society than any other group.

Given the affinities between some of the basic themes of the satire and the integuments of the black experience, there remains little wonder why Schuyler embraced it with such enthusiasm. Along with his efforts to encourage greater skepticism in his audience, Schuyler always attacked notions of racial inheritance, whether these justified Anglo-Saxonism or black nationalism. He gloried in what he regarded as the deeper truth of racial intermixture that remained hidden behind America's myth of race. Seidel's theory helps to explain why satire constituted the perfect literary mode for this project. It also explains why Schuyler spoke in the voice of the happily alienated individual who maintained his race loyalty only to violate its boundaries. As the "Ten Commandments" shows so well, Schuyler's work in the 1920s sought to liberate blacks as a whole by liberating black individuals from the constricting hold that racism and conformity within the group had over their minds. For him this implied the embrace of a mind-set attuned to the disjunctions and inconsistencies of empirical reality rather than blueprints, habits, and formulas. It required the adoption of a sensibility harmonized with the ugly and uncomfortable truth and a method of delivering these truths in an ironic and contradictory fashion, a dart here and a shaft there.

For this reason it makes little sense to expect from Schuyler a solution to the so-called Negro Problem as it came down to him from Du Bois, Washington, Randolph, Miller, Garvey, and others. Nothing could be more out of step with his guerrilla method of fighting racism than judging his importance as a black public intellectual by the internal coherence of his schemes or by his consistency in selecting targets. As we shall see, Schuyler never escaped the inherent contradictions of his satirical method, nor did he transcend the built-in paradoxes of the race discourse. Like many other black intellectuals, he would throughout his career remain an expert on a problem that he regarded at its root to be false. In other words Schuyler never escaped the dilemma of "twoness" that Du Bois stated so profoundly in *The Souls of Black Folk*. In his own way Schuyler was also explaining what it feels like to be a problem. Still, by *not* solving the "Negro Problem" in his own distinctive manner—through irony, satire, and humor—he made a critical intervention in the race discourse of his time that still remains relevant in ours. Satire and humor made it possible for

him to point out the shortcomings of both old and New Negroes alike without pretending that he could entirely break the cultural code that locked
him and other blacks—and whites also—in a prison house of absurdity.
His attacks on race melodrama and sentimentalism, on the race man's
revealing discomfort with laughter, on the illusions of white and black
racial inheritance, on the crippling myths of black victimhood and white
superiority strike at the very core of values that American society continues
to hold. With this in mind let us now turn to some of the specific battles,
the record of sneak attacks, internal purges, and infiltrations of enemy
lines, that constituted Schuyler's individual guerrilla war on American
racism.

CHAPTER THREE

"The Right to Laugh"

WHEN ASKED DURING AN interview in the late 1960s about George Schuyler, A. Philip Randolph, the leader of the *Messenger* circle in the 1920s, declared: "Schuyler was a socialist when I met him. But he never took it seriously. He made fun of everything—including socialism. But he had an attractive writing style." This statement might have been less dismissive if a political chasm had not developed between Schuyler and Randolph during and after the 1930s.[1] Had Schuyler remained on the left throughout his career, Randolph probably would not have found it necessary to distance him by recalling what marked Schuyler as an insincere socialist. Still, despite his bias, Randolph makes an important point concerning the substance of Schuyler's radicalism during his years with the *Messenger*. While most of Schuyler's contributions to the magazine, as both a writer and an editor, fit within the black socialist framework set forth by Randolph and his collaborator Chandler Owen, they also spill over the edges of that ideological container, often through sheer force of laughter.

Thinking back on the 1920s in his autobiography, Schuyler emphasizes his freethinking spirit: "I . . . always thought dangerously, believing there should be no limit to thought, that the mind should be free. I could entertain any idea without accepting it. Anarchism, feudalism, communism, republicanism, monarchy, vegetarianism, cannibalism, monogamy and polyandry—all had their points."[2] It is telling that socialism did not make this list. During the 1920s Schuyler certainly accepted it to a greater degree than those ideas he merely entertained. Still, a close look at his writings in the *Messenger* reveals that socialism constituted one element within a larger network of ideas that impressed him as alternatives to boring and straight-laced convention, especially on the race question.

Of his various stories, feature articles, plays, essays, and other writings for the *Messenger*, nothing illustrates this point better than the series "Shafts and Darts," which Schuyler began in April 1923 and cowrote with theater critic Theophilus Lewis between April 1924 and August 1925. In their first "Shafts and Darts" column together Schuyler and Lewis announce it as their purpose to "slur, lampoon, damn, and occasionally praise anybody or anything in the known universe, not excepting the President of the Immortals or the gifted editors of this great moral magazine." They explain their dominant motive as malicious, and say that they will go much farther to expose stupidity than to praise anyone. They also deny any reformist intent for fear that success in such an endeavor would reduce the number of laughter-producing spectacles.[3]

In another "dart" called "The Right to Laugh," Schuyler and Lewis express the same thought in another way: "One can laugh at the violent impact of a portly posterior on an icy pavement, the crushing of a derby hat or the squashing of a lemon meringue pie on some citizen's physiognomy, but to laugh at an undertaker's funeral, a marriage, or the annihilation of a battalion of wage slaves fighting to make the world safe for democracy, is sufficient to bring down upon our heads an avalanche of curses and calamities. We may smile broadly at the incantations of a Buddhist, but not those of a Baptist. We may chuckle at the fetish worship of an African, but we must maintain a straight face at the flag worship of an American." As Schuyler and Lewis acknowledge, some readers will consider laughter at the annihilation of a battalion of soldiers gratuitously cruel. Indeed, some measure of coldness in that idea seems hard to deny, but Schuyler and Lewis regarded nationalistic sentimentality and reverence for soldiers as no less cruel for promoting mass murder and capitalist exploitation. They realized, perhaps better than most, the dark side of humor, which they stated in a characteristically playful manner: "The essence of humor lies in the contrast of ours and the other fellow's position with the advantage of course, on our side."[4] At the same time that they used humor to promote a democratic agenda, they realized that the smaller side of human nature, the desire for advantage and dominance, played an undeniable role in the process.

Why, they asked, should we allow social pressure to limit the scope of humor to such mindless rituals as pie-throwing contests and the sentimental "drolleries of Will Rogers?"[5] In any social order the acceptable boundaries for the humorist will, like other social codes, tend to the maintenance of the status quo. It follows, therefore, that those who want to change society must resist pressure to produce canned forms of comedy and find their own objects of laughter. If they are brave and creative, perhaps they will find the formula that leaves the advantage, as Schuyler and Lewis would have it, on the side of the lowly and the downtrodden.

Read even more broadly, "The Right to Laugh" ventures a challenge to the relegation of humor to unimportant or light subject matter. Against this prejudice Schuyler and Lewis claim laughter as a useful mode of resistance against modern forms of repression, including the gloomy reign of seriousness over everything recognized as a matter of significance. The prejudice against humor has constrained discourse as much on the left as it has with defenders of the status quo. However liberating for the downtrodden, genuine and open laughter has always undermined the grip of ideology. This has made it an object of suspicion on the left, which has generally held to a grave seriousness concerning all matters related to the class struggle.

For different reasons the public posture projected by the black "race man" or "race woman" has also eschewed humor for more stern, courageous, earnest, thoughtful, or sympathetic options. One might even regard the portrayal of a certain earnestness and sincerity as an informal requirement of black American leadership, which has always taken upon itself the burden of representing the highest hopes of the race. This burden brings with it a particularly keen concern with exposure because the failings of a black leader are not merely his or her own. A sex scandal, for example, reveals more than individual lust. It places the lascivious nature of all black people on display. A misused word corroborates the ignorance of the group. The use of humor, especially racial humor of the low and common belly-laugh variety, indicates something similar. It evokes images of the happy darky of the minstrel stage and "plantation school" lore, a laughing Uncle Tom possessing insufficient dignity to fight for his freedom.

One can read into Randolph's statement concerning Schuyler this kind of equation. He hints that the conservatism of Schuyler's later years bears a strong relationship to the free and open laughter of his youth. Yet we might find in Schuyler's laughing socialism something different and more important than this.

Schuyler understood that the race man's fear of laughing "at the wrong thing" required him to accept conventional ideas about race. His general avoidance of levity, especially concerning the "Negro Problem," revealed his deeper fear of seeing a cackling coon or a snickering darky staring back at him in the mirror of other people's eyes. Schuyler thought that one so conventional and so faint-hearted could never bring himself sincerely to laugh at whites, nor could he laugh with them. And yet what could be more ridiculous than the patent falsehood of race ideology? Schuyler believed that the New Negro needed desperately to insist on the right to laugh openly and audaciously. His satirical contributions to the *Messenger* represent one of the best attempts in the history of black American letters to realize such a vision.

Randolph's apparent disapproval of Schuyler's propensity to laugh at everything, "including socialism," might give the impression that the leader of the *Messenger* group strongly objected to such transgressions. But thinking back on his days with the *Messenger*, Schuyler recalls that behind the scenes, when no one was looking, Randolph found as much to laugh at in socialism as he did: "Well, naturally, we were in the office together, and we used to laugh over these things. He, of course, wouldn't have done it in public, but we were very close together, and sitting in the same office, and I acted as his secretary. And of course he would dictate these usual stock socialist phrases full of the usual clichés and claptrap, and—well, we both had to stop and laugh at it. . . . I think he had seen through a lot of the socialist posture, as any intelligent person will if they're not True Believers."[6]

In his autobiography, *Black and Conservative*, Schuyler notes Randolph's keen sense of humor along with his impeccable attire in casting him as a member of that rarest breed of men, the civilized minority. No doubt, Randolph's long-established anticommunist record helped Schuyler to arrive at this conclusion, but it took more than politics to make the conservative editor pay tribute to Randolph as an exemplar of those qualities he thought blacks ought to conserve. He remembers Randolph as among the "finest and most engaging men I ever met . . . undemanding and easy to get along with . . . leisurely and undisturbed, remaining affable under all circumstances."[7] In other words Schuyler considered Randolph the very picture of civilized self-possession and decency, a consummate example of one whose intellectual gifts had shaped an entire approach to life. Both personally and intellectually, Randolph continued to make a mark on Schuyler, even after the passage of years had made the gulf between them impassable.

Like most statements of adulation, Schuyler's fulsome praise of Randolph in *Black and Conservative* excludes as much as it reveals. In the early 1920s Schuyler became attracted to Randolph as a friend and as a model of New Negro style and comportment not only for his dignified demeanor, but also for his charismatic embodiment of idealistic opposition to injustice and his willingness to do battle with all comers, big and small. No one took a stronger stance against World War I, spoke out louder for the downtrodden, advocated more strenuously for the self-determination of darker peoples, nor risked more for his opinions than the well-dressed and deep-voiced leader of the *Messenger* group. For an angry and talented young black man just emerging from a difficult encounter with the U.S. military and inclined already toward satire, the combination of suit, tie, and balled fists embodied by Randolph and his associates must have seemed like the natural answer to a series of natural questions: How could he write and fight at the same time? How could he reconcile his basic disdain toward authority with his desire for socially recognized distinction? How could he elevate his race and transcend racially imposed limitations at the same time?

In the 1920s Randolph presented himself as both a visionary and an iconoclast, as a faithful idealist and as the consummate modern man of science and economic realism. He was both a polite gentleman intellectual and a pugnacious antagonist to his enemies, whom he constantly peppered with rhetorical rabbit punches and blows below the belt. A man of the people, Randolph advocated a doctrine whose fundamental practicality most members of the black working class could not see. By the late 1920s he would have to admit that the people had a point. Where the special problems of blacks were concerned, the Socialist Party offered little help. Racists in the ranks made it difficult for the more racially enlightened in the party to act on their egalitarian principles. Also, inclined to construct the so-called Negro Problem as a mere reflection of the larger working-class struggle, its leaders tended to discount the special features of black American oppression and refused to support blacks' independent efforts with enthusiasm. Harried and weakened by schism and by the repressive anti-Red policies of the U.S. government after World War I, the party offered little hope to the white working class, much less to blacks.

Despite their trajectory toward failure, and the marginality of their presence on the sinking ship of socialism in the 1920s, Randolph and the *Messenger* circle made a unique and lasting contribution to black American consciousness. Throughout its eleven-year existence, from 1917 to 1928, the *Messenger* circle included some of the best young black minds in America. In its early years, such figures as the West Indian radical W. A. Domingo, World War I veteran William Colson, Detroit minister Robert Bagnall, and theater critic Lovett Fort-Whitman contributed regularly to the magazine. Later, the *Messenger* attracted the services of historian J. A. Rogers, economist Abraham Harris, writer Wallace Thurman, and theater critic Theophilus Lewis. Under the leadership of Randolph and Owen these thinkers formulated a mode of economic radicalism that would remain an important part of the black freedom struggle throughout the twentieth century. Along with *Opportunity* and the *Crisis*, the *Messenger* also played a central role in defining black cultural politics during the Harlem Renaissance. In a watershed period the writers associated with the *Messenger* invented a unique vision of the New Negro as a political, economic, and moral force.

A child of World War I and of the radical ferment among Harlem's street-corner orators in the years just before the war, the *Messenger* began in November 1917, seven months after the United States entered the war and one month after the October Revolution in Russia. The titles of the editorials in the first issue of the *Messenger* provide a good outline of what the magazine would be in the five years between its inception and 1922, when Schuyler joined the staff. Of the fourteen editorials in this issue, five elaborated different sides of the magazine's radical position on the war: that blacks should refuse to fight until the United States became a democracy. Like many of their white socialist allies, such as Scott Nearing, who contributed "Business and the War" to the first issue of the magazine, Randolph and Owen denounced the war as a capitalist and imperialist sham whose false slogans could not hide the truth revealed in the simple equation of mounting bourgeois bank accounts and the rising death toll of the working class. Another editorial in the first issue, "The Friends of Irish Freedom," extended this analysis to the question of national self-determination, which would become a staple issue of the magazine, especially in connection with the "darker races" in Africa, Asia, and the Caribbean. Other editorials in the first issue encouraged blacks to vote for socialist candidates, join the Socialist Party, become members of the International Workers of the World, and form their own unions and worker-oriented community organizations.[8] Along with the war these were the issues that dominated the *Messenger*'s editorial page in its first years of existence. These were also the issues that secured the young George Schuyler's interest in the *Messenger* circle and provided the staple concerns of his articles and editorials for years to come.

With the end of World War I came several events that would help to shape further the *Messenger*'s identity as a radical New Negro organ. The "Red Summer" of 1919, the Red Scare, the postwar depression of 1920, the Pan-African and Versailles Conferences, the developments in postrevolutionary Russia, and the rise of the American Communist Party each added to the atmosphere of crisis, catastrophe, and opportunity that granted the journal its unique flavor of intellect on the verge of fisticuffs. Of these events none had a greater shaping influence on the *Messenger* than the "Red Summer" of 1919, which exploded in the form of riots in Chicago, Washington, D.C., and other cities just after the return of the soldiers in the winter and spring of that year.

The most graphic depiction of the *Messenger*'s approach to the "Red Summer" appeared in a drawing in the September 1919 issue.[9] On the left this two-page illustration depicts three "Old Crowd Negroes"—Howard math professor and essayist Kelly Miller, Tuskegee president Robert Russa Moton, and the *Crisis* editor W. E. B. Du Bois—telling two black men to turn the other cheek, to be "modest and unassuming," and to "close ranks." All the while, a white mob led by a soldier and a gun-wielding scholar attacks them in front of the Statue of Liberty. The opposite page depicts the New Negro alternative to this problem in the form of a muscular black soldier in an armored car spraying gunshot into a panicked white mob. Above the crowd the sentence "Giving the 'Hun' a dose of his own medicine" hovers in the billowing gun smoke. Above this message appears a quote from Woodrow Wilson: "Force, force to the utmost—force without stint or limit!" Below the illustration, in large bold letters, the phrase "The 'New Crowd Negro' Making America Safe for Himself" delivers the main message.

Disgusted by this display of aggression from the *Messenger* editors, a reader claiming to be the son of "black abolitionists" observed fearfully that the illustration was "enough to make the blood of every white man who is not a Bolshevist or a professional Negro-lover, stir and quicken very perceptibly." Accusing Randolph and Owen of wanting to provoke a general armed conflict, the reader warned them that a "sensible Negro should not be so unwise as to be deceived by the insane ravings of any Bolshevist, any I. W. W.'ist, or anarchist or socialist of any class." He urged them not to "betray their race into the hands of men who would wreck the government." Such criticism only inflamed the editors of the *Messenger*. Their official response, penned by business manager William Daly and endorsed by Randolph and Owen, took the reader to task for accepting segregation and for his apparent inability to understand the connection between racism and capitalism. Rather than admit some wisdom in the reader's caution, they painted him as a defeatist and as the real betrayer of the race.[10] Such was the all-or-nothing quality of their political rhetoric in these years. In preaching caution and in suspecting the left, the reader fell on the wrong side of the *Messenger* binary. Of the stark choices Randolph and Owen presented to their audience—Old Negro/New Negro, capitalism/the people, science/superstition, courage/cowardliness—he had chosen the wrong option in every case. Although Schuyler would in future years handle challenges from his readers with more irony and humor, his dismissive style of address always harkened back to Randolph and Owen's highly charged rhetorical provocations.

In the early years of the *Messenger*, Randolph defined his concept of the "New Crowd Negro" in rigidly antistereotypical terms against everything he understood as characteristic of the black past. Only a racist could have painted a more disparaging picture of the "Old Crowd Negro" than Randolph, who cast aspersions on his intelligence, honesty, and courage. In contrast to his pitiful precursor, the New Crowd Negro was a modern heroic knight armed with the truth and riding the swift-moving current of history like a trusty steed. An economic determinist, a rationalist, a materialist, and a champion of the working class, he possessed "calm and dispassionate poise" and understood that the tough facts of power held sway over the tender-minded wishes of idealists. Because he knew how to look through the surface of ideological appearances to the economic truth lurking underneath, racism presented no mystery. It existed simply because the rich profited from it and would disappear when the working class separated this evil group from its property. Thus the truth about race stood revealed as all surface and no depth, an ideological mystification of capitalism that remained powerful only because so many people insisted on believing in it.[11] Although this epiphenomenal understanding of race represented an advance over the biological and cultural essentialism that dominated the race discourse of the period, it imposed a gnawing dilemma on the New Crowd Negro. Although he devoted himself to exposing the falsehood of race in all of its many manifestations, race remained his only real basis of organization. Despite all of their protests against the concept, Randolph, Owen, and later Schuyler remained devoted race men, dedicated to amending a social identity that they could not fully embrace.

Six years before Harlem Renaissance cultural critic Alain Locke published his famous statement on the New Negro, Randolph in "A New Crowd—A New Negro" pronounced the passive, unscientific, and uninformed Old Crowd Negro not only useless, but "like the veriform appendix ... decidedly injurious." Randolph applied this characterization to a wide range of leaders across the entire spectrum of black American political thought, including such venerable figures as Du Bois, Miller, Moton, and Republican Party functionary Charles "Chas." W. Anderson, all of whom Schuyler would take up later as prime targets for his own political smart bombs. Regardless of their differences, Randolph regarded all of these leaders as equally servile lackeys of the capitalist "White Old Crowd," which provided them with money and marching orders. In opposition to this, Randolph called for young men possessing "ability, radicalism, and sincerity" who would have "no armistice with lynch-law; no truce with jim-crowism, and disfranchisement; no peace until the Negro receives complete social, economic and political justice." Striking a high point of moral indignation at the Old Crowd traitors to the Negro cause, Randolph declared that working-class blacks should join the Egyptians, Germans, Hungarians, and Russians in sweeping away compromised traditional leaders and their "false, corrupt and wicked institutions of oppression and cruelty."[12]

In "The Failure of Negro Leaders," Randolph's close associate Chandler Owen presses the same case while demonstrating his talent for a more playful brand of vitriol. In accusing the Old Crowd leaders of ignorance, which he calls "the worst indictment of the modern world," Owen condemns them for provoking laughter among whites. Citing specifically the uninformed views of the leading black professors concerning socialism, Owen rises to his rhetorical apogee: "It makes us ashamed to think what men like Professor Charles A. Beard, Scott Nearing, Overstreet, Albert Bushnell Hart and E. R. A. Seligman must think when they read these pigmy opinions and this puerile, credulous interpretation of history from men who are supposed to have given their lives to the study of science, but who are little short of mental manikins and intellectual lilliputians."[13]

Between Randolph and Owen, both of whom specialized in overblown rhetoric, the latter always provided the greater dose of humor and cynicism. One can see some of the difference between them in their statements on black leaders. While Randolph prefers to paint the Old Crowd as a group of criminals and lackeys, Owen dwells on their shame-provoking foolishness. Randolph sets black leaders against the black masses, whose inevitable rise he seems to believe in without question. In contrast, Owen sets the black professors against white professors, whom he imagines looking down on their inferior dark counterparts. Eventually Schuyler would develop the suggestion of satire in Owen's writing beyond invective into a full and self-conscious approach to the race question.

The *Messenger* group's radical denouncement of established black leadership reached its greatest intensity between mid-1922 and late 1923, during another defining moment in its history, the infamous "Garvey Must Go" campaign. By 1920, Marcus Garvey, a fiery and inspirational Jamaican admirer of Booker T. Washington, had captured the popular black American imagination with his bold plan to establish an African empire through the agency of a shipping fleet called the Black Star Line. The Universal Negro Improvement Association (UNIA) publication *Negro World* projected the organization's intellectual voice while mass meetings, conventions, and parades made Garvey's vision accessible to its ever-expanding working-class membership. Although no one knows the precise figures, estimates of membership in the UNIA at the height of its popularity in 1920 have ranged from four hundred thousand to four million. The editors of the *Messenger* could only dream about that kind of appeal among black workers. Yet it required more than simple jealousy to make them call lustily for Garvey's political emasculation.

Initially, Randolph and his *Messenger* allies objected to the Garvey Movement in polite and measured tones, but when Garvey admitted in mid-1922 to having met with the Imperial Wizard of the Ku Klux Klan, the rhetorical ground shifted significantly. After Garvey's startling announcement, all of the unspoken differences between the Garvey Movement and the socialist radicals began to surface. Also, thanks to Garvey, Owen and Randolph found themselves for the first time in agreement with Old Crowd black leadership, especially Du Bois, who carried out a determined campaign to undermine support for the "provisional president of Africa." In July 1922 the *Messenger* joined a chorus of black leaders, including William Pickens, Du Bois, and New York Alderman George Harris, in condemning the Jamaican nationalist as a fraud and race traitor. The lead editorial in that month's *Messenger* announced "Marcus Garvey! The Black Imperial Wizard Becomes Messenger Boy of the White Ku Klux Kleagle." It declared that the *Messenger* had decided to fire "the opening gun" in a campaign to drive the "sinister viciousness" of Garveyism off of American soil.[14]

Although the opposition to Garvey reflected well many of the *Messenger* group's defining values, the willingness to cooperate with Old Crowd black leadership did reflect a subtle shift in values. So did the willingness to join the NAACP in drafting a letter to Attorney General Harry M. Daugherty requesting Garvey's deportation and the acceleration of court proceedings against him for mail fraud. For the *Messenger* group this letter represented a particularly egregious departure from principle. To support the prosecution and deportation of Garvey, Randolph and Owen had to pretend that they had never spoken out against the Red Scare, whose foundation consisted in the principle of deporting dangerous foreigners. To make matters worse, the *Messenger* appealed to the lowest form of anti–West Indian feeling in its pursuit of Garvey, associating him with ignorance, odor, and other age-old black stereotypes. This kind of rhetoric represented a retreat from the *Messenger*'s earlier internationalist position, especially its advocacy of self-determination for the darker races of the world.[15]

Owen and Randolph's willingness to abandon principle in the case of

Garvey naturally leads one to question the intensity of their attachment to the ideals they pronounced so eloquently in the early days of the *Messenger*. Like all of those who shift with the political sands, neither would have detected in the "Garvey Must Go" campaign anything but absolute consistency with their black socialist program. Whether the *Messenger* group's effort to erase Garvey from the black American political scene represented abandonment of principle or temporary practical adjustment to immediate political circumstance, one fact remains certain: In the two years after 1923 the *Messenger* changed markedly as both of its editors lost faith in socialism and drifted away from the publication.[16]

Randolph's journey away from socialism was less personal than that of his collaborator. Through the early to mid-1920s he became convinced that socialism offered no practical possibility for organizing black workers. Therefore he turned to the next best thing, the union movement. As president of the Brotherhood of Sleeping Car Porters, which began in 1925, he became too busy to edit the *Messenger*. By this time Owen's role on the *Messenger* had also changed drastically. In 1922 he began to conduct national fund-raising tours for the magazine that effectively ended his active participation as editor. Owen's diminishing faith in socialism received a final blow in 1923, when his brother Toussaint died penniless. For years he had attempted to secure a union job for Toussaint, but he ultimately failed to prevail over the racism of his white socialist allies. For Owen this delivered in a personal and painful way the fundamental difficulty of joining race advocacy and socialism. If he could not get one black man a job, what hope could there possibly be in a large-scale class movement across racial lines?

According to Schuyler's somewhat tendentious but useful recollection, Owen's inclination to doubt had prepared him to abandon socialism many years before this tragic episode. Schuyler remembered Owen's streak of cynicism in positive terms as an indication of his intelligence and his superiority to all "True Believers," including Randolph. In his autobiography Schuyler recalls Owen as "a facile and acidulous writer, a man of ready wit and agile tongue endowed with the saving grace of cynicism." He emphasized that "Owen was gifted with hyperbole and his sarcasm was corroding." But Schuyler also recalled less praiseworthy aspects of Owen's character. Claiming that "Owen was interested more in saving Owen than in saving the masses," he pointed to the streak of opportunism that kept Owen from taking the stated project of the *Messenger* too seriously. Randolph's biographer Jervis Anderson corroborates this point in describing Owen's obsessive concern with becoming wealthy.[17] More a devotee of the late-nineteenth-century sociologist Lester Ward than of Karl Marx, he always hoped for personal fame and fortune, despite his many impassioned statements in the *Messenger* to the contrary.

As with his comments on Randolph, Schuyler had other reasons besides politics to recall fondly Owen's cynicism and wit. Of those writing for the *Messenger* when Schuyler joined the staff in 1922, Owen came closest to sharing his sensibility. Although most of Owen's *Messenger* articles addressed the same range of economic and political issues as those of Randolph, he also ventured outside of the standard subjects to pronounce on broader cultural themes. Of these themes love and romance were his favorites. In the first issue of the *Messenger*, Owen attempted in "Passing of Novelty" to explain the eternal appeal of infidelity. He published four other articles in a similar vein in successive months at the beginning of 1923. Each part of Owen's four-month love tutorial attempted the same essential intellectual trick: the reduction of the unruly dynamics of the heart to the materialist and evolutionary logic of the New Crowd Negro. Deriving most of his sensibility, if not his material, from Lester Ward's attempt to wed collectivism and evolution, Owen claimed that romance and love ultimately reduce to physical desire, or, as he put it, to "the crave for sex."[18]

Despite their tendency to reduce human beings to the level of highly complex animals, Owen's statements debunking romance need not be viewed as entirely cynical. Ultimately, they hinge on an optimistic notion concerning the relationship between nature and the "good." Also, like many writers in the 1920s devoted to the cause of sexual freedom, Owen counted himself a rebel against repressive Victorian cultural values. His battle against repression on the sexual front complemented his struggle against race and class oppression. In "The Black and Tan Cabaret—America's Most Democratic Institution," Owen combined his sexual, racial, and class politics in arguing that the cabaret plays a central if unrecognized role in the battle against racism. In asserting this, he sought at once to challenge the black bourgeois politics of respectability, racist opposition to interracial sexual contact, and the narrow definition of political behavior that sometimes prevailed on the left in the 1920s. As an alternative to

these limiting and negative perspectives, he held up the unpretentious actions of ordinary people answering the multifaceted call of Eros—dancing,
drinking, listening to music—as the epitome of democracy and as one
powerful answer to the "Negro Question": "Fundamentally, the cabaret
is a place where people can abandon their cant and hypocrisy just as
they do in going on a hike, a picnic, or a hunting trip. They get close to
earth where human nature is more nearly uniform. The little barracks of
hypocrisy and the prison bars of prejudice are temporarily at least torn
down, and people act like natural, plain human beings—kind, cordial,
friendly, gentle—bringing with them what Walt Whitman called 'a new
roughness and a new gladness.'"[19]

Although he insisted in uncompromising fashion on total social
equality between the races, Owen's collaborator Randolph never made
this kind of direct connection between sexual, cultural, and racial liberation. The constant appearance of such ideas in Schuyler's 1920s and
1930s journalism, especially the insistence on race mixing as the key
to "solving" the race question, appears in large part a matter of Owen's
influence. Although Owen engaged in economic determinism with nearly
the same vigor as Randolph, his articles on such subjects as romance
and the cabaret demonstrate clearly his struggle against stock socialist
themes. But it would take Schuyler to advance this struggle to a new
level of "roughness" and "gladness." Where Owen employed unmerciful
invective against black leaders, Schuyler used satire to paint them as fools;
where Owen debunked love by reducing it to sex, Schuyler found in the
acts of lovers further grounds for human folly; and where Owen saw
beauty and democracy in nightlife, Schuyler recognized a less sentimental
play of the beautiful and the grotesque, a democratic stew with more than
a few unsavory elements.

The *Messenger* hovered on the edge of satire from its first issue. Its fundamental perspective was ironic, confrontational, embattled, iconoclastic,
and heavily anchored in a hermeneutics of suspicion and unmasking. The
practical position of its black socialist writers—unacceptable to socialists
because of their race, unpalatable to the black masses because of their
socialism, and unable to view blackness, their only real basis of organization, as something other than an elaborate illusion—also suited them well
to the production of satire. That they produced little more than colorful
pieces of invective in the years before Schuyler joined the staff attests to

the absence of a writer with the full range of skills and interest to develop the *Messenger*'s courtship of irony into a full-fledged marriage.

Schuyler joined the *Messenger* at a turning point, just after the most telling and vituperative shots of the "Garvey Must Go" campaign had been fired and when the two principal voices that had shaped the publication found themselves doubting the faith of earlier times. His contributions to the *Messenger* during the next five years turned the doubt and contradiction that characterized the journal into a virtue. Writing almost always in a satirical voice, he spoke from the standpoint of the self-proclaimed fake, the literary hack, the impostor, the neurotic, the drunkard, and the criminal. From this position he sought less to preach a doctrine than to glory in the distance between empirical reality and any idea invented to explain it. As a result, he took the demystifying and suspicious orientation of the *Messenger,* rooted in demonstrating economic reality behind ideological appearances, in a new direction.

Initially, Schuyler joined the *Messenger* staff to replace Owen in the office rather than in the pages of the journal. Owen's frequent fund-raising trips left the magazine's offices shorthanded and in need of organizational help. Schuyler provided this for almost a year before he began to write. His first article appeared in the September 1923 issue. Called "Politics and the Negro," it reflected his past as a socialist street-corner speaker in Syracuse much more than his future as a leading satirist. Written in a didactic tone, it contained a note at the end apprising readers that they had just read "a basic analysis of economic determinism in the realm of politics." This was certainly true. "Politics and the Negro" showed that Schuyler, a veteran of numerous socialist forums, lectures, and discussions, had learned his lessons well: "The methods of supplying the needs of life and the relationship between individuals growing out of the associations required for the production of the vital necessities form the basis upon which are built up the laws, customs, morals and theology of any human group." This opening sentence establishes the major theme and the prevailing tone of the article. Objective and straightforward in style, it relates the twice-told tale of base/superstructuralism in a manner that belies its almost evangelical mission: the banishment of the owning-class philosophy from the minds of the workers so that "the pure free air of economic truth can lead the way."[20]

Although "Politics and the Negro" delineates some of Schuyler's basic early values, it reads more like a *Messenger* club membership requirement than a typical product of his pen. His next piece, a two-part article called "Hobohemia: The World of the Migratory Worker," departs markedly from the boilerplate style of this initial effort. Although it contains neither satire nor humor, "Hobohemia" sets forth a fundamental vision that would remain central to all of Schuyler's best efforts in the 1920s. In "Hobohemia," Schuyler draws on his past as a Bowery bum to describe an underground community of despised and oppressed men and women whose rejection of conventional bourgeois values allowed them to construct a model of democracy on the margins of American society. He writes: "By the snobs of society and those who ape them . . . [Hobohemia] is considered the very lowest social group—the mudsill. The Hobohemians themselves, as in all other things, depart from convention in considering themselves the best people on earth. As the snobs scoff at them, they look with scorn on 'the society stiffs,' 'psalm-singers,' [and] 'white collar slaves.'"[21]

Despite their diversity—they are young and old, male and female, white and black, clever and stupid—Hobohemians have two broad characteristics in common, wanderlust and revolt against the regimentation of machine civilization. The Hobohemian's freedom-loving instinct earns her Schuyler's praise, but her unique brand of self-consciousness marks her as truly superior. The Hobohemian's skill in turning language to the requirements of her chosen existence provides particularly strong evidence of her superiority to the standardized mainstream. The expletives "dumb," "tramp," or "vagabond" that respectable citizens heap upon her like blows serve as emblems of pride to the Hobohemian, who uses them in self-description. Adding to their positive qualities, the experience of oppression combined with incessant travel help to make Hobohemians less provincial and less racist than other Americans. Anarchists, communists, syndicalists, athiests, socialists, and representatives of many nationalities all dwell among them. Because of this, and despite its inconveniences and occasional cruelties, Schuyler regards Hobohemia as the kind of community any truly moral person would want to join. It features freedom of movement, freedom of expression, and true Christian generosity, with no strings attached.[22]

"Hobohemia" remains one of Schuyler's most important essays because more than any other it shows the connection between his individualist values and a communal ideal. While imperfect, the world of the hobo represents for Schuyler the ability of downtrodden people to answer difficult challenges with dignity and creativity. Although the world frowns on them, the hobos consider themselves the best people on earth. By the way they treat each other, they provide strong evidence that they might well be right.

Despite its focus on a multiracial group, and in another sense because of it, "Hobohemia" suggests a broad analogy between the life of the hobo and the black American condition in the 1920s. Like the hobos, blacks in this period lacked economic resources, had their own ways of using language, appeared in one guise primitive and in another ultramodern, played an indispensable and unappreciated role in the economy, and represented almost everything despised by those who saw themselves as "respectable." But in Schuyler's view the citizens of Hobohemia possessed something that too many black people lacked: a strong sense of group identity based in the clear and constant perception of their humanity. Because of this, the hobos, who constituted neither a class nor a race, represented an ideal for both black people and the working class. Constitutionally opposed to the direction of machine civilization, they regarded no other group as worthy of imitation. Instead, they formed a confederation of naysayers and skeptics, the best individuals in the world, despite all outward appearances.

One might say that during the 1920s, and especially during his early years with the *Messenger,* Schuyler considered himself more of a Hobohemian than a straight advocate of the black proletariat. Unlike members of the working class, Hobohemians chose their outsider status in defiance of everything official society considered valuable. Their problem with capitalism went beyond inequities of resource distribution and the theft of surplus value right to the philosophical core: How should people live? What did they need to lead truly civilized lives? For their willingness to give a tangible social meaning to their vision while eschewing all talk of utopia, the Hobohemians—a group with no claim to tradition, racial heritage, wealth, belief, or expectations of a glorious future—constituted Schuyler's spiritual community of preference.

Schuyler's next appearance in the pages of the *Messenger* would develop the position of cultural and social outsider, proclaimed in playful but sincere tones in "Hobohemia," into what would become his trademark mode of expression. In September 1923 the *Messenger* published the first installment of "Shafts and Darts," which begins appropriately with a short satirical dialogue intended to signal to *Messenger* readers that they have entered a new world. The brief exchange between a Martian and a Harlem host in 1973 introduces the reader to the strange and nearly unrecognizable world of the future. The Martian asks his host: "Who were those fellows, Kinknomore and Facebleach[,] to whom you have erected these great monuments?" The host answers: "They are the gods of our parents. They solved the race question!"[23]

Thus Schuyler begins his new column with the issue that would remain its central concern throughout the five years of its existence: the relationship between the race problem and the larger human tendency to embrace comforting and self-justifying fantasy. Can the users of skin lighteners and hair straighteners solve the race problem? That idea seems just as ludicrous as the notion of a Martian touring Harlem in 1973. By placing such a ridiculous and exaggerated scenario in the future, Schuyler makes fun of the progressive expectation of ever-brighter days to come. Instead of sincere and earnest reformers "solving" the race problem, Schuyler fantasizes that those with the least amount of race pride, those who would do anything to acquire the external characteristics of the white man, will eliminate the problem altogether. This requires them to uphold the mythology of race even as they abolish it. Thus appears the central irony of Schuyler's short dialogue: race pride and its opposite stand revealed as aspects of the same mind-set. Even the raceless world of the future will build monuments to race, if only to define itself against it. As the humorous fantasy goes, even the Martians, the ultimate racial other, will have to learn something of our racial past, and the folly that made it possible, to understand our humanity.

After this startling beginning, Schuyler turns to more routine work: pelting the *Messenger* group's favorite targets, including Garvey, whom he calls the "Self-Styled Emperor of Africa" and the "Imperial Blizzard"; Negro Communists of the African Blood Brotherhood, whom he chides for their greed and lack of membership; Du Bois, whom he calls a self-serving windbag and friend of the Ku Klux Klan for his emerging nationalism; and Miller, whom he calls the "Mouthematician of Howard." The German fascists, the Ku Klux Klan, black northern machine politicians, and "the hat-in-hand Negroes of the Washington snobocracy" who attended Warren

Harding's funeral procession all get a few choice drops from Schuyler's acid-dipped pen.[24] The list of Schuyler's targets seems almost as long as the nasty arsenal of insults he uses to undermine its unlucky members, all of whom he portrays in true *Messenger* style as greedy, stupid, self-serving, petty, and barely fit to have a voice in the public discourse.

Next to Randolph's and Owen's statements concerning Old Crowd black leadership, Schuyler's playful vitriol may have struck *Messenger* readers as light fare. In the pieces written in the immediate aftermath of the "Garvey Must Go" campaign, Schuyler's humorous and ironic tone in attacking leaders tended to balance the self-righteous and self-justifying rhetoric that prevailed in the *Messenger* group at that time. In Schuyler's hands Garvey, Du Bois, Moton, and other typical *Messenger* targets seemed no more attractive than they did when Owen wrote about them, but their faults appeared less morally offensive for being part of the larger human circus. As an expert spectator, Schuyler appreciated this show for the pleasures it made possible. He also relished the opportunity it provided to undermine conformity, convention, and untested faith.

The attack on black leaders, especially on Garvey and Du Bois, would continue as a staple of "Shafts and Darts" throughout its existence. After Garvey's conviction for mail fraud, Schuyler seized unmercifully on every opportunity for laughter. In the December 1923 "Shafts and Darts" he announces that among the new records from the Moron Phonograph Company, which include a solo by Major Robert "Rusty" Moton called "Dodging the Issue" and a comic dialogue between Democratic Party leader Ferdinand Q. Morton and Imperial Wizard Evans called "We Vote the Same Ticket," Garvey sings a spiritual called "Nobody Knows the Trouble I Have," accompanied by judgments and warrants. The next month Schuyler announces that the Cap and Bells Publishing Company of Ward's Island, New York City, will publish, along with conservative Fred R. Moore's 999,999,999-page book *Empty Editorials* and Du Bois's *Europe In Winter: Or the Value of a Pan-African Conference in Raising the Price of a Vacation*, Garvey's 41,144-page dialogue with U.S. Judge Mack, entitled *Atlanta or Leavenworth: Their Relative Merits as Havens of Rest*, at the bargain price of two rubles.[25]

In addition to Du Bois and Garvey, Schuyler also lampooned the communists of the African Blood Brotherhood with particular relish in the first year of "Shafts and Darts." In one particularly well-pointed piece, he estimates the membership of the workers party at twenty thousand, using as his source a confidential report to a "high mogul of the faith in Berlin" known only to "the Department of Justice, the Civic Federation . . . and other such uplift organizations and preservers of democracy." Mocking the paranoid anti-Red sentiment prevalent at the time, he wonders what would happen to this fair country if the communist rebellion actually took root. He speculates that the honest farmer would be forced to toil all year and get nothing in return, the hard-working urban dweller would have to live in apartments stuffed with eight or more people, and the women would be nationalized and thus could not marry for love. In other words the communists would change nothing of note. Of the twenty thousand disruptive revolutionaries in the Workers' Party, he estimates that at least fifteen hundred speak English, and can therefore "carry on the vicious propaganda from Holy Moscow that much more effectively." He observes that in addition to the 1,494 whites, all of the other English-speaking insurgents are members of the African Blood Brotherhood. For those fearful of the damage that these six dangerous Negroes can cause, Schuyler recalls the "Garvey Must Go" campaign, noting that only one of them is a naturalized citizen.[26]

To reward black leaders and intellectuals for particularly outstanding displays of hypocrisy, exaggeration, stupidity, or Uncle Tomism, Schuyler inaugurated in December 1923 a monthly prize of a "beautiful tissue-paper overcoat." Over the years the prize changed from "an elegantly embossed and beautifully lacquered dill pickle" to a "genuine cut glass thunder-mug," but the requirements for winning it remained the same. The first winner, Kelly Miller, earned the tissue-paper overcoat for the following "delicious tidbit": "Dr. Du Bois is fostering the Pan-African Conference composed of representatives of the mother continent now scattered among the various nations of the earth. Marcus Garvey heads a more positive and dramatic movement with a program of immediate or early effectiveness. He startles the world with the self-assurance and finality of his proposal. He puts the world at a gaze like a new comet that blazes suddenly in the heavens." Although Schuyler did not give specific reasons for awarding the prize for this statement, Miller's exaggerated romantic tone probably set it above other candidates in the black press on the same general topic. Following the long-established *Messenger* habit of pelting Du Bois, Schuyler often chided the *Crisis* editor for his vaunted but sparsely attended Pan-African Conferences.[27] Next to the somewhat humbling and decidedly inauspicious reality of Du Bois's conferences, Miller's rhetoric appeared either delusional, dishonest, or unbelievably ingratiating. His attempt to cast Garvey's "Back to Africa" embarrassment as an improvement on Du Bois's already bad idea, even to the point of comparing the UNIA leader to a comet, struck Schuyler as the very epitome of laughable wish-fulfillment. Still, if Miller had made the same substantive statement without the worshipful pose, Schuyler probably would not have awarded him the prize.

Over the years most of Schuyler's favorite targets managed to garner at least one tissue-paper overcoat, dill pickle, or thunder-mug. Du Bois, Alain Locke, and the writers and editors of *Negro World* each won once. Benjamin Davis of *The Atlanta Independent* had the special honor of winning three times, the first for a "dose of wangdoodle" congratulating the Coolidge administration for providing a "clean, honest, and upright government" and praising the country for having a "Chief Magistrate whose patriotism and devotion to public duty stand him four-square with every American citizen."[28] Again, as with Miller, the thought ranked lower than the rhetorical gesture in meriting the award.

Although Schuyler spent most of his satirical energies in the first year of "Shafts and Darts" pointing out the foibles of black leaders, he devoted one of his best and longest "darts" to lampooning the pretensions of white racists. In "Caucasophobia" he parodies the condescending tone of a typical white liberal antiracist in "viewing with alarm" the rising tide of black prejudice against the "uncolored" brethren. At the same time, he left-hooks such white Anglo-Saxonists as Lothrop Stoddard and Madison Grant, uppercuts black nationalists like Marcus Garvey, and jabs moral suasionists who believe that they can win the battle against racism using only reason and appeals to sympathy.

Schuyler begins "Caucasophobia" with a humorous appeal to his black readers to ignore the propaganda circulated by black supremacy advocates. He points out that white people are in this country through no fault of their own, the great majority of them having been kidnapped and sold into slavery in their home countries, just like blacks. Building his ludicrous case for sympathy on deftly twisted facts, he observes that many whites had been "brutally torn from the jails of England and sent to this wild land, while a few were run out of Great Britain because of fanatical religious beliefs." Mirroring perfectly the condescension of both black and white liberals of the day toward the black masses, he says of whites: "It takes time to civilize such poor stock."[29]

Pushing his argument further, Schuyler attests to white potential for civilized behavior, using whites' ability to copy the best technical innovations of the darker races throughout the ages as proof. He also points to the much-vaunted capacity of whites for fair play, so evident in the treatment of American Indians and "the uplift movement in Georgia and other foreign countries," as an indication of their potential to feel some of the same fine sentiments as blacks. After a long and humorous romp through most of the other possible arguments for white inferiority, including gullibility, deep sexual attraction to blacks, the inability to survive in a wide variety of climates, and the unwillingness to compete with blacks on an equal basis, Schuyler concludes: "If we would have a better world free from race hatred, we must meet all the arguments of the Caucasophobes with irrefutable facts. Only in this way can race prejudice be scotched."[30]

Through such statements as "Caucasophobia," his criticisms of black leaders, and the "monthly prize," Schuyler established in the first year of "Shafts and Darts" every major theme and target that would appear in the column after he began his collaboration in December 1924 with the theater critic Theophilus Lewis. During their sixteen-month collaboration Schuyler maintained primary control over the column, although the greater emphasis placed on religion and electoral politics may well have resulted from Lewis's efforts. Still, it is difficult to tell who wrote what. Many years later Schuyler recalls a highly team-oriented and open mode of production. He reports that he and Lewis would individually write a few lines of one "dart" and perhaps add a few to another. At the end of this process he would combine the elements and provide them with what coherence he could.[31] Besides this, little exists on the specifics of Schuyler and Lewis's creative collaboration except their own satirically inflected comments in the pages of "Shafts and Darts."

In "In Imitation of Yahweh," Schuyler and Lewis demonstrate a wonderful capacity for self-directed laughter. Referring to themselves as the "compilers of this page of bushwah," they focus on their many disagreements, both important and minor. In doing so, they describe their relationship in the same manner that they cast everything else—as a comic discontinuity. Playing their self-ironizing role to the hilt, they give the general impression of insufficient principle to take their relationship seriously, or even to tell the whole truth about it. Exaggerating their political distance from each other, they reveal that Lewis inclines "far to the left," while Schuyler is as reactionary as "a man owing money to his landlady" can be. Nor can they agree on the best way to approach a woman, with Lewis preferring the "realistic modern" method and Schuyler "inclining toward the mid-Victorian romantic school." They also disagree on the relative merits of D. H. Lawrence and Theodore Dreiser, synthetic gin and corn liquor, home versus restaurant cooking, Will Rogers, and the Book of Proverbs.[32]

Despite these disagreements, Schuyler and Lewis do manage to concur on one issue—atheism. They agree that the rejection of a theological god should lead naturally to the dismissal of all others: "Our revolt against the Almighty resulted in an abandonment of faith," they say, "not merely a transference of faith from the Lord of Hosts to some other deity; say Socialism, or democracy, or Communism or science." Despite this pledge of 100 percent atheism, Schuyler and Lewis do admit to some sympathy for believers. Parodying the biologism of popular race theory, they reason that the human desire to believe evolved to help the species survive under harsh conditions in the prehistoric past. Although the circumstances that made belief relevant disappeared long ago, the primitive feelings remain. Therefore believers deserve sympathy from their evolutionary superiors. Like the insane, they suffer the ravages of instinctive forces too powerful to resist. Still, notwithstanding their enlightened and sympathetic style of atheism, one kind of believer still manages to incur their wrath: the "emotional atheist; a sort of John Roach Stratton of the left . . . who, while denying that the second coming of Christ is at hand, passionately believes that the spirit of Lenine [sic] goes marching on."[33]

The next month, in "If We Were King," Lewis and Schuyler reiterate their playful distance from the "true believer" style of left politics while satirizing the Republican Party, Marcus Garvey, and a long list of favorite targets. With Kal Koolidge (Calvin Coolidge) headed for an inevitable downfall at the hands of the working class in the election of 1924, they declare that the time for their "revolution against revolution" has arrived. They expect the rebels of Pittsburgh and Youngstown to declare the communist leader William Z. Foster "Caesar of triumphant oclocracy" and anticipate that this will open the door for them. Mocking the rhetoric of inevitability common among revolutionists on the left, they assert the counterrevolution as their destiny because the highest-priced astrologers and fortune-tellers have confirmed it. Empowered by destiny, they expect no earthly force to stand in their way. Filled with confidence, they feel no sense of danger in announcing the reforms that will follow their rise to power. Taking a jab at Garvey, they pledge to do away with all of that "*sic semper tyrannis* stuff" and immediately declare themselves joint kings of Aframerica and Cuba, emperors of Liberia and Alaska, "Everlasting Protectors of Puerto Rico, and Almighty Rulers of Haiti, Santo Domingo, and the National City Bank." To ensure domestic tranquillity, they will immediately declare a foreign war against Montreal, which they expect to be too weak and "boozy" to put up much resistance. Although their army will consist of mostly white troops, they think they can win the war anyway given the weakness of the projected enemy. While the courage of white troops remains questionable, they say, Schuyler and Lewis still have faith that their long experience in defeating weak and technologically backward foes will pay off.

With the war over they will surround themselves with a "Mongolian Guard" and proceed to "drink and rule." After satisfying their personal animosity against radical Richard B. Moore of the African Blood Brotherhood and conservative Fred R. Moore of the *New York Age,* they will turn to the less exciting work of legal reform. Because the rich can get around any legislation intended to limit the complete exercise of their will, Schuyler and Lewis propose to abolish all of the petty distractions and persecutions that currently pester them. In addition to making every person worth more than $1,000,000 exempt from half of the current statutes, they will declare anyone worth more than $31,000,000 an "anarch" empowered to ignore all laws "except those prohibiting trespass against royal persons, revenues, liquor, and women."[34]

Schuyler and Lewis extend their satire of American politics in a four-part series featuring the presidential campaign of two fictional black newspapermen, the Honorable Amos Hokum of Maryland, editor of the *Baltimore Afro-American,* and his running mate Bungleton Green of Illinois, editor of the *Chicago Defender.* These two unlikely but confident candidates reason that the maze of political interest groups has made it impossible for anyone except the most morally dubious individuals to attain the presidency. Therefore the field has become ripe for that most unsavory character, the black newspaperman. Only he can hope to "appease the chronic discontent of the alleys of Pittsburgh, kowtow to the prejudices of every considerable racial group, promise the moon to everybody who asks for it, and soothe the prevailing hysteria of the Cro-magnon people of the great open spaces."[35]

Following the standard requirements for election to national office, Hokum and Green offer a platform calculated to please every significant group in the country. In writing this platform, Schuyler and Lewis attempt to satirize every significant political interest group. Appropriately, the platform contains thirteen points. Together these points provide good entertainment and a good overview of the range of political issues Schuyler discussed in his other articles and columns in the 1920s. Some of the points are as follows:

1. Given the great expense to the nation of falsifying income tax returns and the exorbitant expense to the government involved in detecting cheaters, Hokum and Green pledge to abolish the tax all together.
2. Intending to "be ever working to the best interest of patriotic Americans," Hokum and Green vow to transfer all linen to the South at government expense. They also say that if the Nordics demand the surrender of such anti-Nordics as Franz Boas, J. A. Rogers, and A. A. Goldenweiser they will remember that "the voice of the people is the voice of God."
3. In order to make it less expensive for Congress to communicate with Wall Street, they will move the capitol from Washington D.C. to New York City.
4. Under the Clean Books Act, which they give their full support, they will ban distribution of the Bible.
5. They will stop all immigration. Since there are enough restaurants and laundries, Chinese immigration will be stopped. The French will be prevented from entering the country in order to safeguard the morals of the nation. In order to prevent the depopulation of the West Indies, immigration from these islands will be limited to 2% of the population in 1492. Since there are enough policemen and politicians, all immigration from Ireland will also be cut off.[36]

Like most of the satirical statements in "Shafts and Darts," the Hokum and Green election series has many targets, both important and unimportant. The Ku Klux Klan, American sexual paranoia, the Immigration Restriction Act of 1924, fundamentalist Christianity, the Republican Party, and big business all receive jabs. The black press, one of Schuyler and Lewis's favorite targets, receives special treatment for its sensationalism and for its willingness to promote rather than criticize politicians. Hokum and Green rather transparently represent Carl J. Murphy of the *Baltimore Afro-American* and Robert Abbot of the *Chicago Defender*, two owner-editors that Schuyler and Lewis regarded as prime offenders in this direction.

Although they delivered it in humorous form, Schuyler and Lewis's characterization of Murphy and Abbot in the "Hokum and Green" series followed the outlines of many *Messenger* editorials on the relationship between politicians and the masses.[37] As Schuyler explained in his early article "Politics and the Negro," American politicians and the press served moneyed interests. The two-party system provided the masses with only the illusion of choice. Without anything of significance to debate, politicians simply pandered to the lowest popular tastes, ingratiating themselves with clownish antics to a maze of deluded interest groups and retrograde prejudices. The media profited from amplifying this circus, which the civilized citizen can only respond to with the ironic resignation of a captain cast adrift in a sea of fools with no land in sight.

Striking this note of resignation most directly, Schuyler and Lewis announce in "The Civilized Minority" that "the uncivilized folk are overwhelmingly in the majority. Nearly everything is on their level: the newspapers, the movies, the schools and colleges, politics and religion." Against this, they describe their own "civilized" alternative: "Civilized people are seldom moral, but generally honest, which accounts for their scarcity. They abhor cant, humbug and hypocrisy. As a rule they are never hot to save humanity from any of the thousand and one imbecilities with which the *genus homo* has surrounded itself. To them life is an interesting spectacle in which they are at times willing and unwilling actors. They do not lie awake nights worrying over the morals of their fellow men. . . . The civilized folk are generally agnostics and largely cynics. They are not 'joiners' or 'viewers with alarm.' Hence it is apparent that they are rare animals." This ideal of civilization excludes almost everyone, including "Baptists, Methodists, Mormons, Catholics, Communists, Spiritualists, and Theosophists, to say nothing about the Christian Scientists and the cattle who flock around the standards of the Ku Klux Klan and their lamp-black edition, the U.N.I.A."[38]

Although "The Civilized Minority" does pay homage to the perspective of Randolph and Owen, it reflects very little faith in the working class. From Schuyler and Lewis's superior standpoint, no one can save this group from the imbeciles and idiots that dominate its ranks. While "true believers" and other sentimentalists might pity such buffoons or regret their sad state of confusion, Schuyler and Lewis's "civilized minority" welcomes the opportunity they provide for mirth and merriment. Still, despite their unmerciful and elitist pose toward the majority of humanity and their apparently severe curtailment of socialist hopes and dreams, Schuyler and Lewis promote a radically egalitarian standard. All anyone has to do to join their exclusive caste is to laugh along with them.

At the end of "The Civilized Minority," Schuyler and Lewis turn a critical eye toward the group that would bear the brunt of the antibourgeois aspect of their message. They ask simply: "Is there any more side-splitting spectacle than the sight of so-called educated Negroes struggling to ape the buffooneries of the Nordic bourgeoisie?"[39] The answer to this question would have been obvious to their audience long before they asked it here, because from its inception "Shafts and Darts" attacked the black middle class with special dedication. In some ways this mirrored the standard *Messenger* attack on the owners of the means of production and their lackeys for exploitation and for promoting false consciousness. As socialists, Owen and Randolph pointed out the importance of class distinctions among blacks whenever and however they could. "Shafts and Darts" embraced the same goal, but from an angle more amenable to its satirical perspective. Instead of castigating members of the black middle class for fiendish exploitation of the helpless, it ridicules them for their hypocritical and self-defeating imitation of whites.

Although "Shafts and Darts" offers many examples of "civilized" laughter at the antics of the Negro "booboisie," the best statement of this sort occurs in a short satirical dialogue that Schuyler wrote alone. "At the Darktown Charity Ball" opens with two gossips resting in the corner of a ballroom rented for the evening by the Hand-to-Mouth Club, an exclusive organization whose roster features the names of the very best people of black society. As one might gather from the name "Hand-to-Mouth," "At the Darktown Charity Ball" capitalizes on the distance between the aspirations of the black middle class and its social practices, which reveal it to be common, not so much for its vulgarity as for its willingness to imitate people who do not merit emulation.

"At the Darktown Charity Ball" misses nothing in its selection of targets. Naturally, the affair begins two hours late, at ten o'clock instead of eight. This results not only from black people's legendary aversion to punctuality, but from the financial needs of the so-called best people. "Don't fool yourself," says one gossip, "there are more of those ladies of the upper ten sneaking out to domestic service to make ends meet than you can shake a stick at. Work for a half a day often keeps the wolf away." The men have similar troubles. The first gossip wonders why none of them have well-fitting suits. The second gossip, who knows Harlem well, answers: "You can't always rent a suit to fit you. Give these fellows credit for doing the best they can—five dollars is a lot of money." The first gossip then asks: "Who is the shabbily dressed fellow over there with the dull, tired, hungry look?" The second gossip answers: "You'd look tired, dull and hungry, too, if you were in his shoes. He is one of our Negro journalists—campaign funds were awfully scarce this year. . . . If he worked to improve his sad lot he would lose caste." The second gossip continues: "Anyway, as a college graduate he has no marketable skills, so he might as well stick to his four page newspaper."[40]

The reporter's lot reflects that of everyone at the ball. Unable to make true economic progress, they struggle for status in an artificial black hierarchy. In a "dart" called "The New Aristocracy," Schuyler and Lewis further accentuate the artificiality of this hierarchy by emphasizing the ease with which numbers runners, bootleggers, and pimps "made it into Negro society." In a flurry of comic exaggeration they speculate that the numbers runners might even become the predominant group among the social elite: "With the 'numbers' more popular than the cross-word puzzle was a short time ago, the Numbers Bankers will soon have everything their own way. . . . Yes, strange changes take place in Aframerican society. Who knows but the time may come when carpenters, bricklayers and concrete finishers will be among the social dictators or—are all but parasites forever barred?"[41] Schuyler and Lewis did not mean to "view with alarm" the association of numbers runners and the "best people" of black America. In fact, they enjoyed the opportunity the association provided to expose false dignity.

However ardent and consistent with his socialist values, Schuyler's habit of attacking the black middle class in "Shafts and Darts" and other places did not stop him from shamelessly boosting black business. Although he pelted the black bourgeoisie in such articles as "The Darktown Charity Ball," his statements in other articles concerning such black business figures as Mme. C. J. Walker and Mortimer Harris of Washington, D.C., could have easily qualified him for one of his own "elegantly embossed and beautifully lacquered dill pickles." Although his ironic and playful relation to ideology makes it difficult to regard any of his statements as strictly inconsistent with his principles, Schuyler's sketch of Washington, D.C., realtor Mortimer Harris comes closer than anything else he wrote to contradicting the spirit of his satirical voice. Instead of depicting a greedy capitalist dedicated to crowding his own people into small apartments at exorbitant expense, Schuyler casts Harris as a hero who has established an ultramodern black business using the latest organizational and managerial techniques. In justifying this position, Schuyler reasons that in a machine civilization a man's value to his community corresponds to the quantity and quality of food and shelter he brings to it. He even quotes approvingly Harris's philosophy: "Man leads because he yearns, hopes, longs, desires, dreams, visualizes, makes mistakes, corrects them. But—always—he finally creates. . . . As with the individual, so with the business."[42] In "Shafts and Darts" this statement could have competed seriously for a cut glass thunder-mug, but here Schuyler seems to embrace it without question. The *Messenger* obviously had some bills to pay.

Paying these bills continued as a constant worry throughout the existence of the magazine. Although money and subscriptions from the Brotherhood of Sleeping Car Porters Union provided some relief between 1925 and 1928, the editors still needed to court the black business elite to keep the *Messenger* afloat. This is what made Wallace Thurman, who edited the magazine during Schuyler's nine-month trip to the South in 1926, comment that the *Messenger's* politics in these years reflected whoever happened to be paying the bills. Although this exaggerates matters a bit, practical considerations did significantly dull the edge of the *Messenger's* radicalism during the period between 1923 and 1928, the years when Schuyler, Lewis, and Thurman had primary editorial control. When challenged on this matter, Schuyler pointed out that strictly speaking, private business ownership did not conflict with socialist principles.[43] The truth of this statement probably did little to deter the most critical readers of the *Messenger* from marking the vast distance between Schuyler's pragmatism and the ringing advocacy of the Russian Revolution that characterized the *Messenger*'s early years.

At this point, with Schuyler locked in a somewhat awkward embrace with capitalism, we might return to where we started: to A. Philip Randolph's memory of him as an insincere, laughing socialist. At no point could Randolph's suggestion of a connection between Schuyler's laughter and the conservatism of his later years seem more plausible. Yet the implicit contrast that Randolph sets up between himself and Schuyler does not hold up. Schuyler's critical but pragmatic relationship to black capitalism in the mid- to late-1920s constitutes a moment in the larger movement of the *Messenger* from its early existence as "The Only Radical Negro Magazine" to its later incarnation as "The World's Greatest Negro Monthly."[44] This movement reflects the intellectual and political journey of the magazine's originators, who began with hopeful expectations that the war, the Russian Revolution, and colonial rebellions would alter racial politics all over the world and set the stage for positive changes in the United States. Riding the wave of anger and expectation among blacks following the war, they developed a combative and distinctive radicalism, only to find with every passing year of the 1920s more evidence that the forces of retrenchment had won.

Government paranoia turned communism into a dangerous option. Socialism continued to have little appeal among working-class blacks, and blackness proved distinctly unattractive to socialists. Garvey demonstrated that the black masses preferred a more nationalist and conservative message than the *Messenger* group could stomach. Randolph and Owen could help to remove him, but they could never replace him. All of this dictated that the *Messenger* would have to make compromises to hold onto as many elements of its socialist message as it could while maintaining its relevance and extending its popularity. Randolph's private laughter with Schuyler while spouting his socialist stock phrases in the office seems a perfectly natural reaction to the discontinuities of this situation.

Schuyler's early career with the *Messenger* mirrors the larger history of the magazine, moving from the sincere tones of "Politics and the Negro" to the more ironic but serious "Hobohemia" to the full-scale satirical play of "Shafts and Darts." In "Shafts and Darts," Schuyler made the private laughter he shared with Randolph a public matter as he developed the satirical voice and perspective of the *Messenger* into a self-conscious literary mode. In doing so, he took over the invective and name-calling style common to Randolph and Owen's broadsides against such targets as Du Bois and Garvey and, by eliminating its self-righteous tone, turned it into a subtler weapon of cultural politics. In the process he added intellectual flexibility and literary flair to a journal that could have easily become brittle and inflexible in a new political atmosphere. "Shafts and Darts," and most of Schuyler's other contributions to the *Messenger,* promoted the lasting and important ideas that Owen and Randolph brought to the discourse of race and radicalism—skepticism, materialism, realism, and the avoidance of race essentialism—while resisting in both style and substance such sentimentalizing tendencies of left politics as romanticizing the folk and exalting the revolutionary. In accomplishing this, Schuyler played a central role in navigating the journal from an earlier posture dominated almost exclusively by economic and political radicalism to the kind of cultural politics that would make it a force in the Harlem Renaissance. Certainly, Schuyler did not make this move without sacrificing some of the crusading spirit of the *Messenger's* originators, but he did this only after they ceased to crusade for socialism themselves.

CHAPTER FOUR

Debunking Blackness

IN *THE OUTLINE OF BUNK*, E. Haldeman-Julius—the publisher of
George Schuyler's 1928 Little Blue Book series pamphlet *Racial Intermarriage in the United States*—pays homage to a long line of 1920s journalistic satirists, including H. L. Mencken, William E. Woodward, James
Thurber, and Donald Ogden Stewart, by attempting to capture their collective philosophy. He traces the origin of the term "buncombe" to a nineteenth-century congressman and "man of the people" from Buncombe
County, North Carolina, who achieved distinction for the "flood of bombas-
tic nonsense that he poured forth."[1] So exemplary were the efforts of this
politician to swindle the masses through the clever use of tricky language
that the name of his county, shortened to the pithier term "bunk," became
synonymous with manipulative, mob-charming rhetoric. Haldeman-Julius
uses the term "bunk-shooter" to indicate the most dedicated practitioners
of this art, among whom he distinguishes two groups: crooks who pur-
posely mislead the crowd for personal gain and fools who actually believe
their own nonsense.

As the sardonic reference to H. G. Wells's *The Outline of History* in
the title *The Outline of Bunk* makes clear, Haldeman-Julius regards human
history as a long and sad testament to the power of bunk. He insists
that from the caves of the Neanderthals to the trenches of World War I,
the majority of humankind has preferred the iron cage of comforting

fantasy to the open exploration of the world around them. Rather than face life directly and rationally, employing reason to improve the quality of existence, men motivated by greed and fear have invented religion, morality, tradition, superstition, and prohibitions of every sort to cajole and co-opt their counterparts into submission. Haldeman-Julius labels the small minority of truth-seekers who have dared throughout human history to question the bunk-embracing mob and its bunk-shooting leaders "debunkers." To these few unpopular souls he attributes all human progress, from the discovery of fire to the theory of relativity. Counting scientists, philosophers, inventors, poets, and satirists alike as general participants in the spirit of debunking, he praises them for saying no to tradition and thereby increasing human expressive powers and the ability to harness nature.

Specific chapters of *The Outline of Bunk*—such as "Bunk in Sex," "Bunk in Morals," "Man's Creative Art," and "The Modern Spirit"—present the program of the debunker as a constant struggle to achieve freedom. Haldeman-Julius follows John Dewey and other philosophical pragmatists in conceiving of freedom as a constant expansion in the number of ways people realize and perceive liberty across a variety of individual and communal experiences representing creative engagement with a dynamic universe. In this way he attempts to go beyond the more common idea of freedom as a mere absence of restraint. Given Haldeman-Julius's concern with the connection between freedom and debunking, one might expect his book to contain a culminating chapter on race as a supreme example of how one kind of bunk can employ almost all of the other forms—sexual, historical, moral, religious, political, and scientific bunk—in radically limiting human potential. Despite his familiarity with Schuyler's work, and that of H. L. Mencken, Franz Boas, and other debunkers of race ideology, however, the author has little to say about the race question. Still, no single work articulates better the central concerns of Schuyler's journalism in the 1920s, as Haldeman-Julius's account of the value of laughter makes clear: "As a debunker it is proper for me to say that bunk-shooters fear laughter more than anything else. Indeed, the most important significance of laughter is when it takes the form of satire directed against bunk—against evil and at the same time foolish institutions—against the things that discredit human nature and obstruct or obscure its better possibilities. Humor as mere entertainment is valuable. Yet the humor that is intelligently critical, the humor that is iconoclastic, the humor in which man laughs (seriously, one might say) at man is humor at its greatest."[2]

If Schuyler had chosen to state his viewpoint systematically, rather than simply practicing the art of the debunker, he could not have done much better than this in explaining the role of laughter in "Shafts and Darts" and in his other satirical writings for the *Messenger*. Schuyler hoped that iconoclastic, intelligently critical humor would help to open the minds of his readers to a thoroughly debunked and realistic perspective impervious to the efforts of even the most skilled bunk-shooters. Although he regarded this perspective as its own reward, and as the best salve for the psychic wounds caused by racial exclusion and subordination, he also thought that it would provide the best preparation for rational economic and political action aimed at improving the black condition.

When Schuyler moved this project—rooted in the perception of a crossroads between science, truth, freedom, irony, and laughter—from the cozy ideological confines of the *Messenger* to the *Pittsburgh Courier,* he changed none of its essentials; but the new context did require him to adjust his message somewhat to accommodate the peculiar faults and possibilities of the black newspaper in the 1920s. From the standpoint of a debunker the black press in this period had two opposing tendencies. On the positive side it served an emancipating and cosmopolitanizing purpose by promoting wide-ranging intellectual debate and by leading the charge for equal rights. Still, no institution in black America proliferated bunk more powerfully than the black press. Schuyler defined his mission around this two-sided reality. He endeavored to undermine the force and effect of bunk so that the better aspects of the black press could prevail with maximum effect.

By accepting Robert Vann's offer in late 1924 to write a column for the *Pittsburgh Courier,* Schuyler agreed to join forces with a consummate bunk-shooter, a man whom only three years earlier the fiery editors of the *Messenger* had called a "hat-in hand" office-seeker and typical "old crowd" lackey. Certainly Vann—a lawyer, an entrepreneur, a Republican, a former candidate for a Pittsburgh judgeship, and a staunch antisocialist—qualified well as a natural target for A. Philip Randolph and Chandler Owen. In fact, he opposed almost everything they supported. During the World War I era Vann sought to advance the black cause in Pittsburgh and around the country by promoting anti-immigrant feeling. Hoping that by donning a bold mask of red, white, and blue he could make whites forget the blackness underneath, Vann insisted on unstinting, 100 percent loyalty to the flag. His positions on individual issues flowed from this impera- tive. Vann enthusiastically promoted black participation in the war, sup- ported legislation limiting immigration, opposed unions, encouraged strike-breaking, and applauded the most repressive antiradical actions of the federal government.[3]

Vann's enthusiasm for the flag and for law and order even extended to blacks arrested for defending themselves in race riots during and af- ter the war. Although he did not fail in any case to attribute the major cause of violence to white racism, he invariably supported prosecution and even execution of black offenders.[4] By the standards of the day Vann's willingness to interrupt his retreat on issues of racial justice with a few face-saving lunges at the enemy qualified him as a moderate. As such he remained committed to lawful and dignified protest aimed at the eventual achievement of full equality for blacks but only at the deliberate pace that the existing American economic and political system would allow. For radicals like Owen and Randolph, such moderation seemed little better than the accommodationism of black conservatives like Robert Russa Moton, who accepted segregation in order to ingratiate themselves with the "good" whites of the South. From their perspective Vann appeared to achieve similar ends through a slightly different strategy. He scapegoated immigrants and radicals in an attempt to curry favor with the "good" whites of the North.

As his many satirical darts aimed at submissive "handkerchief head" black leaders in the *Messenger* indicate, Schuyler held a humorous version of the same opinion; but he recognized no conflict of interest in writing for the moderate *Courier* and editing the radical *Messenger* at the same time. If Vann had asked him for ideological concessions, Schuyler would have certainly refused his offer, but he did not have to change at all to please the *Courier* owner. More of a pragmatist than an antisocialist, Vann viewed Schuyler's leftist orientation, vigorous pen, keen sense of humor, and affection for verbal combat as valuable additions to his effort to reshape the *Courier* into a newspaper of national significance.[5]

At the time that Vann hired Schuyler, the *Courier* had achieved only local fame. Riding a wave of black migration to Pittsburgh in the years surrounding World War I, the newspaper evolved from a badly edited sheet when Vann assumed control in 1911 to a reputable publication circulating more than 30,000 copies per week by the early 1920s. Such a rapid rise to respectability made Vann hungry for more success. Robert Abbot's *Chicago Defender,* the largest black publication of the day, with a national weekly circulation of over 150,000, demonstrated clearly the heights a black newspaper could reach when it combined a national distribution network, a strong protest orientation, and a sensationalistic method of reporting the news. While Vann aspired to the national standing and success of Abbot's newspaper, his conservative, almost Victorian, moral sensibility bristled against the lurid appeal of crime and sex news, bold red headlines, and other devices of the Hearstian method. Although economic necessity dictated the use of sensationalism, Vann tried when he could to find a different way to gain the ear of new working-class readers.[6]

This made Schuyler, a prominent and exciting writer with a black magazine known for its vigorous interest in the plight of black workers, a logical addition to the *Courier* staff. His writings in the *Messenger* demonstrated clearly his ability to attract readers by using comic juxtaposition to produce strong emotions ranging from laughter to outrage. In other words, by placing before readers a spectacle of exaggerated conflict and rhetorical violence, Schuyler's satirical method provided a gut-level appeal capable of competing with sensationalism, without the anti-intellectual undertow. Of course, Vann would have settled for much less than this. Like most owners and editors of black newspapers, he wanted a column on his editorial page that would add color, style, humor, and contrast for readers who found editorials too serious and boring. "Shafts and Darts" showed clearly that Schuyler could far exceed the standard of other comic columnists like S. B. Williams, who penned "Cimbee's Ramblings" for the *Houston Informer,* or Ralph Matthews, whose "Amos Hokum Says" provided the readers of the *Baltimore Afro-American* with a bit of laughter to balance the editorial reflections of owner, Carl Murphy, William Jones, and Kelly Miller.

While Schuyler's efforts for the *Messenger* made him an easy bet for success as a columnist, Vann still could not have known in late 1924 what a wonderful addition he had made to his staff. By the end of 1926, as a result of a nine-month tour of the South, Schuyler had personally increased the circulation of the *Courier* by one-third. When Vann asked him to start writing the regular *Courier* editorials in the same year, Schuyler's gift of phrase, deft selection of subject matter, and uncanny ability to write convincingly what he did not believe immediately improved what had always remained mediocre under Vann's control.[7] But it was in "Views and Reviews," where he expressed his own unvarnished opinions, that Schuyler made the distinctive mark that would place him at the pinnacle of black journalism by the late 1920s. In this column, which translated the playful and fantastic style of "Shafts and Darts" into a more prosaic mode appropriate to commentary on weekly events in the news, Schuyler demonstrated a unique ability to make black readers like and respect him even as he criticized them without mercy.

Schuyler's critical wit and affection for confrontation certainly earned him enemies in his first years with the *Courier,* but his detractors did not represent the dominant response to his work. This says as much about Schuyler's audience as it does about the author himself. Schuyler's readers appreciated the symbolic importance of his self-presentation as a bold, informed, and defiant black thinker above compensatory rhetoric and ego salve. They also showed a special appreciation for irony and cutting humor. In other words they demonstrated qualities that the author himself always associated with intellectual sophistication. Yet Schuyler's method required him to address his readers as he would a group of yokels in need of instruction from a city slicker. However much this enabling fiction departed from empirical reality, and however much Schuyler's readers knew this, they appreciated very much the show it made possible.

By 1930, Schuyler had risen to such heights among black journalists that even Theophilus Lewis, his sardonic former colleague with the *Messenger,* felt compelled to declare him "the preeminent personality in Negro journalism."[8] Yet in keeping with his caustic orientation, Lewis spent the rest of his *Amsterdam News* editorial explaining why this exalted position appears so much less impressive than in former years. Writing in response to a letter from a journalism student, Lewis reveals several unsweet truths behind the heroic exterior of the black press. Without a hint of mercy for the innocent hopes of his young correspondent, he bemoans her bad timing in choosing to enter a field that bureaucracy, standardization, sensationalism, and the profit motive had spoiled over the past fifteen years.

At one time, Lewis says, editors and other newspapermen had power in the organization and direction of the black press. But of late, owners like Vann, P. B. Young, and Carl Murphy— businessmen with negligible journalistic talent or experience—had begun to follow their white counterparts in running their newspapers like money machines. In streamlining their publications for profit, these owners hired only yes-men as editors and treated columnists as clowns who existed only to add an entertaining touch and perhaps a bit of controversy to increase sales. Lewis admits that columnists like himself receive a certain "cheap notoriety" for adding a bit of personality to an otherwise thoughtless product, but he laments the passing of such genuine and substantive journalist/owners as T. Thomas Fortune of the *New York Age,* who truly deserved the attention they received. He complains that corporate control has eliminated such charismatic figures and put in their place columnists like himself, who imitate the form of "personal journalism" without the substance: "The columnist runs a sort of journalistic sideshow while his superior, the editor, manages a three-ring circus. Like his boss, the columnist thrives on various kinds of social sickness. Heywood Broun's best days are those on which he belabors the stupidities of the D. A. R. or some numbskull of a city magistrate. George Schuyler never appears so brilliant as when he lampoons the imbecilities of colored preachers or business men. The reason why Frank Byrd has not arrived yet is because he has not turned jackal like the rest of us."[9]

By presenting this dim inside view of the black press, heavily colored by personal disappointment and perhaps even envy at Schuyler's rapid rise, Lewis hoped to disabuse his young correspondent of all romantic notions regarding the role of the black newspaper in the black freedom movement. His main complaint—that the black press had joined the mainstream American press in abandoning its democratic mission for the naked pursuit of profit—might seem more applicable today than it did seventy-five years ago. For this reason Lewis's analysis still retains some of its original debunking effect. Also, Lewis challenges the idea of the black press as a "fighting press" righteously and heroically engaged in the struggle for equal rights, a proposition that even the most recent histories of black newspapers put forward with special conviction.[10]

Still, Lewis's view has obvious faults. In recalling a golden age of black journalism before World War I, when charismatic figures dominated the scene, he appears to idealize the efforts of the preceding generation. Although the black press of the Progressive Era could boast of such outstanding paragons of protest and charisma as Ida B. Wells and William Monroe Trotter, it failed to match the example of forceful opposition set by Frederick Douglass, Henry Highland Garnett, David Walker, and other nineteenth-century abolitionists who invented the black newspaper to serve as a weapon in the struggle against slavery and second-class citizenship.

During a period of rapid expansion in the late nineteenth century, the black press became less defined by protest and turned more toward serving the practical needs of segregated black communities. In this period it addressed itself more to the needs of black elites than it did to those of the masses, whose literacy rate fell below the level necessary to support newspapers built around their special concerns. Between the turn of the century and World War I, the conservative Booker T. Washington used his considerable financial and political influence to control the ideological center of the black press. Eventually he even won the allegiance of Lewis's favorite "personal journalist," T. Thomas Fortune, whose *New York Age* carried the torch of conservatism well into the 1920s.[11] In his zeal to debunk the New Negro press of the 1920s for its greed and bureaucracy, Lewis seems to forget that black journalism after World War I became more heavily identified with protest against segregation, Jim Crow, and racist violence largely by defining itself against the efforts of the preceding generation. However tainted by business concerns, the black newspaper of Lewis's own period pushed the fight for equal rights much harder than its immediate forebears.

In fact, by the 1920s protest had become a kind of routine and necessary gesture of the black newspaper and more intimately connected with the profit motive than ever before. Black migration provided the main impetus for this change. The movement of 1.2 million blacks from the rural South provided new readers for newspapers based in northern industrial centers.[12] These new readers, who had made a conscious break with southern segregation, demanded publications that expressed the drama of their struggle for freedom in terms that confirmed their rising expectations. Even blacks who remained in the South wanted to read about the fate of those who had left home and the tantalizing possibilities of big city life, not the least of which included the freedom to speak out directly against racial injustice. Appealing to these new readers required the New

Negro newspaper to project itself as a loud promoter of the group cause. The louder and more strident the protest, the greater the chance of attracting readers. The more these readers regarded themselves as part of a large and unified struggle for emancipation and justice, the greater their loyalty to the black newspaper, which acted more than ever before as a powerful force in creating this impression. Thus for the major players in the black press after World War I, which included the *Chicago Defender,* the *Baltimore Afro-American,* the *Pittsburgh Courier,* the *Norfolk Journal and Guide,* the *Amsterdam News,* and several others, the endgame was clear: protest drove popularity and popularity increased profit.

During the period between the wars the formula of protest, popularity, and profit implied a strong relationship with exaggeration and sensationalism. Practical realities dictated this. The size of the black population always prevented black newspapers from competing with mainstream dailies in reporting day-to-day events. With no option except to appear weekly as a supplement to the regular sources of news, these publications always stood on precarious ground. Like all weeklies, black newspapers placed a great emphasis on editorials and commentary while presenting the news only in highly edited form. Because the black press served a relatively small, despised, and impecunious market niche, major advertising dollars always proved difficult to attract. This left circulation as the only road to profit and placed editors and owners very much at the mercy of a largely working-class readership. Whatever the owners and editors of the black press thought about sensationalism did not matter. Their readers liked the excitement of crime, sex, and gossip news. Getting these readers to pay attention to protest-oriented commentary, which also had its sensational aspects, required a large dose of sweetener. Those that did not provide it did not survive.[13]

In his analysis of the black press, Swedish economist Gunnar Myrdal makes this point as he reflects on some of the characteristic pressures that granted the black newspaper its special character: "Sensationalism . . . occurs in the Negro press because it is an 'additional' Negro paper. Its excuse for existing is to select those items with a race angle and to 'play them up,' as they are 'played down' in the ordinary white press. In hammering the Negro protest week after week, the press is constantly in danger of becoming abstract and tedious. It must, therefore, attempt to 'personalize' the news as much as possible. It must accentuate the human-interest angle, and create a feeling that people are fighting and that big things are happening." Black newspapers found crime, sex, and gossip news just as useful in promoting protest as in relieving readers of abstraction and tedium. Stories about salacious and illicit interracial love affairs, which appeared almost every week on the front page of such best-selling newspapers as the *Baltimore Afro-American* and the *Chicago Defender,* implicitly contradicted racist myths about white aversion to blacks even as they provided titillation. A large headline, for example, about a white policeman going on a shooting rampage highlighted a legitimate community concern with state violence even as it satisfied morbid fascination with dramatic and transgressive violence.[14]

Not all items in the black press employed sensationalism in this way. Some stories appealed to the lurid curiosities of readers without promoting protest at all.[15] Others, such as the ones that "played up" the deeds of black athletes or social events in black communities, often employed exaggeration but did not involve sensationalism in the strictest sense of the term. They existed simply to convey the impression that black people were "making it," usually in conventional terms. They also emphasized by way of exclusion that segregated black society had its own special claim to social and cultural sophistication and excellence. If one only read the sports page of a typical black newspaper, for example, one would learn in great detail the heroic deeds of black baseball teams but might not ever find out that the Yankees had won the world championship. One might read all about the great football rivalry between Howard and Grambling without the slightest inkling of Red Grange. As Myrdal points out, this kind of reporting constituted an important weapon in a game of tit for tat. By amplifying what the white press attempted to render invisible, the owners and editors of black newspapers hoped to increase black group consciousness and self-confidence. Naturally, they also hoped that this would increase sales and promote the black struggle for civil rights at the same time.

Although Schuyler understood well the need for protest and for compensatory rhetoric aimed at healing the injured consciousness of oppressed people, he remained skeptical that an excessive focus on either would actually help to emancipate anyone. He worried that by exploiting alarmism, emotionalism, hysteria, and excessive race patriotism, the black newspaper powerfully aided forces that threatened to mold blacks into a crowd of weak-minded conformists, spiritual slaves to the dogma of the group. Yet in "Views and Reviews" he rarely stated this criticism of the black press directly. Instead, he hoped that by expressing controversial opinions in a provocative manner and by naming his targets directly, he could set an example of independence and skepticism that would stand in bold relief against the psychological junk food that his readers encountered in the rest of the newspaper. Schuyler regarded such "crowd-mindedness" as a sort of occupational hazard for the downtrodden, whose condition of oppression brought with it a psychology of inferiority. Following the psychologist Alfred Adler, Schuyler held that victims of the inferiority complex almost never faced the source of their problem directly.[16] Instead, they "protested" against feelings of inferiority through a wide variety of compensations and avoidance behaviors, some obviously neurotic and others more subtly maladjusted.

According to Schuyler, gaining a sense of confirmation and conviction in the thrilling experience of unquestioning and uncritical agreement with a large group has always stood as one of the most common of these strategies. Stalwart crowd-thinkers regard the assent of the group, however ridiculous, as truth and the actions of the group, however cruel, as justice. Because they think of the crowd in absolute terms as a self-confirming reality, they view all threats to it, however minor, with a great and unrelieved sense of alarm. Schuyler regarded this constant sense of alarm, especially when it rose to the sublime heights of paranoia, as yet another classic mode of compensation for feelings of inferiority. The more pervasive and cosmic the source of threat, the more compensated group members feel for their psychic pain.

While he focused far more often in his writings on deterring the effects of defeatism and crowd-mindedness among blacks, Schuyler recognized the basic phenomenon as a pervasive fact of American society. Although he had many guides in forming his views on this matter, none had a greater effect on him than Everett Dean Martin, a popularizer of social psychology and a lecturer at The People's Institute at Cooper Union in New York City. During his early years wandering around New York, Schuyler attended Martin's lectures and read his book *The Behavior of Crowds* with special attention.[17]

In this polemic against mass culture, Martin attributes the special attraction of crowds to a seductive illusion. Because they involve many people moving in concert, such large gatherings can give the false impression that social rules and prohibitions requiring the repression of primitive drives have been relaxed. According to Martin, only the strongest and most rationally balanced souls can resist the win-win proposition of primitive release and social reinforcement. Thus individuals who display perfect comportment within a civilized and ordered atmosphere might find themselves releasing murderous rage or engaging in some other form of symptomatic behavior in the context of a crowd. The role of the crowd in providing compensation for feelings of inferiority adds to its seductive appeal. Because they exist only to enable emotional release, crowds thrive on slogans and dogmatic generalizations that members accept without examination, often in a spirit of elated submission.

Those inclined to irony might recognize in Martin's perspective a kind of counterparanoia. Startled by the sight of the paranoid herd all around him, Martin conceives of himself as a member of a small crowd of reasonable people who need to defend themselves against chaotic and destructive forces. It never occurs to him that there might be some humor in the predicament of the thoughtful man surrounded by fools or that there might be something obsessive and compromising in his need to define himself so thoroughly in opposition to them. This is where Schuyler and Martin part company.

Although he agreed very much with the main thrust of *The Behavior of Crowds,* Schuyler did not share its author's earnest spirit. Like Martin, Schuyler hoped that education rooted in the reality principle would help stem the tide of foolishness that threatened democracy. In fact, he built his *Pittsburgh Courier* column around this vision. But the didactic and activist thrust of his column always remained intimately connected with the project of the jester and trickster, with the desire to recognize the many sides of bitter experience and to have some fun in the process. He makes this abundantly clear in his opening column for the *Courier,* where he introduces himself to his audience by humorously denying almost everything he intends to accomplish: "In contributing this column to the Pittsburgh COURIER, I am actuated by no desire to assist in the rescuing of humanity from the bow wows. . . . Nor am I doing this for the purpose of getting rich, as I have no illusions about the rewards of journalism. If

I wanted to get rich quick I would start brewing grape juice and raisins, selling lucky charms and jade stones, go into the real estate or undertaking business or start another movement to solve the Negro problem. . . . I don't intend to deal with heavy stuff like philosophy, logic and facts. I learned long ago that people will do anything to keep from thinking, so why try to make them do something unpleasant."[18]

Of their many consequences for black life, Schuyler regretted most the detrimental effect that black crowd-mindedness and paranoia had on the scope of public discussion about the problems of the group. Too often, he thought, intellectuals, journalists, and political leaders preferred comforting race pride rhetoric to frank discussion concerning how blacks might improve their condition within the context of a rapidly changing machine civilization. In a "Views and Reviews" editorial on the black tendency to avoid criticism, which he called the "ostrich attitude," Schuyler stated his case on this matter in typically controversial style: "Psychologists inform us that in order to cure a complex, the victim must be taught its cause and history. The inferiority complex is no exception to this rule. Rather than deny charges made against us, we should inquire of those making them the cause for the existence of the alleged shortcoming. We should ever keep in mind that Aframericans constitute an artificial race. Neither ethnologically nor culturally are we a race or even a nation. We are more or less a caste like the untouchables of India, the Etos of Japan, the slaves in Mohammedan countries, the peasants in Europe and the Jews in Poland."[19]

Pressing the comparison between black Americans and their international counterparts to the point of provocation, Schuyler asserts that just like the peasants of medieval Europe and the untouchables of India, black Americans offer little resistance to members of the ruling group. In most cases even whippings and lynchings fail to inspire in them any will to fight back because they secretly agree with their oppressors, who regard them as little more than dogs. To support this harsh position, he points to the actions of black Southerners, whom he describes in the most disparaging terms as a people showing every sign of regarding themselves as inherently inferior.

Although he does not like their actions, Schuyler refrains from blaming black Southerners for their corruption. He reasons that if the English peasant after several hundred years of freedom still feels inferior to the nobility, then why should blacks less than a century removed from slavery entertain different notions. "Why play the ostrich," he says, "and deny that most Aframericans similarly conditioned by similar environment, respond similarly." Rather than succumb to outrage or shame about their condition, Schuyler proposes that blacks understand their circumstance in objective terms as the logical result of tangible economic and political forces and not as the outgrowth of a biological or spiritual essence. If his readers abhor "natural human responses" to the caste line and wish to end them, he says, they should face the source of these problems directly and stop denying them merely to save face.[20]

In addition to Schuyler's affection for provocative generalization, his editorial on the "ostrich attitude" conveys how useful he found the idea of the inferiority complex as a key to the black American mind-set. During the 1920s he attributed to it almost everything he found objectionable in black life. Skin color prejudice, gullibility, crime, the dependence on charismatic leadership, the inability to cooperate, political passivity, hustlerism, excessive race patriotism, uncritical public discourse, the mad dash for social distinction, and the tendency to self-aggrandizing rhetoric all in one way or another reduced to that single idea. Even when Schuyler criticized black institutions like the church, the National Association for the Advancement of Colored People (NAACP), the Universal Negro Improvement Association (UNIA), or the black press, he usually had in mind their tendency to promote herd ideas and dogma whose appeal depended ultimately on black defeatism and convictions of inferiority.

Given its heavy focus on black southern attitudes, it is instructive that Schuyler wrote the "ostrich attitude" editorial only two months after his nine-month tour of the South. This tour, which gave rise to the series "Aframerica Today," took Schuyler to every city and town in nine southern states—West Virginia, Virginia, Kentucky, Arkansas, Tennessee, Louisiana, Texas, Oklahoma, and Mississippi—with a black population greater than two thousand. Although the condition of individual southern towns and cities constituted the main subject of these articles, the fascinating juxtaposition of Schuyler's New Negro identity against the iron cage of black southern life provided the main point of interest. The statement circulated by the *Pittsburgh Courier* to advertise the series presented Schuyler as a purely objective observer, a "lifetime student of the race question," "neither an optimist nor a pessimist" but a "realist . . . leaning more toward science than sentiment." Rather than the slanted accounts of the South found commonly in the black press, the advertisement promised that "Aframerica Today" would present a "word-photograph" that would impress readers with its "judicial poise, its keen penetration, its sophistication and urbanity."[21]

Had it not conflicted with the idea of cool and controlled scientific observation, the *Courier* advertisement might also have boasted of the sheer energy Schuyler expended in producing "Aframerica Today." In all he visited more than one hundred localities, taking one or two days in each to gather the information for his articles, which he wrote on weekends along with his "Views and Reviews" columns and the regular *Courier* editorials. This crash course in investigative reporting proved quite a learning experience for a young man who had never ventured south of Philadelphia. In every town he visited, Schuyler would pick up the fifty copies of the *Courier* waiting for him at the post office and distribute them to the agent he had contacted in advance. Then he would proceed directly to a taxi, which he would hire to take him on a tour of the town. Often Schuyler would use the information he milked from the cabdriver to find out whom he might interview besides the obvious suspects: preachers, school principals, and other representatives of institutions. Typically he gathered his best information in local barbershops and pool halls.[22]

Using the information he gathered in his quick but thorough investigations, Schuyler reported in each installment of "Aframerica Today" on conventional points of sociological interest, such as the number and condition of black-owned homes, black businesses, schools, interracial relations, intraracial relations, and the state of black political power. He also commented on areas of personal concern, such as where one might get a good drink or what the women looked like. Although he took note of the ravages of white racism in all of the cities he covered, he focused mainly on what black Southerners had done to improve their lot within the limitations of racial oppression. Against the expectations of those who viewed the South as a monolithic horror, and against the main thrust of his own editorial on the "ostrich attitude," he discovered a wide diversity of political and economic situations. Even in racist Texas, for example, Schuyler found cities like Fort Worth, where blacks had made impressive economic progress. In many of these localities he encountered complex social relations between the races. He learned about such anomalies as the southern tolerance for interracial sexual contact, the codependence of black and white gangsters, the existence of "friendly" southern whites, and of sophisticated, erudite, and wealthy blacks. He also discovered cities like Tulsa and Muskogee, Oklahoma, where blacks showed an admirable willingness to resist white violence directly through the barrel of a gun. Still, despite these pleasant surprises, Schuyler visited few cities where he thought blacks had taken full advantage of opportunities to improve their condition. His disappointment with this provided the overall theme of "Aframerica Today." The titles of some of the articles in the series make this clear. For instance, Schuyler described the residents of Morganstown, West Virginia, as "Just Makin' Time," while those in Paris, Winchester, and Richmond, Virginia, were "Bivouacking in the Blue Grass."[23]

Schuyler's account of Clarksburgh, West Virginia, reflects well the overall approach of "Aframerica Today." Called "Asleep at the Switch," this article tells the story of a town where blacks do fairly well. They work, pay their rent, and buy homes. But this is not enough for Schuyler. What he finds wrong with the black citizens of Clarksburgh, he would find wrong in almost every southern town with a sizable black population: pessimism and fear prevent them from taking advantage of opportunities to advance themselves. He describes the whites of Clarksburgh as "quite cordial" because they patronize the black businesses of the town, and unlike the black upper class "they don't blink and walk out of the door with chin elevated when they see a Negro behind the counter." So what explains the problems of black Clarksburgh? Schuyler cites the black inferiority complex as the main culprit. In support of this contention, he quotes a leading black citizen who blames the problem on "jealousy, shiftlessness, and suspicion of their own people among them."[24]

By blaming black Southerners rather than racist whites for black social and economic problems, Schuyler hoped to debunk the hyperbolic, melodramatic, and comforting rhetoric of southern evil that often accompanied, and partially justified, the protest orientation of the most prominent black newspapers. Without denying southern racism, Schuyler wanted to emphasize the opportunities for black agency in the South rather than whining too loudly about the debilitating constraints and inhibitions of segregation. Also, writing for an audience composed mostly of migrants to the North, he wanted to inspire a conversation about what they could do to improve their own circumstances rather than having them shake their heads over the insoluble problems of their brethren. By accusing black Southerners of wasting opportunities to gain economic and political power, Schuyler wanted his northern readers to wonder how many more chances they wasted themselves.

To call greater attention to his countervailing view of the South, Schuyler sometimes exaggerated the rosy side of his message. Upon Schuyler's return to New York in the summer of 1926, his *Courier* colleague Floyd Calvin commented that the normally corrosive columnist could not utter ten words without eight of them being in praise of the South. In a 1930 editorial Schuyler confirms this comment by claiming a warm place in his heart for the South despite his many articles on its faults. Labeling the black population of the South the most civilized and "lovable" in the United States, he declares that they alone "save Dixie from being like Vermont, Indiana, Illinois and Iowa." To corroborate this, he cites conversations with working-class blacks all over the region that offer clear reason for hope. He declares "that the average Negro worker is nobody's fool and is the superior of the white man of similar status and training." Schuyler continues: "There are millions of such Negroes. . . . All they need is intelligent, capable leadership and they will accomplish wonders in group advancement."[25]

Schuyler believed that the oppressive conditions of slavery and segregation provided blacks with rare virtues to go along with their vices. Surviving on the bottom of American society and maintaining group pride and coherence at the same time required a strong capacity for realism, opportunism, and humor, and for capitalizing on the hidden ironies within oppressive situations. In the same editorial just cited, he recalls a conversation with an old grizzled farmer in Lawrenceville, Virginia, whom Schuyler found to be absolutely sound on almost every question relating to blacks. He describes this man as "proud, capable, fairly well-to-do and with supreme confidence in his black brethren and yet a fellow who had but three years schooling."[26] To Schuyler, this represented the black caste mentality at its best—resilient, proud, determined to survive under any and all circumstances. Nothing could be further from the characteristics that Schuyler attributed to black Southerners in his editorial on the "ostrich attitude."

Like many observers of the social scene in the 1920s, Schuyler expected that the relatively "freer" conditions in the North would allow blacks to amplify and perfect their virtues. For him this meant that the independence, common sense, and faith in other blacks that the grizzled old man in Lawrenceville had displayed in a rough way, blacks in northern cities should exhibit with increasing determination, sophistication, and militancy. Perhaps this is why Schuyler railed so persistently, and so humorously, against all lingering indications of the opposite, of what he saw as the black mob mentality.

If sheer volume of words could measure such matters, Schuyler's campaign against hair straighteners and skin lighteners constituted his most avid crusade against the values of the black mob. Nothing seemed to him more clearly motivated by the desire for conformity through self-effacement than the plethora of advertisements in the black press for products to remove "kink" from the hair or to "beautify" the skin by making it lighter. It may well have been the prominence and frequency of such advertisements in black newspapers that drove Schuyler to criticize the black desire to become white nearly every week, even when it seemed somewhat remote from the main issue at hand. A "true story" he told about a visit to a Harlem barbershop provides a good example of the kind of rhetoric he normally brought to the topic:

> I was sitting in the barbershop the other day when a young
> Harlem[ite] entered and announced to the white-coated
> beard remover that he wanted his hair "done" in Aframerican.
> This means to have the reluctant kink removed by powerful
> persuader and a high patent leather gloss installed. While
> the interesting process was taking place, I listened to the
> following conversation between the recumbent lounge lizard
> and the tonsorial artist.
>
> The Sheik: Where is the manicurist you had here?
> The Barber: Oh, she's gone.
> The Sheik: Why don't you get another one? I want my nails
> done. And when you get one, don't get any brown skin or black
> gal, get a yallah. . . . I want my money's worth![27]

For Schuyler the urge to whiteness evident in the attitude of the Sheik differed little in fundamental motivation from its apparent opposite—the overemphasis on race pride. In his view both positions shared the tendency to read too much significance into externalities. By locating the most transcendent meanings in the greatest superficialities, he thought that the black glorification of blackness served the same basic psychological ends as the mad dash of the mob for the chromatic advantages of lightness. In a 1926 statement Schuyler explained why he regarded black race chauvinism as little more than compensation and pretense: "When you come to think of it, why are most of us bellowing for NEGRO art, NEGRO literature, NEGRO music, NEGRO dancing, etc.! . . . Is it because we wish to be considered a separate group, a different group? Are we not thus agreeing with Imperial Wizard Evans and the late lamented Harding? If this is not true, why do we continually emphasize color the same as the apostles of Nordicism? . . . A social psychologist might conclude that we emphasize color in everything because we hate it—a protest against a feeling of inferiority! Can this be true, Oswald?"[28]

In another editorial on the black inferiority complex Schuyler comments on the debate surrounding the capitalization of the "n" in *Negro*. Contradicting almost everyone in the black press, he characterizes the debate over the issue as an exercise in futility, a mere symbolic gesture that does little more than "throw a bouquet at the feet of the well-known inferiority complex." Because of this, he characterizes the desire for a capital "n" in *Negro* as an empty compensation for the absence of real economic and political power, "a superficial dodge . . . somewhat akin to whitening skin and straightening hair." He concludes that such purely symbolic gestures will never provide a substitute for the attainment of real power or genuine group unity, nor will they make whites respect blacks more. With this challenge to his audience, he closes his column and confidently awaits the "shower of brickbats and ancient vegetables."[29]

Because he so often ran against the mainstream of black opinion on important issues and did so in a dismissive and cocksure manner, some readers resented Schuyler for his irreverence and for his deficit of race pride. One reader complained that on "every other page" of Schuyler's column, he found a statement gratuitously critical of black people. "If you are so ashamed of black tincture in your skin and you don't want to be known as a black," the reader wrote, "then get off the staff of *The Pittsburgh Courier* and stop taking the money of those you despise and are ashamed to be one of." In response, Schuyler reversed the tables on the reader by rating group criticism as the obligation of true race loyalty: "Yes, I do frequently 'pan' Negroes, but probably not as much as our correspondent imagines. I can do it pretty well because I have always been a Negro, am so black that swallowing arsenic would not make me light enough to join the race of Gyp the Blood and Harry the Thaw, come from a poor family that did laundering, cooking and laboring and I have studied the Ethiop closely and continually. Among the things white people have that I want to see Negroes get are money, health, knowledge, power and the ability to organize for something besides praying and parading. I am not quite as loyal as my friend Max; when the race is wrong it certainly is not right, and I believe in telling them so, even if I do have to go back to dish washing."[30]

Despite Schuyler's ardent claims to authenticity and group loyalty within the bounds of rightness and honesty, some members of his audience still found reason to question his race pride, and those sympathetic to Marcus Garvey found special reason to do so. In "Views and Reviews," Schuyler continued his personal "Garvey Must Go" campaign long after the nationalist leader entered prison in Atlanta. Fearing a rise in sympathy for Garvey after his imprisonment, Schuyler tried not merely to prove Garvey wrong, but to make him look unworthy of respect. After Garvey's conviction in 1925, for example, Schuyler could not wait to launch a cruel joke: "Uncle Sam not only got Garvey's number—he gave him one. While Marcus is working, all his followers are playing—that number. The number barons of Harlem aver that there are more people playing the combination of 19359 than ever before." In another cruel but humorous statement Schuyler pretended to have tender hurt feelings over Garvey's deportation in 1927: "Alas! the tears pour upon my typewriter as I pound out these lines with heavy heart. All the world seems dark and dreary. Disconsolate, I glance ever and anon out of the window at the gray sky, wondering if life is really worth living. How can it be, I ask myself, when our good friend, Marcus Garvey[,] is to be deported to Jamaica? God, what a shame to deprive us thusly of our greatest source of mirth."[31]

Although such statements, taken one at a time, evoke smiles and chuckles, they begin to lose their effect after a while. Schuyler probably knew this, but he never seemed to get tired of administering lashings to Garvey and his followers. He viewed Garvey as a consummate mob orator, a megalomaniac and bunk-shooter of the highest order whose paranoid followers fed off of the acrimony surrounding his name. Because of this, Schuyler decided that laughter would undermine Garvey more effectively than denouncement. But Schuyler never really succeeded in making a clown of the popular nationalist leader. In fact, his incessant lashings probably had the opposite effect. They gained for his favorite whipping boy more sympathy than disapproval.

One representative reader expressed her anger at Schuyler's unyielding attacks on Garvey in no uncertain terms. Mary Jackson of Pittsburgh threatened to stop reading the *Courier* if Schuyler did not curtail his "mean, despicable, and tratorious [*sic*] references to Marcus Garvey." Although Jackson did not expect her angry letter to "see the light of publicity," Schuyler enjoyed it enough to quote it in his column. In response he asked her with mock seriousness, "So why do you read my 'nasty stuff' anyway?" Taken aback by the discreditable implication of Schuyler's question, Jackson answered the following week that she read his column "for the same reasons that the movie and book censors view obscene pictures and read filthy books." Schuyler could not have planned a more perfect response. Uncharacteristically, he allowed his correspondent the last word.[32]

Just as Schuyler used "Views and Reviews" to extend the attack on Garvey that he began in the *Messenger,* he employed his *Courier* column to carry on a protracted scrimmage with all of his old targets. Kelly Miller, Robert Russa Moton, Robert Abbot, Eugene Kinkle Jones, W. E. B. Du Bois, and a long list of others all became the victims of periodic attacks in "Views and Reviews." Sometimes these attacks would lead to debates featuring Schuyler and his interlocutors firing at each other week after week in their respective publications. These exchanges helped Schuyler to develop his combative reputation. They also allowed him to emphasize by example the kind of skepticism and tough-mindedness that he regarded as a corrective to the blind faith that followers of the crowd accorded to those in charge. Usually Schuyler attempted in these debates to expose his opponent, often through unfair accusation and ridicule, as a subrational faker or as a crook whose anger, emotionalism, and dishonesty disqualified him from serious consideration.

One such debate began in 1930, when Gordon Hancock, a professor at Virginia Union University, a columnist for the *Norfolk Journal and Guide,* and a target of a long series of jabs from Schuyler throughout the 1920s, advised black workers to do everything they can to hold on to their jobs. The next week Schuyler denounced Hancock's advice as woefully insufficient because it did not address the underlying conditions that give whites control over black jobs. No matter how hard blacks work, Schuyler charged, powerful whites would always displace them in tough economic times. This sensible but dismissive response provoked Hancock to strike back with a full barrage. In a long series of accusations, he charged Schuyler with "fourth-rate iconoclasm" and "near Menckenism," of wishing to see all black churches destroyed and "all black ministers drowned," of desiring to make all blacks into socialists and communists, of leaving blacks in the South "holding the bag" for his desire to wear spats and tuxedos, of speaking down to struggling folk, of being a "Black Nordic," and finally of being an "ear-tickler" for profit.[33]

Predictably, Schuyler responded with a long barrage of his own. To Hancock's contention that the race needs fewer "Black Nordics" like him and more "honest-to-goodness Negro men" who will take the practical approach to solving the problems of black people, Schuyler delivered his most telling blow: "What the Negro race needs is fewer cloistered apostles of timidity and super-caution and more honest and intellectually unfettered students of economics, history, mass behavior and the sociology br'er Hancock professes to teach, who will be capable of formulating programs and policies holding out real hope to the struggling masses of Negroes who as yet are more familiar with jail than with Yale, and who prefer to be addressed as adults, and not as half-witted infants. . . . Saying which, the 'Black Nordic' brushes a speck of dust off the lapel of his tuxedo, passes the perfume atomizer over his silk handkerchiefs, dons his derby, lights a fat El Producto and saunters down Seventh Avenue twirling his silver-headed stick."[34]

With this, Hancock's contention that Schuyler liked beautiful clothes and fake superiority does not even seem worthy of serious consideration. Having turned the tables on his adversary, Schuyler likens him to a dust speck on his lapel, the removal of which presumably restores his tuxedo to its original pure blackness. Somehow the performance of trampling Hancock has made blackness, superiority, radicalism, working-class advocacy, and an elegant gentility possible. Having exposed his opponent as a coward and a hypocrite, Schuyler glories in his freedom to be a vicarious gentleman for his working-class readers, the ultimate embodiment of their complex and conflicting aspirations.

*

By rebuffing Hancock, Schuyler saw himself doing the good work of the debunker, disposing of a popular bunk-shooter who threatened black American freedom and individuality with his ridiculous and submissive conservatism. Still, strictly speaking, Schuyler did not consider himself an advocate of freedom. He always considered such vague and moralistic abstractions a sure sign of the crowd-mind. Far more often than he spoke out for high-minded notions, Schuyler debunked ideals like freedom, justice, and morality as impediments to the realization of the best possible society. Rather than regard these ideas as metaphysical givens, he encouraged his readers to think of them as socially constructed concepts, no better than the people who created them. In a playful statement on the subject of freedom, Schuyler explains in humorous terms why the crowd-minded reform attitude has made freedom in America a moot point: "Although I have been in every civilized corner of this land of liberty I have failed to find any. So I have come to the conclusion that freedom is just another of our great American myths." To support this point, Schuyler recites a long list of repressive laws and customs. He complains that anytime a movie threatens to depict real life, the censors turn it back to fantasy. If a man wants to take his girlfriend to a resort in another state, the Mann Act threatens him with a jail sentence. Blacks who find their way into money cannot move to white neighborhoods. A man cannot even take a drink without being threatened by state action. "Why is it," Schuyler asks, that in "the very country that yelps about having free institutions, freedom of speech, press and assembly, and a lease on all the personal liberty in *terra firma,* none of these things exist?" Echoing Everett Dean Martin and H. L. Mencken, he finds democracy itself at the root of the problem: "As soon as you tell a yokel that he is one of the rulers of the country—one of the hundred million sovereigns—his ego becomes inflated and he wants to exercise his great authority by preventing his neighbor from doing anything the fellow wants to do, which is why we are so deviled with reformism, which is why we are surrounded with intolerance, which is why we have no freedom. If this be treason, make the most of it."[35]

In an editorial on the Florida flood of 1928, when the National Guard forced black workers into labor camps to repair the damage, Schuyler reflects more seriously on the impact that a notion of relative freedom should have on the black attitude toward injustice: "It seems to me that the individual Negro ought to derive a great deal of satisfaction from contemplation of the fact that nobody really is free. Indeed, this whole idea of liberty and freedom is an illusion. Man, regardless of his race, color or creed, is imprisoned in a hundred different ways. . . . So few of us realize that it is really impossible to 'get ahead,' that there is no such thing as progress in the sense of definite improvement; that advancement, like everything else in the universe, is merely relative." Applying this insight more directly to the race question, Schuyler asserts that most blacks worry too much about freedom. He offers that social problems do not have definitive solutions because advantages and disadvantages exist everywhere. Thus the whole game of human freedom reduces to one of adjustment.[36]

Schuyler brought a similar attitude to the question of justice. In one editorial he urged his readers to stop agitating against injustice: "The civilization in which you live is founded on injustice, sin and wrong. Without this foundation we would be unable to visualize the ideals of justice, virtue, and right (the main characteristic of ideals, you know, is that they are never attainable)." Schuyler hoped that by rejecting an abstract idea of justice, blacks would stop expecting it to act automatically and would therefore be more inclined to seek power by whatever means served the end. Thus he wrote: "It is quite possible for us through intelligence, information, faith and, above all, organization, to create our opportunities. We might as well quit looking for justice to intervene in our behalf. Moreover, if a lot of us received justice we would be worse off than we are. The meaning of justice at best is very vague. It is probably all right to read about and be the subject of a philosophical dissertation; but for practical purposes, i.e., surviving in a hostile civilization, we can toss it overboard and place our main dependence in our organized power and strength intelligently directed."[37]

Convinced that radical doubt and protest formed an unbeatable pair, Schuyler wrote editorials questioning conventional conceptions of sexual morality, the value of federal elections, medical science, popular superstitions, and just about everything else. In place of brute faith in these matters, he advocated a habit of mind broadly based on the scientific method. Following the behaviorist John Watson, Schuyler regarded thinking as a physical process, "the same as breathing, swimming or dancing and as much a part of our bodies as the fifth vertebra, the fallopian tubes or the eyeball." Applying this materialist conception of the mind with the consistency of a zealot, he compared the untrained mind struggling with a new thought to a stiff body straining to turn a somersault. To remain flexible in the face of ever-shifting reality, he claimed, the rational person had to exercise mentally—and the younger he started the better. Putting himself forward as a professional athlete in this regard, Schuyler offered the example of his own youthful exertions: "Very early I found out that the first step in making the mind pliable, capable of assimilating unusual mental fare and not wholly a slave to the emotions, is to [test] everything. Anything I was unable to prove was immediately thrown in the trash basket and every one of the sacred and moral tenets turned completely around to see how it sounded that way. I have used this method very effectively in rendering myself shockproof and at the same time not averse to considering new ideas or tossing obsolete views overboard."[38]

In *Terrible Honesty: Mongrel Manhattan in the 1920s* historian Ann Douglas describes this very attitude as a central intellectual theme of the period following World War I. Having rejected the faith of their nineteenth-century intellectual forebears in the oneness of modernity and progress, thinkers in the 1920s embraced the idea of a dynamic, relative, and inhospitable universe of abstract forces and energies. More often than not, these forces mocked human wishes more than they fulfilled or reflected them. This framework suggested to them a conception of intellectual integrity rooted less in the articulation of rules and regularities than in honest reportage of the chaotic and sometimes terrible reality behind the appearance of order. According to Douglas, the ability to face such unsettling forces—whether in the form of Einstein's Theory of Relativity, Freud's id, William Fielding Ogburn's theory of cultural lag, T. S. Eliot's *The Waste Land,* Mencken's "Carnival of Buncombe," or Langston Hughes's "Weary Blues"—and to communicate something of their power and subtlety proved central to the intellectual and spiritual mission of a large number of thinkers in this era.[39]

While the success of Douglas's ambitious attempt to characterize a tremendously diverse era by reducing it to a single overriding spirit remains doubtful, her ideas do provide insight into how Schuyler could claim some of the comforts of faith in relativity and doubt. Douglas's idea of "terrible honesty" also helps to explain why Schuyler went so far in boldly relating unvarnished truths that he imagined most others incapable of facing. When this tendency in his thought reached high tide, Schuyler could sound downright lugubrious: "Very few people can face the hard fact that there is no meaning to life; that their coming and going is of no consequence in the universe; and that they are quite as insignificant as the mosquito that we kill with a blow of the hand." In the effort to demonstrate his tough-minded ability to face the deepest tragedy without fear and trembling, and thereby negate the image of the fearful and superstitious Negro of the past, he sometimes employed exotic literary and historical sources. For example, one of his 1930 editorials began with a quote from the gloomy Aztec prince Nezhaulcoyotl, king of Tezcuco, who asserted that "all the round world is but a sepulcher; and there is nothing which lives on its surface, that shall not be hidden and entombed beneath it. . . . The things of yesterday are no more today; and the things of today shall cease, perhaps on the morrow."[40]

By quoting approvingly the doomed prince of a doomed people in the midst of a reflection on the power of death, Schuyler asserted a strange kind of optimism. Armed with his philosophy of death, the prince must have interpreted the imperialist Spanish as just another force in the big round world rushing like the rivers, streams, and the Aztecs themselves toward an inevitable demise. Such a man could never truly lose a war, nor could he ever regard his conqueror as his better. Able to stare directly into the horrible face of reality, he secured the only victory possible in a tragic world: the ability to accept the fleeting character of existence with equanimity and grace. As an advocate of "terrible honesty," Schuyler could only hope the same for his readers and for himself.

Schuyler's tough-minded advocacy of doubt as a way of life provided the main backdrop for his discussion of religion and of the role of the Black Church. Challenging directly what he regarded as the gullibility of his average audience member, Schuyler constantly attacked the religious mind-set as a mental crutch for those lacking the capacity to negotiate directly life's varied dissatisfactions. In one of his many editorials on the subject of religion, he wrote: "All religions, past and present, are merely so many philosophical expressions of the desire of hopeless humans[,] mere specks wafted by chance down the corridors of destiny, to become superior to their environment, to find something permanent and tangible in the eternal flux of things. All humans have this yearning which we know as the desire for immortality. . . . Specific religions, and the churches their adherents found, just serve the purpose of partially satisfying these yearnings and thus making apparently worth while an existence that would for most of us be a perpetual mental torture. Thus, I believe for the broad masses of society . . . some religious belief and organization is absolutely necessary, and consequently I am led to think that the Negro church is a necessity."

Hoping to separate the desire for mastery, which he saw as a usable kernel, from the husk of superstition, Schuyler measured religious institutions by a highly practical and simple Darwinian calculus. To the extent that they aided men in the struggle to master environmental circumstance, Schuyler regarded them as good. Otherwise, he had little use for them. His assessment of the Black Church reflected this bottom-line attitude. On the negative side of the ledger he counted a long list of characteristics that he regarded as politically, culturally, and economically retrograde. These included listening to ignorant preachers, substituting otherworldly rewards for "this-worldly" action, praying to a white god, and wasting precious resources on large and unnecessarily elaborate church buildings. Still, in spite of these criticisms, Schuyler regarded the church as one of black America's brightest hopes. Because of its mass appeal and institutional entrenchment, he believed that it could act as a powerful economic force and thereby aid blacks in adjusting to the requirements of machine civilization. If it served this function, addressing the material needs of its members, Schuyler could live more easily with its more mob-oriented characteristics. Thus in a 1927 editorial he proposed that every black church should study consumer cooperation, which he thought of as the key to addressing the fundamental economic problems of black America. In this way he thought that for the first time the Black Church could provide members with a tangible reason to believe.[41]

Throughout the late 1920s and early 1930s Schuyler filled "Views and Reviews" with incessant appeals for various kinds of cooperative business. After the 1929 stock market crash this appeal became decidedly more urgent, even angry. In response to a 1930 Urban League report showing the dismal condition of black labor, Schuyler compared the black economic predicament with an all-out race war: "When all of the nice words have been uttered, all of the reports written, the fact remains that we are at war and have been for 300 years. Only occasionally does this war bring sudden death to one of us, save in the case of lynching, hanging, electrocution, and industrial accidents due to lack of worker protection because of color; but it is war nevertheless. Furthermore, it is war between white and black. Camouflage it all you please, that is a fact. This is a war that blacks are not waging in a smart manner because they are making no efforts to procure economic power. They allow themselves to become too dependent on white people."[42]

The idea of an economic race war implied to Schuyler the need for young troops trained in a new military discipline by a new kind of black leadership. Believing older blacks too set in their ways to provide these necessities, he made a direct appeal to the youth of black America. In an article appearing in his column two months before the declaration of war just mentioned, Schuyler asked why there were "no Negroes today under the age of 30 who are as outspoken and militant as were Drs. Du Bois and Monroe Trotter at that age?" In response to this deplorable circumstance, he offered to organize a "corps" of five thousand militant black volunteers from fifteen to thirty years old who would pledge to "take a manly stand for full social equality." This group would act as a "spearhead for the black struggle to avoid pauperism." To qualify, the members had to be "emancipated from religious superstition, political tradition, patriotic vaporings, superracialistic blah-blah, race and color prejudices and . . . [to] keep abreast of the best thought of the day."[43]

With this statement Schuyler began the Young Negroes' Cooperative League (YNCL), his first attempt at creating an organization to respond to black people's needs. Schuyler's romantic and ambitious vision for this organization featured a vanguard of young radicals thoroughly trained in the principles of cooperative economy. These young soldiers would spread their economic gospel by teaching classes and starting cooperatives in cities all over the United States. Schuyler hoped that the actions of this vanguard would help to provide some relief from the problems of the Depression and ultimately help to bring about a much larger "cooperative commonwealth" throughout the United States. Even Schuyler had to admit that the idea sounded fanciful, but he sincerely believed that Depression-ravaged black Americans could enhance their collective economic security by following his "Five Year Plan."[44]

Although Schuyler wanted very much to see this five-year plan real-ized, he did not intend to remain in charge of the YNCL long enough to implement the scheme himself. Fearing that older blacks would infect the organization with submission and corruption, he set the age limit for membership at thirty-six. Because he was thirty-five at the time, Schuyler made it clear that he had no plans to remain the general of his young army very long. Instead, he only wanted to get things started and then go on to his writing career. Thus the person in the YNCL who had thought the most about the larger aim and vision of the group would be gone after only one year.[45]

Schuyler's ambivalence about leadership combined with other factors to kill the YNCL shortly after its birth. Although he claimed intimate knowledge of the black masses, his naiveté concerning the plight of the black working class during the Depression contributed most tellingly to this outcome. People living one meal to the next have never provided a good market for economic planners, even those with left-oriented inten-tions. Schuyler simply overestimated the willingness of such people to invest in the future. The five thousand young radicals Schuyler hoped for never materialized. In December 1930 the YNCL started out with thirty members. By mid-1931 the organization reached its apogee with about four hundred members, with study groups in Arizona, the District of Columbia, Louisiana, Ohio, Pennsylvania, South Carolina, and Virginia. During its short life the YNCL held two national conferences. The second conference, which convened in Washington, D.C., in 1932, exemplified the problems of organization, membership, and recruitment that plagued the league. Some of the discussion topics for this meeting included "Getting the Members to Pay Dues to the National Office," "Does Discussion of Religion and Politics Make for or against Harmony within the Council," and "How Has Impatience and Intolerance Led to Disharmony between Officers and Members?"[46] One might expect an organization led by a professional satirist to come to this.

If nothing else, the history of the YNCL demonstrates clearly how far Schuyler's skill as a cultural provocateur surpassed his ability to run an actual organization. It also placed in bold relief conflicting ideological commitments, which in the context of satire proved enabling but would cripple any group attempting to foster practical social change. The conflict between Schuyler's desire for black economic independence and his socialism appears the most glaring of these tensions. Although he advocated cooperation with white socialists who wanted to change the whole American economy, he never explained how the YNCL should define this relationship to achieve these larger goals and black economic independence at the same time. Schuyler also failed to address adequately the relationship between the YNCL and the black business community. Initially he encouraged members of his organization to cooperate with the National Negro Business League and the Colored Merchants Association program, but competition for the consumer dollar in black neighborhoods combined with Schuyler's general hostility to bourgeois "fat cats" did not bode well for these tentative ties. Perhaps this would not have mattered much if the businessmen had not represented the only element of black society possessing enough money to buy YNCL stock. These contradictions, together with the somewhat romantic idea of having a group of economic "shock troops" mostly in their twenties running a national organization against all odds, combine to make the YNCL seem even more fanciful than the schemes of leaders like Marcus Garvey and W. E. B. Du Bois that Schuyler had such fun satirizing.

Although Schuyler liked cooperatives for what he saw as their practical potential, his deeper reason for promoting them reduces to ideals. The notion of black youth, unencumbered by the defeatist past, rising up to light the torch for blind and broken elders, simply fit his vision for a better world to come. With the YNCL he hoped that black political and economic activity could finally shake itself free from the client mentality, pandering, intragroup economic exploitation, sentimentalism, melodrama, and other formulas of the crowd whose main manifestations he debunked weekly in "Views and Reviews." He insisted that through materialism, rationality, organization, individualism, and most centrally through embracing each other, black people could overcome the worst problems facing them even if they could not entirely solve them.

Schuyler knew that blacks could not control their destiny alone, that they could not by their own efforts make America more integrated and democratic. Nevertheless, he did think that they could prepare themselves for almost any eventuality, that they could, to use his phrase, "render themselves shockproof." In "Views and Reviews" he devoted himself to this project by debunking everything he thought his mass audience believed. As his failure with the YNCL amply demonstrates, the value of this project remains squarely in the realm of cultural politics, in its energizing effect on the public discussion about race. Schuyler attempted to inspire a broad, dynamic, self-reflexive, and flexible intellectual exchange with his readers on the central issues facing them. By doing so, he hoped to promote the development of strong, creative, independent, socially engaged individuals. He did not doubt for a moment that these individuals would lead black people toward material and spiritual progress even within the boundaries of American apartheid. At the foundation of the large edifice of irony, laughter, exaggeration, and derisive commentary that he constructed in the *Pittsburgh Courier* stands this cornerstone of faith in black resilience and potential. What would white America do when faced with a large group of "shockproof" black people, battle-hardened by slavery and segregation, and adept at navigating the swift currents of modernity? Above all else, Schuyler wanted to see this question answered if only for the amazing show it would produce.

CHAPTER FIVE

"The Rising Tide of Color"

ALTHOUGH GEORGE SCHUYLER APPEARED most often as the author of editorials in the *Pittsburgh Courier* written for and about blacks, he made his biggest impression in the black press for what he said in a mainstream publication about whites. By the time Schuyler published "Our White Folks" as the lead article in the December 1927 edition of the *American Mercury,* he had already established himself as a star among black columnists for his provocative views and muscular writing style. Yet before 1927, even his most artful, insightful, and vitriolic statements failed to inspire more than occasional commentary among his peers. "Our White Folks" changed all this. Upon its appearance Schuyler's became the most recognizable name in black journalism. Suddenly, with the publication of this single article, Schuyler had gone from commenting on the news to *being* news; he had risen from the status of talented but youthful contender to the rank of race representative.

Although black writers had begun to publish more frequently in mainstream journals in the 1920s, they still did so rarely enough for the occurrence to merit special attention in black newspapers as evidence of the emerging New Negro voice. A lead article in the highly respected *American Mercury* went well beyond the standard for special notice of this sort. For many blacks such recognition of intellectual excellence appeared to be a victory not only for the individual writer but one for the race as well. Some black writers of the period, including Schuyler, pointed out the irony of supposedly self-possessed New Negroes looking outward to whites for confirmation of their independence, but this did little to diminish the value of black writers and leaders who could get whites to listen. Regardless of the compromising ironies, blacks had to take notice of another member of the group if whites noticed him, especially if he gained attention as Schuyler did, for telling whites how ridiculous they looked to informed and intelligent black people.

Less than four weeks after "Our White Folks" appeared on newsstands, Geraldine Dismond of the *Interstate Tattler* arranged a testimonial dinner in honor of Schuyler's achievement at Harlem's Venetian Tea Room. At the event Schuyler responded to the copious praise lavished on him by a crowd of more than seventy well-wishers, including William Pickens, A. Philip Randolph, and Charles S. Johnson, by assuring his audience in a wry tone that his new status would not change him. He declared that the organizers of the dinner had made a great mistake in thinking that they could purchase him for the price of a "feed" and that he would probably "knock" them all in his next column.[1]

This event, which marked Schuyler's social and intellectual arrival, confirmed the wide praise that "Our White Folks" had already garnered all over black America for its fearless, frank, and brisk dismissal of white pretense directly in the face of a white audience. The *New York Age* declared that Schuyler had in his remarkable article succeeded in "Out-Menckening Mencken." The *California Voice* referred to Schuyler as the "splendid voice of the New Negro," and the *Chicago Bee* called him "one of our most prolific and virile writers" who has produced "a classic of its kind." In citing Schuyler's use in the article of such terms as "nordic," "cracker," "pinks," "ofay," "Caucasian," "Anglo-Saxon," "peckerwood," and "red neck" to describe whites, the *Baltimore Afro-American* referred to his syncopated and entertaining hurling of epithets as "jazz literature." Although Schuyler also used such terms as "Ethiop," "shine," "blackamoor," "chocolates," "moke," and "smoke" to describe blacks, his enthusiastic reviewer took no offense. Instead, he regarded the playful and inventive display as an example of consummate virtuosity by a writer in cool and superior control of his destructively beautiful art form. Still, despite his keen cultural perception, the reviewer might have come to a much different conclusion if Schuyler had not placed between the epithets a copious outpouring of praise for his own people. In "Our White Folks," Schuyler leaves no doubt that he regards the average "moke" as the white person's clear superior. His pose of lordly confidence before his white audience flows directly from this conviction: "The Negro is a sort of black Gulliver chained by white Lilliputians, a prisoner in a jail of color prejudice, a babe in a forest of bigotry, but withal a fellow philosophical and cynical enough to laugh at himself and his predicament. He has developed more than any other group, even more than the Jews, the capacity to see things as they are rather than as he would have them. He is a close student of the contradictory pretensions and practices of the ofay gentry, and it is this that makes him really intelligent in a republic of morons."[2]

Schuyler points to the rigid training and discipline imposed on blacks under slavery and segregation as the main factor in reducing the number of "weaklings and incompetents" in the group. He maintains that oppression, which forces upon blacks "more trying situations in a week than the average white citizen faces in a year," has made the average "Ethiop" far more alert, tactical, and skillful than his "pork-colored" competitor.[3] In other words, by exploiting blacks for more than three hundred years, whites have unwittingly created a resilient and in some ways superior being that might soon displace them in the harsh struggle for superordinance and survival.

Because differences in intellectual capability played a central role in popular arguments supporting white superiority, Schuyler made a special point in "Our White Folks" of criticizing decadent white intellectuals. Although white thinkers generally possess a great deal of information, he says, they lack common sense. They also lack the quintessential intellectual quality of "gentle cynicism," which even the most ordinary black person has in abundance. Pushing this assertion even further, Schuyler observes blithely the white thinker's penchant for shallow enthusiasm so evident in her ability to bounce from one fad to the next, from mah-jongg to "Ask Me Another," with great facility. Of the various fads that attract them, Schuyler argues, none appeals to white intellectuals more than psychoanalysis, which places their pathetic "sexual debility" on display for all to see. In contrast, he maintains, the "lusty, virile . . . shine, is too busy really living to moon overly much about the processes of life." The same applies to black intellectuals, whom Schuyler cannot imagine standing around in a drawing room "consuming cigarettes and synthetic gin" while discussing their complexes and inhibitions.[4]

Sexually repressed and bored intellectuals represent an extreme manifestation of a more general emotional constipation among whites. Exploiting the stereotype of the repressive and puritanical Anglo-Saxon to the hilt, Schuyler laughs at the white people's pathetic attempts to have fun. Somehow, he says, the fanatically competitive and congenitally bored Nordic always manages to turn the pursuit of pleasure into work: "[Nordics] cannot swim without attempting to cross the English Channel or the Gulf of Mexico; they cannot dance without organizing a marathon to see which couple can dance the longest. They must have their Charleston contests, golf contests, coffee-drinking contests and frankfurter eating contests." All of this shows that unlike blacks, white people demonstrate a marked inability to experience even the most common pleasures without extremes of self-consciousness and exhibitionism. Schuyler contends that the so-called emancipated whites display these symptoms to an even greater extent than their more conventional counterparts. He points to their "antics" in Greenwich Village as proof. Because whites cannot have genuine fun with each other, Schuyler says, they venture to Harlem in search of easy, guiltless pleasure. Although they enjoy themselves most while among blacks, they fail to take the right message home from their pleasurable excursions across the color line. Schuyler regards the desire to punish those who provide joy as one of the most curious features of the white mind-set. Unable to live comfortably with their natural desire for pleasure, whites project upon blacks the ambivalent but guilt-relieving image of a happy-go-lucky, childlike fool that they both love and hate with pathetic shallowness. It only makes matters worse that they turn to charlatans like radio evangelist Billy Sunday, race pseudoscientist Madison Grant, and Imperial Wizard of the Ku Klux Klan Hiram Evans to help them further enhance their fantasies.[5]

Could it be that everything the popular mind associates with white strength really signifies the opposite? In revaluing, exaggerating, and redeploying a long series of white stereotypes, themselves the product of racist theories, Schuyler hoped to make his white audience ask this very question. By skillfully manipulating stereotypes, rather than indignantly rejecting them as morally wrong, he shows that a skillful satirist can twist race prejudice to a new purpose: he can use it as a tool for the display of black superiority. In "Our White Folks," Schuyler shows that all of the qualities commonly put forth as white virtues—a strong work ethic, a deep moral concern, a preponderance of worldly power, and intellect—can with only a bit of exaggeration serve the case for white decadence just as well. The same goes for the negative qualities commonly attributed to blacks, which appear tremendously positive with only a slight shift in perspective. To Schuyler, the close proximity of good and bad, virtue and vice, fitness and unfitness implied that racists, who claimed to occupy the Archimedean standpoint for making absolute judgments about whole groups, could not win the game that they had set in motion. At best they would find themselves marked with the very stain they excluded and de-spised. At worst they would make dangerous enemies of the people they dominated by force of arms.

In many of Schuyler's writings this thought, rooted in the celebration of ironic turnabout, took on the pitiless character of the most extreme rac-ist writings of his day. War, genocide, race competition, and amalgamation all played their role in his reflections concerning why whites could not maintain their fictional racial integrity under the conditions presented by the Machine Age. In an article appearing in the February 1930 edition of the *American Mercury* called "A Negro Looks Ahead," in which Schuyler attempts to shock his audience by proposing amalgamation as the most practical solution to the race problem, he summarizes some of the reasons for his ominous prognosis: "Breaches in the social barriers will become harder to repair with the softening of the Caucasians and the passing of the professional Anglo-Saxons, and will widen with the flow of ambi-tious blacks. The Aframerican, shrewd, calculating, diplomatic, patient and a master of Nordic psychology, steadily saps the foundation of white supremacy. Time, he knows, is with him. A few Caucasian alarmists cry shrilly, and ever and anon rally considerable forces to the defense. The Negro suffers a reverse, loses a position, but when the dust is settled he has the ball on the Nordic's five-yard line. He has learned one thing well: that the Caucasian is human before he is white, and he orders his attack accordingly. Ten, twenty or forty years hence he may not be in possession of complete social equality and all that follows in its path, but he'll be nearer the goal. By 2000 A.D. a full-blooded American Nordic may be as tanned naturally as they are now striving to become artificially."[6]

As we have already seen, Schuyler regarded the ability to adjust and adapt to the ironic realities of oppression as the most praiseworthy aspect of black American identity. He saw black Americans as a racially mixed and downtrodden caste—as opposed to a class or a race—whose struggle for rights and material prosperity represented one instance in the larger contest between human diversity and the closed values of inbreeding and rigid hierarchy represented by whiteness. By placing his evolutionary bet on blacks, Schuyler declared in characteristically bold terms his belief that entropy and dynamism would always defeat contrived order and pretense. Ultimately, he thought, the race question reduced to how long Nature would take to announce her inevitable verdict.

Of course, most racists believed that Nature had already announced her verdict. According to them, whites ruled the darker races as farmers ruled pigs and horses: with a dominion underwritten by the irresistible force of superior biology. One long-held racist belief posited that blacks would soon die out if circumstances ever forced them to compete with whites as free men. Some theories of this sort emphasized race war; others declared blacks intellectually deficient. Still others pronounced blacks constitutionally unfit for the chilly North American climate. Even when they did not predict black extinction, racist theories often held that for the greater good of humankind the government should prevent such inferior types from reproducing.

During the Progressive Era and throughout the 1920s a motley mix of these dangerous ideas circulated in the forefront of the American mind.[7] In addition to the many sources for these notions in popular lore, novels, and songs, a group of "professional Anglo-Saxons" led by Madison Grant, Lothrop Stoddard, and Thomas Dixon attempted to translate the arcane racial pseudo-science of the day into compelling and accessible statements for a mass readership. In celebrating the idea that whites rather than blacks would be the next victims of natural selection, Schuyler countered these thinkers with a series of propositions diametrically opposed to theirs. Where they held a natural Anglo-Saxon aversion to the lower races, he emphasized the mutual attraction of light and dark. Where they claimed the inferiority of mixed types, he asserted their superiority. Where they affirmed the primacy of heredity, he cited the centrality of environment. Invariably, such point for point inversions achieve their ends at the cost of adopting the structure of the models that they set themselves against. Schuyler's ideas about the competition of the races provide an excellent illustration of this rule. Rather than directly contradicting thinkers like

Grant and Stoddard, Schuyler selectively employed their racist ideas, especially the belief in a weakening or dying Nordic race, to promote his antiracist ends.

In *The Passing of the Great Race,* Grant provides a classic statement of the tragic and alarmist turn that the most virulent racist literature began to take under the influence of World War I. With the spectacle of mass slaughter in Europe to prod his reflections, Grant held that the Nordic race, which he thought of as the latest and greatest of human groups, would die out both because of its warlike nature and because of a distinct genetic disadvantage: recessive traits accounted for all of the refined characteristics that made Nordics superior to other races. Therefore, mating with the other two European races—the Alpine and the Mediterranean, whose traits derived from a more ancient and dominant genetic legacy—would eventually drag the big-boned, blond, intellectually gifted Nordic type down the evolutionary ladder. For this reason Grant regarded eugenics as a necessary protective measure for the greater good of humanity.[8]

Grant's ideas set the agenda for many post–World War I champions and protectors of the highest and best whites, including Stoddard, who applied the logic of *The Passing of the Great Race* to a broad analysis of the world political situation after the war. In *The Rising Tide of Color against White-World Supremacy,* for which Grant wrote the introduction, Stoddard argued that world supremacy had created a crisis for the white race. Having modernized the yellow, brown, red, and black races through conquest, whites had unwittingly augmented the powers of their natural enemies, all of whom reproduced at a faster rate. Although Stoddard regarded blacks as the most fertile among the races, he did not think that they presented much of a threat on their own. The real danger came from Asians, Arabs, and Indians, who might use the highly impressionable black population to supplement their armies. He feared that an inbred desire for submission made blacks easy converts for any other group with a coherent worldview. Intellectual weakness and doglike loyalty, combined with superior physical vitality and reproductive power, made them the perfect body for a brown or yellow brain to thrust into battle against the hated blond beast.[9]

To his credit, rather than granting such ideas the dignity of serious intellectual engagement or succumbing to the indignant response typical of most black protesters against racism, Schuyler usually administered a calm and humorous rhetorical whipping. Of his many articles on this theme, "The Negro and Nordic Civilization" provides one of the best examples of the sheer fun Schuyler could have laughing at the ridiculous pretense inherent in the views of such men as Grant and Stoddard. In this short satire Schuyler employs an unexpected inversion to provide comic tension. Instead of arguing directly against the belief in white superiority, and thus fulfilling the typical expectation for a black writer, he argues the opposite case: that blacks are indeed laughably inferior. In the process he calls into question the tendency of Grant, Stoddard, and others to confuse the "lateness" of human groups with greatness. With this aim in mind Schuyler declares the inferiority of Africa obvious on the basis of its small number of insane asylums, Rotary Clubs, YMCAs, toothpick shoes, bell-bottom trousers, French heels, derby hats, and corsets. Continuing along these lines, he laments that Africa has no Fords, "no snugly packed subways, no healthy steel mills, coke ovens, or brass foundries; and no well regulated coal mines in which to be gassed." In another place he declares with mock admiration: "Long live such scientists as Lothrop Stoddard and Madison Grant."[10]

Although "The Negro and Nordic Civilization" represents Schuyler's most typical mode of response to the professional Anglo-Saxons, he did on occasion offer more direct and serious statements challenging their claims. In one "Views and Reviews" column, for example, he questions a statement by intelligence researcher Alfred Binet guaranteeing the accuracy of intelligence tests, which had by the 1920s become the main weapon in the arsenal of racist pseudo-science. While granting the general importance of intelligence tests, Schuyler questions their ability to give a pupil's true mental rating. He urges teachers to rely on their own judgment, using standardized tests as conveniences rather than crutches in the larger project of educating young people. Schuyler juxtaposes this moderate attitude concerning the place of testing against the eugenicist overestimation of standardized measures as sure guides to the how, why, and whom of genetic cleansing. Expanding this argument, Schuyler declares: "It would be exceedingly dangerous to allow any group of people to say who shall be allowed to have offspring. I am sure I do not know who is the most unfit, Henry Ford or one of his workers. Should John Sapp, the ashman who carts away our trash, be castrated while the idiotic Prince of Wales continues to be thrown off horses?"[11]

In most of his editorials on eugenics Schuyler preferred to poke fun at its advocates by agreeing with them in the manner of Jonathan Swift's "A Modest Proposal" rather than dwelling on how much damage the application of their ideas would cause. In this spirit he often pointed out what a wonderful world it would be if some benign agency really could eliminate the idiots and the unfit. In one editorial of this type Schuyler praises a Canadian lawmaking body for discovering the perfect form of population control, one even better than abortion: a law providing for the sterilization of the feeble-minded. Taking this as an opportunity for a bit of choice debunking, Schuyler wonders what effect such "wise and efficient" legislation would have in America. He speculates that groups like the Ku Klux Klan, the Southern Democrats, and the Universal Negro Improvement Association (UNIA) would immediately oppose the passage of such a law for fear of losing the majority of their members.[12]

In his unceasing effort to call Nordicism comically into question, Schuyler constantly pointed to the existence of a large population of idiotic white people. To support this claim, he often repeated stories from the press featuring a white person falling for a cheap swindle or doing something stupid beyond belief. After telling the story, he would commonly point out that if the person were black the deed would cause whites to call the whole race into question. Sometimes these stories featured interesting inversions, as in the case of a white person being caught in a black person's chicken coop. In another tale of white stupidity, he told of a selfish American, appropriately named Fred Hogg, who tried to sneak a few puffs from his cigar aboard the hydrogen-filled Graf Zeppelin. Schuyler commented that Hogg would have been the first to complain if he saw a black person doing the same thing.[13]

Although they reveal some of his enthusiasm for the game of turnabout with white supremacy, Schuyler's gentle comic reflections on white foolishness provide little indication of his more punitive extremes. For this one must read his editorials on race and international politics. Among these none contains more direct expression of anger than Schuyler's editorial on the decline of the British Empire, in which he claims to be "tickled to death" over the humbling of "bigoted, arrogant color-phobic England." Schuyler happily reports statistics documenting the precipitous increase of the insane population in Wales and England and delights in the prospect of British authorities passing a sterilization law in order to avoid building new asylums. In response, Schuyler rejoices that eugenics has come full circle: For the greater good of humanity, the mighty Anglo-Saxons have agreed to prevent their own increase. Delighting in the "chickens coming home to roost" character of the British predicament, he asserts that in order to dominate foreign peoples, the British ruling class had to cannibalize its own working class. With the blindness of Grant and Stoddard clearly in his mind's eye, Schuyler declares the degradation of the British as the real legacy of the British Empire. Having employed economic analysis to arrive at the same basic conclusions as Stoddard, he celebrates white decadence and the rising tide of color: "The empire is disintegrating. The mother country is rotten from top to bottom because of poverty, vice and weakening of the old moral code. She is gradually passing out of world power. Another nice big war and she will be a gone gosling. The darker peoples should rejoice. An ancient enemy is falling. There is a lesson in this to us Negroes in America, for this country is on top of the heap, but it won't be long before she too will follow in the footsteps of Greece, Rome, Turkey, Spain and England. . . . As the single, intelligent, homogeneous group in this country our time of power is almost here as it is for the darker peoples everywhere."[14]

In a review of *The Twilight of the White Races*, by French historian Maurice Muret, Schuyler offers a few speculations on some of the astonishing events that will accompany the rise of dark and downtrodden masses of the world. Combining the basic logic of Stoddard with a twist of economic determinism, Schuyler optimistically asserts that in the mad scramble for colonies, European nations have planted the seeds of their own destruction through the introduction of modern weapons, modern methods of human organization, and modern aspirations to darker peoples. By coincidence, he says, the imperialist exploiters happen to be white, while the exploited natives are yellow, brown, and black. For this reason "the struggle against expanding capitalist imperialism is resolving itself into a struggle between the white and colored peoples of the world."[15]

Schuyler's review of *The Twilight of the White Races* demonstrates clearly the importance of international politics in his overall assessment of race relations. Like Chandler Owen, A. Philip Randolph, J. A. Rogers, and other members of the *Messenger* group, he always analyzed American race relations in light of the larger drama of class and race around the world. Throughout his long career Schuyler distinguished himself among black journalists for the scope, detail, and frequency of his commentary on a wide range of international events, especially those bearing on the race question. In the 1920s Schuyler used his column "Views and Reviews" to raise black consciousness concerning expanding American imperialism in Haiti, Mexico, and Nicaragua. He also commented on events in China, India, and South Africa, especially when they demonstrated evidence of the rising tide of rebellion so feared by Stoddard and his followers.

Of the various threats to white dominion, Stoddard worried most about the Japanese, who had broken the Nordic winning streak against the darker races of the world in the Russo-Japanese War. For Stoddard this victory signified something much more than the emerging military power of a single nonwhite nation; rather, it betokened a general upsurge in military capability for the entire yellow race. By his alarmist and reductionist method of calculating such matters, this placed China second in line as a potential threat to humanity. More than anything else this probably explains Schuyler's unbridled enthusiasm for Chinese militarism in the mid-1920s. In a 1927 editorial on the Chinese Revolution, he praises Chiang Kai-shek for military strategy "worthy of Napoleon." Triumphantly he cheers on the advancing Chinese military machine: "Bolshevism! cry the imperialist powers, but they dare not make too much of a show of force for fear of inflaming all China with its four hundred millions of people. Down with Imperialism! On with the Revolution! cry the victorious Cantonese." Carrying these enthusiastic reflections on China forward, he reflects on the prospects for an African rebellion of similar proportions: "There is one more thing that I would like to see before the morticians start fussing over my remains, and that is the same thing happening in Africa. Just imagine all Africa seething with revolt and the missionaries . . . speeding down the Nile, the Niger and the Congo seeking the safety of foreign cruisers! That, my friends is not as far off as one might think. . . . Twenty years ago hardly anyone dreamed that China would in such a short period go anti-Christian, anti-imperialist and, what's more, Bolshevik! It makes a whole lot of difference when you get a few rifles, cannon, machine guns and such toys on your side."[16]

Although this statement reveals a considerable enthusiasm for revolt in Africa along with a strong sympathy with Pan-Africanism, it neglects to mention black Americans for a reason. Schuyler regarded the notion of black Americans "returning" to Africa, put forth most famously by Marcus Garvey and his followers, as inimical to African self-determination. In an editorial on the Jewish homeland in Palestine, he expands on this theme in the course of opposing the British-aided imposition of Jews on Muslims and Christians, whom he describes as having lived together peacefully for fourteen hundred years. Taking the political tangle of the Middle East as his point of departure, Schuyler comments that black Americans going "back" to Africa will encounter the same problems as the Jews going "back" to Palestine. He uses Liberia as a case in point, describing black American settlement there as an "invasion" and the resistance of the native tribes as both vigorous and righteous. Because of this, Schuyler asserts, black Americans wishing to go "back" to Africa must do more than entertain romantically motivated notions of a return to origin; they must understand that political and economic complexities do not end where race begins.[17]

Along with debunking romantic expectations of international racial harmony among blacks, Schuyler also relished opportunities to challenge romantic myths about the benign intentions of colonial powers. Of the nations he criticized in this regard, none surpassed France, whose reputation among black Americans for benevolence on racial issues Schuyler attempted to spoil at every opportunity. Again focusing on the Middle East, he reports in "Views and Reviews" on a "gentle" fifteen-hour shelling that the French occupying troops had perpetrated on the helpless city of Damascus, destroying three hundred houses. This, he says, should cure those "innocents" in his audience who constantly "rhapsodize" about the French for their generosity toward black Americans in World War I. To bring his point a bit closer to home, Schuyler follows these comments with few observations on Africa: "In Africa, too, whenever any of the natives get out of hand, the punishment is severe and swift. . . . Move five or six million Negroes into France and it wouldn't be long before you would hear of Negroes being lynched in the Versailles gardens."[18]

Schuyler brought this debunking spirit to bear even more powerfully in discussing the American effort to make the world "safe for democracy." In "Views and Reviews" he seized every opportunity to expose this well-known Wilsonian conceit as a transparent piece of mob-minded rhetoric intended to obscure the spread of American-style racism to Europe and to the darker nations of Central America, South America, and the Caribbean. In pursuing this theme, Schuyler kept a particularly close eye on the southward expansion of the American Empire to Cuba, Haiti, Nicaragua, and other nations presumably requiring kind white masters to teach them how to govern themselves. In a 1925 statement on the occupation of Haiti, he reflects with biting humor on the obvious ironies and self-mystifications involved in racist Americans presuming to give Haitians a lesson in the application of democratic values: "If the Haitian is primitive, so are most of the Americans I meet; if the Haitians practice voodooism and fetishism, these are just as valuable as Christianity. . . . If the Haitian dislikes hard work, he is no different from the rest of humanity (the American ideal, remember is a Long Island or Miami bungalow with a yacht, swimming pool, expensive motor, breakfast in bed at nine o'clock and dinner at eight in soup-to-nuts regalia—in all of which there is no mention of hard work). So it is quite doubtful whether the Haitians will be better off in factories than in forests, and there is little belief that the National City Bank alias the U.S. Navy will evacuate the black republic any time in the near future."[19]

The idea that whites do not belong in such places as Haiti not only receives political and moral justification in Schuyler's editorials; it also receives the validation of biological destiny. In a 1929 editorial on the tanning craze, for example, Schuyler explains why the Nordic blond places himself at a distinct evolutionary disadvantage whenever he ventures below the forty-fifth parallel. Following the theories of Charles Woodruff and other investigators into the effects of sunlight on the white race, Schuyler claims that the white man's constitution disagrees violently with tropical conditions. Woodruff, who feared the immigration of "swarthy" Eastern and Southern Europeans to the United States, explains in 1905 in *The Effects of Tropical Light on White Men* that light skin allows the most harmful wavelengths of light to penetrate the body, causing debilitating harm to the nervous system and the internal organs. Therefore, in geographic regions below the forty-fifth parallel, darker types always appear healthier, reproduce better, and live longer. Proving once again his willingness to employ any theory that allows him to turn the tables on the promoters of racial purity, Schuyler uses Woodruff's theory to predict colored dominion over most of the globe, including the United States. He claims that the Italians, Arabs, and Spanish acquired dark skin by mating with darker people, but white Americans, with their anti-intermarriage laws, are waging an impossible war against Nature, which is demanding "a change of colors."[20]

Such statements reveal where Schuyler's environmental explanations of racial difference, rooted in a mixture of Darwinian logic and class analysis, spilled over into biological determinism. In part, this tendency stemmed from Schuyler's desire to provide race mixture with the same aura of inevitability that granted the arguments of the professional Anglo-Saxons such popular appeal. Also, in stretching the arguments of his enemies to his own purposes, Schuyler played the role of the satirist even when he gave the appearance of more straightforward explanation and commentary. Schuyler's penchant for biological determinism also stemmed from the influence of his good friend and colleague J. A. Rogers, whose voluminous historical research into interracial sex throughout the ages informed his ideas about nature's role in fomenting sexual contact across the color line.[21]

From Rogers, Schuyler borrowed the idea that throughout history ruling classes, whether light or dark, have perpetuated themselves by taking the strongest and most desirable women of the exploited group while allowing subordinate males to mate only with weakest and least attractive. For Rogers this implied something bordering on a general law of human relations: that military, political, and economic conquest proceeds through sexual domination. In his various studies on this subject, most notably his three-volume study *Race and Sex,* Rogers argued that this general rule explained why lighter and darker peoples have always held a special mutual attraction. In *As Nature Leads* he elucidates further the mechanism of this interaction through a four-part scheme borrowed from Lester Ward's *Pure Sociology:*

> 1. The women of any race will freely accept the men of
> a race which they regard to be higher than their own.
> 2. The women of any race will vehemently reject the men
> of a race which they regard as lower than their own.
> 3. The men of any race will greatly prefer the women of
> a race which they regard higher than their own.
> 4. The men of any race, in default of women of a higher
> race will be content with women of a lower race.[22]

Rogers assumed that the desire for evolutionary progress constituted a universal human motive and a fundamental principle of nature. He also thought that men pursued this end differently than women, seeking to maximize the number of sexual encounters while women sought the best chance of survival for their offspring. For him this general law proved sufficient to explain why women of less powerful groups prefer ruling-class men while ruling-class men take whatever attractive women they can get regardless of origin.[23] Thus the mixed-race types derive mostly from the mutual attraction of upper-class men and lower-class women. Taken as a transhistorical process repeated in every epoch, this tends to improve the entire human race. The less successful types advance through amalgamation while the more successful types avoid diminishment caused by excessive inbreeding.

Rogers derived this theory from a long study of many race theorists, but none loomed larger in his reflections than Ward, whose ideas concerning the beginnings of civilization provided a model of inevitable conflict between the races.[24] As mentioned in chapter 2, Ward strongly influenced all of the members of the *Messenger* group, especially Owen. Himself a product of humble origins, Ward developed his social theory to counter the Social Darwinism of Herbert Spencer and William Graham Sumner, which justified conservative ideas of natural incremental social change and limited government intervention to relieve social maladies. Against the Social Darwinist glorification of individualism and survival of the fittest, Ward championed the ideals of social cooperation, planning, and the rights of workers.

While he generally resisted the biological reductionism that justified seeing downtrodden workers as "unfit" and therefore deserving of their condition, Ward tended to slip into biological determinism when discussing relations between blacks and whites. In speculating about the causes of lynching, for example, he applied the same four-part scheme that Rogers found so useful in *As Nature Leads* to explain why black men naturally wanted to rape white women and why white men should want to kill them for it. Also, Ward accepted the theory of Lamarkian inheritance, which held that acquired characteristics could be inherited, to provide further support for his belief that improved social conditions would produce better men.[25] Although Schuyler and Rogers did not follow Ward in accepting this idea, one can still recognize its influence in their assertions, especially in Schuyler's tendency to attribute rapid societywide biological changes to economic, social, and historical factors.

Ward's race theory, most of which he borrowed from two nineteenth-century German sociologists, Ludwig Glumplowicz and Gustav Ratzenhofer, attributed human progress to an endless cycle of racial conflict occurring in a series of stages: Two races engage in warfare. The winning side either exterminates the losers or, more commonly, reduces them to slavery or some other form of servitude. Forcing the conquered into servitude requires the winners to enter into an agreement involving reciprocal duties and obligations. This results in a caste society. Over time the dominant group finds it increasingly difficult to maintain the discipline necessary to police the lower caste through direct force. To make their task easier, they enlist members of the lower group to aid in the policing function. As more time passes, the walls of caste become more porous as individual members of the two groups engage in informal contact. Eventually the upper caste discovers that it needs to enlist the lower caste to aid in the struggle against a foreign enemy. This requires further compromise of caste barriers. As interbreeding and intermarriage between the two groups intensifies, separation becomes moot. Ultimately the former enemies merge into a single homogeneous people only to fight another war and go through the same cycle of conquest and amalgamation with some other group, playing the role of winner or loser depending on battlefield fortune. Ward held out hope that one day this violent and wasteful process would end in a world marked by cooperation and productive intermixture between races, but he saw no reason in his own time to think that the cycle would end any time soon.[26]

Although Schuyler never directly mentioned Ward as an important source for his ideas, one does not have to stretch very far to see how the theory of race conflict served him as a broad model. It provided a clear basis for the simultaneous emphasis Schuyler placed on the seemingly opposed categories of amalgamation and race war. It also stands behind his insistence on referring to black Americans as a caste, rather than a race or a class, and on his corresponding confidence in their ability to fight successfully a war of attrition against the white man's will to maintain the color line. Some of Schuyler's irony about the race question, especially his insistence on the race problem having no ultimate solution, seems in part derived from the image of perpetual worldwide race conflict central to Ward's outlook. Schuyler's ultimate hope and expectation that through its racial conflicts the United States would become a more cooperative and racially intermixed nation appears to be the mirror image of Ward's desire to see the cycle of conflict end in the inauguration of a new era of perpetual peace.

Following the general outlines of Ward's conflict theory, and Rogers's application of these ideas, Schuyler promoted any action that he thought would weaken white resolve to maintain strong caste barriers, especially ones involving stealth and trickery. This made him a loud advocate of such actions as blacks "passing" for white. Periodically he would tease his audience by claiming the existence of an increasing population of blacks permanently crossing over to the white race. Knowing that many of his readers would find such reports shocking, Schuyler attempted to shock them even more by questioning the very idea of a person being able to pass for white. Rejecting the notion that race had any meaning under the skin, he claimed that a person simply is what he appears to be. Those who look white are white and those who look black are black. Considering a person white because he has one drop of white blood would seem nonsensical, he says, so why accept the opposite so readily? Occasionally Schuyler took this rejection of conventional American cultural "logic" even further by maintaining that blacks should applaud any member of the group who benefits from "passing." Denouncing blacks who "out" their chromatically advantaged brethren, Schuyler asserts: "We ought to be glad when anybody can better his or her chances in life by hurdling the obstacle of color. . . . Unless a voluntary Negro has a fat job or a good graft among the sable brethren, I think he is a dolt to stay with them."[27]

Hoping to anger the race patriots in his audience, Schuyler predicts happily that as time goes on an increasing number of blacks will journey across the color line. So long as the biological attraction between blacks and whites continues, and Schuyler says that this will be forever, the population of mulattos will increase. Reflecting humorously on the meaning of this trend for his personal situation, he speculates that by the time he grows old, a very dark black man will have become something of a novelty. He envisions being captured for display in the sociological zoo with a headline appearing in the newspaper to mark the occasion: "Surviving Full-Blooded Negro Captured in the Wilds of Harlem after Tremendous Struggle."[28]

Schuyler's reasoning on the issue of racial intermarriage also shows the marks of Ward's conflict theory. He thought it childish to expect that blacks could attain social and economic equality with whites without marrying them. Against the widespread belief that whites found blacks unattractive, that only the lowest whites married blacks, and that mixed couples always suffered ostracism, he promoted the opposite: that whites and blacks found each other overwhelmingly attractive, that mixed couples generally managed happy marriages despite social difficulties, and that the best of both races commonly fell in love and had begun to marry with greater frequency. With the last of these points in mind he told the story of John Rankin, a black man, and Bertha Soffer, his white lover. This pair had grown up together, fallen in love, and run away to New York City. When the girl's parents finally caught up with the couple, they had poor John arrested and charged with abduction. At the trial Bertha resisted the tearful pleas of her family and refused to testify against her lover. Without evidence the court had no choice but to release the young man. As one might imagine, this did not soften her family's position on the matter of matrimony. At the time of Schuyler's report the pair stood in limbo. Despite Bertha's pregnancy, her family still refused to see her marry a black man. Schuyler reported that both were from "good" families. In a somewhat hopeful tone, he concluded: "Now there you are. Despite all the social taboos, these young people got together. There is much more of this going on in the South than in the North. It used to be said that the only free people sexually in these United States were white men and colored women, but that is no longer as true as it used to be."[29]

Stories about couples like John and Bertha, many of which Schuyler published in his 1929 pamphlet "Interracial Marriage in the United States: One of the Most Interesting Phenomena in Our National Life," helped to increase his faith in a rising tide of resilient and determined interracial love, but his most powerful feelings of confirmation stemmed from much more intimate sources. When placed next to Schuyler's ideas on interracial marriage and on the biological and economic forces behind race mixing, his own torrid romance with Josephine Cogdell appears an almost surreal instance of self-fulfilling prophesy. As a couple, George and Josephine eventually came to represent a strong antiracist symbol, a kind of public and tangible proof of deep and abiding love in black and white. In this way they defied the most important racial myths and shibboleths of their day. Yet they never really transcended race. Rather than colorblindness, their relationship depended on a long list of transvalued racialist ideas, which they used to enhance their love. Within the complex dynamic of their mutual attraction, an abiding consciousness of blackness and whiteness intensified the mutual recognition of personal virtue that made them admire each other with dogged conviction. Allowing for all of the other reasons each found the other singularly fulfilling, one wonders, upon reading Josephine's diary, which provides the only record of their intimate life, whether George and Josephine would have ever met or gotten married if they had had the same racial background. Racial difference provided them with a framework of overcoming, with a reason to invest in each other intensely and defiantly in the spirit of "the world be damned."

If Josephine and George did not fall in love at first sight, they certainly managed to generate immediate and powerful lust. Having come to New York from San Francisco in part to meet Schuyler, whose writings she had greatly admired, Josephine arrived unannounced at the door of his *Messenger* office on a hot August day in 1927. In the midst of a particularly hectic editorial rush, nothing could have surprised and delighted Schuyler more than the sight of a shapely white woman standing before him awaiting his attention. He told her that he regarded himself as something of an expert in the detection of racial identity, but could not tell her race from the articles she had submitted to the magazine. Of course, Josephine knew Schuyler's race, and this made a great difference to her. In hopes that her office visit would inspire the proper feelings in the hard-boiled satirist, she had chosen her best blue dress, the one that matched her eyes. When she finally saw him, she found him attractive as only a dedicated romantic racialist could: "He was stunning," she later wrote in her diary. "His black skin gleamed like satinwood and his hands were as long and graceful as the wings of a raven."[30]

In his travels Schuyler might have encountered women who felt the same way, but few would have been able to articulate their feelings in the elaborate and dramatic voice that Josephine employed in her diary and in her various letters and poems. Like almost everything else in her life, her diary spoke to her artistic aspirations, which she developed early in life as the spoiled youngest child of a rich Texas rancher and banker. Through individual tutoring, music lessons, and other luxuries of a privileged upbringing, Josephine learned to reject both the provincial values of her fellow Texans and the rugged pioneer capitalist framework of her arrogant, cruel, and reckless relatives. As an aspiring lady in a harsh world built on cottonseed, animal flesh, naked ambition, and improvised justice, she longed for escape to more beautiful surroundings, which she found in her dreams and in her early attempts at artistic expression. Like many other rich southern children, Josephine also found escape among black servants, who taught her to ride and to hunt, to sing and to tell compelling stories. Because of them, she always associated blackness with art and with spiritual freedom. During her most formative and impressionable years she learned through her family's servants to love blacks for the antithesis they offered to the cold and unvarnished money-grubbing of her father and brothers, who only wanted to see her marry someone who could bring money and status into the family. It only increased her feelings of kinship with blacks to hear of the sexual excursions of her father and brothers across the color line. These feelings of closeness became intertwined with rage and guilt as maturity brought knowledge of the systematic cruelty that her white relatives perpetrated upon the black men and women who represented the saving grace of her youth.[31]

In her diary Josephine relates a dream that she had in 1919 while living in San Francisco that brought together all of the conflicting themes of her early encounters with race and family. In the dream Ainky, her favorite servant on the ranch in Texas, introduces her to a dark young man for whom she feels an instant and deep sexual attraction. After kissing the young man on the mouth, she becomes frightened that he might assault her "cruelly and revengefully." Then, trembling with fear, she says to herself: "Now I will pay that long due debt which the white race owes the black race for the centuries of cruel assault." The realization of her willingness to pay this debt thrills her "exquisitely." But nothing terrible occurs. Instead, she and the black youth begin to dance "wildly, ecstatically . . . whirling and leaping together with joined hands and arms." While dancing she beholds "with an inexpressible sensation the magnificent contrast" of black and white skin. Possessed by the deepest joy, she feels as if all opposition in the world has been overcome.[32]

Josephine had this dream just as she gained her initiation to socialism, communism, feminism, and to the statements of black intellectuals in such journals as the *Crisis* in the explosive political context following World

War I. Despite its occurrence eight years before she thrust herself into Schuyler's office and into his life, this dream represents well the agenda that made Josephine so perfect for confirming his views about race. In describing their frequent dates between August 1927 and January 1928, Josephine paid particular attention to dancing. On one occasion she recalled that her skin "burned" under Schuyler's touch even though he made no sexual advances. On another she described more elaborately the feelings of sublime joy mixed with titillating fear that possessed her as she moved and swayed in Schuyler's arms at the Savoy: "He executed the bumpety-bump with a sensual African grace that is full of savagery yet urbane and dignified. . . . He undulated his lean dapper body to the accented movement flowing almost without effort through him. His arms held me softly and loosely but the smile of insolent possession he [sent] upon me riveted me to him. At such times I could kill myself for his pleasure. The concentrated power in his face is absolute, voluptuously cruel, diabolical."[33]

Josephine's fear of Schuyler had almost as much to do with his satirical and literary talents as it did with his race. In keeping with the theme of sacrifice in her 1919 dream, she thought that Schuyler could through his keen critical abilities reduce her Anglo-Saxon pride. By doing so she hoped that he could help her become a better and more productive writer. In one particularly poignant moment of confession she wrote: "I want him to browbeat me, I want him to destroy my superiority complex[,] I want him to laugh at my white affectation and rationalize my fears. . . . To my mind the white race, the Anglo-Saxon especially, is spiritually depleted. America must mate with the Negro to save herself. . . . I need Schuyler. Without him I shall quit growing and solidify."[34]

In exchange for Schuyler's aid, Josephine vowed to "give him greater confidence in himself" and to make sure that he did not become too bitter. "I will make him certain of his superiority," she pledged. "He needs to be cherished and inflated as I need to be pruned." Two days before the wedding day she took her desire for "pruning" to a level that must have alarmed even her shockproof fiancé. Referring to one of her moments of misbehavior, she said: "When I get like that beat me. There's nothing like a good beating to cheer a woman up. Beat me and then love me and I'll be as docile as a lamb." She complained that her old boyfriend could not perform this essential deed, but she thought that she could depend on Schuyler. The bewildered editor answered at first that he could not do such a thing, but after Josephine persisted, he relented: "I'll try," he said reluctantly.[35] No evidence exists that he ever followed up.

After two weeks of dating, George and Josephine made love for the first time. For her this proved an almost religious experience quite similar to that which occurred in her 1919 dream. The next day she noted in her diary: "My blood is still ringing from it. Somehow, strangely enough, I feel ennobled. I cannot explain why except that a complete satisfaction fills me with wholesomeness and gratitude towards life." Later she wrote: "The prowess of the fellow is classic. There is always something new to his performance. He is subtle, masterful, bold, tender, seductive, imaginative. I come from his arms as from a religious experience. . . . No wonder the white man fears the Negro. Yes, he is a menace to their civilization."[36]

Apparently Schuyler, who pronounced the gospel of sexual pleasure in many editorials and whose 1930 lecture tour included a talk entitled "Love as an Art," knew how to practice what he preached. Like Josephine, he often said that the white man's great fear of blacks reduced to sex. Although he believed in feminism for many other reasons, in "Emancipated Women and the Negro" he held that white women's emancipation would aid the black cause considerably. Given the choice, he thought that many white women would, like Josephine, take a black lover and would do so for similar reasons. In "Some Unsweet Truths about Race Prejudice" he went even further, claiming that this attraction might have a biological root. He wrote that "there are certain physical differences between the sex organs of Caucasians and Negroes that are reported to greatly increase the pleasure of coition between the two." He declined to discuss them but declared that "the fact is known in a general way by the masses of people." Although Schuyler gathered the evidence for this statement from several official and unofficial sources, including sex researchers like Havelock Ellis, he also found it confirmed in his most intimate experiences. In breaking the bad news of her new relationship to her old boyfriend, an artist named John Garth, Josephine made sure to mention that her new black lover was "ultra-sexual" and despite his stature "was possessed of the most gigantic anatomy."[37] During their five-year relationship in San Francisco, Garth had often used the term "supersexual" to describe her. He also referred to her as "Delilah."

Given the emphasis Josephine placed on expressing her feelings

openly, Schuyler probably knew the full extent of her thoughts and fantasies about him and, judging from his reaction to her, liked them very
much. After all, Josephine's fantasies seem the perfect balm for some of
the injuries he suffered as a talented black writer in a racially stratified
field of endeavor. While Schuyler never whined about problems, he fully
recognized the unfair limitations that his extremely dark skin color placed
on his ability to achieve social recognition among blacks and whites. The
anger concerning these unfair restrictions smolders beneath the surface
of all his writings. In contrast to almost everyone else, Josephine chose
to see him as something of a superman, both mentally and physically
superior to other men, singularly fulfilling, and one for whom she could
be a perfect complement—a wife and an intellectual partner.

Although Josephine began to love Schuyler soon after meeting him,
she did have the good sense to doubt whether she wanted to suffer the
social isolation and rejection from family members that would follow a
marriage. Recognizing this, on more than one occasion Schuyler offered
her a chance to back out.[38] The presence of Josephine's old boyfriend,
who came to New York in the fall of 1927 with sincere professions of
love, increased the difficulty of her deliberations. She decided during this
period to arrange a double date where she, Garth, and Schuyler would all
go out together in Harlem, with her and Garth as one pair and Schuyler
and his date as the other.

At the Savoy while dancing with Josephine and looking over her shoulder at Schuyler, Garth decided to give artistic form to his jealousy. He suggested that the black reporter, with his black skin and his crooked nose,
looked like a satyr and that he wanted to paint him that way along with
Josephine depicted as a nymph. Josephine agreed. She called Schuyler
the next day to ask him to pose for the picture. Ever wry and sardonic, he
asked Josephine if she thought this was not "running it into the ground."
Josephine countered with a humorous statement of her own, pointing out
the poetic justice of her old lover enjoying the satisfaction of proclaiming
her "faithlessness" in paint.[39]

The following Sunday, Schuyler found himself in a scene reminiscent
of Langston Hughes's story "Slave on the Block": posing nearly naked, a
participant in a strange act of homage and revenge. No doubt, as he stood
there wearing a cloth around his waist, the endless ironies of the situation ran through his mind: the heavy suggestion of racist condescension,

Josephine's complicity in the matter, his own desire to please his lover and to show his superiority to the whole incident by treating it as if race had nothing to do with it. Regardless, he could find comfort in one sure fact: he had Josephine and Garth did not; in the battle of male one-upmanship, he was "one up." Sensing himself "one down," Garth could not contain his need to speak disparagingly of Schuyler's stature. A violent argument with Josephine ensued. He yelled, "I hope you are pregnant and have a black baby!" She shot back: "I hope I do too!" John shouted: "You'll probably end by committing suicide!" She responded: "Undoubtedly."[40] Neither could know at the time that both wishes would eventually come true.

On 6 January 1928, Josephine accompanied Schuyler downtown to the Municipal Building for a discreet and perfunctory civil wedding. Although she had a few lingering doubts about going through with the act, she leaned on Schuyler for support and guidance. Fearing that her relatives would find out what she had done, she signed the marriage certificate as Josephine Lewis, her name from an earlier marriage in Texas. To further conceal her identity, and perhaps to seal her symbolic passage across the racial divide, she reported her race as "colored." Her mind turned to the blacks back on her father's ranch. "Ainky," she said, "you won." Then she imagined that "all of the cotton pickers and mill hands stood smiling at me, and all of them shouted—joyously."[41]

Schuyler told Josephine later that just after they had finished their vows, his mind turned to the scene in "All God's Chillun Got Wings" in which "they come out of the church and the people are gathered on either side with their hands out pointing at them." In this way he revealed his concern with what his marriage with Josephine would mean to the rest of the world. The next day he said more directly: "Do you know, Josephine, we stand absolutely alone? We can't count on anybody. The whole world is against us, the negroes as well as the whites?" As if to confirm this statement, the *New York News* announced three months after the wedding day in a small article, with the headline "Schuyler Marriage Shocks Elite," that only a little more than a week after his testimonial dinner for "Our White Folks," Schuyler had made an "irretrievable fall to lighter hue." By marrying a white woman, the article claimed, he had implicitly rejected the black women of Harlem and had dismayed black society "to the point of frigidity." According to Josephine's account in her anonymous article "The Fall of a Fair Confederate," this captured the majority opinion. Still, not everyone in the black press disapproved of George and Josephine's bold move. Ever willing to swim against the current, W. P. Dabney of the *Cincinnati Union* reported the identity of Schuyler's wife with glee and fanfare. Proving that some people could find delight in the symbolic meaning of their bond, he dedicated a bit of doggerel to them in his column almost two years after their wedding day:

> George and Josie jogged along
> The path of domestic life;
> The world for them seemed one glad song,
> So free was it from strife.
> But thus it had not always been,
> The past had taught them well,
> So when they met they did begin,
> To make Paradise out of Hell.[42]

The pressure of the world watching rarely has a good effect on a celebrity marriage, but one might say that George and Josephine fed off of their importance to others. The prospect of disapproval from without imposed a certain discipline on their relationship and with it a certain harmony. In a poem called "Taboo," which she wrote for Schuyler in 1930, Josephine openly acknowledged just how far the sense of their relationship as a social and symbolic force penetrated their most intimate communications:

> When I lose my temper
> Or talk a bit too free
> He will call me to him
> And quietly lecture me:
> "If we stoop to brawl
> They will say Mixed Marriage
> Is what has caused it all."[43]

In a beautiful love letter written on the third anniversary of her visit to Schuyler's office, Josephine assures her husband that their attempt at mixed marriage had proven the world entirely wrong. In expressing her love "audibly," she testifies that the "perfection" they have achieved as lovers and friends has more than offset the costs and pressures of their interracial marriage. She tells Schuyler that she "worships" him not only because he pleases her physically and intellectually, but for his ability to improve her character by the example of his own indomitable spirit. Claiming to have been improved as a person by 50 percent in the three years she has known Schuyler, Josephine dismisses his "few flaws" as "mere fly specks on the classic body of my black Zeus."[44]

If this letter were only half true, more a product of Josephine's romantic temper and desire to buttress Schuyler's ego than a balanced assessment of how she felt about him, it would still provide some insight into their bond. Even as Josephine appears to objectify her husband through constant reference to his "classic black body" and "saturnine countenance," the broader range of complex characteristics that make him uniquely attractive remain in view. She describes him as alternately aesthetic, idealistic, cynical, bawdy, practical, cautious, reckless, kind, and cruel.[45] And still, in spite of this recognition of Schuyler's broader human virtues, one would be hard pressed to find anyone, white or black, who could have loved his blackness like Josephine.

In a letter written during a three-month stay in Mississippi in 1935, Schuyler matches the feeling of Josephine's 1930 letter as he testifies to his loneliness and longing for her love. "As time goes on," he says "the conviction grows deeper and firmer that you are the one companion in the world for me." Claiming to have been shaped into a better man by Josephine's influence, he lauds their decision to marry "bravely and resolutely" rather than settling for more convenient and less noble options. Rising almost to the level of his wife's swooning romantic reveries, he assures her that the sacrifices she has made for their interracial bond have raised her to the highest possible position in his eyes: "Atheist though I be, there is one god I worship, and that is my Josephine. Like Jehovah, my god has been eccentric at times and righteously wrathful, but I only worship the more ardently, for my adoration can only be properly termed worship. . . . Your respect for and confidence in and reliance upon me have long since become psychological food and drink without which my spirit would waste away like wheat in a drought and curl up and perish. I would not exchange you for all the other women in the world rolled into one. Beside you even the best become dwarfs."[46]

In this letter Schuyler not only testifies to his love for Josephine, he congratulates her efforts in raising their four-year-old daughter, Philippa, who by this time had already made headlines for her precocious intellect. When she was only two-and-a-half, an article by Lincoln Barnett declared in the *New York Herald Tribune:* "Negro Girl, 2½, Recites Omar and Spells 5-Syllable Words." Another article, appearing in the same newspaper six months later, announced: "Harlem's Youngest Philosopher Parades Talent on Third Birthday." In February 1936, at Josephine's behest, both Columbia and New York University measured Philippa's intelligence quotient as somewhere between 179 and 185. Suddenly Schuyler, who had always questioned such tests, could not have been more proud. Although he promised Josephine that he would keep Philippa's astonishing test scores private, he could not suppress his desire to share this marvelous vindication of his interracial marriage with a reporter from the *Houston Informer.*[47]

Like everyone else, the Schuylers were stunned and at a loss to explain the phenomenon they were raising. Following the way of most befuddled parents of exceptional children, they resorted both to nurture and nature to account for their good fortune. In keeping with the general thrust of the Schuylers' editorials and articles on race mixing, and borrowing from theories Josephine learned from her experiences with horticulture and animal breeding, the Schuylers speculated that Philippa's stunning intelligence had derived in part from hybrid vigor. Products of mixture, they thought, could profit from the good characteristics of both parents while minimizing the bad ones.[48] At the same time they believed that the extraordinary efforts they put into shaping Philippa's environment gave her native gifts the best chance to develop.

As thoroughgoing environmentalists, the Schuylers followed the child-rearing edicts of the behaviorist psychologist John Watson with assiduous attention. Watson's manual on this subject, *Psychological Care of Infant and Child,* encourages the creation of ultraindependent, rugged, punctual individuals capable of responding to challenges with as little assistance as possible. Toward this end it directs parents to keep such rearing practices as bathing and potty training on a specific and strict schedule. It also insists that parents keep hugging and kissing to a minimum, provide daily sunbaths on a regular schedule, rarely bounce their child on their knee, avoid talking down to them regardless of age, reveal all of the facts of sexuality as early as possible, and shake hands with their child every morning. In addition to following these and other suggestions from Watson, the Schuylers also carefully engineered their daughter's diet. From her teenage years Josephine had been interested in new medical discoveries on the connection between eating and the maintenance of health and vigor. Through her researches she came to believe that cooking had a bad effect on the vitamin content of food. For this reason she served raw vegetables and raw meat to her family. She also found modern chemicals, sugar, starches, dyes, and other common additives in processed food to be detrimental to health. To her, the avoidance of these substances, which only existed to maximize profit for capitalists, amounted to something of a crusade. She avoided them like poison.[49]

Whatever the ultimate reason for her success—pure food, sunshine, superior breeding, doting parents, or dumb luck—Philippa became a remarkable woman: an author, a humanitarian, a feminist, and a world-renowned pianist. In other words she could not have represented more perfectly her parents' hope for a new generation of superior mixed-raced Americans who would lead the country out of its racist past toward a truly democratic future. Yet Philippa never found a place of belonging in the world nearly so perfect as her position in her parents' dreams. An almost total absence of friends her own age, her status as a globe-trotting child star, an intense codependent relationship with her obsessed mother, the constant absence of her busy, globe-trotting father, and the overwhelming effort that both of her parents put into making her the perfect symbol of their interracial love affair combined to produce a profound lifelong identity confusion. In a country where race meant almost everything, Philippa never really developed a secure sense of racial identity. Unable to find recognition in the United States for her talent, she traveled constantly to play concerts abroad. This compromised her sense of national identity. As she grew older, Philippa's national, racial, and personal identity confusions combined to play havoc with her attempts at romantic attachment, granting her story a somewhat haunting resemblance to that of a classic "tragic mulatto." Considering that her parents made every effort to fashion her into a pure negation of that stereotype, it becomes possible to recognize in her story some of the flaws of perfectionism, whether of the racist or antiracist variety.

At his best Schuyler certainly recognized these flaws. In "Our White Folks" he praised the "lusty virile shine" for his ability to perceive discontinuous and ironic realities in his own terms. Because this character could live directly and honestly without imposing fast frozen ideals, especially moral ideals, on ever-shifting circumstance, Schuyler thought that he would in good time displace the narrow and decadent white racist. He also believed that this resilient character would achieve his ends by any means necessary, employing love, sex, violence, and protest alternately. His biological advantages, which derived ironically from his African heritage, his hybrid vigor, and his environmental circumstances, would significantly aid this effort. Where whites allowed it, he would integrate. Where they made it necessary, he would gladly live with his own, build black institutions, and bide his time. Ever ready to adjust and overcome, this protean character would through trickery and stealth, through direct assault and strategic retreat, achieve his ends by exploiting every blind spot of white supremacy. A pure antithesis of perfection and a master of irony, he would win by capitalizing on contradiction.

Described this way, Schuyler's "lusty virile shine," whom he attempted in his own way to embody, emerges as a thoroughgoing attempt to invert racist values and thereby offer a counterideal. In this we might find both his flaw and his promise. Schuyler succeeded through his writings and through intimate relationships in realizing a beautiful interracial vision. This occurred partly through his willingness to utter a loud and impractical "no" to the world around him. His satirical talents also appear in part the result of this willingness to set himself against his fellow men as the defender of high and rare ideals. In this way he appears the perfect negation of the realistic and pragmatic "moke" of "Our White Folks." And yet it remains hard to imagine anyone better suited to articulate the virtues of that character and, against the odds, to grant those virtues a tangible, if imperfect, reality.

CHAPTER SIX

The Black Mencken

GEORGE SCHUYLER'S FIRST EDITORIAL for the *Pittsburgh Courier* in his new column called "This Simian World" features among its short satirical sketches a fictional interview with Mr. G. Orilla, dean of the Simians, held at Mr. Orilla's uptown residence in the Bronx Zoological Garden. Although Schuyler had shown no indication in his previous writings of any ability to speak the Simian tongue, his conversation with Mr. Orilla on the occasion of William Jennings Bryan's retirement from the podium demonstrates clearly his skill in cross-species communication. Upon hearing the news of the great man's retirement, Mr. Orilla leans against the bars of his residence, shakes his head, and utters in a sorrowful voice, "I fear we are losing our best friend." Schuyler asks, "How so?" The monkey replies with a short speech: "You see ever since Darwin's time, the so-called scientists have spread the canard that we monkeys are in some way related to the human race. They claim in fact, that humanity descended from us, or rather our forefathers. Of course it is evident that humanity descended from something because it has never shown any evidence of ascending. At first all the people who had ever studied us in our natural habitat and noted our intelligent mode of living, rebelled against the idea. Nobody had ever seen us carry on war, lynching each other, filling up jails, or working our little children."[1]

Schuyler responds incredulously: "You don't mean to say that you consider your people superior to the human race?" The monkey urges him to contemplate the facts. "Did you ever see monkeys straightening their hair or whitening their skins? Did you ever hear of monkeys allowing one of their race to appropriate all of the trees in the jungle, and then pay rent to him?" Somewhat trumped, Schuyler shifts the conversation back to Bryan, whom the monkey considers a great man for rising above the human norm in recognizing his own inferiority. Reasoning that apes constitute a distinct and superior group, he praises Bryan for becoming a fundamentalist and fighting the injustice done to his kind by the evolutionist canard. Speculating that Bryan's nobility could well derive from superior breeding, Orilla adds: "[Bryan] is the only man who thoroughly understands monkeys. In fact I believe he has a lot of monkey in him. Didn't he run for president four or five times? And only a monkey could dominate every convention for the Democratic party the way he has. . . . In short, if there was any truth to the statement that we are related to the human race, Bryan would be the best evidence of it." After calling the monkey a bigot, Schuyler wonders how a resident of a cage could express such confidence. "That's the biggest point in our favor," Orilla declares, adding that people serve the apes night and day. Sensing victory, he strikes his final rhetorical blow: "Isn't that sufficient evidence that you yourselves acknowledge our superiority?"[2]

Although Bryan, the leading voice for the prosecution in the 1925 Scopes trial, remains the most explicit focus of this short sketch, several secondary issues combine to define its overall practical purpose: introducing Schuyler to his new audience. Given this aim, Schuyler's invention of Mr. G. Orilla, a signifying monkey of the highest order, seems the perfect calling card. His black audience would have immediately recognized the reference, especially in light of Orilla's interpretive tricksterism. Courting irony to the hilt, Schuyler juxtaposes this image of an articulate intellectual monkey against the characterization of blacks as near-monkeys so common in the works of race pseudoscientists Lothrop Stoddard and Madison Grant, who ranked blacks lower than whites on the evolutionary scale. Playing around the many humorous possibilities inherent in the relationship between monkeys and men, Schuyler implicitly poses the idea of science as a discourse of truth, a bulwark against superstition, fundamentalism, fanaticism, and racism against the tendentious distortions of the professional Anglo-Saxons and their less distinguished followers.

Schuyler's role as an interviewer, a translator of the Simian language, and one of Orilla's old acquaintances adds to the irony of the sketch. His venture uptown to the Bronx Zoological Garden represents a black version of the journey a white New York reporter might make from his downtown office to observe blacks in the urban habitat of Harlem. This analogy, suggested within the terms of the sketch, conveys Schuyler's clinical distance from other blacks. Yet the author's suspicious and somewhat discreditable intimacy with the denizens of the monkey house exposes this claim as mere pretense. Schuyler can understand the monkeys and report their doings because he is a monkey too. As a kinsman, he proves supremely able to reveal their thoughts, which reflect the most foolish wisdom.

Mr. Orilla, the ultimate ghetto-dweller, inverts everything. He regards the cage as a room in a palace, zoo-keepers as servants, and all evidence of human superiority as sure proof of the opposite. Yet despite his delusions concerning himself and his "people," he can see clearly the flaws in humans that they refuse to see in themselves. In other words his false consciousness, so apparent in his deep race pride and contentment with ghetto life, does not prevent him from thinking like a radical. He even recognizes the element of monkey blood in "the Great Commoner" Bryan, the quintessential turn-of-the-century Democrat and man of the people, whose career as a public figure represented so well the contradiction of democratic pluralism and the rhetoric of purity.

For all of its playful irony, Schuyler's fictional interview with Mr. G. Orilla leaves one idea absolutely unambiguous. Bryan, a fool of the lowest order, deserves the kind of rhetorical whipping that only the most civilized man can administer: a thorough and humorous application of abuse that manages nonetheless to avoid all of the characteristic vices of the herd, especially moralism, paranoia, mawkishness, and fascination with the pleasures of cruelty. Schuyler shared the conviction of Bryan's foolishness with many thinkers on the cultural left in the 1920s, including his *Messenger* colleague Chandler Owen, but his playful and satirical approach to expressing it underscored most of all his formative relationship to H. L. Mencken, who pelted Bryan with ridicule at every available opportunity. Charles Fechner, a Mencken biographer, rates Bryan with Woodrow Wilson and Franklin Roosevelt as one of the political figures Mencken most loved to abuse with his famous vicious jabs. In *Damn! A Book of Calumny,* published just after World War I, Mencken reduced Bryan's philosophy to two assertions, both of which he regarded as pure foolishness. The first insisted on the wisdom and honesty of the common people. The second labeled as scoundrels all doubters of this ironclad faith. Take away these two propositions, Mencken claimed, "and all that would remain . . . would be a somewhat greasy bald headed man with his mouth open."[3]

In "In Memoriam: W. J. B.," Mencken shows his capacity for unmitigated and pitiless assault by dancing a rhetorical jig on Bryan's grave. At the beginning of this obituary, he notes Bryan's last secular act on Earth as catching flies. How appropriate, he says, that Bryan "spent his last days in a one horse Tennessee village, and that death found him there." As the reference to rural and small-town life in this passage indicates, Mencken disdained "the Great Commoner" as his personal antithesis, as a super-rustic overcome with hatred for all things urban, sophisticated, and cosmopolitan. He even described Bryan's charisma as a second-order effect of hatred and smallness, the product of a superior ability to distill the resentment of the average small-town dweller into an intoxicant of unbelievable power and purity. Mencken speculates that Bryan achieved this feat by exaggerating ignorance and stupidity to a degree that the ordinary American rustic could not match. Thus he became a representative man for whom the "simian gabble of the crossroads was . . . wisdom of an occult and superior sort," and he lived for the sole purpose of leading the "anthropoid rabble" against the men of the city who regarded him quite rightly as a laughingstock.[4]

Mencken's treatment of Bryan grants language and laughter a central place in political power play. Although Mencken by no means discovered this ancient method of gaining political advantage, he practiced it with a proficiency rarely matched in the history of American arts and letters. His rhetorical expertise and his skill as a humorist allowed him to place an indelible and distinctive stamp on intellectual life in the 1920s. For this reason, and because he profoundly affected both the form and substance of Schuyler's thought, we must take closer look at the "Sage of Baltimore," especially regarding his views on race.

Of the important concepts at work in Mencken's worldview—such as civilization, cosmopolitanism, realism, and irony—none surpassed race as a recurrent focal point. Through the years race, along with the related issues of tradition and cultural inheritance, remained a central category in his battle against the narrow elite of New England–bred Anglo-Saxon critics who ruled the cultural scene during his youth. Using mimicry, parody, and other weapons of the satirist, Mencken opposed this Victorian elite, which represented to him little more than an organized effort to deny everything vital and interesting about the United States. Next to such realities as rampant political corruption, "big-stick" imperialism, the violent exploitation of workers, increasing prejudice against immigrants, and organized racial violence against blacks, the sentimental values of such "cultural custodians" as Stewart Sherman, Paul Elmer Moore, and William C. Brownell struck Mencken as irrelevant and laughable denials of reality. He disdained their narrow Anglo-American literary canon and detested their effort to promote the appreciation of moral values within it. That these gentleman critics also denied the crucial cultural contributions of regions other than New England and of ethnic groups other than their own seemed to him both ridiculous and deeply wrong.

In pressing his criticism of this elite, Mencken developed a set of intellectual values and a mode of self-presentation that inverted everything they represented. Against their insistence that art promote morality, he championed the works of realists who undermined and questioned accepted values. In opposition to their narrow American canon of mostly New England "classics," he located the roots of American literary achievement in a wide range of regional and ethnic expressions. He insisted that this art, which represented the most vital and insightful products of the American mind, would remain forever hidden to such men as Sherman and Brownell, whose sentimentalism and worshipful Anglophilia inclined them to disdain most things American. Against the assumption of Anglo-Saxon superiority informing the attitudes of these self-proclaimed humanists, Mencken promoted the ideal of America as a mosaic of many races and ethnic groups striving toward a cosmopolitan, worldly, broad-minded, and sophisticated nation.

Rather than preach against the evils of such men as Sherman and Moore, Mencken parodied their pretension to gentlemanly status. Claiming to represent the "civilized minority," he lampooned his enemies as fakes and as thinly disguised yahoos who deserved the disdain that only the true man of culture can have for those who portrayed ignorance as wisdom. In pressing his satire of the gentlemen critics, Mencken employed a language all his own built from a synthesis of the clean, direct prose of the well-trained journalist, the cultivated tone of the man of letters, and the protean creativity of various regional styles of American English.

Mencken not only employed this style in satirizing pseudoaristocrats, he also used it like a battering ram against a wide array of targets, including the Ku Klux Klan, political reformers, churchgoers, preachers, politicians, Prohibitionists, sexual prudes, and anyone else he deemed a member of the vast crowd of conformists who lacked the common decency to mind their own business. Such intolerant souls seemed to him out of step with the sensibility necessary to sustain the dynamic polyglot multiplicity of the United States. Against the narrowness of those who would have the entire nation march in lockstep to their own values, Mencken promoted the ideal of the ruggedly independent and tough-minded individual with strong but cultivated prejudices. As his own best example of this kind of person, he advocated a set of classical liberal values intended to make the United States a safe place for the man of talent and intellectual attainment to live and thrive without the interference of the mob or of the fake aristocrats who controlled nearly every institution of worth. This liberal streak in Mencken's thought often expressed itself as a profound suspicion of all reform, especially those efforts that threatened to increase the size of the state. On one side he opposed the hegemony of the rich and spoke out loudly for an elite based on honor and cultivated sensibility. Against the dominion of crass and standardized material values, he defended both the sanctity of high culture and the importance of minority rights and cultural diversity. Yet Mencken remained content with capitalism so long as it observed basic rules of honor and fair play. Despite the emphasis he placed on fairness and cultural openness, he remained eternally suspicious of democracy and complacent about inequality, sometimes to the point of blaming the victim.

As author Richard Wright attests in *Black Boy*, Mencken received his greatest recognition among blacks not so much for his pluralistic fair-mindedness as for his blistering attack on the South, which he carried out most famously in "The Sahara of the Bozart." In this unrelenting assault on southern values, Mencken characterizes the South as a cultural wasteland ruled by inferior men incapable of understanding the glories of southern aristocracy before the Civil War. In opposition to the self-serving racism of these Southerners, Mencken offers by way of parody his own racialist explanation for their utter inferiority. Against the myth of white southern descent from the best strains of Anglo-Saxon blood, he claims that the Civil War wiped out all of the genetic superiors, leaving mostly descendants of the low-born Celts, with whom the Anglo-Saxons always refused to intermarry. Rather than sully themselves through sexual contact with repugnant Celts, the better strain of whites preferred the highest types among their slaves. This left the mixed breeds, the mulattos, as the natural superiors of both their darker counterparts and the dirty whites of the southern majority: "It is commonplace that nearly all Negroes who rise above the general are of mixed blood, usually with the white predominating. I know a great many Negroes, and it would be hard for me to think of an exception. What is too often forgotten is that this white blood is not the blood of the poor whites but that of the old gentry." As a result of this mixture, Mencken says: "It is not by accident that the Negroes of the South are making faster progress, economically and culturally, than the masses of whites. It is not by accident that the only visible aesthetic activity in the South is wholly in their hands. No Southern composer has ever written music so good as that of half a dozen white-black composers who might be named. Even in politics, the Negro reveals a curious superiority."[5]

For Mencken's black readers, especially the darker ones, embracing this vision of black superiority came at a cost. Certainly Mencken's attack on the South presented tempting possibilities, but sincerely accepting it required tacit assent to a romantic myth of the glorious old South and acknowledgment of the ultimate racial superiority of slaveholding Anglo-Saxons. Recognizing this, James Weldon Johnson offered an alternate explanation for southern intellectual deficiency. He speculated that the excessive energy the South put into maintaining segregation and Jim Crow explained its cultural failure, not racial deficiency. Mencken never responded directly to this suggestion.

"The Sahara of the Bozart" places an important question in front of anyone pondering the much-debated issue of Mencken's racism. It demonstrates well Mencken's preference for slippery irony in mocking racist frameworks through imitation rather than direct counterargument. Still, Mencken's willingness to give the racist some of his own medicine through parody leaves room for doubters to wonder whether he makes for the antiracist an entirely secure ally. Even those who understand Mencken's ironic methods and intentions have expressed doubts concerning just how much of the racist remained in the man behind the satirical mask. In his writings on racial and ethnic issues, Mencken commonly employed reductionist and Social Darwinist language in referring to minorities. He also employed a wide array of pejorative names for ethnic groups, referring to Jews as "kikes," Italians as "dagoes," and blacks as "nigaros," "sambos," or any other distasteful appellation that came to mind. This method of challenging "respectable" names for groups, and the narrow-mindedness of those who enforce such linguistic codes, has always made racial progressives more than a bit uncomfortable with Mencken. Of course, Mencken liked making such people feel uncomfortable because he regarded their crusading reformism as a large part of the American problem.

Whatever his doubters thought, Mencken always regarded himself as completely devoid of racism. However accurate in fact, this self-characterization did express his intentions and many of his actions, which reveal him as a bulwark against the most vulgar manifestations of racism in his era. Although he delighted in Social Darwinist rhetoric regarding groups, he never used such language in connection with individuals. Despite the emphasis he placed on culture and heritage, Mencken cared most deeply for the emancipation of the individual, especially the heroic, realistic, intellectual, doubting, self-creating individual. He regarded this independent modern type as an insurance policy against the lynch-mob mentality that inclined people so often to justify treacherous crimes that they would never perpetrate on their own. He once wrote: "Personally, I hate to have to think of a man as of a definite race, creed or color; so few men are really worth knowing that it seems a shameful waste to let an anthropoid prejudice stand in the way of free association with one who is." In addition to making such statements, Mencken repeatedly published antiracist writers like Franz Boas and Melville Herskovits in the *American Mercury* and denounced mightily the efforts of such racist groups as the Ku Klux Klan. Whether he lived up to his own vision in every case, the fact remains that Mencken regarded racism as a feature of the American herd mentality, an idea indicating charter membership in the rabble that he always lambasted with supercilious contempt.[6]

Mencken's enlightened views on the racism of the herd amplify the irony of his own racialism to the point of sublime ridiculousness. Through a strategy of playful imitation and reversal, Mencken found racist reasons for regarding racists as idiots. Yet to accomplish this feat, he adopted the terms of the racist in ways that make him a suspect for those inclined to more straightforward styles of antiracist advocacy. For such advocates it probably provides little comfort that Mencken never sounded more racist than in his denunciation of Anglo-Saxons, especially the ones he regarded as dirty and lowborn. In "The American Tradition" he states his case as an offended member of the pure, unmixed Anglo-Saxon minority and as one highly qualified to recognize those who do not make the grade: "It so happens that I am myself an Anglo-Saxon—one of far purer blood, indeed, than any of the half-bleached Celts who pass under the name in the United States and England. I am an Angle and I am a Saxon, and I am very little else, and that little is all safely white, Nordic, Protestant and blond. Thus I feel free, without risk of venturing into bad taste, to regard frankly the *soi-disant* Anglo-Saxon of this incomparable Republic and his rather less dubious cousin of the Motherland."[7]

Mencken describes the two main characteristics of this so-called Anglo-Saxon as an inability to do anything difficult and a susceptibility to fears and alarms. With no real ideas of his own, this exhausted and weak strain among men, who "fears ideas . . . cravenly" and remains "palpably third rate" even when educated, succeeds only by appropriating the strengths of less exhausted types through racial mixture. Mencken cites such literary heroes as Edgar Allan Poe, Walt Whitman, and Mark Twain as examples of mixed types who tried to "shake the old race out of its spiritual lethargy, and introduce it to disquiet and experiment." Against these hearty types the so-called Anglo-Saxon succeeds only through plodding practicality and his unmatched ability to remain perpetually alarmed. Thus, Mencken says, at the height of his triumph the Anglo-Saxon still looks "shabby": "England trembling before one-legged France, the United States engaged in a grotesque pogrom against the wop, the coon, the kike, the papist, the Jap, the what-not—worse, engaged in an even more grotesque effort to put down ideas as well as men—to repeal learning by statute, regiment the arts by lynch-law, and give the puerile ethical and theological notions of lonely farmers and corner grocers the force and dignity of constitutional axioms."[8]

To emphasize emphatically his own resistance to the Anglo-Saxon herd, Mencken always announced proudly his attachment to his German ethnic roots. He employed a wide array of references to German language and culture in his writings and often asserted directly the superiority of this heritage to that of his low-caste Anglo-Saxon enemies. During World War I he paid heavily for these gestures when Stewart Sherman accused him, in a review of *A Book of Prefaces,* of sympathizing with an enemy of the United States. Sherman's review capitalized so effectively on anti-German hysteria that when Mencken returned from service as a war correspondent in March 1917, all newspapers and magazines except the *New York Evening Mail, The Seven Arts,* and his own magazine, the *Smart Set,* had closed their pages to him.[9] Rather than intimidating him into silence, however, such rough treatment redoubled his resolve. Mencken emerged after the war with an even greater contempt for the Anglo-Saxon elite and with a more embattled sense of identification with immigrants and other socially marginal groups, including blacks, whose art and cultural peculiarities had always interested him. As an expression of this interest, he opened the pages of the *American Mercury* to a long list of black writers, including Walter White, James Weldon Johnson, Countee Cullen, and of course George Schuyler.

In keeping with his observations concerning immigrants and with his racialist critique of the American majority, Mencken always encouraged blacks in his various articles on the race question to insist on themselves, strive for superiority, and resist the desire to imitate decadent whites. He also recommended a pragmatic, two-sided approach to politics. In "The Curse of Prejudice" he praised the "shrewder among the younger Negroes" who followed the strategy of edging as close to whites as they could while simultaneously glorying in their "Negroness." This, he says, "will probably bring them far nearer to equal rights and dignities, in the long run[,] than the effort of other leaders to obtain for them the complete equality that they can never really get. Besides, it is more self respecting than the other scheme, for it involves neither charity nor patronage."[10]

Reflecting on the precarious situation of his own ethnic group during the war, Mencken reasoned that the Germans, who held their ground "calmly and correctly, making no effort to conceal their race or their feelings," got more respect after the war than those who waved the flag and misrepresented themselves. He charged that these "cowards and mountebanks" gained neither the respect of Anglo-Saxons nor that of their own kind. Therefore, at the same time Mencken preached individualism, he also maintained a faith in group loyalty, which also flowed from his philosophy of the "civilized minority." In the United States, a society ruled by an intolerant and uncivilized majority, Mencken believed that thinking this way would always come at a cost. Minorities insisting on their own identity against the great herd would always experience persecution, especially if they demonstrated a capacity for higher achievement. Against those who wanted to cast ethnic and racial antipathy as an aberration incompatible with American democracy, Mencken regarded prejudice as an inevitable by-product of life in pluralistic societies, which owed their dynamism to the creative violence of competing groups jousting for advantages that they could in turn deny to others. To live happily in such a society and to enter its competitive realities fully, individuals had to accept prejudice as something to be managed and manipulated rather than denied or disdained. For this reason Mencken always admired groups that endured difficult circumstances with dignity, honor, patience, and "without protesting too much."[11]

This idea always stood behind Mencken's admiration for blacks, which he stated in his own distinctive terms: "That Negroes, in more than one way, are superior to most American whites is something that I have long believed. I pass over their gift of music (which is largely imaginary) and their greater dignity . . . and point to their better behavior as members of our common society. . . . No one ever hears of Negro wowsers inventing new categories of crime, and proposing to jail thousands of their own people for committing them. Negro Prohibitionists are almost as rare as Catholic Prohibitionists. No Negro has ever got a name by pretending to be more virtuous than the rest of us. In brief, the race is marked by extraordinary decency." To this characteristic of decency and greater sociability, Mencken adds a strong capacity for humor and cynicism, both of which he regards as wonderful characteristics. To their credit, he says, blacks approach experience with a perspective suffused with doubt: "His view of race-leaders who prey on him—for example, the clergy—is full of doubts and dubieties. I often wonder how many pious blackamoors really believe that they will turn into white angels post-mortem—probably no more than a few imbecile old women. The Negro spirituals, taking one with another, are anything but confident in tone, and after singing the most hopeful of them the congregation often turns to 'I went down the rock to hide my face; / The rock cried out, "No hiding place, / No hiding place down here."'"[12]

In perhaps his greatest compliment to blacks, Mencken declared in

1927 that the United States had emerged from "the Age of the Rotary" and entered "the Coon Age." Mencken's idea of the fundamental cause for this—the abatement of race prejudice among upper-class whites—seems naive in retrospect, but the assertion at the center of this article that everything original in American culture has a black origin remains remarkable for its boldness. In "The Coon Age," Mencken recognizes the ubiquitous appeal of jazz, the superiority of black culinary achievements, and trenchant black contributions to the American language, especially in shaping the southern dialect. He also notes the black origin of American styles of dance and religion. Although some of these achievements, such as the black contribution to Methodism, which he calls "African from snout to tail," receive less credit from him than others, Mencken does not waiver in attributing them to blacks.

Of course, Mencken would not be Mencken if he only offered praise. Although he complimented black cultural contributions in general, he still complained about religion. In "The Burden of Credulity," Mencken characterized the black attachment to religion as "extraordinarily stupid, ignorant, barbaric and preposterous," and he stopped just short of calling it "downright simian."[13] Notably, in this article he contradicted his contention in "The Coon Age" that white religiosity originated in Africa. In "The Burden of Credulity" he attributed the origin of black religion to "the lowest class of southern whites." Mencken did not worry so much about historical details so long as he could be sure that the target of his comments would feel the sting.

Mencken's most famous and most controversial critical statement concerning blacks appeared in his "Hiring a Hall" column in the *New York World*. In this article he endeavored to tell the harsh truth concerning black artists. Prefacing his remarks on the quality of black art with the same optimistic assessment of American race relations informing "The Coon Age," Mencken complained that blacks have become less worthy as a result of mixing too quickly and too enthusiastically with decadent whites. He began by attacking what most of his readers would have thought of, quite correctly, as a black cultural stronghold: "It may be, as they say, that the Negroes invented ragtime, and jazz after it, but certainly it would be absurd to say that they have surpassed or equaled the whites in writing the new music. The best jazz of today is not composed by black men, but by Jews—and I mean best in every sense. Why did the Negro composers wait for George Gershwin to do his 'Rhapsody in Blue'? Why, indeed, did they wait for Paul Whiteman to make jazz a serious matter?"[14]

Mencken's error of judgment in these remarks can make his main point easy to miss. Although he appears in these remarks to undercut the idea of a special black contribution to American culture, he focuses in the bulk of the article on something closer to the opposite. He wonders whether increased contact with inferior whites, and increased racial inter-mixture, will erase the social preconditions necessary for genuine black artistic expression. Mencken believed that so long as it did not compromise dignity, the struggle against hardship increased the ability of groups to perceive the basic truths of human experience and that this inclined them to the production of great art. He feared that mixing socially and sexually with whites could make blacks complacent, or, as James Weldon Johnson's Ex-colored Man put it, prone to selling their souls "for a mess of pottage." In pressing this point, Mencken pans black literature. He contends that no black author has written a novel even remotely comparable to *Babbitt* and that no black writer of short stories has risen above the level of "white hacks." He speculates that blacks may have ventured into the arts too soon and that they may find their greatest success in the more practical realm of business; but he warns that black businessmen can only achieve success if they displace the clergy, whom Mencken accuses of having made a "terrible botch" of their leadership.[15]

By telling blacks, in essence, that they need to build a strong economic foundation among their own and that this would in turn provide the independent means necessary for future black artistic contributions, Mencken played a dangerous game. Although he regarded it as simply pragmatic for blacks to think of racism as a permanent feature of American society, he flirted with a kind of segregationist complacency in putting the issue the way he did. Although Mencken's critical statement on black life and leadership inspired a large volume of response in the black press, the range of the commentary remained fairly narrow, focusing mainly on his denouncement of the black clergy and his disparagement of black art. The high volume of negative commentary on these issues compelled Mencken to return to the issue again in the same column two months later, but only to modify his opinion in one respect. He admitted that one black artist, Professor R. Nathaniel Dett (of Hampton Institute), had written a good spiritual. Beyond this, he only reiterated and reinforced his old position,

most notably by criticizing harshly Walter White's *Fire in the Flint,* a novel
that Mencken played an important role in promoting. Perhaps to balance
the harsh treatment of White's novel and offer his black readers a sliver of
hope, Mencken followed his critical barrage with a ringing endorsement
of Schuyler as a leader in the movement toward "realistic stocktaking"
and "unsentimental self-analysis" needed to rid blacks of the archaic and
barbaric folkways that made them such easy prey for "exploitative frauds
and mountebanks."[16]

This strong praise from the dean of American arts and letters did not put
Schuyler in the best position to criticize Mencken in his usual vituperative
tone. Also, Mencken's article repeated many elements of the case Schuyler
had been bringing against black middle-class intellectuals for years. Thus,
in his response to Mencken in the *Courier,* Schuyler voiced strong agreement even on the controversial points: "Indeed I have said much the same
thing myself. That a number of so-called Negro Literati are mere hacks is
quite apparent to the most casual reader. When Prof. Mencken says that
the literary and artistic accomplishments of the Sons of Ham in these
United States 'have been very modest,' he is telling what God loves."[17]

Schuyler said that this also applied to the realm of music, despite the
popular faith in black peoples' natural rhythm. He challenged his readers
to compare any black American poet to such greats as Tennyson, Swin-
burne, Shelley, and Keats, or even to such lesser lights as Longfellow, Frost,
or Sandburg and come away from the experience with anything other than
the conviction that the blacks are second rate. Until blacks build enough
wealth to support the arts properly, he wrote, they cannot hope to equal
or better these whites in technique or ability. Still, he pointed out that this
cannot serve as an excuse for America's white writers, who have not produced anything nearly as good as any number of Europeans. Because of
this, he said that Mencken's attitude concerning blacks struck him as "a bit
too pontifical." Schuyler wrote: "He forgets it seems to me that American
writers generally haven't contributed much timeless literature, nor have
any American composers, white or black, rivaled Beethoven, Wagner, or
Liszt. Our American poets, too, with the possible exception of Whitman
and Poe, are decidedly not of the first water. The fact is that this is a young
country just emerging from the pioneer stages. Heretofore, it has been
absorbed with building a civilization and has only begun to criticize and

interpret it. In the future [it] is quite probable that our American artists and writers will create just as lovely poems, books, sculptures and paintings as any of the European masters, but up to the present time . . . we have not done so."[18]

This criticism really does unravel Mencken's case. It is important that Schuyler accomplishes this feat by agreeing with the *Mercury* editor and then taking the view to extremes toward which its originator would not venture. One could say that by doing this, he out-Menckens Mencken. By turning the light of analysis back to artistic production in America as a whole, he weakens Mencken's position as a critic of black culture. Moreover, by pointing to the oneness of black art and American art, he exposes Mencken's lapse in regarding the two as so easily separable. He also turns the rhetorical tables by bringing the same condescension to American literature, and to Mencken, that the "Sage" brings to black literature and music. In this way Schuyler challenges Mencken's somewhat limited and presumptuous attitude toward blacks even as he courts the *Mercury* editor as an ally. In politely calling him "a bit too pontifical," he shows that no matter how honest Mencken's interest in blacks, the *American Mercury* editor could not presume to tell the unvarnished truth about them without seeming to imply his superiority as the great white dean of American arts and letters. In this way Schuyler's answer to Mencken on the issue of black art served to remind his readers of the costs involved in Mencken's special brand of hubris.

The occasion of Schuyler out-Menckening Mencken provides a good place to begin the consideration of Mencken's impact on Schuyler's general posture and outlook. In his book *The Sage in Harlem* author Charles Scruggs documents the trenchant effect that Mencken's ideas and patronage had on a large number of 1920s black intellectuals, including James Weldon Johnson, Walter White, Theophilus Lewis, J. A. Rogers, Wallace Thurman, and many others. Although Scruggs tends to overstate Mencken's effect on the Renaissance, he does document the relationships between black intellectuals and Mencken more clearly and in a more detailed manner than anyone before him.

Of the black intellectuals affected by Mencken, none employed the form and substance of his perspective with more enthusiasm and precision than Schuyler. In recognition of this fact, some of Schuyler's readers used the moniker "the black Mencken" to describe him. Although this name does capture an important dimension of Schuyler's approach, it grants too much to his status as a Mencken imitator and too little to the effect Schuyler had on Mencken over the years. Also, as Schuyler himself often pointed out, the characterization of him as a mere imitator of Mencken ignores his attraction to satire and irony before he had ever read the *Smart Set* or the *Mercury* and discounts the possibility that he and Mencken constructed issues in similar ways because they shared a similar temper. If Schuyler did imitate Mencken, he did not do so more than Sinclair Lewis, W. E. Woodward, Ring Lardner, or a long list of other thinkers who grew up in the general atmosphere of deflating and debunking to which Mencken made an important and formative, but not exclusive, contribution.

Still, Mencken had a strong and deep effect on Schuyler's ideas and general intellectual approach. Looking at Schuyler's journalism as a whole, one can find no editorial, no article, and hardly a sentence where Mencken's influence does not seem somehow evident. Schuyler's criticism of religion, morality, Prohibition, feminism, the South, and the corruption of the political system all demonstrate his debt to Mencken. One can also see Mencken's influence in Schuyler's ideas concerning the decadence of the white race and in his disdain for Britain, which informed his idea of the darker races of the world rising against white supremacy. Although this idea has many other sources among Schuyler's intellectual influences, it does reflect in part the influence of Mencken's polemic against the fake and decadent Anglo-Saxons of the United States and Britain. Schuyler's condemnation of the black inferiority complex bears a crucial relation to Mencken's criticism of the American inferiority complex. His promotion of black independence as well as his disdain for mendicancy and patronage reflect Mencken's emphasis on ethnic groups in America maintaining their way of life and their independence even in tough times. In addition to these more substantive contributions to Schuyler's outlook, Mencken provided Schuyler with a methodological clinic in the uses of satire for the outsider in American culture. Mencken showed that a clever critic could win the cultural upper hand without really arguing against conventional standards. Using parody, he could reverse them or reject them wholesale as the ridiculous creations of ridiculous men.

As many examples in the preceding chapters of this book have shown, Schuyler did not hesitate to use this weapon on his own people in a style that often followed Mencken so closely that his insulted victims sometimes suspected him of being the worst kind of white man's Negro. One critic writing in the *Washington Eagle* spoke for many angry blacks in referring to Schuyler's "picturesque 'apish' Menckenese." Another complained that in trying to conform to Mencken's style, Schuyler often "forgot himself," using such terms as "Sambo" and "Sons of Ham" to ingratiate himself to white readers. An article in *Heebie Jeebies* entitled "Schuyler-Mencken" attempted to out-Schuyler Schuyler by referring to Mencken as the "Mahomet in Mr. Schuyler's garden" and as "George's Great White God." In "Our Negro Intellectuals" literary and cultural critic Allison Davis provided the most prominent and sophisticated statement in this spirit, accusing all of the black followers of Mencken, especially Schuyler and Eugene Gordon, of scandal-mongering and of emphasizing black eccentricities over virtues. He casts these "little Menckenites" as dangerous posers whose "specious liberalism" may succeed in misguiding a whole generation of black thinkers.[19]

Although they tended to undermine the force of their claims with exaggeration, Schuyler's critics did have some grounds for questioning his pose of radical independence. When Schuyler called Robert Russa Moton "Rusty Moton," or referred to Kelly Miller as the "Mouthematician of Howard," or labeled Marcus Garvey the "Imperial Blizzard," he seemed only the slightly darkened and distorted image of Mencken calling Warren G. Harding "the numskull of Gamaliel," or Woodrow Wilson "the archangel Woodrow," or Calvin Coolidge "a dreadful little cad."[20] Schuyler's habit of combining this kind of invective with exaggerations of polite, scientific, or archaic terminology mirrored Mencken's method of creating comic incongruity by placing formal modes of English next to the more informal and direct language of everyday Americans. Like Mencken, Schuyler heightened incongruity by employing outrageous exaggeration almost as if to say that no amount of overstatement could match the ridiculous reality that he endeavored to describe. Schuyler also repeated many of Mencken's coinages and pet phrases, such as "booboisie," "buncombe," "of the first water," and referring to misguided foes as "brother."

A mere perusal of Schuyler's "Shafts and Darts" column in the *Messenger* reveals its close relation to the "Clinical Notes" section of the *American Mercury*, with its short satirical titles printed in the same italic style and its aphoristic mode of commentary. Also, just as Mencken teamed with theater critic George Jean Nathan in writing "Clinical Notes," Schuyler collaborated with the theater critic Theophilus Lewis in writing his column of calumny and satire. Occasionally one can even spot an item in "Shafts and Darts" or in one of Schuyler's essays that seems to mirror directly the "white" version in "Clinical Notes." For example, Schuyler's short dialogue "At the Darktown Charity Ball," which satirized the black "booboisie," appears as the dark twin of Mencken and Nathan's "The Greenwich Village Ball," which poked fun at the foibles of the corresponding class of whites. The same pattern applies to Schuyler's "Reflections of a Bachelor at Thirty," which bears a striking similarity to the series of observations Mencken made in "Clinical Notes" under the title "Reflections of a Bachelor at Forty."[21]

Despite the compelling testament they give to Mencken's strong influence, such examples do not justify glossing over the important differences between the two men. Taking account of the occasions on which Mencken and Schuyler reviewed the same book provides one good way to measure these differences. The publication of *God's Stepchildren* by the South African novelist Sarah Gertrude Millum provides one such occurrence. *God's Stepchildren* tells the story of a South African family that endures everything to become white. The family finally achieves its goal when the last descendant, Barry, marries a British woman. When she becomes pregnant, his conviction of inferiority gets the best of him. Overcome by shame, he tells his pregnant wife of the "harm" he has done by marrying her. He insists that the expected child remain in Britain, on the white side of the color line, with his wife. Bringing the story full circle, he returns to Africa to preach and seek atonement in the very district where his great-great-grandfather—the weak, incompetent, and sentimental Rev. Andrew Flood—began a hundred years earlier.

Impressed by the psychological truth contained in Millum's depiction of the black South African inferiority complex, Schuyler praised the novel. He recognized these merits despite the racism of its author, who in telling the story of the whitening of a South African family through successive generations reinforces such notions as the intellectual superiority of lighter peoples. Schuyler concluded on an ironic note that Lothrop Stoddard and Imperial Wizard Evans would read Millum's book with "great gusto and agree with its conclusion: Thou shalt not practice miscegenation."[22]

In contrast to Schuyler, Mencken gave *God's Stepchildren* much more credit. He spent most of his review relating the novel's plot, which he liked very much for conveying the "searching and mordant" sociological insights of the author concerning the negative effects of racial mixture. Acknowledging none of the qualities that Schuyler found objectionable, Mencken declared the novel "an extremely artful, knowing and moving piece of work."[23] Thus both critics interpret Millum's novel as a cautionary tale, but Mencken regards it as a treatise on the dangers of race mixing, while Schuyler appreciates its usefulness as a guidebook on the South African version of the black inferiority complex.

This puts Schuyler and Mencken on opposite sides of the same intellectual thoroughfare. Schuyler's reading emphasizes ideas and imperatives that he shared with Mencken, such as the rejection of self-deprecating modes of consciousness among minorities and the repudiation of racialist thought. Yet he rejects the more hard-core version of cultural pluralism and the hint of Social Darwinism that grants Mencken's review its slightly malodorous air. Still, to Mencken's credit, his propensity to doubt the efficacy of amalgamation had more to do with his uncertainty concerning the white American majority than any misgivings about blacks. He thought it unwise, impractical, undignified, and ultimately self-negating for blacks to protest for mere inclusion within a social and cultural mainstream that badly needed their most critical contributions. That he could not say this without placing himself in the paternalist position of the white man who "knows what's good for the black folks" gives ample testament to how difficult it can be, even for a consummate ironist with the best intentions, to escape the endless ironies of American race relations.

Schuyler's social position and critical posture also imposed its ironies. He agreed with Mencken that blacks should not debase themselves with fantasies concerning the superiority of white society and should insist on the equality of their group life with that of any other. Yet he also thought it romantic and unrealistic to emphasize too heavily the differences between so-called races that had lived in close proximity and experienced high amounts of social, cultural, and sexual contact throughout American history. For him American race relations presented a slightly different irony than the one Mencken stressed. Schuyler saw black and white Americans as substantially alike, especially in their propensity to declare their differences from each other. Of course, this made it difficult for him to give a compelling account of the differences that did exist between blacks and whites, even when he wanted to acknowledge them and use them to justify the pride he thought blacks ought to have in themselves. However awkward, this weakness in Schuyler's perspective on race did purchase for him certain advantages over Mencken and over many pluralists of his era. His review of *God's Stepchildren* makes this apparent. His familiarity with the many forms that racialist discourse could take made Schuyler bring a much higher quantum of suspicion to writers like Sarah Gertrude Millum than "the Sage of Baltimore" ever thought necessary. Had Mencken awakened one day with his skin suddenly dark, he might have made similar judgments himself.

The 1924 publication of Upton Sinclair's *The Goslings,* a book debunking the American education system, provides another occasion on which Schuyler and Mencken produced opposing opinions on the same book. In his review for the *Messenger,* Schuyler endorses Sinclair's book so strongly that he devotes the majority of his remarks to repeating and rhetorically enhancing the author's main points. Sounding a bit like Mencken criticizing the subintellectual New England professoriat, Schuyler argues that the schools and universities do little to promote knowledge. He proposes that a great change must take place before education can improve: the people supposedly most interested in the advancement of knowledge, the teachers and professors, need to organize themselves against the plutocracy that attempts to "throttle real education." He writes: "I am in perfect agreement with the author . . . (both of us are violent Reds!)." But Schuyler does not want to stop with the construction of a national teachers' union: "If the majority of people in this country, white and black, are to be anything besides propertyless, exploited morons, then all workers must unite in One Big Union and see that this country of the people, by the politicians, for the plutocracy, is returned to those who perform the useful labor—the Workers."[24]

Although the phrase "propertyless, exploited morons" reflects Mencken's influence, the opinion Schuyler expresses here could not contrast more with the *Mercury* editor's mocking reflections on Sinclair. Although he grants Sinclair the basic truth of his argument, Mencken objects to his underlying reasoning. Detecting in the author a certain narrow ideological enthusiasm and extremism that he always regarded as sure signs of allegiance with the herd, Mencken denounces *The Goslings* as a product of "a great deal of false reasoning and vain indignation."[25] He attributes most of Sinclair's false reasoning to an idealistic assumption: that the public education system actually exists to create knowledgeable democratic citizens. Sounding for a brief moment like a Marxist himself, Mencken asserts the real mission of state-run education as the opposite: to wash every semblance of individuality out of the minds of the young in creating standardized citizens. Mencken offers the swelling numbers of such organizations as the American Legion, the Ku Klux Klan, and the Rotary Club as undeniable proof of government's efficiency in this matter.

As he scoffs at Sinclair's lack of realism, Mencken also denounces his foolish liberalism and his even more foolish "bolshevism," accusing him of desiring mere schoolmarms to decide what they want to teach "their little flock of morons" and, even worse, wanting schoolmarms in Congress to make decisions about educational policy. Showing his supreme contempt for bureaucratic jobholders, Mencken denounces congressional schoolmarms as natural followers who only know how to do the boss's bidding. He doubts that such people could possibly know anything concerning the creation of independent minds. Because of this, he concludes that Sinclair's ideas would make matters worse. He congratulates the author for gathering a vast mass of "scandalous and amusing facts" but chides him for employing a wrathful tone in relating what everyone knows already anyway.[26]

Mencken's review of *The Goslings* reflects perfectly his larger view of socialism and socialists, whose "believing minds," he said, disqualified them from conceiving social problems realistically. He joked that the socialist tendency to believe would not have been so bad if socialists did not feel so compelled to give such credence to falsehood. The socialist "yearns" for falsehood, he once wrote, "as a cow yearns for the milkman." Mencken also could not take the socialist concern for the poor seriously. He denounced socialism as "the degenerate capitalism of bankrupt capitalists."[27] Certainly Schuyler and the *Messenger* group could not have presented much evidence to make Mencken doubt his claims. The attempts to promote black capitalism in the *Messenger* would have provided excellent grist for his mill. Still, however much he corresponded with Mencken's idea of the money-hungry socialist, Schuyler fundamentally disagreed with "the Sage" on matters of politics. Although he would come around to Mencken's position in time, during the 1920s Schuyler believed in the possibilities of collectivism and regarded it as an answer to social problems in the United States.

✻

Mencken probably did not have Schuyler's socialist advocacy in mind when he wrote a letter to him in 1927 asking the *Messenger* editor if he could write an article for the *American Mercury*, something "done realistically and fearlessly," like Schuyler's "excellent stuff in the *Pittsburgh Courier*." Mencken suggested that Schuyler do an article on how whites look to an "intelligent Negro" and added that several "dark literati" of his acquaintance had attempted to write this article for him but they "couldn't get rid of politeness." In a letter written three days later Mencken commented that he would love to see the Nordic dosed with his own medicine, for he must surely be "ridiculous seen from without." Less than three weeks later Schuyler's article "Our White Folks" arrived at Mencken's office with a letter from Schuyler declaring that in accordance with Mencken's request, he had "thrown politeness in the garbage can," spit on his hands, and "laid around with great gusto." In case Mencken found the diatribe too strong or crudely done, Schuyler enclosed a self-addressed stamped envelope, "in accordance with the venerable traditions." Mencken accepted "Our White Folks" for publication immediately, congratulating Schuyler for a "capital article."[28]

With this exchange Schuyler had begun the most significant and extensive correspondence of his career, spanning nearly thirty years, from 1927 until Mencken's death in 1956. The early years of this correspondence, from 1927 until Mencken's exit from the editorship of the *American Mercury* in 1933, a period during which Mencken published nine articles by Schuyler, reveals the negotiations of an editor and a much-respected writer. In almost total opposition to critics who viewed Schuyler's relationship with Mencken as one of crass imitation, the letters between the two men document an association based on mutual high regard that over the years developed into an important friendship. Of course, as a major editor and cultural figure, Mencken held the preponderance of power in the relationship, but his dealings with Schuyler—at first as editor of the *American Mercury* and later as a friend—remained remarkably fair and straight. Recognizing Mencken's power, Schuyler certainly did not stretch to emphasize his disagreements with "the Sage," but his broad agreement with Mencken on most subjects made it fairly easy for him to be himself within the boundaries of the relationship.

From the late 1920s to the early 1930s all of Schuyler's letters to Mencken focused on ideas for articles or on criticism of his many

submissions to the *Mercury*. Although Mencken accepted some of Schuyler's articles without reservation—like "Our White Folks," "Black War-
riors," "Keeping the Negro in His Place," and "Traveling Jim Crow"—he
could be quite frank in objecting to some of Schuyler's more questionable
efforts. For one of Schuyler's early submissions, a collaboration with a
Pullman porter on the technique of extracting tips, Mencken did not hesitate to point out flaws: "I am sorry indeed that you put in any work on this,
for I fear it won't do as it stands. The introduction is rather too long and
obvious, and there are too few illuminative anecdotes. It would be better,
indeed, if it started with an anecdote. The reference to Terre Haute, again,
might be developed into an amusing discussion of regional liberality. In
brief, the thing shows some good material, but it jogs a bit, and so is not
effective. I scarcely know whether to advise reworking it or scrapping it.
And I am sorry that I put you to trouble about it."[29]

Over the years Schuyler submitted many articles that Mencken turned
away, some of which appeared in other places. Sometimes, as in the case
of "Southern Idyll," an article on Okaluna, Mississippi, Mencken feared
the accusation of libel. On other occasions, as in his response to Schuyler's
short story "Fair Flower," Mencken objected to Schuyler's moralism. In
turning away Schuyler's "Devil Town," a short story about missionaries in Liberia, Mencken scolded him for "once again" spoiling a good
story with too much indignation and reminded him that irony serves
the cause of advocacy much better than anger. This was Mencken's most
common objection to Schuyler's fiction, which he generally regarded as
inferior to his articles and essays. In rejecting two articles from Schuyler
on interracial marriage in 1928, which later appeared as the Little Blue
Book series pamphlet "Interracial Marriage in the United States" and
"Emancipated Women and the Negro" in *Modern Quarterly*, Mencken
questioned Schuyler's information and his argument. He also wondered
if the columnist were not wasting his time trying to prove sexual attraction
between blacks and whites, which he regarded as something everyone
knew already anyway.[30]

With the exception of "Black America Begins to Doubt," which he
edited with Schuyler in person to correct bad organization and excessive
length, Mencken usually rejected all but the strongest submissions, which
he did not edit extensively. His main editorial contribution to Schuyler's
work came in the form of title changes. For a few of Schuyler's submis-

sions to the *Mercury*, Mencken employed his gift of phrase to improve Schuyler's titles. Schuyler's "The Decline of the Negro Church" became "Black America Begins to Doubt." His "Sambo Craves Recreation" became "Keeping the Negro in his Place." Mencken improved "The Negro Traveler" by transforming it into "Traveling Jim Crow." Schuyler gladly assented to all of these improvements.[31]

Whatever objections or improvements he made to Schuyler's submissions, Mencken always expressed the greatest faith in Schuyler's overall abilities. Almost simultaneously with the publication of "Our White Folks" Mencken began to consider him a regular contributor to the magazine. Throughout the late 1920s and early 1930s he encouraged Schuyler to submit article ideas to him on both racial and nonracial topics. In a 1930 letter he even encouraged Schuyler to stay away from racial topics and "meet the whites in open competition." Schuyler responded to this encouragement with a flurry of suggestions. In addition to the ideas for the articles Schuyler eventually published, he suggested articles on such diverse topics as misinformation about blacks in grammar school textbooks, Beethoven's racial background, why Montezuma refused to crush the Spanish, the hypocrisy of racial philanthropists, racism among socialists, the myth of Negro rule during Reconstruction, and black humor "as it is." He also suggested a series of sketches focusing on Harlem eccentrics and a burlesque of a socialist local. Of these ideas Mencken expressed the most interest in the ones that would allow Schuyler to relate interesting anecdotes without excessive analysis. For these purposes he liked the proposed series of Harlem sketches, the satire of the socialist local, and the article on textbooks. Of these Schuyler eventually produced the socialist satire under the title "Local Zenith," but Mencken rejected it as ineffective although he could not describe the flaw that had rendered it so weak.[32]

By the mid-1930s the correspondence between Schuyler and Mencken had moved from its narrow focus on Schuyler's article ideas to a broader discussion of the issues of the day. In these letters both men appear to glory in performing for each other as they ridicule Franklin Roosevelt, the South, communists, Methodists, World War II propaganda, and other favorite targets. Of these recurrent inspirations to biting ridicule, none surpassed the southern cracker as an object of denouncement. In one exchange Mencken and Schuyler seem to enter a veritable competition to see who can utter the most colorfully ugly phrase concerning the poor whites of the South. In the course of congratulating Mencken for his anti–New Deal diatribes, "The New Deal Mentality" and "Dole for Bogus Farmers," Schuyler, who resented deeply the racial inequities of government relief policy in the 1930s, makes several disparaging observations concerning the "ignorant and shiftless" southern "clodhopper." Mencken responds by declaring the southern cracker "so low" that he would not object to a proposal to "proceed against him with machine guns." He announces: "There has never been a more miserable white man on this earth, nor black man, nor yellow man." In the course of the attack, he mentions that he reads Schuyler in the *Courier* and enjoys him constantly.[33]

In his answer to Mencken, Schuyler stretches so far to show his disdain for poor white Southerners that he begins to sound like a white racist railing against blacks. In a lengthy statement he claims that "generations of semi-starvation and sexual promiscuity, coupled with rural existence, poverty, abysmal ignorance and a pathetic race consciousness have developed a human type not to be found elsewhere." At one time, he declares, the chances looked good that the cracker would fall victim to "pallagra [*sic*], hookworm, rickets, malaria, and other maladies to which he is heir" and thus become extinct like "the Maoris and Tahitians." He complains that lately "the Uplift has . . . invaded the eroded habitat of the cracker, teaching him to read True Stories, the funnies and the current Ku Klux weekly, fetching him salvarsan, quinine and tomato juice, instructing him in the use of soap and water, douche bags and condoms." He laments that these efforts, along with "rural electrification" and other reforms of the New Deal, will unfortunately prolong the cracker's miserable existence. But he doubts that these efforts at improvement will do any good. "He may sew up and wash his overalls. He may go to work steadily. He may move from his sagging shack to a new WPA cabin. He may cease his incestuous ways and even do away with his rutting camp meetings and his prodigious sessions with the jug, but let him sniff the frying carcass of the blackamoor and at once he will revert to his true self and scramble for a big toe or a knuckle."[34]

In his next letter to Schuyler, Mencken reports being struck "very forcibly" by his remarks, having just returned from a trip to Daytona, Florida, where he made "two trips into the jungle lying behind the town" and encountered the "ghastly spectacle" of "a great many crackers in their native wildwood." He reports with disgust that "their houses were filthy, their children were in rags, and their farming operations were of the most meagre sort." While riding along one of the back roads outside Daytona, he reports comparing one of the cracker settlements to an "African kraal" to the tremendous delight of his black driver.[35]

Schuyler was certainly aware of the performative element of his exchanges with Mencken. After writing a letter to Mencken during his long stay in Mississippi in 1935, Schuyler told his wife Josephine that he had just written Mencken the "sort of letter one ought to write Mencken," one detailing his sojourn in "the worst American state." By all indications both men enjoyed their exchanges very much. They shared stories and lore, colorful phrases and slang, all in a jovial spirit. For example, in one letter Mencken shares a scientific study with Schuyler on the bite of the "blue-gummed niggah," which southern lore had declared more deadly than that of the crocodile or hyena. Pretending not to notice the preposterous foolishness of such scientific investigations, he confesses to having believed the myth "implicitly" before reading the article. Following in this pattern, Schuyler apprises Mencken in one of his letters of two new pieces of slang he encountered in his travels through Aframerica. He defines "freebie" as "a free ticket to a game or a dance" and "grief" as synonymous with "price" as in "The grief is fifty cents."[36]

Throughout the 1930s and 1940s Mencken repeatedly invited Schuyler to his home in Baltimore for "sessions" on the topics of the day. As the term "session" indicates, Mencken, who reserved such events for the most worthy members of the "civilized minority," intended these meetings to involve something more than mere chatting, eating, and sampling his ample cellar. In his typical style he wanted them to resemble something more like a grand meeting of great men engaged in cultivated discussion of the issues of the day. As Mencken became more intellectually isolated because of his peculiar stances on the New Deal and World War II, his meetings with Schuyler, who agreed with him more than any other writer of stature in the United States, appear to loom larger for him in importance. Much of the correspondence between the two men during the 1930s and 1940s involves their attempts to find meeting times that would fit into the busy work schedule each liked to keep. On several occasions they did manage to squeeze in a session, usually on weekend nights at nine o'clock, always with Mencken's brother August present to participate in the fun. After one session in 1940, Mencken penned the following report:

"George S. Schuyler, the colored journalist, was here last night and August and I had our usual pleasant session with him. He came in just as we were eating our meagre Sunday night supper and we invited him to join us. His talk, as usual, was lively and amusing. He is a shrewd and somewhat bitter critic of the quacks who now posture as leaders of the American Negro. He sees clearly into their self-seeking and seems to be convinced, as I am, that the number of honest men among them or even half honest men is quite negligible."[37]

As one can tell from the somewhat distant tone in this note, Schuyler and Mencken never became intimate friends. In their twenty-nine years of association Mencken always addressed his letters to "Mr. Schuyler," and Schuyler appears to have attempted nothing warmer than "Mr. Mencken." Their relation, built on intellectual convergence and mutual professional respect, never became "chummy" and always avoided the exchange of quotidian commonplaces and personal emotional revelations. And yet over the years each provided for the other an important and personal sense of confirmation and support.

As Mencken's health declined in the years leading to his death in 1956, he could no longer write to Schuyler or host him at his residence. Schuyler's notes inquiring into Mencken's health had to go through Mencken's secretary, who always shared them with the bedridden satirist and reported his responses. On one occasion, only five months before Mencken's death, Schuyler sent him one of his articles, which the secretary read to Mencken as he reclined weakly in bed. After listening to the familiar cadence of Schuyler's prose, Mencken commented on the tremendous respect he had for Schuyler and on the great pleasure he received from reading Schuyler's *Courier* articles over the years.[38] This statement, made through his secretary, was the last substantial communication Mencken made to Schuyler in his life.

Whatever else we might derive from the story of Schuyler's relationship with Mencken, one fact stands out clearly: ideas of white intellectual domination, or more specifically of Schuyler "aping" the great "Sage of Baltimore," fail to capture the dynamic of mutual recognition and respect that transpired between them. Mencken, for whom the subject of race remained a central point of meditation, found Schuyler's writings uniquely insightful and compelling, not just for reflecting his own ideas, but for adding to them. Schuyler's regard for Mencken goes almost without saying. Still, it remains important to recognize that Mencken made a crucial but by no means exclusive contribution to the *Courier* editor's intellectual development. Certainly Schuyler learned a great deal from Mencken, but he had his own purposes for those lessons. Like many writers, he borrowed from the unique comic style of the "Sage of Baltimore" and repeated some of his ideas. Yet, as his answer to Mencken's "Hiring a Hall" editorial makes clear, Schuyler could use Mencken against Mencken. Also, he valued cultural pluralism less than Mencken and, in the 1920s and early 1930s, when he published the bulk of his articles for the *American Mercury*, he esteemed socialism more.

More than any other black writer, Schuyler recognized that Mencken had established a beachhead for all outsiders contending for cultural recognition. Not only did "the Sage" satirize the "custodians of the culture," he also castigated Southerners and anyone else he regarded as an undereducated member of the herd. Although he could sometimes take a condescending position concerning blacks, the fact remains that Mencken stood first as one who regarded the average white man as America's true nigger. As the first major voice in American history to present matters this way, he certainly deserves the homage Schuyler paid him while crafting his own darkly humorous view of "This Simian World."

In his column "The Big Parade," Ralph Matthews of the Baltimore *Afro-American* coined the mellifluous moniker "Sage of Sugar Hill" after Mencken's nickname, "Sage of Baltimore," both in derision and in praise of his *Pittsburgh Courier* colleague.[39] On one side of this name stands the obvious suggestion of imitation and on the other the highest recognition of originality, individuality, and wide-ranging intellect. Even more important, as it implicitly chides Schuyler for his pretentious desire to stand above the crowd, Matthews's nickname acknowledges the satirist's unique role as a situated public intellectual, as one who pronounced on important issues from the special vantage point of his perch atop Harlem's Sugar Hill. From this perch Schuyler simultaneously played the role of consummate insider and disaffected outsider. For this reason the name "the Sage of Sugar Hill" appears most apt indeed. By evoking Schuyler's relationship with Mencken as it proclaims the *Courier* editor's distinctly black intellectual location, it highlights the inadequacy of racial authenticity as a framework for understanding his cultural contribution. And yet, in evoking laughter at Schuyler's expense, it suggests that the ability to rise above such categories may well require an appreciation of the nexus between violence and comedy, a nexus where Mencken and Schuyler achieved broad ideological agreement and genuine mutual regard from opposite sides of the color line.

CHAPTER SEVEN

Hokum and Beyond

IF STUDENTS OF BLACK LITERATURE recognize George Schuyler
for nothing else, they know him as a notorious naysayer to the general
ideological thrust of the Harlem Renaissance. Yet a close analysis of his
varied statements on culture during the period reveals this as a half-truth.
Schuyler did indeed denounce many aspects of the Renaissance, especially
its faddish and nationalistic dimensions, but he also affirmed many of its
individual artists as he made his own contribution to its diverse outpour-
ings. In large part the perception of Schuyler as a stark opponent of black
cultural progress during the Harlem Renaissance stems from the larger
dominance of a black/white, for/against melodrama that continues to
hold an important place in critical works on the period.[1] Yet the reassess-
ment of Schuyler's place in the cultural history of the 1920s depends on
a fuller appreciation of his unique ability to utter an artful satirical "no"
to its most melodramatic tendencies even as he instigated polarizing
controversy. In doing this, Schuyler provides good reasons to resist our
own current temptations to elide the complexity of the American cultural
past through the hasty application of historical frameworks that in the
name of racial progress only return the basic terms of the problem that
they claim to oppose.

Typically, Schuyler's satire "The Negro-Art Hokum" plays the evil dark twin in black literature anthologies to "The Negro Artist and the Racial Mountain," Langston Hughes's famous response to Schuyler in the *Nation*. One does not have to read very far into "The Negro-Art Hokum" to understand why the *Nation* editor Freda Kirchwey set Schuyler's bitingly humorous essay aside for special treatment. Fearing that it might offend racial sensitivities and deliver the wrong message about the relationship of her journal to the cultural claims of the Harlem Renaissance, she passed the article around to several prominent black intellectuals. One of these was James Weldon Johnson, who suggested Hughes as a good candidate to write a response. Following Johnson's suggestion, Kirchwey—who found Schuyler's essay "rather flippant in tone" but "provocative in point of view"—asked Hughes to craft "an independent positive statement" of the case for a true Negro "racial art" that would stand against "The Negro-Art Hokum" without attempting to refute it directly.[2]

The first few lines of Schuyler's essay, which establish clearly his challenge to the very possibility of racial art, demonstrate the necessity of Kirchwey's face-saving maneuvers. "Negro art, 'made in America,' is as nonexistent as the widely advertised profundity of Cal Coolidge, the 'seven years of progress' of Mayor Hylan, or the reported sophistication of New Yorkers. Negro art there has been, is and will be among the numerous black nations of Africa; but to suggest the possibility of any such development among the ten million colored people in this republic is self-evident foolishness." In this passage Schuyler dismisses the whole idea of a separate black American culture in a humorous and cocksure tone as an ideological reflex of the mob. Along with this he rejects the concept of a black spiritual essence as worthy of no more consideration than the utterances of children or the mutterings of the insane. In making this point, Schuyler asserts the mixed-race character of black Americans, who in this case he refers to as "colored." He declares the primacy of nation over race in determining black American cultural identity and equates belief in the existence of a peculiar black art with the silly popular desire to see so-called racial differences confirmed: "This nonsense is probably the last stand of the old myth palmed off by Negro hobbyists for all these many years, and recently rehashed by the sainted Harding, that there are 'fundamental, eternal, and inescapable differences' between white and black Americans. . . . On this baseless premise, so flattering to the white mob, that the blackamoor is inferior and fundamentally different, is erected the postulate that he must needs be peculiar; and when he attempts to portray life through the medium of art, it must of necessity be peculiar art. While such reasoning may seem conclusive to the majority of Americans, it must be rejected with a loud guffaw by intelligent people."[3]

Counting the majoritarian American mind incapable of acknowledging cultural differences between the races and respecting equality at the same time, Schuyler rejects the cultural pluralist approach to the race question as a concession to racism. To the majority of whites, he says, "the mere mention of the word 'Negro' conjures up . . . a composite stereotype of Bert Williams, Aunt Jemima, Uncle Tom, Jack Johnson, Florian Slappey, and the various monstrosities scrawled by the cartoonists." Schuyler contends that minds possessed of such foolishness could not possibly show interest in the creations of black artists, except to confirm convenient and childish wish fulfillments. Against black stereotypes so common in the American popular culture of the period, Schuyler declares that the average black person resembles these unbecoming caricatures no more than "the average American resembles a composite of Andy Gump, Jim Jeffries, and a cartoon by Rube Goldberg."[4]

In arguing against the racist tendency to ignore differences among blacks, and the black tendency to profit from confirming white prejudices, Schuyler emphasizes both black cultural diversity and the racial intermixture of certain well-known black thinkers. He maintains that such cultural creations as the Sorrow Songs, ragtime, and jazz, which many observers attribute to black Americans as a whole, "are foreign to Northern Negroes, West Indian Negroes and African Negroes" and express the fundamental character of black Americans no better than the music and dancing of Appalachian highlanders or Dalmatian peasants express the soul-spirit of Caucasians.[5]

In addition to pointing out cultural differences among blacks, Schuyler underscores the Western European origins of the best-known black literature and visual art to undermine further the tendency to equate race and culture. He observes that W. E. B. Du Bois, "the dean of the Aframerican Literati," received his schooling at Harvard and that the foremost Aframerican sculptor, Meta Warwick Fuller, trained at leading American art schools and under Rodin. Although both of these leading intellectuals show obvious evidence of grounding in the Western European tradition,

Schuyler says, neither expresses "the Negro soul" any better than the scribblings of racist white humorists such as Octavus Roy Cohen and Hugh Wiley. Schuyler's most controversial statement in "The Negro-Art Hokum"—that "the Aframerican is merely a lampblacked Anglo-Saxon"—comes as a corollary to these observations.[6] Above all of his other attempts at provocation, this statement captures best his willingness throughout "The Negro-Art Hokum" to court controversy by shocking all "right thinkers" on matters concerning race.

By 1926, Schuyler—whose ideas about black emancipation still remained within the ideological orbit of the *Messenger* group—had concluded that the wide attention being given to black culture among black and white intellectuals had begun to detract from more crucial economic and social concerns. He also suspected that the "vogue of Negro Art" had crystallized into a comfortable ideological bargain between condescending whites, who wanted to preserve their racist beliefs without feeling bad about them, and cynical blacks, who valued the cheap rewards of victim status over real equality. In stating his strong disapproval of this state of affairs in satirical form, Schuyler could sometimes appear to accuse all whites who expressed an interest in black culture of romantic primitivism and all blacks who accepted their attention of greed and self-hatred. Although he penned many editorials in the *Courier* denouncing the paranoia of blacks who suspected all whites of racism, he still appeared at times to fall into the trap himself. This grants a certain note of irony to the publication of his best-known statement of this sort in the *Nation,* a mainstream liberal white journal.

Although "The Negro-Art Hokum" takes an aggressive, even destructive, approach to exposing and ridiculing black and white racism, we might recognize in its corrosive style a constructive aim. Rather than following the "correct," condescending, and dishonest strategy of avoiding the mention of distasteful racial designations, Schuyler follows his standard practice established in "Shafts and Darts" and in "Views and Reviews" of using them to indicate his supreme imperviousness to the petty inventions of white and black inferiors. More important, by reusing stereotypes and hurtful terms for his own purposes, Schuyler attempts to diffuse them through entropy. After all, not using an offensive term or concept can represent a much greater confession of its terrible truth and power than recontextualizing it through reuse. Left dormant such terms do not die; rather, they remain in reserve for special moments of racial high drama. Recognizing this, Schuyler strategically redeploys hurtful terms and concepts within the context of satire and humor. Rather than leaving racial fears and taboos repressed and unaddressed, he calls attention to them, hoping to outrage and shock those who make racists feel powerful by regarding them with alarm. The use of the term "lampblacked Anglo-Saxon" provides an excellent example of this strategy. It calls to mind the clownish antics of white minstrels as it evokes the ugly possibility that blacks do nothing more than imitate the white mob that oppresses them, that they are empty and retrograde with no culture of their own.

Schuyler sets his own rhetorical performance in "The Negro-Art Hokum" against this fear. In striking contrast to the shrill anger of an insecure political dependent, Schuyler affects the posture of an insistently individual black radical employing complex irony and a controlled will to destruction. Even more than the substance of his argument, Schuyler's tone conveys the confidence of one who cannot accept racist condescension because he regards himself as the superior of most white people. As one who stands impervious to the racist discourse of the mob, he uses for his own purposes the terms and formulas that its members either employ sincerely or avoid like a plague. Rather than a manifesto aimed at stating in clear and final form his position on race and culture, Schuyler envisaged "The Negro-Art Hokum" as a discursive smart bomb. Aimed at what he thought of as an emerging orthodoxy among intellectuals, he hoped that his acerbic essay would provoke open critical discussion not only about the existence of a separate black American culture, but about the very possibility of addressing the American race problem through art. By attempting to force critical debate on an important issue facing blacks, "The Negro-Art Hokum" served the same general purpose as "Shafts and Darts," "Views and Reviews," and Schuyler's other writings in the 1920s.

Given the satirist's goal of constantly returning the terms of racial discourse to the open arena of democratic deliberation and debate, the publication of Hughes's "The Negro Artist and the Racial Mountain," which disputed almost every claim Schuyler made, might be considered a powerful argument in his favor. Although Hughes took Kirchwey's advice of avoiding a direct debate with Schuyler, the power of his rousing declaration of black artistic independence appears to derive in part from his attempt to oppose Schuyler's corrosive rhetoric with a language of hope, regeneration, and fulfillment. That Hughes does not even mention Schuyler in his "rebuttal" says more than any gesture of direct denouncement could concerning the poet's conviction of the satirist's irrelevance to those actually engaged in the faithful and constructive chores of the black creative writer or visual artist.

Employing an array of biblical metaphors against Schuyler's iconoclastic rhetoric, Hughes evokes the image of a "racial mountain" that the black artist must scale before he can produce art that will attest to the beauty of his people. This mountain, which represents the urge to whiteness within the race, threatens the artist lacking the faith to scale its heights with a lifetime of blind, dishonest, and self-alienating expression. Although Hughes does not mention directly Moses standing atop Sinai viewing the Promised Land—God's gift to a race of former slaves—the momentum of this dominant image carries his essay to an inspiring conclusion: "We younger Negro artists who create now intend to express our individual dark-skinned selves without fear or shame. If white people are pleased we are glad. If they are not, it doesn't matter. We know we are beautiful. And ugly too. The tom-tom cries and the tom-tom laughs. If colored people are pleased we are glad. If they are not, their displeasure doesn't matter either. We build our temples for tomorrow, strong as we know how, and we stand on top of the mountain, free within ourselves."[7]

Thus Hughes makes his implicit case against Schuyler. Climbing the racial mountain is first and foremost an act of faith in one's own human potential. The logic of this position implies that those possessed of such faith, and hard at work building "temples for tomorrow," cannot bother themselves with the railings of professional doubters and cultural infidels. Nor should they worry about what whites think of their efforts at self-expression. Such distractions cannot inspire much more than empty naysaying because outsiders, especially if they are racists, must by their very definition distort the meaning of what black people do by themselves and for themselves. From this the implicit case against Schuyler seems clear. In Hughes's eyes Schuyler's pose of self-possession appears false. Instead of the sure-footed black individual he wishes to portray, the satirist emerges in "The Negro Artist and the Racial Mountain" as a weak-willed doubter who destroys black temples as he peers nervously over his shoulder at the white mob hot in pursuit.

In his response to Hughes, published as a letter in the *Nation* the next week, Schuyler—who many years later would complain that Hughes never "joined issue" with him—followed his standard debating practice of reiterating his position rather than addressing the most important arguments of his adversaries. If the spirituals and the blues reflected a racial origin, he reasoned, then blacks from Zanzibar and Sierra Leone should have been able to catch the intricate rhythms of these songs. Their inability to do so demonstrated clearly enough for him the foolishness of "racial art" as an idea. Defending his claim in "The Negro-Art Hokum" of a strong black inclination to imitate whites, Schuyler pointed to the popular practices of hair straightening and skin lightening as prime examples of how ridiculous this self-effacing desire can become, especially in light of overwhelming cultural similarity between the races. Going further, Schuyler accused black artists who promoted the idea of racial art, especially through "primitivist propaganda-art," of doing little more than protesting against feelings of inferiority. These artists felt so inferior to the white man, he said, that they exaggerated the value of their so-called cultural origins in a pathetic attempt to reverse the tables in fantasy where they could not in fact. Following this line of reasoning, Schuyler found the urge to whiteness evident even in the "blackest" black American art. Of course, this included by implication the most soulful pronouncements of his adversary from the peak of the racial mountain.[8]

Had he chosen to do so, Schuyler could have criticized Hughes more directly, but the indirectness and civility of the poet's attack on his position, and the location of the debate in a white journal, tended to undermine the attractiveness of bare-knuckled assault. If Schuyler had chosen this route, he may well have pointed out Hughes's dependence on melodrama and on logical sleight-of-hand. In his opening gambit, Hughes denounces an unnamed fellow poet (Countee Cullen) for saying that he "wants to be a poet—Not a Negro poet." Hughes translates this into "I want to write like a white poet" and eventually into "I would like to be white."[9] Although Hughes's rhetorical skill makes this ride down the slippery slope tempting, a reasonable reader might well wonder if he ought to go along. Does the desire of the black writer to be recognized as an artist in universal terms really translate into the wish to be white? Believing Hughes's case depends on answering a narrow "yes" to this question. It depends also on assenting to an all-too-simple binary of black working-class originality and white ruling-class standardization. The romantic heroism of the black artist in turning away from the "urge in the race toward whiteness" and in affirming the beauty of his own people flows directly from this controlling dichotomy. Long experience in the army, in the streets, and as a journalist made such romantic thinking about black culture impossible for the hard-boiled Schuyler, who knew the black masses better than did Hughes in 1926.

In his rejoinder to Schuyler's letter, which appeared a month later in the *Nation,* Hughes really did attempt to "join issue" with the satirist, but on terms that emphasized matters of substance rather than the questions of form and tone that remained implicit in Schuyler's attack. Rejecting Schuyler's claim of overwhelming similarity between the white and black masses as "absurd," Hughes asserted confidently that "as long as the Negro remains a segregated group in this country he must reflect certain racial and environmental differences which are his own." Even if blacks did straighten their hair and lighten their skins, he said, this made them different from whites in important ways. Until America had completely absorbed blacks and until segregation and racial self-consciousness had ended, Hughes concluded, "the true work of art from the Negro artist is bound, if it have any color and distinctiveness at all, to reflect his racial background and his racial environment."[10]

In the long run Hughes's hopeful and defiant position on black American culture prevailed decisively over Schuyler's acidulous skepticism; but in the short run, at least where the readers of the *Nation* were concerned, the satirist had won a decisive victory. Although none of the letters from readers of the *Nation* on the Schuyler/Hughes debate reflected Schuyler's view exactly, and some took positions on black art whose details he would have rejected, the unofficial verdict fell clearly in his favor. In supporting Schuyler's doubts concerning the quality of New Negro art, one reader of the *Nation* argued that the Old Negro, who produced the spirituals, surpassed his modern counterpart in creativity and depth. A second reader equated Hughes's laudation of black folk culture with a celebration of black poverty in such neighborhoods as Seventh Street in Washington, D.C. In opposition to this somewhat slanted characterization of Hughes's intentions, she maintained that almost all of the lower-class blacks that the poet lionized for their authenticity wanted to get out of the ghetto and into the American economic mainstream as fast as possible.[11]

A third *Nation* reader, no better versed in the cultural politics informing "The Negro Artist and the Racial Mountain" than the second, indicted Hughes for underestimating the repressive force of racism. Convinced that good art only appeared under harmonious social conditions, he thought that Hughes had failed to take full measure of white racial hostility. Following Schuyler, this reader questioned the existence of an independent black culture, but he offered reasons for doubting it that the satirist would have found entirely sentimental. He asked: "Where is the motif, where are the symbols, where is the sympathetic background upon which every true art develops?" To this somewhat genteel objection to Hughes, a fourth reader, the Marxist editor of *The New Masses* Michael Gold, added a criticism from the opposite end of the ideological spectrum. Rounding out the anti-Hughes outpouring in the letter section of the *Nation*, Gold self-righteously reprimanded the poet for his irresponsibility to the masses. Agreeing with Schuyler in emphatic terms, Gold pronounced a separate black culture "in this huge America" absolutely impossible. If black intellectuals such as Hughes really cared about their brethren, he announced, they would "leave the cabarets of the jaded dilettantes and the colleges of the middle-class strivers" and join the class struggle.[12]

Except for J. A. Rogers, who predictably defended his friend, ally, and lunchtime companion against Hughes in the *Amsterdam News*, no reviewer in a black publication came close to questioning Hughes in the aggressive style of the readers of the *Nation*. In fact, many black reviewers found Hughes's position preferable. Responding to Rogers in the *Amsterdam News*, the poet Fenton Johnson defended Hughes's conception of literature as "a mass affair." If Homer and Shakespeare sang the songs of peasants and farmers, Johnson reasoned, then black artists could achieve greatness by returning to their own folk roots. In the *Baltimore Afro-American* columnist William N. Jones repeated and amplified Hughes's contention that American racism had provided the necessary groundwork for the emergence of distinctive black American art forms. Applying this argument directly to Schuyler, he contended: "The very stinging and effective thrusts of [Schuyler's] pen . . . show a background from which NO WHITE MAN COULD WRITE."[13]

The most balanced and diplomatic opinion on the Schuyler-Hughes debate came from editor of *Opportunity*, Charles S. Johnson. As one of the custodians of the Harlem Renaissance, he found in the contention between the poet and the satirist a generally positive "mental fermentation" on the issue of black art that surpassed in importance the conclusions of either writer. Casting both Schuyler and Hughes as polemical, overstated, and imprecise, he observed in a tone at once avuncular and academic that neither author bothered to distinguish between art and culture. While one focused his case on artistic form, Johnson said, the other concentrated on content; one railed against the black middle class while the other attacked intellectual parvenus. Attempting to draw an intellectual circle around both Schuyler and Hughes, Johnson pointed out the "peculiar difficulty" that blacks expressed all of the contradictions and paradoxes reflected in "The Negro-Art Hokum" debate: Some blacks wanted to be white, Johnson said. Others expressed black cultural difference unself-consciously and simply in the way they lived and expressed themselves. Still others adopted the approach of black artists who attempted to portray in many different ways the beauties of their people. Underwriting the gestures of artistic independence made by Schuyler, Hughes, and all of the other artists involved in shaping the energies of the new black cultural movement, Johnson concluded: "These black artists should be free, not merely to express anything they feel, but to feel the pulsations and rhythms of their own life, philosophy be hanged."[14]

In emphasizing the issue of artistic and intellectual freedom, Johnson advanced an important insight into the commonalties between Schuyler and Hughes. As the satirist and the poet thumbed their noses at each other, they each declared independence from all representatives of the cultural establishment, both black and white, who attempted to tell them what to say or how to say it. This included Charles S. Johnson, W. E. B. Du Bois, James Weldon Johnson, and almost every other source of elderly wisdom. The rhetorical and substantive distance between Schuyler and Hughes in "The Negro-Art Hokum" debate makes this and other points of convergence easy to miss. Although he rejected Hughes's belief in "truly racial" artistic expression, Schuyler—who published some of Hughes's work in the *Messenger*—joined him in criticizing middle-class American standardization and in calling for an independent black voice that stood for something better than the American norm. Schuyler also shared Hughes's disdain for black middle-class conformity and his condemnation of blacks who feared the appearance of anything in art that they regarded as uncomplimentary to the race. As the previous chapters in this book have shown, Schuyler staked a large part of his satirical approach to the race question on the great fun one could have offending such people. Although he departed from Hughes's romanticism concerning the black lower class, especially where this involved hearing tom-toms cry and laugh, Schuyler heartily agreed with the poet's contention that black artists should seek to understand the black masses and depict their lives and thoughts realistically.[15]

In a review of *Fine Clothes to the Jew* nearly a year after the "The Negro-Art Hokum" debate, Schuyler emphasized his points of agreement with Hughes, especially regarding the poet's critical attitude toward the black middle-class establishment. Because Hughes endeavored in *Fine Clothes to the Jew* to express in direct and unvarnished fashion the perspective of the black working class, Schuyler believed that the highly conventional black intelligentsia would greet his collection of poetry with a "shower of bricks." This gave him ample reason to grant Hughes's book a generous measure of credit despite his objections to it on formal grounds. Revealing his somewhat old-fashioned ideas about poetry, Schuyler declared Hughes's experimental verse "both too free and too blank." Despite this, he insisted that Hughes receive credit for showing an intimate knowledge of the Negro proletariat and for standing up to the establishment: "It is precisely because [Hughes] knows this type of Negro and portrays him that the Negro bourgeoisie, reviewers and readers, will fall on him like a ton of bricks. I notice the tendency among Negroes (and whites, too) to become very indignant at such portrayals. The truer the pictures are, the louder the good fellows yelp."[16]

In addition to indicating the "positive" element in his view of Hughes, this quote gives a good indication of the kinds of values Schuyler brought more generally to the artistic works of the Harlem Renaissance. In keeping with the satirical framework of "The Negro-Art Hokum," he valued works of art first and foremost for their ability to destabilize the conventional values of black and white custodians of culture. Regarding the repressive and sentimental values of these critics as part of the problem, he proposed unvarnished realism as the solution. When artists portrayed black life in terms that he could see reflected in the world around him, he offered praise; otherwise he tended to poke fun at their lies and flights of fancy. This critical style matched his satirical outlook in bringing the ironic and unsystematic qualities of the world of action to bear in denouncing excesses of artistic invention. As one might gather from his quick dismissal of Hughes's literary experimentation, Schuyler did not always bring subtle ideas of "the world" or of art to bear in his judgments. Although he made valuable observations in criticizing art, he lacked the sensitivity and range of satirist/critics like Bernard Shaw or H. L. Mencken, who understood better the common ground they shared with aesthetic mavericks and innovators.

Schuyler's wholesale rejection of modernist formal artistic innovation came mostly from the influence of the *Messenger* group. Like many other thinkers on the left in this period, he associated high modernist impulses with bourgeois boredom and decadence. He also thought of them as frivolous and escapist, precisely the opposite of the hard-nosed and ironic realism that he hoped black Americans would adopt as a general political outlook.[17] Schuyler believed that the best kind of art helped men and women in the struggle to adjust to environmental circumstance by providing realistic and useful ideas about the world. As a corollary to this, he believed that the best kind of art produced by or about blacks should promote the black struggle for economic and political equality, although he avoided the temptation of thinking that one and only one point of view would serve this end. In the debate that raged during the period over the merits of art versus propaganda, this placed him distinctly on the side of propaganda. Although he never squared this allegiance entirely with his insistence on unvarnished realism, he did want it to serve the same fundamental end: the liberation of diverse cultural, political, and social potentialities that remained dormant within black life. Again, this emphasis had its foundation in Schuyler's fundamental commitment to the destructive methods of satire, which he employed in casting doubt on all claims to pure racial lineage, whether cultural or biological.

Still, Schuyler did occasionally employ melodramatic appeals to achieve his ends. In an unsigned *Courier* editorial written in 1926 called "Art and Propaganda," he provided the best example of this tendency. Abandoning the satirical tone he normally employed in his own voice, he expressed the need for black propaganda/art in the sincere manner of a call to arms: "We need more capable Negro men and women to sear with white-hot words the conscience of white America and rouse from ignorance and indifference the masses of black America. We need the services of these talented people, not in singing sorrow songs or depicting the cheap, squalid, raucous life of unsanitary slums with a sad tint of hopelessness and futility; but we need them to cogently reveal the reasons and remedies for our ills to the end that the group, enlightened and encouraged, may emancipate itself from its present position."[18]

This statement demonstrates clearly Schuyler's agreement with such figures as W. E. B. Du Bois, James Weldon Johnson, and Charles S. Johnson that art could and should play an important role in the black freedom movement. Yet, in contrast to many advocates of black culture in the 1920s, Schuyler placed more hope in the potential role art could play in augmenting black working-class self-confidence than he did in its ability to mitigate white racism. Although he wanted black artists "to sear with white-hot words the conscience of white America," he never really had much faith in the practicality of "freedom by copyright." The idea, expressed most famously by James Weldon Johnson in *The Book of American Negro Poetry*, that white racism would abate as blacks demonstrated the capacity for high culture, always struck him as laughable. In a 1926 editorial he stated this idea in his characteristic cocksure tone: "Many simple people imagine that by writing books, yelping the spirituals, shouting the blues and producing plays and poems, we can engender a kindlier feeling among the whites toward us; the idea being that the better you know a person and of what that person is capable the more tolerant and just you will be toward him."[19]

Although he oversimplifies the logic of Johnson's position in this passage, Schuyler does offer compelling and unusual reasons for rejecting it. Reversing conventional wisdom, which considered white racism a natural protective response to the threat of contact with an inferior people, he holds that whites hate blacks for fear of their betters. Echoing Mencken's argument in "The Sahara of the Bozart" and "The American Tradition," Schuyler contends that the white mob experiences its allergic reaction to excellence in particularly virulent form where blacks are concerned. Thus he insists that discrimination finds its root in the supreme resentment inferior people have for their natural superiors. "[Whites] realize that given free rein, the Negroes would very likely be running the country in less than half a century. . . . The average white man of sense knows the average Negro is his equal and very often his superior; that is the reason why he limits the Negro's sphere of activity. One does not seek to handicap and hamstring one's inferiors: one doesn't purchase a cannon to shoot pigeons."[20]

Schuyler's doubts about the Harlem Renaissance reduced in many ways to his desire to see blacks claim their superiority to whites without special pleading. Rather than promoting an exclusive discourse of black cultural expressiveness, which he could only perceive as a tacit acceptance of victim status, he wanted independent black thinkers to fight an aggressive and offensive battle with whites. Instead of complaining about white power and making appeals for sympathy based in an artistic discourse of racial feeling, Schuyler wanted black creative artists to ridicule white pretense and undermine the rhetorical basis of inequality.

Schuyler made this point on many occasions in many different ways, but nowhere more playfully than in a 1928 editorial on the staging of *The Mikado* at the Manhattan State Hospital for the Insane. Although he made no great claims for the quality of the performance, Schuyler joked that it had eliminated any excuse for the absence of a prosperous Little Theater "in every black community." Pressing the comparison of blacks and the insane toward a criticism of white condescension, he quoted the reporter covering the event, who seemed unaware of the sad truth in his amazed realization that the insane "for the most part are just folks." Reaching a crescendo of sentimentality, this reporter speculated that the only difference between the inmates of the asylum and the people "outside" may have been in how "nice" they were. "Walking through the streets of that lovely island," he said, the visitor was constantly greeted by inmates "with direct and trusting smiles." He recalled fondly one resident's request to "pray for me." Such warm encounters with the well-mannered inhabitants of the insane asylum made him conclude happily that all the people on the "island" were friends.[21]

By quoting the compassion-filled words of this reformed reporter, Schuyler offers a playful reflection on the idea of "civil rights by copyright." The relevance of race to this scenario becomes apparent when one compares the Manhattan State Hospital for the Insane to Harlem and the reporter to a naive white visitor interested only in confirming his somewhat insane view of blacks. In addition, the spectacle of the insane, who already live in a fantasy world, acting out a fiction to prove their relative sanity appears devastatingly similar to the notion of black people "playing" themselves to prove their humanity. With his characteristic smirk

Schuyler suggests that if a hard-boiled reporter can fall in love with an insane asylum after viewing a play, blacks might have a chance in America after all. Perhaps by imitating the mentally disturbed they can win a few unsuspecting whites over to the cause.[22]

If white condescension and sentimentalism annoyed Schuyler, black complicity with candy-coated forms of racism brought him to a boil. Of his many statements against this trend, which he counted as a major problem of the black American public discourse on racial issues, his essay "Our Greatest Gift to America" made the most telling commentary on the cultural scene. In this humorous essay Schuyler argued that the white "superiority complex" found its true origin in resentment and weakness. Using artful exaggeration, he asserted most centrally that the black man's greatest gift to America had been to bolster his weak-minded white oppressor with flattery: "I submit that here is the gift par excellence of the Negro to America. To spur ten times our number on to great heights of achievement. . . . This indeed is a gift of which we can well be proud."[23]

Although he chided working-class blacks for their willingness to imitate whites, Schuyler focused particularly on black intellectuals, whom he lambasted for flattering the "ofays" even as they scrupulously documented the black contribution to American culture: "On divers [sic] occasions some eloquent Ethiop arises to tell this enlightened nation about the marvelous contributions of his people to our incomparable civilization. With glib tongue or trenchant pen, he starts from the arrival of the nineteen unfortunate dinges at Jamestown in 1619 . . . and traces the multiple gifts of the black brethren to the present day. . . . No Negro meeting is a success without one or more such encouraging addresses, and no Negro publication that fails to carry one such article is worthy of purchase." So general had this practice become, Schuyler said, that even whites had jumped onto the bandwagon. Such groups as the "Tired Society Women's Club" came to regard it as a requirement to invite such speakers as "Prof. Hambone of Moronia Institute, or Dr. Lampblack of the Federal Society for the Explanation of Lynching" to give lengthy speeches on "the blackamoor's gifts to the Great Republic and why, therefore, he should not be kept down."[24]

According to Schuyler, these speakers miss a crucial psychological insight. In demonstrating the black desire to contribute to the tradition that whites see as their own, and as the only legitimate tradition, they reinforce the fantasy of superiority that causes white people to despise them. Once they place themselves in the position of explaining their humanity or their contributions to civilization, blacks enter a losing bargain. Against the assumption of inferiority, no intellectual argument will suffice, especially ones rooted in proving self-evident truths. In "Our Greatest Gift to America," Schuyler attempts through satire to escape the rhetorical disadvantage that blacks find themselves in when they fail to recognize that the terms of racist arguments are loaded.

Although Schuyler attacked many targets in "Our Greatest Gift to America," none stood out more than Du Bois, whose rhetoric of "black gifts" in *The Souls of Black Folk* punctuated a pathbreaking account of black culture as a source of pride, strength, and intellectual insight. Twenty years later, in *The Gift of Black Folk,* Du Bois repeated and amplified this rhetoric while documenting in detail the black contribution to the development of the United States. Perhaps it provides some insight into Schuyler's wily ways, and into his essential ambivalence about Du Bois, that he reviewed *The Gift of Black Folk* quite positively when it came out in 1924. Praising the book for its clarity and for its therapeutic effects on black self-confidence, he announced cheerfully that Du Bois had "obliterated" any excuse for blacks to harbor an inferiority complex. Hinting at Du Bois's tendency to employ flowery rhetoric, he also lauded the book's accessibility. "It is all written so simply," he declared, "that even a Garveyite or a Georgia peckerwood can understand it." Besides demonstrating Schuyler's gift for faint praise, this statement demonstrates clearly where he drew the line in making fun of the rhetoric of black "gifts." While he ridiculed those who sought to prove black worthiness to whites, he tended to praise those who did the same for blacks. Although he doubted that blacks had "gifts" anything like the ones touted by Du Bois, he regarded the history of black contributions as excellent propaganda and took great pains himself to relate this history to his audience in the *Messenger,* the *Pittsburgh Courier,* and the *Illustrated Feature Section.*[25]

Despite the joy Schuyler took in occasionally maligning Du Bois, his position on the Harlem Renaissance—which emphasized the importance of propaganda, black self-hatred, and white racism—made him a natural, if somewhat reluctant, ally of the *Crisis* editor, especially after 1925. By 1926, a pivotal year in the history of the Harlem Renaissance in general, Du Bois began to express his lingering doubts concerning the ability and willingness of black artists to serve the larger protest needs of the black freedom movement. These doubts had many sources, but none weighed heavier on Du Bois than the second-place status of his journal in the battle with Charles S. Johnson's *Opportunity* for preeminence among black publications in matters of culture. As the early months of 1926 passed, the success of *The New Negro,* edited by *Opportunity* literary custodian Alain Locke, made the "also-ran" position of the *Crisis* clear enough for Du Bois to consider a shift in strategy. Rather than continuing to fight a losing head-on battle with *Opportunity,* Du Bois hoped that by seizing the high ground of civil rights activism, and casting his rivals as apolitical aesthetes, he could regain some of his lost advantage. Jessie Redmon Fauset's resignation as literary editor of the *Crisis* in February 1926—ostensibly the result of disagreements over the amount of space the journal granted to literature—made these aims easier to accomplish because it eliminated the one person in the *Crisis* circle who would attempt to limit Du Bois's propagandistic inclinations.[26]

With Fauset gone, Du Bois began quickly to question the role white patrons and publishers had been playing in the production and promotion of black art. Throughout 1926 he ran a symposium in the *Crisis* called "The Negro in Art: How Shall He Be Portrayed?" that featured prominent black and white artists, critics, and editors such as Mencken, Charles Chesnutt, Alfred Knopf, and Fauset answering a list of somewhat leading questions on black art and artists. The questions themselves give a good indication of Du Bois's intentions. One of them asked, "Can publishers be criticized for refusing to handle novels that portray Negroes of education and accomplishment, on the ground that these characters are no different from white folk and therefore not interesting?" Another asked, "What are Negroes to do when they are continually painted at their worst and judged by the public as they are painted?" As cultural historian George Hutchinson has pointed out, this symposium proved more remarkable for the nearly unanimous insistence by the white contributors that black artists portray themselves realistically and boldly. Thus, by fundamentally agreeing with Du Bois, they provided good grounds, in the midst of his own symposium, for doubting his claims about them.[27]

Corresponding with the end of the symposium on black art in October 1926, Du Bois published "Criteria of Negro Art," which set out a new cultural direction for the *Crisis* in terms intended to oppose directly the orientation and influence of Johnson's *Opportunity*. In this programmatic statement Du Bois complained that white artists, who served racist white audiences and greedy publishers, had severely distorted the black image in the popular mind. Du Bois also protested against the tendency of black audiences to hamper black artists by judging them according to white standards, which he called the "narrow second-hand soul clothes of white patrons." In opposition to this self-alienating trend, he trumpeted the development of black artistic institutions, the cultivation of a sophisticated black audience, and the creation of black standards for judging black works of art.[28] Yet notwithstanding his enthusiasm for black artistic independence, Du Bois did not expect his largely tactical proposals to inspire a distinct black aesthetic. Instead, he held out hope that by honoring black humanity and beauty, a black artistic sphere would help to sustain the possibility of the eventual emergence of a truly democratic and beautiful America.

In adopting a skeptical posture concerning white incursions on black cultural territory in "The Criteria of Negro Art," Du Bois indicated more than dissatisfaction with events in the cultural arena. He also signified his displeasure regarding the sudden social transformation of Harlem. By 1926 it appeared to some black thinkers that Harlem had begun to suffer for its faddish appeal among whites. Signaled in satirical form by Rudolph Fisher's *American Mercury* essay "The Caucasian Storms Harlem," new complaints emerged in black newspapers and magazines concerning the antics of thrill-seeking whites who threatened to transform the intellectual capital of black America into a romantic racialist playground. For Du Bois nothing indicated better the dangers inherent in this movement than the publication of *Nigger Heaven*, Carl Van Vechten's novelistic exposé of Harlem life, late in 1926. In the spirit of a bull charging a red handkerchief, Du Bois described the white-authored novel as a "blow in the face" for its sensationalist focus on the sordid aspects of Harlem life. No doubt, this blow stung Du Bois even more as the amazing marketplace success of *Nigger Heaven* became apparent in subsequent months.[29]

With the example of *Nigger Heaven* to spur him, Du Bois voiced more frequently in the late 1920s his doubts concerning the pronouncements of white artists and critics on the Negro question. Ironically, this made him less relevant to younger black artists, whom he frequently chided for their bohemianism and primitivism, behind which he always detected the influence of nefarious white patrons. Against this group of artists, which included Wallace Thurman, Bruce Nugent, Claude McKay, and others, Du Bois touted the middle-class oriented works of Jessie Redmon Fauset and Nella Larsen as models for the future direction of black literature. As we shall see, Schuyler made similar critical judgments, although he did so for his own reasons.

For Schuyler and other members of the *Messenger* group, Du Bois's shift to a more vocal promotion of propaganda over art, to black control of black cultural institutions, and to a suspicious attitude toward patronage signaled an important concession to their way of thinking. With Du Bois moving in the late 1920s toward an emphasis on institution-building among the black masses—evident, for example, in his establishment of the Krigwa Little Theater movement in 1926—and away from the high-toned bourgeois emphasis on art by and for the "best people," they saw potential for common ground.[30] Although Schuyler, whose cultural sensibilities matched those of the younger "bohemian" crowd in many ways, continued to disagree with Du Bois, he could still see the good sense in occasionally taking sides with the powerful *Crisis* editor on the shifting cultural battleground of the mid-1920s.

While Du Bois's sincere critical spirit always remained opposed to Schuyler's playfully ironic orientation, the *Crisis* editor did influence the timing and substance of Schuyler's 1926 assault on the Harlem Renaissance both in the pages of the *Messenger* and in the *Pittsburgh Courier*. Spanning the whole year, this campaign reached its high point with the publication of "The Negro-Art Hokum" but included many other choice pieces of vitriol directed at black artists, white patrons, and the very idea of a separate black culture.[31] Generally these statements reflected the tone, substance, and purpose of "The Negro-Art Hokum" as they applied some of Schuyler's standard themes such as antisentimentalism, realism, and the criticism of "the best people" to the question of culture.

In January 1926, Schuyler's acerbic "Advice to Budding Literati" ridiculed the money-hungry ways of black writers and publishers. Focusing on the black literary scene, Schuyler offered aspiring writers surefire advice guaranteed to secure financial success. As one might guess, refinement of writerly craft did not rank very high on Schuyler's list, which included joining the right social circles, ingratiating oneself with the "two or three literary dictators of Aframerica," learning to do a "mean Charleston," and avoiding at all cost writing anything realistic about black people. If budding writers followed these easy directions, Schuyler promised, they would find success, even if they possessed little talent.[32]

In April, just two months before the appearance of "The Negro-Art Hokum," Schuyler turned his attention in "Shafts and Darts" to the question of black culture. Writing from one of the many southern towns he visited during 1926, he claimed that his trip had yielded little evidence of Negro "art," except "the patchwork on faded overalls, the dissimulation of shrewd black peons and the weekly gymnastics in the pulpits." Not long after this, in "Views and Reviews," Schuyler challenged the reputation of the spirituals as a privileged expression of the black soul. Rather than religious songs, which he imagined working-class and poor blacks singing only at the command of a preacher, Schuyler proposed the blues and jazz as the music most expressive of the black experience. This also included the middle-class black experience, despite the tendency of the "Talented Tenth" to ignore the records they played at home when waxing philosophical on the subject of their beloved racial heritage: "The highbrow Negroes who gush over the spirituals as 'Negro' music, have ten 'blues' records in their phonograph cabinets for every record of the spirituals, while all over the land (even the most obscure hamlets in the Black Belt) the blackamoors are singing and playing such Rabelaisian ditties as 'Shake That Thing,' 'Papa De-Da-Da,' 'My Daddy Rocks Me' and 'Aggravatin' Papa.' . . . After all, are not the 'Blues' and work songs more expressive of the soul of the Negro masses than the spirituals?"[33]

Following a characteristic pattern, Schuyler placed a surprising twist on this observation. At the same time that this music expressed perfectly the black soul within the fast-moving and liberating energies of machine civilization, he said, it could not have been more popular among whites. Schuyler explained that this phenomenon, which might have seemed like a contradiction to a racist mind, occurred for a simple reason: the new music expressed the white American soul too. "Save for a greater diplomacy, timidity and sensitiveness wrought by the color caste system," Schuyler claimed, "the Aframerican's psychology is identical with that of the white Americans."[34] Rather than elaborate this assertion, or even attempt to account for its apparent contradiction with the black dominance of blues and jazz music, Schuyler left this polemical claim to do its provocative work on the minds of his readers.

In August, corresponding with his letter in the *Nation* concerning "The Negro Artist and the Racial Mountain," Schuyler published two pieces of playful but cutting mock poetry called "Ballad of Negro Artists" and "The Curse of My Aching Heart," which he aimed in part at Hughes, but also more broadly at pretentious black artists and the patrons who supported them. A few lines of "Ballad of Negro Artists" convey well its main message and spirit:

> Now old Merlin the wizard had nothing
>   on us.
> Though he conjured a castle up out of
>   the dust;
> For with nothing but gall and a stoutness
>   of heart.
> On the public we've foisted this New Neg-
>   ro Art.[35]

Schuyler delivered the same playful but cutting sentiment in "The Curse of My Aching Heart," a ballad of disappointed love written by "Carl Von Victor," a name intended to make the target of the satire obvious to even the most uninformed *Messenger* readers. If "Ballad of Negro Artists" directed its shafts at writers like Hughes, the "Curse of My Aching Heart" aimed its darts at Carl Van Vechten and other white patrons who assisted them in foisting their questionable art on an unsuspecting and long-suffering public. The obvious reference to Germany in the name "Von Victor" extended Schuyler's habit, evident in *Black No More* and in many playful sketches in the *Messenger* and the *Courier,* of continually linking Germans with the idea of illicit race mixing or unusual forms of black/white interaction. The allusion to victory in the name "Von Victor" indicated Van Vechten's Pyrrhic victory in his struggle to promote black art beyond any reasonable estimate of its value. As a piece of sentimental doggerel, the poem reflected this message in both form and substance. Its subtitle declared its status as "A Very Touching Love Lyric Dedicated to the New Negro Artists":

I've made you what you are today,
   Yet I'm dissatisfied.
I boosted you until it was said,
   No one so glibly lied.
Now book men print your puerile trash;
   Your jongleurs dine *à la carte.*
Though your vogue's nearly through,
   To think I boosted you—
That [is] the curse of my aching heart.[36]

Two months later, corresponding with the publication of Du Bois's "Criteria of Negro Art," Schuyler announced in "Shafts and Darts" a fictional debate between Van Vechten and David Belasco, the white producer of the hit play *Lulu Belle,* to decide who would garner the title "Santa Claus of Black Harlem." Combining references to Alain Locke, Van Vechten, and the recent white uptown invasion, Schuyler added snidely that Harlem was once called "the Mecca of the New Negro" (Locke's term) but lately this had changed to "Nigger Heaven." He imagined the scene as one where plainclothes officers would have to search "all Negro literati and members of the Lulu Belle Company for deadly weapons," which they would surely use in "belligerently backing their respective benefactors."[37]

Surely some of those who regarded Schuyler as the "Black Mencken" must have wondered while reading this if the satirist himself would not have concealed a few deadly weapons to defend the reputation of his own "Santa Claus" during such a debate. Although Schuyler had not yet begun his unprecedented publishing run with the *American Mercury* at the time of this statement, he still knew that support from influential whites could prove helpful to black artists and did not always require them to engage in sycophancy. He also knew that these relationships could help the patrons. His broader perspective, rooted in the importance of interracial contact, especially among black and white members of the "civilized minority," implied as much. But his role as a satirist generally conflicted with a consistent rendering of ideas. Schuyler regarded the production of controversy around the cultural issues of the Harlem Renaissance as a more important goal than perfect fidelity to any line of argument.

*

Given Schuyler's harsh opinions on upper-class white "literati and dilet-tanti" and the nasty satirical barbs he aimed at Van Vechten in the *Messenger,* one might expect him to have followed Du Bois in severely criticizing *Nigger Heaven.* Yet, despite his suspicions regarding the majority of the white upper class and the intentions of white art promoters, Schuyler chose not to join the crowd of black critics who greeted the novel with nega-tive and sometimes hysterical reviews. Instead, he seized on the publica-tion of *Nigger Heaven* as an opportunity to cause controversy among the "best people" of the black upper class who felt offended at Van Vechten's focus on gambling, violence, and prostitution. Befitting this goal, Schuy-ler's review of *Nigger Heaven* paid more attention to the alarmed black reaction to the novel than it did to matters of plot, style, or dramatic con-tent: "New York Negroes are all wrought up over Carl Van Vechten's latest book 'Nigger Heaven.' . . . What the author has seen he reports faithfully and truthfully. Therein lies the rub. Negroes, like other folk, don't like the truth. For debauchery in all its forms, ancient Babylon could not possibly have had anything on modern Harlem, and Van Vechten frankly reveals existing conditions. Hence the howl."[38]

Making the most of the opportunity to contrast his shockproof New Negroism against the sensitivity of Van Vechten's detractors, Schuyler criticized *Nigger Heaven* for not being devastating enough. He said that Van Vechten's book pales next to the reality it emulates, one where under-world figures and the so-called best people commingle more closely than in any other community. Still, Schuyler pointed out, many Harlemites live above this level. They have no contact with dope peddlers, numbers men, or pimps. He noted that these upstanding types have no place in Van Vechten's novel, which exploits sensationalism for its main effects. Despite this, however, Schuyler praised the novel for the truth it contains and labeled it "capable reportage" even as he denounced it as a bad piece of art.[39]

In asserting that Van Vechten should have been even more explicit about Harlem debauchery than he was, Schuyler emphasized the destruc-tive side of his view on cultural matters. As an apostle of the ugly truth, he refused to give in to what he thought of as excessive black sensitivity stemming from the all-pervasive racial inferiority complex. Like his em-phasis on "realism," this aspect of Schuyler's outlook strained against his interest in propaganda aimed at buttressing black self-confidence. At the same time that Schuyler wanted Harlem Renaissance artists to produce books depicting devastating racial realities without apology, he hoped that they would make black people proud of themselves. As one might imagine, such contradictory requirements combined with Schuyler's satirical voice to make him a rather unwelcoming critic.

Nevertheless Schuyler did, on occasion, encounter a piece of literature worthy of his unqualified endorsement. One such work was Du Bois's romance *Dark Princess,* which Schuyler could not even finish before dashing off a letter to the *Crisis* editor attesting that after reading only 127 pages, he had seen enough to conclude that "other contemporary writers hailed as 'great' pale into insignificance." Schuyler gushed: "Not only do I think 'Dark Princess' is a fine work from the literature standpoint, but it is also great as a portrayal of the soul of our people." This letter, which Schuyler wrote in 1928, might appear a radical departure from the tone and perspective of "The Negro-Art Hokum," but Du Bois's melodrama did suit some aspects of Schuyler's cultural and political agenda better than most other books written in the period. Schuyler's satirical commitments never deterred him from praising works that he thought would make blacks proud of themselves, especially if these works encouraged productive political directions. Schuyler published many such stories himself, both under pseudonyms and in his own name, in the *Illustrated Feature Section* and in the *Pittsburgh Courier* from the late 1920s through the 1930s. Because *Dark Princess* promoted the anti-imperialist fantasy of the darker races rising up—in part as a result of an interracial romance between a black American and an Indian princess—Schuyler considered it excellent propaganda well suited to the political and literary needs of the black masses. Yet, in deference to his hostile past with Du Bois, Schuyler declined to mention *Dark Princess* in "Views and Reviews." Instead, he buried a short, anonymous but positive review in the *Illustrated Feature Section.*[40]

While Schuyler could not disclose in full public view his affection for Du Bois's fiction, he could proclaim loudly his approval of Jessie Redmon Fauset, whom he joined the *Crisis* editor in praising. Departing from the emphasis one might expect given his constant railings against the black middle class, Schuyler found in Fauset's staid and genteel performance in *Plum Bun* inspiration for a full, sincere, and rare declaration of group loyalty: "I may be naive, but I long to see the day when all Negroes will be satisfied to be what they are—hair, color and features; proud of the silent courage, grim tenacity and remarkable achievements of the group. . . . It may sound like 'sour grapes' to the superficially-minded, but knowing what our people have been, are today and are going to be, I wouldn't be anything else but a Negro." In what might have been his most gushing review, Schuyler raved that *Plum Bun* had established Fauset as "the greatest novelist the American Negro group had produced." He particularly applauded the novelist's sensitivity to the details of "real human relationships" and the unconventional features of *Plum Bun*'s plot, which he commended for breaking with the melodramatic commonplaces of the tragic mulatto tale. Even worthier of praise, he insisted, was that the novel avoided the common flaw of making the white world appear preferable to the black one. He also noted Fauset's deft avoidance of the common problems of protest literature. Rather than mere "pegs . . . [for] her opinions," Schuyler said, Fauset's characters in *Plum Bun* resembled "real men and women that you know and meet every day."[41]

Schuyler added that Angela, the light-skinned principal character, represented a much greater achievement than the psychological types of Eugene O'Neill. In contrast to O'Neill's brittle characters, Angela—a "lovable, restless, and ambitious girl"—appeared to Schuyler believable and lifelike. Although Fauset subtitled her book "A Novel without a Moral," Schuyler found an important lesson in the main character's discovery that the white world offered no more than the black one. Taking this idea even further, he speculated that more interracial contact would increase race pride by making blacks more aware of their superiority. For her ability to deliver this excellent piece of propaganda with artistry and realism, he awarded Fauset his highest marks.[42]

Schuyler found many of the same virtues in Nella Larsen's *Quicksand*, which he praised for presenting a variety of black types, not just the ones that primitivists and racists wanted to see. In contrast to *Plum Bun*, however, *Quicksand* did not inspire Schuyler to rhapsodize about his race pride, but it did earn high marks from him for combining art and propaganda. Sounding very much like Du Bois, who reviewed Larsen's novel to the same effect two weeks later, Schuyler announced that in *Quicksand* he found "no story of bulldikers, faggots, slums, cabarets, prostitution, gin parties and whiskey socials, such as we have received from the pens (or typewriters) of too many writers of late years." Instead, he found in the pages of Larsen's novel a variety of black types: "the professional type, the gay metropolitan crowd . . . Negroes of culture and refinement who wear good clothes, eat well, live in fine houses." Although he considered the main character, Helga Crane, "unreal and incredible" for her willingness to leave a perfectly good life in Europe for a self-destructive marriage with a southern preacher, Schuyler found the saving grace of realism in *Quicksand*'s "biographical overtones," which grant the novel a level of objectivity achieved by few black authors.[43]

Like Du Bois, Schuyler appreciated Fauset and Larsen for counterbalancing what he thought of as the undue emphasis in black literature on the sordid and the tragic. Although he did not say it explicitly in his reviews of their books, he also liked these authors for their interest in the ambiguities involved in the interplay of black and white identities. Also, Schuyler liked Larsen and Fauset because they were women. In this way his critical attitude toward them appears similar to that of current feminist critics, although he did not analyze the gender dynamics within their works with anything like the current level of enthusiasm. Still, for his day Schuyler was a strong proponent of women's equality. As such, he made women's issues a major recurrent topic in "Views and Reviews" throughout the 1920s and 1930s.

Schuyler's interest in promoting black feminism and black women's literature shows itself most prominently in his 1937 review of Zora Neale Hurston's *Their Eyes Were Watching God*. In contrast to most male critics of the novel, and diametrically opposed to Richard Wright's dismissal of *Their Eyes Were Watching God* for its insufficient emphasis on protest, Schuyler praised Hurston's deep knowledge of black folk traditions and her mastery over "the homely everyday stuff out of which great literature is made." Calling this work "one of the best novels of Negro life ever written," Schuyler—who had published some of Hurston's early work in the *Messenger*—enthusiastically assured the members of his audience that they would "read breathlessly" the story of Janie Starks, "the brown feminist who did as she pleased and didn't regret it." Just as he praised Hughes for his ability to capture the cadences of black lower-class life in his review of *Fine Clothes to the Jew*, Schuyler applauded Hurston for expressing the genuine voice of the "black yokelry" of the South. While Schuyler always took extra care not to essentialize or celebrate this voice, he did appreciate it, especially in its more humorous dimensions, as evidence of the black will to survive under difficult circumstances. For her grasp of the stories, folkways, and "pawky wit" of ordinary black people, Schuyler valued Hurston as a genuine and honest writer with a depth of life experience at the foundation of her unique writing style.[44] In viewing Hurston this way, Schuyler anticipated the largest vein of current Hurston criticism, which casts her in similar terms.

If Hurston, Larsen, Fauset, and Du Bois were Schuyler's favorite writers of the Harlem Renaissance, Claude McKay was his number-one whipping boy. Although Schuyler could, in the effort to oppose black insecurity and excessive sensitivity, ignore Van Vechten's flights of primitivism and sentimentalism in *Nigger Heaven,* he could only condemn the same tendencies in McKay's exposé of Harlem life, *Home to Harlem.* In one of his nastiest book reviews of the 1920s, Schuyler quipped that the several members of the Negro intelligentsia who sought a publisher for McKay's novel had wasted their time. "If this is the Harlem Claude McKay knew," Schuyler wrote, "then he knew very little about Harlem." To drive his point home even further, he compared *Home to Harlem* unfavorably to *Nigger Heaven,* casting it as not simply bad, but worse than the relatively naive production of a white man with no experience as a Harlem insider: "McKay . . . hits the nail on the head as far as he drives it," Schuyler said, "but he certainly does not drive it as far as one would expect of a Negro who resided in Harlem so long and supposedly knew the life of the people there."[45]

In pressing his attack to yet more insulting proportions, Schuyler compared *Home to Harlem* unfavorably to two novels by white author John W. Vandercook, *Black Majesty* and *Tom Tom.* Despite the occasional racist overtones of Vandercook's stories, Schuyler still ranked them above McKay's effort, which showed him that whites could sometimes do more for blacks than blacks would do for themselves. Finding strong propaganda value in the heroic rendering of Haitian king Henri Cristophe at the center of *Black Majesty,* Schuyler wanted to send the book to every person he knew, white and black. In contrast, he gave the distinct impression of wanting to confiscate and burn *Home to Harlem.*[46]

As one might surmise from his tone in reviewing *Home to Harlem,* Schuyler also disliked McKay's second novel, *Banjo,* which he characterized as a book made to order for racist whites. Returning once again to his preoccupation with the black perpetuation of black stereotypes, he complained that not one "respectable" character appeared in the whole book. Least "respectable" of all, Schuyler said, was the main character, whom he described humorously as "a roustabout . . . a shiftless, worthless Negro who sponges off a Negro prostitute when he is broke and spends his extra francs with a white prostitute who quits him when he got broke." Still, Schuyler admitted, McKay deserved credit for exposing the increasing trend of European racism and for stressing the common interests of blacks everywhere; but in doing this, he treated mulattoes and educated blacks too harshly. In some places, Schuyler declared, McKay even sounded like racist senator Tom Heflin or race pseudoscientist Lothrop Stoddard. Because of the simplicity and one-sidedness of his efforts, Schuyler proposed that the author of *Home to Harlem* and *Banjo* could learn much from Fauset.[47]

Schuyler's reviews of *Home to Harlem* and *Banjo* bring us back once again to the dominant negative tendency in his commentary on the Harlem Renaissance. Instead of entering into a careful and close reading of McKay's fiction, which attempted to transvalue primitivism rather than promote it, Schuyler chose to dismiss both the art and the artist in caricatured terms. This affinity for exaggeration and dismissal flowed naturally from his commitment to the satirical mode. Even when Schuyler did not engage in formal satire, he applied a tough and dismissive tone as a matter of course in the manner of a distinctive personal signature. For him and for his audience, this signature implied honesty, integrity, independence, and bottom-line common sense. Quite often Schuyler employed his unique style, which constituted his best contribution to the diverse outpouring of black American modernism in the 1920s, to utter truths about the ambiguities of American race relations and culture that few thinkers could articulate with anywhere near the same pinpoint accuracy, or humor. Yet Schuyler's commitment to satire also inclined him, perhaps even doomed him, to underestimate the complexity and creativity of the Harlem Renaissance, even as he made his trenchant contribution to it.

Schuyler's commitment to satire also stands behind his unwillingness to offer anything like a synthetic statement about the place of art or culture within the context of the black freedom movement. In fact, an overview of Schuyler's cultural politics reveals strong commitments to opposed positions. He argued for both art and propaganda; for unvarnished and devastating realism and uplifting stories to soothe the black collective psyche; for a suspicious attitude toward white patrons and for deeper interracial understanding; for uncompromising artistic independence and for art devoted to the promotion of a political cause. In almost every case he argued these opposed positions with laughter and with the intention of dislodging conventional accounts of the relationship between race and culture. With this in mind we might say that he used the cultural politics of the Harlem Renaissance as a space for play and for the further liberation of new political and artistic energy.

Certainly, Schuyler attacked some positions more consistently than others. He argued consistently against the existence of a separate black culture, for example, and he inclined more to propaganda than he did to art. Still, these doubts and inclinations never congealed into a blueprint for black culture. Schuyler believed that blacks would solve their problems in America, and their problems as Americans, when they embraced their diverse human potentialities. For him this implied a constant scrimmage with all hard-and-fast conceptions of race, even those that held out the seductive promise of solid and sturdy black cultural foundations. Although he held out hope for black progress, and thought that artistic creation could play a decisive role in bringing it about, Schuyler could not believe in such foundations. They contradicted his whole outlook on life. Nor could he accept the idea, so dear to the popular rhetoric of the Harlem Renaissance, of the black artist as a race hero. Although he often had harsh words for white patrons and publishers, he also rejected the notion of whites as automatic race villains. Deeply aware of the pitfalls and paradoxes surrounding the question of race for all Americans, he fought a shifting battle employing irony and humor as his weapons of choice.

Schuyler's editorials, reviews, and articles on the works and issues of the Harlem Renaissance grant only a partial view of just how he fought this battle. To get a fuller view, we must turn to an examination of his raucously humorous novel *Black No More*, which stands out as his most deeply textured response to the racial atmosphere of the 1920s and to the perennial problems of American race relations. Therefore, in concluding this chapter we must begin the next, where Schuyler comes off of the sidelines and joins the group of artists that he spent so much time criticizing.

CHAPTER EIGHT

"Black No More"

BY THE END OF the 1920s George Schuyler had established himself as a major critical voice on the race question in the most important publications on both sides of the color line. Yet he had not made a reputation as a full-fledged artist. Although he had written a few small fictional pieces for the *Messenger* and penned some of the most artful essays of the Harlem Renaissance, he had yet to join the company of such poets and novelists as Langston Hughes, Nella Larsen, Jessie Redmon Fauset, and Jean Toomer, who had produced one or more lengthy works demonstrating extensive mastery of craft. Also, after six years of taking small satirical shots at almost everything related to the race question, Schuyler wanted to bring his artistic ideas together, and give them focus, between the covers of a single volume. A full-length satire on race would be the first book of its kind and a major showcase for a little-known and severely underrated side of black self-consciousness. Beyond this, the publication of such a book would give Schuyler the best chance to expand his readership and thereby extend the interracial community of laughter that he worked tirelessly to construct around the black/white racial divide.

With these goals in mind Schuyler built his new novel on a favorite recurrent joke that circulated around the *Messenger* office during its heyday. This joke, which combined implicit commentary on a range of race-related subjects—including minstrelsy, the cult of progress surrounding science, and the high value placed on light skin by many blacks—invited playful speculation about what would happen if a scientist invented a formula that would allow blacks to turn white. Combining his own speculations on this matter with the most outlandish postulations of his colleagues, and by reorienting some of his best "Shafts and Darts" and "Views and Reviews" material, Schuyler arrived at the principal elements of *Black No More*, a mock race novel aimed like a precision-guided weapon at the central features of popular 1920s race mythology informing the perspectives of whites and blacks alike. In hitting his target, Schuyler not only challenged racial perspectives in his own time, he also struck hard at many perennial themes of American racial consciousness. Because of this, his satire retains its relevance today and stands up well to the efforts of those who have in the years since its 1931 publication endeavored to follow its lead.

A cursory glance at the plot of *Black No More* immediately reveals its main source of power, which derives from a highly entertaining and suggestive fantasy placed just far enough away from actual events to invite contemplation of the logical core of the American race problem, yet close enough to recognizable situations and personages to place in bold relief the ludicrous quality of everyday racial practices. To this *Black No More* adds biting ridicule concerning a subject that most Americans allow themselves to perceive only in the mode of high moral seriousness or within the narrow confines of ideologically unthreatening humor, melodrama, myths of progress, or fantasies of racial hierarchy. In opposing all attempts to mask the violent foundations of the American racial order, *Black No More* employs wild exaggeration, juxtaposition, incongruity, understatement, and a wide range of satirical devices to undermine all comforting visions of a stable and orderly relationship between black and white.[1] Rather than oppose racial injustice directly, or bring against it a strategy of negation or elimination, *Black No More* celebrates the disfiguring and refiguring energy of interracial desire, whose ironic dependence on a discourse of racial difference it acknowledges even as it works to undermine every fixed notion that such a discourse might employ. In addition, *Black No More* seizes on the anomalous quality of the black American condition—its tenuous positioning between slavery and freedom, inferiority and superiority, culture and silence, outcast and omni-American—for the constant danger it poses to popular accounts of American identity rooted in the high ideals of freedom and equality.

Rejecting all notions of social perfection and the inevitable bow to binary logic that such ideals entail, *Black No More* pursues a strategy of multiplication and dissemination rather than protest and erasure. Hostile to fast-frozen conceptions of race, it depicts a chaotic world of black and white strivers in the only terms appropriate to their unprincipled struggles: those of distortion and disfigurement, of magnification and refraction, of chance and coincidence. In this way it expresses a certain confidence that the unruly subterranean energies of American life remain ultimately incompatible with the visions of permanence and order preferred by racists. Against the appeal to morality and justice common to the black protest tradition, which ironically reinforces the consciousness of racial difference even as it attacks formal and informal barriers to racial equality, *Black No More* exults tricksterism, masking, and power play. At the same time it exposes the limits and imperfections of particular tricks, disguises, and strategies. This provides ample occasion for humor across a great range—from cathartic and wise to cheap and dismissible, reflecting well the sheer obsessive excess of American racial norms. The laughter resulting from this humor, in both its constructive and destructive guises, remains *Black No More*'s strongest suggestion of a proper attitude toward the race question, even as it laughs at the whole idea of a proper attitude.

Yet as it smiles, *Black No More* spreads antipathy liberally against black and white, high and low, the wise and the ignorant. By doing this, it makes an implicit case for human equality, although the terms it employs in making this case—imperfection, wretchedness, scheming, and circularity—would appear to undermine any celebration of the fact. In the end one might say *Black No More* attempts to absorb and implicate its reader in this wretchedness by engaging him in transgressive laughter about one of the dirtiest and most violent subjects that an American can contemplate. Sexual obsession, dehumanization, lynching, genocide, racial invisibility, greed, and impotence all make their appearance in its pages, along with a heavy dose of comic morphine, making the whole ugly scene almost attractive to face. Like many good satires, *Black No More* transacts its most valuable exchanges in the shadow of death and imperfection, which it stealthily employs in the pursuit of an ultimately regenerative vision ironically rooted in the possibility of allowing the monstrous and ugly to sneak through the back door of a piece of literature and run havoc over its pages. In doing this, it embraces a democratic ideal, but one based not so much in the preservation of institutions as in the necessary element of pollution and chaos at the center of a democratic culture staked on newness, dynamic movement, and the untapped possibility inherent in the lives of its lowliest elements.

Black No More relates the events following the invention by Dr. Junius Crookman of a three-day treatment involving "electric nutrition and glandular control" that miraculously erases every trace of the "everlasting stain." The main character in the novel, Max Disher, becomes the first to hand himself over to Crookman after a beautiful blond "cracker" informs him on New Year's Eve in Harlem's Honky Tonk Club that she does not dance with "niggers." Within three years nearly every "Aframerican" follows Disher's lead in seeking "chromatic perfection," making it impossible to tell the "real" whites from the fakes and thus causing a national upheaval. With no one left to fleece, all of the prominent race leaders join the new freedom movement, including Dr. Shakespeare Agamemnon Beard (W. E. B. Du Bois) and Napoleon Wellington Jackson (James Weldon Johnson) of the National Social Equality League (the NAACP), Rev. Herbert Gronne (Mordecai Johnson) of Dunbar (Howard) University, Mortimer Roberts (Robert Russa Moton) of the Dusky River Agricultural Institute (Tuskegee Institute) and the Uncle Tom Memorial Association, Joseph Bonds (Eugene Kinkle Jones) of the Negro Data League (Urban League), Claude Spelling (C. C. Spaulding) of the Society of Negro Merchants (National Negro Business League), and several others. Disher takes advantage of his new identity as the white man Matthew Fisher to become the Grand Exalted Giraw of the Knights of Nordica, a successor of the Ku Klux Klan devoted to eliminating Crookman's Black No More, Inc., and stealing as much as possible from the white working class. Matthew also marries the daughter of his boss, Grand Imperial Wizard Henry Givens, who turns out to be the same woman who injured his ego on the fateful New Year's Eve at the Honky Tonk Club.[2]

When Matthew decides to run his father-in-law for president on the Democratic ticket in the 1936 election, he joins forces with Arthur Snobbcraft, the head of the aristocratic Anglo-Saxon Association, and Samuel Buggerie, a famous researcher for a New York insurance firm. Buggerie concocts a genealogical study intended to identify the "fake" whites and expose the mixed ancestry of the Republican candidates. Instead, he succeeds in demonstrating the mixed ancestry of nearly all Americans, including himself, Givens, and Snobbcraft. With the aid of Walter Williams (Walter White), the Republicans steal the crucial data and use it to expose the Democratic candidates. This eventually leads to the lynching of Buggerie and Snobbcraft at the hands of crazed fundamentalist Christians in Happy Hill, Mississippi. Matthew reveals his true identity only after the announcement of Givens's black ancestry in the newspaper, which convinces his wife that the blackness of their newborn is her "fault." Having been named surgeon general, Crookman, who retains his dark skin throughout, announces that his treatment actually makes its beneficiaries whiter than the original whites. This starts a tanning craze, thus bringing *Black No More* full circle with race-obsessed Americans declaring for the first time that blacker is indeed better. The satire ends with a satisfied Crookman eyeing a newspaper photograph of a brown-skinned Matthew tanning himself on a beach in Mexico surrounded by his dark friends and relatives.

Given its focus on solving the "Negro problem" once and for all, one might say that *Black No More* begins where Schuyler's 1926 "Ten Commandments" editorial ends. But this time, instead of artfully evading the infamous Negro question, Schuyler employs a fantasy to answer it directly, if only to reflect more fully on why it may never go away. In the process of showing why the false problem of race can yield no permanent solution, Schuyler seizes on the ambiguities and built-in contradictions of American race relations to play up the role of the color line as a boundary around which individuals of both races constantly reinvent their public and private identities. By depicting race as a social category like any other, very much in play with class, gender, nationality, and other aspects of shifting historical circumstance, he hoped to encourage his readers to view it practically and complexly rather than dwell on it obsessively as an all-encompassing negative stain, as a mark of chosen peoplehood, or as a mysterious key to the fulfillment of sexual desire. Against both "color-blind" and essentialist accounts of the role of race in American life, Schuyler's *Black No More* puts forth creative engagement of a many-sided and malleable racial reality as an alternative to reification, fetishization, and erasure—all of which it ridicules soundly.

As it pokes fun at the Ku Klux Klan, the eugenics movement, whiteness, black nationalism, cultural essentialism, and many other forms of racist and racialist thought, Black No More celebrates the integrity of black American communal life under segregation, which derides blacks themselves for underrating in their rush to join the greedy and indistinguishable members of the vast American herd. In Black No More taking Crookman's formula is the act of a fool—not just because it involves an overinvestment in the value of skin color, but also for its implicit rejection of an alternative style of American life rich in the flexible enhancement of human potential. Ironically, in becoming white, a choice requiring some insight into how little actually separates the races, Crookman's patients show their overinvestment in the race concept, which makes them turn too easily away from the hard-won values that make their group life worthy of dissemination. Rather than imitating their "pork-colored brethren," "Aframericans," suggests Black No More, find ways to infect whites with their own American values. In his editorials Schuyler used words such as "decency," "civilization," and "gentle cynicism" to describe these values, which represented for him the spiritual fruit of life on the margins of American democracy and on the underside of New World capitalism. Without romanticizing the black American experience, or overemphasizing its particularity, Schuyler found its highest expression in the constant adjustment to harsh environmental circumstance under conditions that encouraged a weather eye on human limitation and evil. Thus he found in the best of black American group values a potential model for a different kind of American modernism, one forward-moving but not blindly progressivist, individualist but not selfish, group-oriented but not tribal, skeptical of morality but at the same time virtuous in its own terms.

This point of view, ever faithful to the possibility of a resilient anti-essentialist black solidarity and ever willing to pit the ugly prospect of black superiority against the racist American mainstream, fit in perfectly not only with the main thrust of Schuyler's political activities in the Young Negroes' Cooperative League, but also with his criticism of the Harlem Renaissance. Corresponding with his criticism of the writers of the Harlem Renaissance for succumbing to the "tragic" theme of sentimental race fiction, Schuyler sought in Black No More to celebrate the qualities that made blacks resilient, one might even say triumphant, under difficult environmental circumstances. In this way he tried to make the black members of his audience more proud of themselves and more power seeking, willing not only to seize what advantage they could, but also to shape the life of the nation in their own terms. His protagonist, the wise-fool Max Disher, learns only after becoming a white man how well his life as a fire insurance salesman and gay blade around Harlem had prepared him for the corridors of power. Disher also learns as Matthew Fisher just how much the mad rush for wealth undermines civilization among whites, in part because of the endless deferral of fulfillment implicit in the progressive American mind-set. As he contemplates just how little whites tend to stylize and embellish the activities of everyday living compared with their darker counterparts, he begins to miss the "almost European" atmosphere of Harlem. Thus, even as he achieves his dream in becoming a wealthy white man, Max/Matthew realizes just how little there is to envy on the other side of the color line.

The antiracist values of *Black No More* have always gotten more attention than its attempt to ironize and deepen the meaning of black pride, although the two always went together for Schuyler, even during his late career as an archconservative. Sensing a potential relationship between Schuyler's post–World War II conservative values and the slippery significations of his satire, most critics between the 1950s and the 1990s have tended to associate *Black No More* with a politically retrogressive desire for assimilation or whiteness. Marking the satire as a key moment in the demise of the Harlem Renaissance, the most well-known of these critics, Robert Bone, even called *Black No More* an "assimilationist" novel. More recently, with the rise in popularity of antiessentialism as a veritable mantra among critics of the race question, it has become more common to associate *Black No More* with progressive racial values, although the taint of Schuyler's late career remains a strong concern. In an apparent attempt to split the difference between the palatable and unpalatable aspects of Schuyler's larger reputation, most critics have found ways to praise *Black No More* while shaking a moralistic finger at it for failing in one way or another to fulfill the requirements for a satisfactory antiessentialist position. For example, one critic finds the fatal flaw of the satire its uncritical embrace of the nation as a foundational category. Another has located this in Schuyler's supposedly conservative view of science. Yet another, seeking to separate *Black No More* as far as possible from what Schuyler became in the 1950s and 1960s, cites socialism as the novel's saving grace. Generally the attempt to boil *Black No More* down to such narrow bottom-line themes as "socialist," "assimilationist," "conservative," or "antiessentialist" has taken place within the larger effort to assess its value as protest literature. Unfortunately, in the effort to weigh the satire by this standard, critics have tended to lose sight of *Black No More*'s deft challenge to the self-undermining qualities of the protest attitude. Still, whatever its short-comings, the new turn in *Black No More* criticism has paved the way for unprecedented recognition of the novel's value. Currently published in three editions, Schuyler's satire has taken its rightful place as the most widely read and appreciated product of his highly productive pen.[3]

In its own time *Black No More* made a reputation similar to the mainly positive one that it has today. Many readers appreciated it for its liberating qualities, with some enthusiasts even hailing it for ushering in a new kind of black literature. Although the Depression kept sales figures low, the book garnered a great deal of attention from critics and even succeeded in causing controversy, especially for its rough treatment of black leaders, which inspired complaints from black and white critics alike. Even H. L. Mencken, Schuyler's model and occasional editor, found the black editor's vitriol a bit too strong for his liking. Having already refused Schuyler's request to write an introduction to *Black No More*, Mencken dismissed the satire in a short and brutally honest review citing plain crudity, espe-cially in the use of low burlesque, as its main flaw. Apparently forgetful of his own tendency toward excessive violence in attacking such favorite whipping boys as William Jennings Bryan, and perhaps revealing his own discomfort with black anger, Mencken characterized Schuyler's work as "excessively savage," implying that the author had failed to balance the violence of his work with the intellectually uplifting qualities that elevate satire above the self-indulgent rant. Unable to see much purpose or re-straint in Schuyler's cuts against other blacks or in the lynching scene near the end of the satire, Mencken could only conclude that its author had failed to overcome his racially motivated attitude of resentment and had thus managed to infect where he intended to inoculate.[4]

Many other contemporary reviewers, both white and black, lodged similar complaints against *Black No More*. In the *New York Herald Tribune* and in a private letter Louis Gannett declared himself disgusted with Schuyler's show of "envious spleen" in libeling the noble leaders of his race. Following the same line of thought and taking the complaint to an even higher level of indignation, P. L. Prattis, writing for the Associated Negro Press under the pseudonym Roger Diddier, called Schuyler a "low-bred ruffian" whose "barroom style" had created a work filled with "the rankest dirt all unnecessary and revulsive." Novelist Rudolph Fisher, one of the most prominent black reviewers of *Black No More,* made the same case as Prattis, but he put the matter more politely. Because of its many errors, he said, *Black No More* succeeded only in "making faces" at the evils of race in America. In denying *Black No More* the status of a novel, and in the process ignoring its inherent mockery of the race novel as a genre, Fisher characterized the substance and approach of Schuyler's satire as "primarily sociological" and "without detachment, without sympathy, without restraint, without clear characterization, and without dialogue that traces crisp portraits." Rather than a work of art, he said, *Black No More* served as a mere vehicle for thinly veiled "Schuyleric opinion."[5] In other words Fisher, whose polite and restrained novel *The Walls of Jericho* (1928) often gains mention along with Wallace Thurman's *Infants of the Spring* (1932) as a classic satire of the Harlem Renaissance, fell into the common error of criticizing a narrative satire by standards more appropriate to the novel.

Writing for the *Nation,* white critic Dorothy Van Doren took the angry spirit of Schuyler's detractors in her own distinctive direction. Seizing on the publication of *Black No More* as an opportunity to continue "The Negro-Art Hokum" debate, she accused Schuyler of writing a "white" satire. By this she meant that instead of searching for the true artistic inspiration of his people, which she found most clearly expressed in music and rhythm, Schuyler imitated white authors. Making ironic use of Schuyler's argument in "The Negro-Art Hokum," she found in *Black No More* a clear message: that black people had emerged from physical bondage only to remain mentally enslaved. Entirely missing the mental enslavement of whites in the satire and the crucial mixture of wisdom and foolishness in such characters as Crookman and Disher, she criticized Schuyler for representing black mental enslavement in contradictory terms, as both inescapable and reprehensible. As a result, Van Doren wondered how the satirist could avoid exemplifying the very problem that his book protested.[6]

With her husband en route to Liberia, and unable to mount a defense against detractors, Josephine Schuyler took up the defense of *Black No More* against Van Doren. In a short letter to the *Nation* she confidently asserted the argument of "The Negro-Art Hokum" while denouncing any attempt to characterize literature in racial terms. Yet in a letter to the *New York World*, written under the pen name Julia Jerome—which she used in her "black" advice column in the *Illustrated Feature Section*—Josephine flirted with just this sort of argument. Claiming all of the privileges of her assumed insider status, she declared *Black No More* the blackest of novels for capturing the deep vein of disillusionment and intelligent cynicism at the heart of the "Aframerican" outlook. Because black life provided strong lessons in grimness and frustration, she said, "real Negro humor is always satirical" and "the Negro . . . must laugh to live." Taking up this spirit, she condemned black writers who pandered to white sentimentality and racist naiveté by writing defeatist accounts of their experience. In contrast to such traitorous intellectuals, she asserted the wisdom of the average black person on the street, whom she imagined swelling with pride over Schuyler's "audacious levity."[7]

If Schuyler's wife, writing in her own name and as Julia Jerome, proved the satirist's best defense against the opinions of Van Doren, his good friend James Ivy made the best counterattack against just about everyone else. In letters to the *New York Herald Tribune* and the *New Republic*, and in reviews in the *Baltimore Afro-American*, the *Timely Digest*, and the *Norfolk Journal and Guide*, Ivy denounced the novel's most prominent black and white critics. Answering the charge of crudity and simplicity lodged by several critics, Ivy praised *Black No More* for capturing the idiocy of American race phobia realistically and in a tone appropriate to its stupidity and cruelty. To the complaint, common among white reviewers of the novel, that Schuyler had unnecessarily libeled the leaders of his race, Ivy pointed proudly to the vigorous criticism of those leaders in the black press. Striking a note similar to that of Josephine Schuyler, and flirting with stereotype, he declared that blacks had an "unfailing sense of humor" that allowed them to chuckle even at their own pet foibles. Ivy emphasized that genuine satire required this quality. It had to rise above the polite slap in ridiculing both "the minnows and the whales." Extending this argument in a later review, Ivy hailed *Black No More* as "the first purely objective treatment of the Negro and his problems in America" and as a harbinger of a confident era of black American literature free from "lacrimal sentimentalism" and erudite but ineffectual syllogism. Like Schuyler himself Ivy hailed the "belly-aching guffaw" as a robust alternative to moralistic protest rhetoric in the struggle against "emotionally held irrationalisms" at the foundation of the race problem.[8]

Although Ivy made important observations in the process of defending *Black No More*, he seems to have overestimated the number of critics who disagreed with him. Actually, Schuyler's satire had more fans than detractors, especially in the black press. Articles and reviews in the *Baltimore Afro-American*, the *Kansas City Call*, the *Palmetto Leader*, the *Cincinnati Union*, the *Norfolk Journal and Guide*, the *Philadelphia Tribune*, the *Amsterdam News*, and the *Pittsburgh Courier* loudly hailed Schuyler's achievement in terms similar to those of Ivy. Notwithstanding Rudolph Fisher's negative review, many black writers and literary critics joined black journalists in unequivocally praising *Black No More*. On the dust jacket of the first edition poet Countee Cullen pronounced Schuyler's status as "the only Negro satirist." In *Opportunity* cultural critic Alain Locke declared that *Black No More* had opened a new vein in black fiction. Triumphantly he announced: "May its tribe increase." Literary critic Arthur Davis declared *Black No More* one of the most significant pieces of black writing since 1925 and urged his audience to read the satire, "even if it hurts." Critic and fellow Harlem Renaissance satirist Wallace Thurman liked Schuyler's satire so much that he led a public discussion on it at the Harlem branch of the New York Public Library. In addition to this public recognition, Schuyler also received personal letters of praise and congratulation from journalist Eugene Gordon, poet Georgia Douglas Johnson, critic and NAACP stalwart Mary White Ovington, activist Mary Church Terrell, Harlem Renaissance patron Carl Van Vechten, historian J. A. Rogers, and many others.[9]

Perhaps the most remarkable positive contemporary response to *Black No More* came from W. E. B. Du Bois, who even seemed to enjoy his own caricature in the satire. Writing in his column "The Browsing Reader," Du Bois declared *Black No More* "extremely significant in Negro American literature" for its courage and for its author's willingness to criticize leaders and thinkers on every side of the race question. This, he said, provided a first among blacks because journals like the *Crisis* avoided satire for fear of being misunderstood and other publications only used it to make fun of enemies in short, insincere sketches. Pointing out that the simpleminded would miss the therapeutic aim of Schuyler's book, Du Bois ended his good-natured review by signing it "Agamemnon Shakespeare Beard," the name of the character in the novel intended to satirize him.[10]

By at least one account, Du Bois came by the good feeling of his review quite honestly. NAACP staffer Henry Lee Moon remembered many years after the fact seeing the editor laugh at recognizing himself in Schuyler's satire. Although it is impossible to know exactly what caused Du Bois to laugh at this, the fact that he did so presents some intriguing possibilities, especially given the devastating contours of his caricature in Schuyler's distorting fable. In *Black No More* the portrait of Dr. Shakespeare Agamemnon Beard takes full advantage of every opportunity that Du Bois's physical appearance, aristocratic manner, and iconic status offered for ridicule. As it lampoons Du Bois, this portrait also plays up some of the larger ambiguities of black leadership and intellect that Du Bois embodied, especially the unavoidable element of fakery and betrayal implicit in his liminal positioning between exemplary blackness and symbolic whiteness, lowliness and aristocracy, distinction and democracy, action and contemplation, black potential and black limitation. These dichotomies all appear in the broad suggestion of Beard's comically haughty name, which refers to poetry, drama, comedy, and tragedy through the image of Shakespeare; to rhetoric, military leadership, fallen kingship, slavery, and the imposter status of the nouveau riche freedman through its triple reference to Agamemnon: the lustful, fallen, but victorious king of the *Iliad;* the dead king of the *Odyssey;* and the trickster, former slave, and teacher of rhetoric of the *Satyricon.* To this the last name "Beard" adds a contrastingly quotidian and complementary final note through its reference to Du Bois's beard, one of the main devices through which he approximated the pose of a European professor.[11]

Other aspects of Shakespeare Agamemnon Beard's description advance even further the negative criticism of Du Bois by calling attention to his distance from the black working class, to political embarrassments such as his support for World War I, and to his penchant for extramarital affairs. A graduate of Harvard, Yale, and "Copenhagen" and a consummate trickster, Beard headed the National Social Equality League and edited *The Dilemma* (the *Crisis*), in which he wrote scholarly editorials denouncing whites, "whom he secretly admired," and praising blacks, "whom he alternately pitied and despised." Although he lauded dark-skinned women in his writings, he hired only octoroons with "weak resistance" to work in his office. In peacetime Beard played the socialist but during war he "bivouacked at the feet of Mars."[12]

As the organizer of the group of black leaders gathered to stop Crookman from solving the race problem, Beard employs his singular ability to say nothing impressively to inspire his colleagues. The result parodies well the vaulting rhetoric of such books as *Darkwater* (1920) and *The Souls of Black Folk* (1903): "I want to tell you that our destiny lies in the stars. Ethiopia's fate is in the balance. The Goddess of the Nile weeps bitter tears at the feet of the Great Sphinx. The lowering clouds gather over the Congo and the lightning flashes o'er Togoland. To your tents, O Israel! The hour is at hand." Having failed to stop the well-organized Crookman, Beard not only becomes a white man, but in true trickster fashion finds a new application of his skills as a social scientist by working as a data analyst for the racist researcher Samuel Buggerie. Later, after Crookman's announcement of the whiteness of the "fake" whites, he resurfaces as Carl Von Beerde, head of the Down-With-White-Prejudice League, thus bringing him back to where he started: somewhere in the ambiguous space between eliminating and exacerbating the race problem.[13]

Although the sheer absurdity of the character Shakespeare Agamemnon Beard might make anyone laugh, we might still wonder, given its emphasis on self-contradiction, corruption, and obsession, how Du Bois himself could have found it a source of healing amusement. Of course, the perceptive Du Bois did not require Schuyler's ludicrous extrapolations to recognize the many ambiguities of his own anomalous existence as a black leader and intellectual, but the humorous context of a ridiculous fable like *Black No More* may have made them a bit easier to face. In his essay "An Extravagance of Laughter," novelist Ralph Ellison reflected at length on his own uncontrollable laughter upon viewing a New York stage play of Erskine Caldwell's *Tobacco Road*. Employing Charles Baudelaire's pithy rendering of the intimate relationship between terror and laughter, "the wise man never laughs but that he trembles," to maximum effect, Ellison attributes his embarrassing inability to stop laughing during the performance to the recognition of his own ridiculous likeness as an American, a black man, and a newcomer to the city to the chaotic, unruly, and incest-ridden poor whites being depicted on stage. The comic rendering of these whites, whom his upbringing had taught him to regard with the greatest fear and trembling, combined with the wide-open opportunities offered by the big city to invent a whole series of experimental masks or "second" selves, provided Ellison with the distance necessary to perceive for the first time the many similarities between himself and a group that he had always regarded as the opposite of everything he hoped to become.

This ethical perception—simultaneously fearful and joyful, ludicrous and wise, bridging sameness and difference, the past and the present, the symbolic and the actual—corresponded with Ellison's maturation into a responsible, self-consciousness, and free individual. Yet portentousness, the normal attitudinal complement to such moments of discovery, would have rendered him incapable of perceiving a lesson that could only convey itself in the unspoken language of laughter. As he shook with this laughter of discovery and democratic possibility, which went far outside the bounds of proper audience response, Ellison found himself becoming more un-ruly and embarrassing, and thus more revealing of the hayseed "nigger" identity whose rejection provided the main context for his attendance at the play in the first place. Therefore the more he laughed, the more his destructive social presence underscored the ridiculous association be-tween himself and the hillbillies on stage. Caught in a vicious feedback loop of laughter, he could do nothing else but howl and shake in the face of social oblivion, joyfully transforming inflexible death-laced fear into the resilient, playful material of human freedom.[14]

Although Ellison's episode of uncontrollable laughter occurred under conditions quite different from Du Bois's chuckling recognition of Shake-speare Agamemnon Beard, it does appear similar enough to suggest a broad analogy. To achieve his epiphany, and his insight into the absurd core of American race relations, Ellison had to face what he feared the most in a dramatic context that made radical otherness, both his own and that of whites, less daunting. In facing Beard—who represented the distortion of his own image in the direction of the common black street hustler on one side and the white racist con man on the other—and the other fakes, criminals, and near-minstrel figures of *Black No More*, Du Bois saw himself depicted in terms of everything he sought to avoid or negate.[15] Of course, his experience in reading Schuyler's satire could not have been dramatically transforming on the order of Ellison's epiphany. Yet sitting there in his office thumbing through *Black No More*, he may well have been moved to face the otherness in himself more fully than usual, and in keeping with his wisdom and insight into the duality of American and black American life, respond in the only language appropriate to its full recognition. If this does not capture why he found *Black No More* irresistibly funny, it is certainly the reason that Schuyler would have preferred.

No doubt, Schuyler found Du Bois an attractive figure to lampoon in his satire not only for his prominence and pretense, but also for his unique elaboration of the construct of doubleness or "two souls" as a framework for understanding black life in the United States. Exploiting the comic potential of this construct to the hilt, and joining it with the traditional satiric deployment of images involving extreme juxtaposition, *Black No More* doubles all of its main characters in a vast network of ludicrous comparisons. This play of opposition and comparison becomes most obvious in the pairing of characters such as Max/Matthew, who is himself double, and his best friend Bunny Brown; the numbers man Hank Johnson and the real-estate dealer Chuck Foster; Arthur Snobbcraft and Samuel Buggerie; and Santop Licorice and Joseph Bonds—each of whom forms a vaudevillian pair in which one of the partners plays the fat fool and the other represents the skinny, tall, and more serious straight man.[16] This repetitive pairing of characters that appear to form opposites but in a deeper sense mirror each other's key qualities follows the larger pattern of the novel in treating the elements of such pairings as black/white, upper class/lower class, or high culture/low culture as mutually reinforcing and in many important ways identical.

Black No More also plays the game of doubling in reference to the real life individuals that its characters represent. For example, the reference to Du Bois, which constitutes one of the satire's main obsessions, appears not only in the character Shakespeare Agamemnon Beard but also arises in the portrait of his nemesis, Dr. Crookman, whose description combines some of Du Bois's characteristics with those of the author. Like Schuyler himself Crookman is a cultivated, dark-skinned man in his midthirties who grew up in central New York State in an atmosphere devoid of the "defeatist psychology so prevalent among American Negroes." Like Du Bois, who grew up in Great Barrington, Massachusetts—and shared Schuyler's northern origin and fatherless upbringing—Crookman enjoyed monotonous academic success despite the death of his father and benefited from a German education, which he acquired with the help of investors. Like Shakespeare Agamemnon Beard, and in another way like Du Bois himself, Crookman embodies a long series of irreconcilable oppositions, many of which link him directly to the *Crisis* editor. On one side he represents the cold calculation of science and on the other the well-meaning blindness of the idealist. He exudes directness and practical wisdom and simultaneously plays the part of a fool caught in the snares of the very problem that he devotes his life to solving. Even in petty ways he appears to reflect the image of Du Bois. While in Germany he ransacks the libraries by day while having liaisons with "fraus and frauliens" (*sic*) by night. Filled with race pride, he is wedded to all things black "but a black woman." His wife, a woman of remote black ancestry, could easily "pass" for white, while his assistant, Sandol, a snow-white African transformed by his treatment, has a greater claim to pure blackness than any other character in *Black No More*.[17]

These similarities to Du Bois invite contrast as well as comparison. In a sense one might say that notwithstanding his many faults and contradictions, Crookman represents a preferable Du Bois. Just as Shakespeare Agamemnon Beard's tricksterish rationality sets him above such leaders as the uncouth and superstitious Bishop Ezekiel Whooper, the accommodating and weak Dr. Mortimer Roberts, and other leaders assembled at the convention of black leaders in the third chapter, Crookman's scientific skill, dark skin, business acumen, amoralism, and willingness to promote his people "by any means necessary" places him far above the leader of the National Social Equality League. Even in the exaggerated form in which these qualities appear in the sketch of Crookman, they still represent a good general outline of the qualities that Schuyler promoted in his editorials as the best attributes of a new kind of black leadership. In this connection the character Crookman conjures up associations with Dr. Louis T. Wright, the first black to serve as police surgeon in New York City, a prominent NAACP board member, and the Du Bois family doctor.[18] When Crookman uses money and knowledge of the inner workings of the American political system to become surgeon general near the end of *Black No More*, he takes on his greatest association with Wright, a genuine doctor—as opposed to the many pretentious fake doctors populating the pages of Schuyler's satire—whose healing touch extended beyond the realm of narrow professional application to the broader political problems of his people.

While it dangles political and scientific rationality in front of its reader as a superior approach to the so-called Negro Problem, *Black No More* also employs the figure of Crookman to expose the limits of cold-blooded reason in solving human problems rooted in hearts, minds, and subjective orientations. To realize this, one only has to consider the violence of Crookman's remedy, which depends on repeatedly shocking his patients in a gruesome chair and infecting them with vitiligo, a pigment-destroying disease. Schuyler's use of such details has caused some critics, in the spirit of promoting "black firsts," to count *Black No More* as the earliest black science fiction novel. Given the flexible boundaries of this genre, the claim seems hardly worth disputing, especially considering how often racial transmutation appeared as a theme in the science fiction of the period.[19] Still, it remains important to recognize that in *Black No More* science merely provides another arena for human folly, one all the more ridiculous for its exalted status as a privileged discourse of truth and as a repository of all-too-human fantasies of total Faustian control. One only needs to contemplate Junius Crookman's name and the twisted fate of his all-encompassing solution to the race problem to see this. In order to save his people, Crookman chooses symbolically to destroy them, and in the bargain to play on their most self-negating desires. Above all else this qualifies him as a consummate crook. He confuses surface with depth, toys with genocide, and regards people as mere instruments of his well-meaning but highly destructive aims.

At the end of the satire, after he has torn the nation apart with his difference-erasing schemes, Crookman seems to achieve a certain trick-sterish equanimity and objectivity as he smiles wearily at the photograph of a dark Matthew Fisher tanning himself on the beach in Mexico.[20] One wonders here if Crookman, who has successfully turned the chromatic tables without affecting racism one bit, has not learned from the experience to balance his scientific zeal with a deeper awareness of the human stain. If indeed Crookman does grow into this kind of awareness, and *Black No More* only hints that he does, he represents most completely of all the characters in the satire the willingness to live and learn in active response to the built-in ambiguities of a democratic nation. With this in mind, his clear association with Schuyler, evident in his skin color, his paradoxical race pride, his background, his affection for rationality, and his attempt to heal through hurt, reflects his corresponding connection with the highest regenerative aims of *Black No More*.

Although the events of *Black No More* only suggest Crookman's growth, they clearly delineate the maturation of the protagonist Max Disher/ Matthew Fisher, who transforms himself from a dapper and slick Harlem striver possessed by a maelstrom of repressed racial resentments into a happier, if not wiser, family man content in his blackness for his hard-won ability to see humanity in what he once regarded as the most remote, superior, and desirable otherness. As a recent migrant from Atlanta and a cutting-edge Harlem sheik, the handsome, upwardly mobile, well-dressed, brown-skinned Max chases "yellow cars, yellow money, and yellow women," which together represent the greatest proximity to whiteness that his ghettoized existence will permit. A paragon of street-level New Negroism, he fetishizes money, race, and sex all at the same time. As a result, he submits himself to excruciating romantic torture in relationships with spoiled light-skinned women who understand all too well their high epidermal value in Harlem's skewed sexual marketplace. The beginning of the satire finds Max paying the price for his obsessions, having been abandoned on New Year's Eve to the company of his buddy Bunny Brown by his high-yellow girlfriend, Minnie. He pays an even higher price inside of the Honky Tonk Club, when the titian-haired white woman of his dreams rebuffs his advances—and defies "the democracy of night life"—despite his best efforts to get close to her. This rejection cuts him even deeper, and etches the color line even more clearly in his mind, for following directly his servile willingness to play the lackey by purchasing liquor for a white male in her party. Angry and confused, Max wonders why whites "didn't want black folks' game but were always frequenting Negro resorts."[21] Soon he would find out that this had something to do with the price they paid for their white masks, which meant little except in comparison to blackness, the very symbol of a freedom that they both desired and despised.

Perhaps it comes as a joke on the whole idea of a democracy of night life that Max, having experienced none, decided that Crookman's chair represented the only way out of the dead end of blackness. After having submitted himself to Crookman's "quiet, swift, efficient, and sinister" treatment, which left him drained and nauseated, Max reflected jubilantly on the vast implications of his rebirth: "There would be no more expenditures for skin whiteners; no more discrimination; no more obstacles in his path. He was free! The world was his oyster and he had the open sesame of pork-colored skin."[22] Max would have to learn slowly that his ordeal of symbolic death and rebirth had not really altered his situation at all; it only made his former living death as a self-hating black man more palpable and obvious.

The first step in this learning process occurs in his encounter with Sybil Smith, a reporter who sits waiting for him in a cab as he emerges from Crookman's laboratory eager to try out his new skin. The date that follows this meeting telescopes neatly all of his future disappointments as a white man even as it adds a few comic twists to his situation. Bored with the white nightclub that they attend and without money, he finds himself unable to command Sybil's serious attentions.[23] Having transformed himself from an exciting and good-looking Harlem "buck" into a standard issue white man, he offers little that the reporter cannot get elsewhere. Also, Sybil's knowledge of his reverse "Oreo" status does little for his romantic chances. To her he remains black on the inside and therefore more of a curiosity than a man.

After providing Sybil with an exclusive story about his racial transformation, Max, who has not yet renamed himself, gets nothing in return but a phone number and a thousand-dollar check from the *Scimitar.* This grants to "William Small" (I am small), the fake name that Max gives to Sybil, a devastatingly personal connotation that goes beyond its obvious ethical and emotional suggestions. The name seems to imply that Dr. Crookman's treatment, which sharpens noses and thins the lips, might be a bit too thorough. Sybil's name also proves broadly symbolic in this direction. An allusion to the Cumean Sybil referred to by the rich freedman and feast giver Trialmachio in *The Satyricon,* this complex name signifies prophesy, the essential unity of life and death, and the braided relationship of impotence and omnipotence. By the time he encountered this immortal witch, Trialmachio says, she had aged so thoroughly that suspended in a glass case and no larger than a worm she could only utter, "I yearn to die."[24]

This allusion reflects more on Max than it does on Sybil, although her cutthroat professionalism, evident in her willingness to exploit Max's pathetic power fantasies, also qualifies well as a thinly masked death wish. Notwithstanding the many connotations that surround this intriguing female character, the most telling suggestion for the encounter of Max and Sybil for the larger meaning of *Black No More* involves the general relationship between difference and desire, especially sexual, racial, and economic desire. Because he understands race in terms of the most extreme difference, and difference stands at the center of what it means to desire, Max conflates racial otherness with all of his deepest wants, especially his craving for sex and superordinance. In other words Max's totalizing relationship to race dictates a certain obsessive desire and yet at the same time appears to defeat the essential differentiation on which desire depends. This places Max between desire and its opposite, thus marking him as a man both living and dead. A walking contradiction in terms, he is at this point in *Black No More* his own comeuppance.

When Max goes back home to Atlanta as Matthew Fisher to pursue his blond object of desire, he follows a retrograde path of reverse migration. Believing that the black man's hell is the white man's heaven, he attempts to move forward by going back, but he finds that as a white man he has to employ the same skills of cunning that he did as a Harlem fire insurance agent in order to get ahead. In fact he finds that in many ways his life as a black man has prepared him to outwit most whites, especially the working-class stiffs of the Knights of Nordica, whom his black background has taught him to despise. Ironically, as a white man Matthew finds greater vent for these "black" feelings than he ever could on the other side of the color line, which offered a much more limited canvas for his schemes. As a white man, Matthew employs his black urban sophistication, which includes an intimate knowledge of the white racist mind-set, in pawning himself off as a New York anthropologist in front of the ignorant Henry Givens. Convinced of Matthew's racist credentials, Givens invites him to speak at an Easter Konklave, where to his delight, he finds Helen sitting in the audience next to her physically repulsive and hopelessly ignorant mother.[25]

Symbolically reborn once again by the sight of Helen, Matthew puts all of his stealth and hatred of the white working class to work for Givens, transforming the Knights of Nordica from a petty scheme to steal the paychecks of its members into a legitimate contender for national power. Having become rich as the Grand Exalted Giraw, and having made Helen's father rich into the bargain, he finds it a simple matter to marry the woman who once made him dream in impotent anger of white men bowing and scraping at his feet. This marriage, which happens on Easter one year after the Konklave speech, represents yet another symbolic rebirth for Matthew.[26] This time, in contrast to his first white rebirth, which places him on the path to power, Matthew's wedding places him on the road to greater self-awareness and greater recognition of the humanity—and blackness—of others.

Much of this has to do with his marriage to Helen, whose name alludes both to Helen of Troy and to Schuyler's light-skinned maternal grandmother, Helen Liedendraught Fischer, from whom he derived his own claim to white ancestry. Although he views his mentally challenged "cracker" wife as an object in the beginning, and thus as a mere appendage of his empire, Matthew eventually realizes just before she gives birth to Matthew Jr. that race has very little meaning in relation to the bond of love that has formed between them over time. This realization, punctuated by Henry Givens's disappointed announcement upon discovering his "true" ancestry—"I guess we're all niggers now!"—sets the blood tie of family, with all of its unruly and sometimes unpalatable racial implications, above the false blood tie of race at the same time that it inaugurates Matthew's life as a mature individual.[27] At this point Black No More can give the impression of putting forth a rather dull and normalizing affirmation of family life somewhat in tension with its more violent satirical aims, but Matthew's continuing trickster status, signified by his susceptibility to the blackness fad and by Crookman's weary smile at the conclusion of the satire, hints at a more consistent interpretive possibility. In the end, one might say, Matthew does not so much transcend his status as a trickster as he matures within it. In broad similarity to Ralph Ellison's epiphany in the New York theater, Matthew advances to an ethical perception of unity within difference; he achieves that sense of democratic hope—inseparable from the ability to face democratic incongruity, imperfection, and even ugliness—that makes it possible through the adoption of a series of experimental second selves to affirm human potential in others.

Matthew's discoveries along these lines stem as much from his engagement with questions of class as they do with issues of gender and race. As the Grand Exalted Giraw of the Knights of Nordica, he learns quickly the relationship between race mythology and the interests of the industrial class, which he takes all the way to the bank. Turning his hatred toward lower-class whites into a virtuoso race-hustling scheme, he uses the Knights of Nordica crusade against Crookman as a powerful lever against his weak-minded charges who value the psychological wage of whiteness above everything they might gain economically from uniting with black workers. Delighted to sell these racist whites down the river, Matthew markets his organization to the white ruling class as the ultimate worker-control mechanism.

When a strike breaks out in Paradise, South Carolina, a depressed mill town owned by two German immigrants named Horzenboff and Blickdoff, Matthew works his plan to perfection. The ethnic identity of these two mill owners highlights the worker/capitalist divide by way of reference to World War I, which according to Schuyler's "Views and Reviews" editorials succeeded only in sacrificing the lives of workers for the enhancement of industrial-class bank accounts. Following this logic, Horzenboff and Blickdoff represent the victory of class interest over national loyalty, which they and their American counterparts manipulate to dupe workers at every turn. This makes the rough treatment they receive at the hands of Matthew, who helps them to maintain their empire, appear ironically appropriate. After intimidating the Germans into paying him $50,000 and sending in his secret agents to agitate among the "undernourished, bony, [and] vacant-looking" workers, Matthew spreads racist propaganda while pretending to support the strike. In the meantime he plants rumors that the leader of the workers, a Westerner appropriately named Swanson (swansong), is really one of Crookman's transformed Negroes. This effectively ends the strike. With this accomplished, Blickdoff and Horzenboff buy off the remaining resistance with such cheap "improvements" as a swimming pool and a shower bath, but they neglect to shorten the workday or increase pay. Although the workers of Paradise suffer objectively from losing their bid for economic fairness, they enjoy a peculiar satisfaction in having won a battle in the larger war to save the white race. In describing their victorious attitude, the narrator adopts a wry but didactic tone: "It did not matter that they had to send their children into the mills to augment the family wage. . . . What mattered such little things when the very foundation of civilization, white supremacy, was threatened?"[28]

Northern "radicals and laborites" enter the scene too late to reverse this damage and prove too "colorblind" to understand the mind-set of the workers. The liberal labor organizer proves so oblivious to the situation in Paradise that he schedules his meeting at Knights of Nordica Hall in complete ignorance of how thoroughly the forces of racism have already trumped his shallow half-stepping unionism. When no one appears, he can do no better than wonder why. When he admits to residing in Harlem, he seals his fate, causing one resident of Paradise to warn that he is not the first "white nigger whut's bin aroun' these parts." The radical labor organizer has an even more difficult time. His Jewish background prevents him from using Knights of Nordica Hall. When a rumor circulates that he is an atheist who wants to divide property and nationalize the women, he admits to the first two charges and laughs at the third. This earns "the disciple of Lenin and Trotsky" an unceremonious ejection from the town with a "crowd of emaciated workers at his heels."[29]

Of all the scenes in *Black No More* the strike in Paradise gives the greatest impression of didacticism. Here Schuyler's socialist politics, which inform several scenes in the satire, make their strongest showing. Yet the failure of the two colorblind organizers to appeal to racist workers carries with it obvious countervailing implications. Rather than a linear reduction of race to class, the scene implies the necessity of a more careful perception of these overlapping social categories based on the empirical realities of American politics. In this way *Black No More* challenges left colorblindness even as it asks its reader to ponder the various forms of class cleavage that contribute to racism. Recognizing this, one might say that it anticipates in its own ironic and refreshingly humorous fashion, what has only recently become a war cry of the multicultural left: "Race matters!"

In fact, race matters so much in *Black No More* that it takes on the quality of an ineradicable American collective psychosis. Dangling somewhere in the space between illusion and reality, it combines easily with other American obsessions—the desire for distinction, wealth, money, conformity, innocence, self-fulfillment, freedom, and equality—in shaping the central conflicts of the national mind-set. Nowhere does this idea come through more powerfully than in *Black No More*'s representation of American politics, which it depicts as a vast democratic cesspool of corruption with the shifting game of black and white at its center. Attorney General

Walter Brybe (Harry M. Dougherty) and head of the Republican National Committee Gorman Gay (William Hays), who both represent major players in the Teapot Dome scandal, make this clear in their willingness to go to the highest bidder among black leaders. This turns out to be Crookman, who pays Brybe to ignore the impassioned letter from Beard and other black leaders demanding an end to his dangerous business dealings.[30] Reminiscent of the letter sent by black leaders requesting an investigation of Marcus Garvey during the "Garvey Must Go Campaign," this moment in the satire combines the idea of black middle-class "race representatives" turning over one of their own to "the Man" with Republican corruption. In this way *Black No More* attempts to undercut simultaneously two forms of traditional black political loyalty: blind devotion to the Party of Lincoln and undue deference to leaders of the race.

Black No More expands its implicit case against the Republicans and against the racism of American politics in general through an extended reference to the presidential election of 1928, when Herbert Hoover succeeded in breaking the "Solid South" by taking several previously impregnable Democratic strongholds. The name for the character representing Hoover, Harold Goosie, alludes directly to this feat, implying that the Republican Hoover flew south like a goose during the election season. In doing so, he followed the dominant strategy of the Republican Party since the end of Reconstruction by colluding with the makers of grandfather clauses and other devices designed to keep blacks as far away from power as possible. As some of the other connotations surrounding the word "goose" might imply, Hoover's ability to woo the southern vote in 1928 derived more from luck than political genius. Mostly he benefited from the inability of Southern Democrats to stomach Al Smith, the Irish Catholic, anti-Prohibitionist machine politician from New York, whose political predicament also plays a role in *Black No More*'s depiction of the race-dominated American political scene of the late 1920s and early 1930s.[31]

Having compromised their appeal to 100 percent Americanism, fundamentalism, and Prohibitionism in nominating Smith as their candidate in 1928, the Democrats rendered themselves practically noncompetitive and left the future of their party in serious doubt.[32] As a joke on the Democratic strategy of 1928, *Black No More* substitutes the Imperial Grand Wizard of the Knights of Nordica for Smith in its version of the election, suggesting that the Democrats might have fared better if they had stayed with their standard appeal to hatred. Also, the substitution of Givens for Smith implicitly comments on the long tradition of northern white ethnics standing in strategic solidarity with the racist status quo of the white South, thus revealing their stubborn unwillingness to regard antiethnic prejudice as a species of the same American xenophobia plaguing their darker counterparts. Unable to claim full "whiteness" and yet unwilling to give up the great American skin game, these ethnics fell victim to forces that made some whites whiter than others. The desperate white-on-white prejudice resulting from the disappearance of the blacks in *Black No More* exaggerates only mildly the social dynamic between white ethnics and the "one-hundred percenters," whom they both despised and supported, mostly at the cost of blacks.

Although the election of 1928 provides the most important reference point for *Black No More*'s improbable but highly realistic portrait of national politics from Coolidge to Hoover, the events surrounding the Democratic Convention of 1924 help to round out a few of its finer points. In that year the Ku Klux Klan parlayed its new position of national prominence into a strong presence at the convention, which took 105 ballots to choose John W. Davis, a compromise candidate whom Calvin Coolidge easily trounced in the ensuing election. Matthew's scheme to run Givens for the presidency in *Black No More* bears a broad similarity to the Klan power grab at this proceeding. Also, the factionalism of Schuyler's fictional convention that nominates Givens alludes directly to the contentious wranglings of the Democrats in 1924. Simeon Dump represents the southern aristocrats, John Whiffle and Bishop Belch stand in for the Drys and the Fundamentalists, Moses Lejewski is a northern ethnic machine politician, and Senator Kretin, the keynote speaker, resembles several racist southern politicians, including Senators Coleman Blease of South Carolina and Francis Vardeman of Mississippi. Unable to select a candidate after twenty ballots, the leaders of the various factions retire to the Judge Lynch Hotel to get drunk and arrive at a compromise. After many hours they still find themselves deadlocked by their motley collection of interests, which render every imaginable candidate unacceptable: "One was too radical, another was too conservative, a third was an atheist, a fourth had once rifled a city treasury, the fifth was of immigrant extraction once removed, a sixth had married a Jewess," and so on.[33] The deadlock provides Matthew with his opportunity. His threat to bolt the convention leads to the nomination of his man Givens for the presidency and Arthur Snobbcraft for vice president.

As part of his two-pronged strategy to win the election for the Democrats, Matthew decides that Givens, the ultimate yokel-charming yokel, should give weekly fire-and-brimstone radio addresses to the nation denouncing Black-No-More Incorporated and rebuking the Goosie administration for refusing to deport its principals. Just before Givens delivers his first long address on the Moronia Broadcasting Company network concerning "the origins of the Republic, anthropology, psychology, miscegenation, cooperation with Christ . . . and many other subjects on which he was totally ignorant," the famous blackface entertainer Jack Albert (Al Jolson) sings his hit song "Vanishing Mammy," accompanied by Sammy Snort and his Bogalusa Babies from the Artillery Café in Chicago. The name "Sam" hints at most of what one needs to know about the band accompanying Albert. Sometimes used as a short substitute for Sambo on the minstrel stage, the name indicates that Snort and his band have only recently become white. Thus the blackfaced Albert, whose race hustle depends on audience awareness of the whiteness beneath his mask, sings to the music of a band whose success depends on concealing a discreditable "real" blackness beneath the skin. Adding to this ludicrous play of racial concealment and exposure, Sammy Snort's band also alludes in an offhand fashion to the exploits of Paul Whiteman, a white jazz musician who managed through superior public relations to become known as the "king of jazz" after playing Gershwin's "Rhapsody in Blue" in a famous Aeolian Hall concert in 1924. Among his many accomplishments, which included a master's knack for removing the "blackness" without completely erasing the jazz, Whiteman also holds the dubious distinction of having written an entire book about jazz without mentioning any black entertainers.[34]

This makes Whiteman, a man whose very name begs for satire, the perfect figure to juxtapose against Al Jolson. Both of these men achieved a level of prominence and wealth that their black counterparts, many of whom surpassed them in talent, could never have dreamed of. This provides the main context for the joke involved in Sammy Snort, who also represents the black bandleader Sammy Stewart, deciding to become white—in effect to become like Whiteman—and procuring a gig on a

national telecast just before the presidential address of a former Klans-
man.[35] All of this plays up the racism of the entertainment industry of
the 1920s, while pointing out a few ironies concerning the American
adoration of black culture. Men like Whiteman and Jolson became famous
out of proportion to their talent by feeding this desire while allaying their
audience's deep fear of becoming black or primitive through excessive
cultural proximity. The play of presence and absence necessary to their
cultural successes, signified in part by Whiteman's exaggerated mask
of white presence juxtaposed against Jolson's dependence on a defining
white absence, mirrors a similar play on the other side of the color line.

In the case of Jack Albert, the concern with presence and absence
takes the form of a strange nervousness about being on the radio. Unable
to gauge the size or racial composition of the unseen millions listening to
the national telecast and incapable of using his mask or his gestures to
communicate with his audience, he must depend exclusively on his all-too-
white-sounding voice. By placing Albert on the radio in this fashion, *Black
No More* playfully inverts the terms of Al Jolson's stratospheric success in
The Jazz Singer, a movie that ironically depicts the Americanization of a
boy from New York's Jewish ghetto in terms of his ability to don a mask
of performative blackness. Symbolically aiding his movement from the
presumably "Jewish" attachment to his father to an "American" attachment to his mother, this mask adds irresistible sentimental punch to
his over-the-top testament of maternal attachment by likening him to a
figure incapable of insincerity due to an almost unfathomable simplicity.
Rendered invisible by the radio, Jolson's *Black No More* counterpart Jack
Albert lacks the proper stage for this kind of performance.[36] Because of
this, he represents perfectly the plight of the nation as it faces the problem of a disappearing black population. Unable to accept black presence,
America also finds it difficult to cope with black absence.

Albert personifies this discomfort in his nervous greeting to the audience: "Oh, hello folks. Awfully glad to see so many of you out there
tonight. Well, that is to say I suppose there are many of you out there. You
know I like to flatter myself, besides I haven't got my glasses so I can't see
very well. However that's not the pint, as the bootleggers say." Given his
situation of unsettling invisibility, when Albert finally gets around to singing "Vanishing Mammy," an entertaining parody of Jolson's "Mammy,"
he appears to be singing for himself. Without depressed and despised

blacks to weep for, his race hustle appears to be in serious danger. Finally Albert, the king of fake sincerity, has a real reason to soak himself in tears. Ironically, this heightens the "soulful" and comic effect of his performance because Albert no longer has to act out his pain.

> I can't help thinkin', Mammy, that you went white
> Of course I can't blame you, Mammy! Mammy! Dear
> You went away, Sweet Mammy! Mammy one summer
> Night
> Because you had so many troubles, Mammy, to bear.[37]

In evoking such figures as Al Jolson and Paul Whiteman, and by placing them in the midst of a complex play of racial mask wearing, *Black No More* accomplishes a deft reversal of the one-drop rule by showing how in the wide-open multiracial arena of American popular culture, the portrayal of the "whitest" white depends on the presence of a crucial drop of black. The implicit criticism of biological racism central to the satire follows a similar logic. Here the dream of pure whiteness gets exposed for its self-undermining dependence on an equally unsustainable and nonsensical notion of pure blackness. This captures in a neat fashion the essential dualism of Dr. Crookman. By eliminating blackness, he appears to commit an act of symbolic genocide against his own people, but he also makes a similar threat to whites and to the whole dream of superiority by decent.

Something analogous occurs in the case of the aristocratic genealogical researcher Samuel Buggerie, except in his case the revelation of racial impurity occurs as the unintended result of trying to rescue the racial binary from Crookman's onslaught. Appropriately, Buggerie's description in the satire alludes to a number of race pseudoscientists, especially Walter A. Plecker, the researcher most closely associated with a series of race integrity bills that passed the Virginia state legislature in the late 1920s and early 1930s. Reflecting Schuyler's vast storehouse of aggression toward figures like Plecker, Buggerie appears in *Black No More* as "a ponderous, nervous, entirely bald, specimen of humanity, with thick moist hands, a receding double chin and very prominent eyes" that shift about in perpetual wonderment behind big, horn-rimmed spectacles. Vastly overweight and possessing a squeaky voice, Buggerie gives the distinct impression of a man incapable of concealment. His rotund body bursts out of his clothes and his pockets bulge with papers and notes. As in the case of Sammy Snort, Buggerie's first name offers a strong hint concerning the researcher's true pedigree. Although he counts himself among the first families of Virginia, Buggerie is by virtue of the one-drop rule a black person. His own research proves this. Upon completing his study, the shocked researcher admits to his partner in crime, the suspiciously dark Virginia aristocrat Arthur Snobbcraft, that the illegitimate daughter of his great-great-grandfather—who had his ears cropped for nonpayment of debts and spent time in jail for thievery—had married a free black veteran of the Revolutionary War.[38]

While Schuyler flirts with the question of homosexuality and male desire throughout *Black No More*, especially in such dyadic pairings as Max/Bunny and Horzenboff/Blickdoff, he makes it an explicit matter in the case of his data-gathering aristocrat. The last name Buggerie not only refers directly to anal sex, but its connection to the archaic English word for the act implies an association with white upper-class decadence and the inability to reproduce and pass down a tradition.[39] Buggerie's homosexuality also represents for Schuyler the ultimate fate of all inbred fantasies of racial dominion, which can never stand against the superior strength of intermixture, crossbreeding, and open adjustment to ever-changing circumstance.

The centrality of Buggerie to the antigenealogical purpose of *Black No More*—which Schuyler dedicated to "all Caucasians in the great republic who can trace their ancestry back ten generations and confidently assert that there are no Black leaves, twigs, limbs or branches on their family trees"—becomes even more apparent upon consideration of the researcher's somewhat doubtful publication list, which includes "The Fluctuation of the Sizes of Left Feet among the Assyrians during the Ninth Century before Christ," "The Incidence of Psittacosis among the Hiphopa Indians of the Amazon Valley and Its Relation to Life Insurance Rates in the United States," and "Putting Wasted Energy to Work."[40] While the first two studies focus on anthropological topics, the last makes a case for harnessing the energy produced by leaves rubbing against each other in the wind. Although this topic appears random and ridiculous, it does bear a relationship to *Black No More*'s dedication. Instead of the relatively neat and highly stratified relationship between limbs, twigs, and branches, it implies that heredity and human sexuality more closely resemble the random rubbing of leaves tossed in the wind.

Just as Buggerie's study proves finally and fully the ridiculousness of his eugenicist schemes, it sets the stage for his cruel demise. Along with Snobbcraft, Buggerie meets his ironic fate at the hands of lower-class whites whose sterilization he would have gladly approved. To add to the irony, both Buggerie and Snobbcraft die in blackface, having disguised themselves to avoid the ugly consequences of being recognized in Happy Hill, Mississippi, as traitors to the Democratic Party and to the white race. When their feeble effort at protective coloration fails, *Black No More* suddenly switches from humor to an almost gothic description of a lynching. This disturbing description, which parodies the many grizzly accounts of such events published by investigators like Walter White and Ida Wells Barnett, derives its power from the juxtaposition of passionate, ritualistic, and primitive bloodlust with a calculating, clinical rhetoric of surgery and dissection: "The two men, vociferously protesting, were stripped naked, held down by husky and willing farm hands and their ears and genitals cut off with jack knives amid the fiendish cries of men and women. When this crude surgery was completed, some wag sewed their ears to their backs and they were released and told to run. Eagerly, in spite of their pain, both men tried to avail themselves of the opportunity. Anything was better than this. Staggering forward through an opening made in the crowd, they attempted to run down the dusty road, blood streaming down their bodies. They had only gone a few feet when, at a signal from [Reverend McPhule], a half-dozen revolvers cracked and the two Virginians pitched forward into the dust amid the uproarious laughter of the congregation."[41]

Here, where the characters of *Black No More* begin to laugh, the readers of the satire feel least inclined to follow suit. With the issues of laughter and blackface in the forefront of the scene, the lynching of Snobbcraft and Buggerie takes on the appearance of a strange and twisted minstrel show at the same time that it highlights the issue of racial violence. In this connection one might see the two unfortunate Virginia aristocrats as symbolic minstrels killed off by the cruelty of a race-hating audience. As it switches in this scene from a lighthearted Horatian mode to Juvenalian invective, *Black No More* declares its distance from the creations of the minstrel stage, whose conventions and gestures it had employed up to that point as part of its comic formula. At the same time, just when the audience of the satire feels least inclined to laugh, the violent origins of

Schuyler's method become clear. Thus one might say that in exposing the laughing savagery of Happy Hill, Mississippi, the satirist uncovers his own claws and fangs.

After the death of Snobbcraft and Buggerie, the image of white tribal savagery in *Black No More* becomes even more intense as the mutilation continues. Little boys and girls bring twigs and small branches while their fathers fetch logs and anything else that will burn. As the bodies of Buggerie and Snobbcraft fry in the laughing flames, the odor of "cooking meat" distends guilty nostrils. Among the guilty stand a few beneficiaries of Crookman's formula. Remembering the pain they suffered during their former days as black victims of American democracy, they wanted to help the two unfortunate racists; but fearing for their lives they joined the rest in prodding and casting stones at the burning bodies. They could not afford for the white mob to think of them as anything else but "one-hundred-per-cent Americans."[42] Thus the two men who thought themselves to represent most perfectly the ideal of pure Americanism, who once believed that they possessed "no Black leaves, twigs, limbs or branches on their family trees" are consumed in the flames produced by the branches, twigs, and dismembered trees that represent best the falsehood and the continuing power of their hateful vision.

Despite its powerful message, and in another sense because of it, those who view objectivity and rational distance as primary virtues of successful satire might rank this scene as one of *Black No More*'s more obvious failures. Such readers might cite its heavy-handed polemics against savage lynchers, minstrelsy, religion, and "one-hundred-percent Americanism," along with the exaggeratedly melodramatic demise of the two "bad guys," as sure evidence of a satire gone awry, spoiled by its author's self-indulgent surrender to moralistic anger and revenge. Yet without denying altogether the force of this criticism, we might acknowledge in *Black No More*'s Happy Hill episode elements that complicate the picture. Unlike conventional depictions of racially motivated mob violence, the lynching episode in *Black No More* blurs the line between black and white, in the case of both the perpetrators and the victims. Also, the scene suspends readers somewhere between sympathy for the unfortunate victims and identification with the persecutors, who send Snobbcraft and Buggerie to their just reward. By blurring the lines in this way, *Black No More* takes the emphasis off of the pathetic black victims obsessively depicted in newspapers, novels, and NAACP pamphlets and places it more squarely on the larger human problem of lynching, which it dramatizes most effectively by causing revulsion for the execution of two men for whom such a pun-ishment might seem most poetically appropriate.

In taking the emphasis off of black victimhood, *Black No More* at-tempts to avoid the inadvertent boost to white feelings of superiority, and the diminishment of black self-confidence, inherent in the promotion of melodramatic narratives of unopposed white power and unrelieved black suffering. By focusing more sharply on the stupidity of the mob than on its power and on the complicity of whites and blacks in the perpetuation of racial violence, the Happy Hill episode in *Black No More* makes a com-plicating and controversial commentary on the discourse of lynching. In this sense it promotes the larger message of *Black No More* even as it departs from the satire's prevailing jovial mood.

The temptation to cry out for closure in the presence of such obvious evils as lynching may well prove impossible to resist. And yet a full understand-ing of such an evil, which would accompany any truly ethical judgment concerning its final meaning, requires the recognition of the complex and contingent humanity of both the perpetrators and the victims. This kind of openness may well be the most difficult challenge of an ethical life. Maintaining it always comes with a certain fear of association with the very evils one is attempting to understand. By itself, satire cannot provide all of the necessary prerequisites for such an understanding. It depends too heavily on caricature and wild juxtaposition to accomplish this end. Nor can it inspire the will to face fully what it highlights so effectively: our umbilical connection to the ludicrous and nonsensical aspects of exis-tence. Yet no mode of literature provides a better set of tools for pointing out how profoundly evil can fall short of profundity. For some readers this will always cause discomfort or disappointment. One measure of human perversity is our desire to seek a certain compensation from destructive forces, to find a strange comfort in attributing to them a depth that they do not always have. Like anything else, evil can be disappointingly paltry.

Ignoring this, one would miss much concerning the distinctive char-acter of a democratic evil like American racism, which places the com-monest of men absolutely above other common men in part to soften the deeply disturbing implications of equality for all. One major part of

American national ideology insists on democratic equality; yet another encourages individual opportunity to achieve wealth and social distinction. But what does striving for distinction amount to if one remains equal to the worst of one's countrymen? In Schuyler's day American society answered this question in part by erecting an aristocracy of commoners ordained by birth to compete and to rise in a land of promise. Below these common aristocrats it subsumed another group on which it projected all of the deepest and most quotidian American fears and desires, almost all of them involving characteristics antithetical to achieving status and wealth. The most extreme of these fears involved limitation by virtue of birth and descent, a condition that American law and custom imposed on blacks with a hypocritical and self-righteous cruelty. What should the lonely democrat do in the face of such cruelty? Should he shake with anger? Should he tremble with fear? Or should he laugh? In *Black No More*, George Schuyler laughs for all of the best and most disturbing reasons. By joining him, we affirm the potential that still remains hidden in the American way of life.

Epilogue

SINCERITY, AUTHENTICITY, AND RACE

THE IDEA OF AMERICA as a good and exceptional nation—synonymous with its symbolic status as a haven for individual aspiration—has always carried with it an implicit commitment to sincerity as a mark of personal virtue. This powerful, popular, and paradoxical version of national ideology imagines American freedom as a function of each individual pursuing his or her "dream" or truest self, whose achievement presumably corresponds with the deepest existential contentment. The peculiar value of the sincere individual to this framework derives precisely from an insistence on the oneness of avowal and actual feeling; or, in other words, from the heartfelt confirmation of the very idea of a "true" self. A successful performance in this direction brings together a complex constellation of such values as earnestness, seriousness, sympathy, and simplicity, but it must avoid at all cost even the mildest brush with irony. Above all else, the sincere individual must say what he feels, feel what he says, and make a convincing show of it.[1]

Because it cruelly complicates the case for a good and exceptional America, the race question has always presented a problematic stage for the performance of "true" American selfhood. This nagging question brings freedom and slavery, equality and mastery, justice and injustice, the American past and the American future into uncomfortable and ironic relation. Nowhere does the sincere American—black or white, racist or colorblind—seem less at one with himself than in the face of these difficulties. Yet on the ground where he finds himself most challenged, this type appears to redouble his efforts. His affirming and comforting symbolic role takes on its greatest importance where the larger narrative it depends on loses credibility. Perhaps this is why sincerity holds such a central place in the American racial imagination. By portraying ourselves as sincere advocates of "blackness" or "whiteness," as honest uplifters sympathetic with black suffering, or as earnest and determined crusaders for equality and freedom, we preserve in the presence of highly compromising complexities the precious idea that we can still be true to ourselves. Nevertheless, it remains in question whether in portraying ourselves so sincerely we do not make it more difficult to be ourselves; whether in showing, and even in having, that we do not undermine being.

In *Sincerity and Authenticity* the critic Lionel Trilling grants sincerity the broadest possible meaning, placing it at the very origin of contemporary conceptions of selfhood, society, and literature. According to Trilling, the sincere posture arose when social mobility became a central feature of Western collective life in the sixteenth and early seventeenth centuries. The ability to move from one class to another provided the basis for both the rise of the modern individual and the invention of society. It also created the possibility of pretending to be above one's rightful place in the class hierarchy. Trilling associates the origin of the modern concept of villainy, and by implication the birth of the melodramatic "bad guy," to this kind of fakery and to the fear of social instability surrounding it. The dangerous distance between what one is and what one pretends to be also implied the opposite: that the individual could and should be true to herself and that she could do this by portraying herself ardently and honestly to others. This new conception of veracity as a mark of personal virtue took the dynamic arena of society as its stage and its testing ground. The individual and society stood coterminous, the truth of one essential to the goodness of the other, joined-at-the-hip allies in the battle against tradition. On the vast intellectual family tree of sincerity, Trilling locates many variants of the theme over a span of more than two hundred years, from the Puritans to the Enlightenment to the Romantics. He finds sincerity fundamental to the posture of the social reformer, the revolutionary, the autobiographer, and to the modern obsession with the question of individual and group identity.[2] One imagines that in all of this Trilling might have said much more about America, a great nation born amid the forces that he defines so carefully. Yet he leaves the deep mark of sincerity on the origin of American collective identity as one of the myriad implications of his highly suggestive analysis.

Although it has never entirely disappeared as an important value in the West, sincerity began to lose ground in the late nineteenth century, when thinkers began to assert a deep and abiding opposition between the self and society. From this simple suspicion—which takes seriously the power of such forces as political propaganda, bureaucratic standardization, democratic conformity, normalizing convention, the machine, and the media to undermine individual autonomy—Trilling derives the value of authenticity. In making their case against the naiveté of the sincere "honest soul" who loses himself in the quest for recognition, the advocates of authenticity posited a "disintegrated self" who employed masks and personas to defend the strength and solidity of being so obviously lacking in their earnest but wildly dishonest contemporaries. On the way to defining authenticity, Trilling names a long line of thinkers and writers from Nietzsche, Wilde, and Freud to the modernists of the 1920s and 1930s, each of whom made distinctive contributions to its rise as an important contemporary value; but he provides the best sense of the concept in pointing out the ridiculousness of questioning the sincerity of a figure like Abraham. Whatever one might think of him, Trilling says, one must begin with the fact that the patriarch Abraham simply "was," that the source of his being had little to do with social recognition. On a different register one might say something similar in speaking of anyone experiencing a thought or feeling of his own without reference to how he might look to others. This person "is" in a way that the sincere individual precludes himself from achieving even in his most private moments.[3]

Although Trilling could have written a penetrating and broad analysis of the wider cultural impact of authenticity, he maintains a careful and concise focus on the intellectual realm. Although he makes several trenchant observations concerning nonliterary authenticity, he remains most interested in the emergence of the modern author, for whom "being" constitutes a defining crusade. At the center of this quest a polemical antagonism to social convention, conformity, economic regimentation, indeed any force giving the remote appearance of threatening the ability of the individual to recognize her own elemental strength, drives a violent will to portray what remains incomplete, incongruous, and horrible in the everyday, the normal, and the well-regulated. This destructive urge also extends to widely accepted conventions of selfhood, especially the ones that offer a fundamental role to conceptions of recognition. As a result, the authentic modern writer typically presents herself to her reader as an author rather than a person. Married to irony, she privileges art and play as the only legitimate vehicles of social perception and remains ever suspicious of beauty, aesthetic pleasure, and easy forms of closure, all of which she eschews in attempting to augment her reader's "sentiment of being." Imperious and alienated, staked on ugliness, terror, and the peculiar possibilities of the well-told lie, this author may be a fascist bent on domination or a tough-minded democrat standing guard against democracy's peculiar threat to equality and individual freedom. Either way she stands solidly with being as her animating faith and as her primary creative charge against modernity's tendency to undermine the very foundation of individual existence.

The quest for authenticity becomes an important American literary value in the nineteenth century but attains prominence in the 1920s, when an unprecedented range of literary and cultural projects from modernism to journalistic debunking carried on a broad and many-sided counterattack against increasingly sophisticated encroachments on the "sentiment of being." In its most fundamental inspiration the Harlem Renaissance participated in this rebellion. Rooted in a positive revaluation of black alienation, it set urban sophistication and authenticity against an older code that conceived of black exclusion in terms of congenital subordination, deformity, and aberration. At their best the artists of the Harlem Renaissance succeeded in employing the idea of alienation successfully in achieving unprecedented inclusion within a cultural mainstream increasingly enamored of the ethical necessity of the outsider. Ironically, this strategy also tended to lock these artists more securely within their "blackness" and into a countervailing posture of sincerity based in the avowal of the "honest soul" claiming to represent the genuine feeling of his group. This posture, which gives the impression of artists *playing* themselves rather than *being* themselves, grants the typical artistic expression of the Harlem Renaissance a certain counterfeit quality, especially from the perspective of those who suspect sincerity and embrace authenticity as a central aesthetic value. This suspicion stands behind the tendency among some current critics to denounce the Harlem Renaissance as a fad or a vogue marked by a distinct absence of self-possession. Other current critics, influenced in one way or another by the postmodern attack on authenticity, have sought to celebrate the inauthentic qualities of the period.[4] For them finding hybridity, transgression, and stealthily ironic opposition to all essentialisms in the cultural expression of the Harlem Renaissance amounts to a rejection of both the naiveté of the "honest soul" and the alienated quest for "being."

As this book has amply demonstrated, George Schuyler stands out as a central figure for any critic interested in taking such an approach to black culture during the 1920s. His emphasis on biting ironic humor, cultural and biological transgression of conventional racial codes, social and metaphysical relativism, tricksterism, shifting ideological standpoints, interpretive freedom, and play serves to make this point. Yet it remains important to notice the centrality of authenticity to Schuyler's aims. Above all else he sought to augment the "sentiment of being" both for himself and for his audience, especially his black audience, whose fundamental sense of strength, solidity, and efficacy required in his view a sophisticated cultivation of alienation against racist conventionality. Schuyler's concern with the black inferiority complex, evident in his criticism of hair straightening, skin lightening, petty squabbling among black leaders, the "ostrich attitude," crowd-mindedness, gullibility, and other manifestations of black self-effacement reflects this aim most clearly. At the same time Schuyler sought to avoid the vortex of sincere racial feeling, which did little more than substitute a black conventionality for the stultifying values of the American mainstream that blacks could not join. For Schuyler strong and principled black political struggle required authentic black individuality, and this necessitated the rejection of sentiment and morality. Something similar held true for American whites, whose sincerity-laced racism reflected for Schuyler a serious deficit of "being" stemming from the tendency of democracy and capitalism to undermine the very individualism that they make possible.

The characteristics that Trilling attributes to the authentic author play a central role in Schuyler's work. The mask, rhetorical violence, irony, the disintegrated self, the rejection of beauty, the emphasis on incongruity, shifting perspectives, and the exposure of the reader to discomforting truth all figure in his iconoclastic assault on the racial standards of his day. In delineating Schuyler's quest for authenticity, this book has placed particular emphasis on his constant resistance to the melodramatic victim/ hero formula. Against the melodramatic affection for stark opposition, Schuyler signified openly and playfully, often vilifying and praising the same people, both black and white. As a counterbalance to sentimental earnestness and seriousness, he offered wide-ranging laughter. He took special pleasure in deflating, among the many targets of this laughter, the exaggerated larger-than-life expectations of the melodramatic mind-set. As an alternative he offered a deflating jocular realism that seized particularly on the all-too-human ridiculousness of those who sought to impose their unexamined beliefs on others.

In offering his alternative to race melodrama, Schuyler took the space between desire and reality, and between truth and falsehood, as a playing field for a game of freedom. In this game a winner could temporarily grasp the prize, but only by recognizing the constant possibility of loss and the ever-present requirement of risk. Because Schuyler viewed matters this way, he never offered his truth as The Truth, nor did he attempt to indoctrinate or to develop followers by promising happy endings or safe havens of moral certitude. Although he enjoyed dismissing his enemies as fools, rubes, and petty thieves, he rejected the moralism of the melodramatic attack. However much he denounced an adversary, Schuyler avoided casting him as immoral or evil. At the same time he attacked his opponents with ruthless abandon, in part to challenge the tendency toward sentimental falsehood and politeness that interfered with forthright and vigorous exchange. In advancing this aspect of his mission, he often bragged of his own violation of conventional morality—his affection for sex, his adoration of alcohol, his disdain for religion—to place a sharp point on how far he stood from the high horse of decency.

In expressing his challenge to "think," along with most of his other ideas, as advice for fools, Schuyler intended to antagonize his audience even as he provided instruction. Although his effort to upset his readers often polarized them, it provided one of the satirist's main weapons in severing the powerful emotional circuit of suffering, revenge, and guilt at the heart of race melodrama. By ridiculing almost everyone, including those who read his work, and by making himself a focus for aggressive feelings, Schuyler created his own emotional circuit aimed at diffusing the bad feelings emanating from racial polarization through redeployment, deflection, and recirculation. In this way he hoped to dissipate racial antipathy, both within and between the races, through a method of confrontation and distortion. Thus even his most hateful and devastating thrusts reflect an overriding concern with healing and hope.

To appreciate fully Schuyler's relevance to current concerns, we must recognize the continuing importance of melodrama as a fundamental grammar of the American race discourse. We need to look no further than the O. J. Simpson trial, the Clarence Thomas hearings, the public fascination with Mike Tyson, the Kobe Bryant trial, or the alarm among contemporary cultural critics over "gangsta" rap to ascertain the continuing importance of the black villain/rapist figure. Black victimhood still makes a strong showing in discussions of reparations and the underclass, and in the contentious debate over affirmative action, especially in the efforts of conservatives to avoid "by any means necessary" the devastating force of the melodramatic equation of goodness and suffering. The affirmative action debate also provides good evidence of how strongly the idea of white victimhood still grips the meritocratic American mind. At its extreme paranoid fantasies of white victimhood and revenge still stand at the center of virulently racist imaginations, even as they animate the secret resentments of some liberal whites who nonetheless feel unjustified in giving full-throated expression to their feelings. Ideas of unmitigated black heroism also continue to play an important role in contemporary accounts of the black experience. They make their appearance at every Martin Luther King Day celebration, just as they inform the most common versions of the civil rights narrative, the black migration narrative, and other black appropriations of the more general American story of progress.

Still, it remains important to recognize that the tradition of protest against racial injustice owes much to the imaginative use of melodrama. The dramatization of black suffering—from the NAACP antilynching campaigns of the early twentieth century to Martin Luther King Jr.'s direct nonviolence campaigns in the 1960s—has served this tradition well as a way to justify claims against the system. When action based on these claims has forced social and legal change, it has undeniably advanced American democracy. Nevertheless, we might ponder the costs of victories won through dependence on race melodrama. However much the use of this mode forces whites to sympathize with the black struggle for freedom, it remains difficult to imagine how an emphasis on black suffering can avoid placing a heavy focus on white power and white evil. Melodramatic narratives of black victimhood, black righteousness, and black political action on behalf of racial justice can hardly exist without narratives that cast whites the same way. An atmosphere filled with black and white counternarratives can hardly fail to inspire deep paranoia even as it produces many genuine examples of interracial sympathy and compassion. We might well wonder whether such compassion could ever prove strong enough to crowd paranoia out of the picture. Given the circular logic of race melodrama, this appears unlikely.

Although virulent racism makes a much less prominent appearance in our post–civil rights period than it did in Schuyler's day, we may be just as vulnerable as previous generations to the bifurcating effects of racial melodrama. For Schuyler, and for many critics and artists of his era, the faith in authenticity, rooted in the quest for a critical and individualistic "outside," provided a beachhead against this powerful force. Today, this faith—for all of its investment in irony and complexity—seems a bit old-fashioned, even quaint. Across a great range of positions, some popular and others more intellectual, some political and others more strictly cultural, our era makes its most distinctive mark in rejecting the tough-minded sacrificial alienation of the authentic individual as antisocial, imperialistic, repressed, or just plain untenable. Most typically the individual of our era makes no effort to hold out for a "sentiment of being" against powerful social forces. Instead, he attempts to gain feelings of strength, hope, and efficacy by turning the self outward toward the world. In this way he represents a return of Trilling's sincere self, but with a crucial difference: Rather than naively expecting a coherent social world to affirm him, this self assumes a fractured world of fractured relations presenting multiple possibilities for identification and recognition. He may commit himself to healing one or another of these fractures, stake himself with steely resolve on an all-or-nothing identification with a particular group or crowd, or simply take advantage of the many possibilities for self-expansion and expression in assuming different masks at different moments. Regardless of his particular strategy, this self makes his most important exchanges in the currency of desire. Unable to depend on agreement concerning grounding categories, he employs a language of compassion and victimhood, sympathy and disrespect, love and rejection to talk across an ever-increasing range of social divisions. This language easily translates into the more specialized terms of melodrama, especially when the social division at issue has the deeply rooted historical and ethical qualities of the race question.

Even in his most skeptical and antisocial guise as the multiple, alienated postmodern subject—where he makes his closest approach to authenticity and his greatest attack on simplifying melodramatic binaries—the inauthentic self of our time still affirms the supreme value of feeling, especially when it derives from rule- and frame-breaking encounters with the irrational or the fantastic. Because of this, he can often give the impression of even greater imperious self-insistence than his modernistic predecessor. In the race discourse the emphasis on tricksterism, hybridity, the signifyin' complexity of the black vernacular, and multiple subject positions all originate in one way or another with the attempt to liberate desire from the constraining effects of race ideology. George Schuyler owes most of his contemporary resonance to the currency of such positions. And yet he also derives some of his claim to our attention from the way he disagrees with them. Schuyler's quirky, stubborn, and unapologetic defense of his own being, evident in his aggressive opposition to all crowds whether mainstream or marginal, provides a particularly cathartic example for an era that feels keenly the value of selfhood but finds that value increasingly difficult to establish within a fractured and confusing array of group identities and social forces. The ethical weight of the race question only adds to this difficulty. Schuyler fought his battle for authenticity on this ground and comes down to us today as one who at his best employed multilayered complexity in simply being himself. This recommends him most strongly to us. George Schuyler has his greatest current value in running against the grain of our time, as he ran against the grain of his own.

NOTES

ABBREVIATIONS

BC: George S. Schuyler, *Black and Conservative* (New Rochelle, N.Y.: Arlington House, 1966)

BNM: George S. Schuyler, *Black No More: Being an Account of the Strange and Wonderful Workings of Science in the Land of the Free, A.D. 1933–1940* (Boston: Northeastern University Press, 1989)

GSSP/NY: The George S. Schuyler Family Papers, Manuscripts, Archives and Rare Books Division, The Schomburg Center for Research in Black Culture, New York Public Library, New York

GSSP/SU: The George S. Schuyler Papers, George Arents Research Library, Syracuse University, Syracuse, N.Y.

HLMP: The Henry Louis Mencken Papers, New York Public Library, New York

JSD: The Josephine Cogdell Diary, The Josephine Cogdell Schuyler Papers, Manuscripts, Archives and Rare Books Division, The Schomburg Center for Research in Black Culture, New York Public Library, New York

JWJP: The James Weldon Johnson Papers, Miscellaneous Correspondence, Beinecke Rare Book and Manuscript Library, Yale University, New Haven, Conn.

LHP: The Langston Hughes Papers, Beinecke Rare Book and Manuscript Library, Yale University, New Haven, Conn.

SS: The George S. Schuyler Scrapbook, The George S. Schuyler Papers, George Arents Research Library, Syracuse University, Syracuse, N.Y.

TL: George S. Schuyler, "Thrusts and Lunges," *Pittsburgh Courier*

VR: George S. Schuyler, "Views and Reviews," *Pittsburgh Courier*

CHAPTER 1: THE PROBLEM OF GEORGE S. SCHUYLER

1. Andrew Buni, *Robert L. Vann of "The Pittsburgh Courier": Politics and Black Journalism* (Pittsburgh: University of Pittsburgh Press, 1974), 137, 171, 325–326.

2. Altogether Schuyler published fifteen articles in the *American Mercury.* Two of these appeared in the late 1920s, eight in the 1930s, two in the 1940s, and three in the 1950s. He also published three times in the *Nation* during the 1920s and twice in *Modern Quarterly* in the same decade; Lewis, a native of Baltimore, was the theater critic for the *Messenger.* Like Schuyler, Lewis had no formal training, but his native intelligence and deep interest in his field made him the best authority on the theater among the black intellectuals of the Harlem Renaissance.

3. H. L. Mencken, *The American Language* (New York: Knopf, 1945), 619, note 1; H. L. Mencken to Blanche Knopf, 7 July 1937, in *Letters of H. L. Mencken,* ed. Guy J. Forgue (New York: Knopf, 1961), 419. Mencken repeats this praise in many other places. See also H. L. Mencken, entry 11 October 1945, in *The Diary of H. L. Mencken,* ed. Charles A. Fechner (New York: Knopf, 1989), 383.

4. The term "Aframerican" was originally coined by James Weldon Johnson. Instead of using race as the defining category, "Aframerican" employs geography, pointing to black people's origin in Africa and their continuing existence in America as a mixed race. Although Johnson coined the term, and Tolson employed it, Schuyler probably put it to the most extensive use of any writer in the period: Melvin B. Tolson, "George S. Schuyler," *American Mercury* 28 (1933): 373–374.

5. The pseudonyms include Samuel I. Brooks, Rachel Call, Edgecombe Wright, William Stockton, Verne Caldwell, Rachel Love, John Kitchen, and D. Johnson. Schuyler also published stories under his own name and on many occasions published anonymously. Robert A. Hill and R. Kent Rasmussen, "Bibliography: George S. Schuyler's 'Pittsburgh Courier' Fiction, 1933–1939," in *Black Empire,* by George S. Schuyler (Boston: Northeastern University Press, 1991), 337–344. See also Hill and Rasmussen, afterword to *Black Empire,* 259–323; and Robert A. Hill, introduction to *Ethiopian Stories,* by George S. Schuyler (Boston: Northeastern University Press, 1994), 1–50.

6. George S. Schuyler, "King No Help to Peace," *Manchester Union Leader,* 10 November 1964.

7. John H. Sengstacke, owner of the *Chicago Defender* and nephew of Robert S. Abbot, founder of the *Defender,* bought the *Pittsburgh Courier* in 1966 from the Republican businessman S. B. Fuller and gave it a much-needed reorganization. Schuyler was one of the first victims of Sengstacke's efforts.

8. The Conservative Party was started in 1960 by two Wall Street lawyers who were impressed by what they saw as Nelson Rockefeller's dilution of true Republican principles. See Daniel Mahoney, *Actions Speak Louder* (New Rochelle, N.Y.: Arlington House, 1968).

9. In his autobiography Schuyler claims to have been a little misunderstood in this matter. When the interviewer asked him about voting for Goldwater, he

NOTES TO PAGES 5–11   257

answered that he always supported the Republican candidate and would support Goldwater despite the candidate's flaws. BC, 349; George S. Schuyler to Elanor Lofton, 13 August 1964, GSSP/SU; quoted in Harry McKinley Williams, "When Black Is Right: The Life of George S. Schuyler" (Ph.D. diss., Brown University, 1988), 362. "Don't send": Williams, "When Black Is Right," 363.

10. "saw red": Reflecting on two radio shows they did together in 1963, writer John A. Williams remarked: "He'd call anyone a communist and even when I rebutted him with facts certifying the contrary, he never let up. He'd just sit back and smile." Williams also implied that Schuyler acted as an informer for the FBI during the 1950s and 1960s in Africa. Williams, foreword to *Black Empire*, by George S. Schuyler, ed. Hill and Rasmussen, x. Schuyler wrote a tribute to Senator McCarthy in VR, 18 May 1957. Three years later he received a letter from the senator's wife thanking him. Williams, "When Black Is Right," 348.

11. "fifty articles": BC, 243; George S. Schuyler, "The Phantom American Negro," *The Freeman* 23 (1951): 457–459; Williams, "When Black Is Right," 341–342.

12. Westbrook Pegler, "Whites Should Read This Negro Writer," *New York Journal American*, 24 July 1961. Pegler was himself one of the great Red-baiters of the post–World War II period. "Opposing philosophy": John P. Diggins, *Up from Communism: Conservative Odysseys in American Intellectual History* (New York: Harper, 1975). For a fuller discussion of the literature on Schuyler, see Jeffrey B. Ferguson, "The Newest Negro: George S. Schuyler's Intellectual Quest in the 1920s and Beyond" (Ph.D. diss., Harvard University, 1998), 90–113.

13. For a thoughtful discussion of the general issue of distortion in black autobiography in relation to Ralph Bunche and other figures, see Nathan Huggins, "Black Biography: Reflections of a Historian," in *Revelations: American History, American Myths,* ed. Brenda Smith Huggins (New York: Oxford University Press, 1995), 94–99.

14. Schuyler's maternal grandmother, Helen Louisa Leidendraught Fischer, of whom he writes lovingly in "Black Art," *American Mercury* 27 (1932): 335–342, was born in New Jersey in the 1830s, the daughter of a slave woman from Madagascar and a German sea captain. Born 28 February 1860, his mother was one of eleven children, and his father, George Francis Schuyler, was born in 1846 in Troy, New York. "Blood relation to his parents": BC, 8; Williams, "When Black Is Right," 5; "meaning for him": BC, 8, 9.

15. BC, 10–11.

16. "America's wars": BC, 47–48; Schuyler reports that he graduated grammar school with a 98 average: BC, 18, 26; "lessons": George S. Schuyler, "Some Unsweet Truths about Race Prejudice," in *Behold America!* ed. Samuel D. Schmalhausen (New York: Farrar and Reinhart, 1931), 88.

17. "obvious authority" and "uninviting lot": BC, 47–48.

18. "appreciate them": Williams, "When Black Is Right," 31. After Schuyler
    finished his first enlistment in 1915, he worked for five months on a military
    transport operating between Hawaii and points east, such as Tokyo, Shang-
    hai, Hong Kong, Guam, and the coast of China. This further increased his
    travel experience and, after a while, contributed to his decision to reenlist.
    William Ingersol, "The Reminiscences of George S. Schuyler," Oral History
    Collection of Columbia University, New York, 1960, 36–43. These three
    stories appear in SS, GSSP/SU, vol. 2.

19. "but himself": BC, 47. The U.S. Army established the segregated officer
    training camp at Camp Des Moines twelve weeks after the declaration of
    war against Germany. Initially many black leaders reacted to this move
    with outrage but eventually cooler—some might say less-principled—heads
    prevailed. At its height the camp had twelve hundred recruits being drilled
    by eighty black noncommissioned officers. Schuyler drilled the Eleventh
    Regiment. By October 1917, 622 officers, including Schuyler, were com-
    missioned. Because the least educated received preference for appointment,
    many black observers feared foul play. Because he shared this opinion,
    Schuyler must have received his promotion with a healthy dose of irony.
    David Levering Lewis, *When Harlem Was in Vogue* (New York: Oxford
    University Press, 1981), 9–12. See also Williams, "When Black Is Right,"
    35–36.

20. Katherine Talalay, *Composition in Black and White: The Life of Philippa
    Schuyler* (New York: Oxford University Press, 1995), 65–68; and also JSD,
    1 January 1928.

21. BC, 93.

22. George S. Schuyler, "From Job to Job: A Personal Narrative," *The World
    Tomorrow* 6 (1923): 147–148; BC, 100–110; George S. Schuyler, "Memoirs
    of a Pearl Diver," *American Mercury* 22 (1931): 487–496.

23. BC, 96–98, 113.

24. BC, 114–115.

25. George S. Schuyler, "A Tribute to Caesar," *Messenger* 6 (1924): 423–432;
    BC, 119–124.

26. A. Philip Randolph and Chandler Owen started the Friends of Negro Free-
    dom in May 1920 to conduct political and labor forums for the education of
    the masses across the United States. The organization never had national ap-
    peal, however. Eventually it became a private intellectual forum for Randolph
    and the friends of the *Messenger*, who met either in Randolph's apartment
    or in an empty storefront next to the Lafayette Theater on weekends. Jervis
    Anderson, *A. Philip Randolph: A Biographical Portrait* (New York: Harcourt,
    1973), 139–142, and BC, 125. "He also frequented": among his many titles,
    Sir Norman Angell wrote a meditation on the costs of war: *The Great Illusion:
    A Study of the Relation of Military Power in Nations to Their Economic and So-
    cial Advantage* (New York: G. P. Putnam's Sons, 1911); Will Durant, author
    of *The Story of Philosophy* (New York: Simon and Schuster, 1926), wrote on
    the history of philosophy for the general reader; Everett Dean Martin wrote

popular books on social psychology, including *The Behavior of Crowds: A Psychological Study* (New York: Harper and Brothers, 1920).

27. "Saint Marks-on-the-Bouwerie": BC, 126–127; Schuyler wrote about these experiences in one of his best articles, "Hobohemia I: The World of the Migratory Worker," *Messenger* 5 (1923): 741–744.

28. BC, 134.

29. On Schuyler's role with the *Messenger*, see Theodore Kornweibel, *No Crystal Stair: Black Life and the "Messenger," 1917–1928* (Westport, Conn.: Greenwood Press, 1975), 57–58; and Anderson, *A. Philip Randolph*, 144–145. Also see BC, 136, and George Hutchinson, *The Harlem Renaissance in Black and White* (Cambridge: Harvard University Press, 1995), 289–312.

30. BC, 136; Kornweibel, *No Crystal Stair*, 50–51, 57.

31. Schuyler also became good friends with A. Philip Randolph during these years. They liked to take walks down Seventh Avenue together on Sunday evenings and attend the vaudeville show at the Ahlambra Theater on West 126th Street. BC, 139–140 and 142–144. Anderson, *A. Philip Randolph*, 141–142.

32. BC, 134. The need for money provided a constant incentive for Schuyler to write wherever and whenever he could. In 1926, when Schuyler returned from his trip to the South, Robert Vann allowed him to write the regular editorials for the *Courier*. When the *Messenger* folded in 1928, Vann helped Schuyler to become the editor of the *Illustrated Feature Section*, a magazine insert appearing in forty black newspapers. Published by the Ziff Company, the *Illustrated Feature Section* attempted to make black papers more attractive to advertisers. It contained such alluring material as fantastic "true" stories, serialized fiction, sensational news items, drawings of sexy men and women, and lots of pictures. The appearance of this kind of material in the magazine caused controversy and debate in the black press. Despite his willingness to defend its practical significance, however, Schuyler was not proud of the five months (from September to January 1928) he spent in Chicago working on the magazine. Later, he described it as "moron fodder" and said that he quit working on it to "preserve what little intelligence [he] had left." Schuyler, "Some Unsweet Truths," 88. These negative feelings did not prevent him from contributing to the magazine frequently even after he quit as editor. For example, see Danton Smith (George S. Schuyler), "Will Negroes Rule Manhattan in 1940?" *Illustrated Feature Section*, 5 October 1929. Schuyler first began publishing under the name Samuel I. Brooks in the *Illustrated Feature Section*. In October 1928 the name first appeared in print to advertise the "Newly Discovered Race Writer" who would be the author of "Chocolate Baby," a serial appearing from 13 October 1928 to 3 November 1928. Schuyler also used this pen name to write a six-part series in the *Interstate Tattler* on Marcus Garvey, running from 5 July to 9 August 1929. See Hill and Rasmussen, afterword to *Black Empire*, 264. Also see Floyd Calvin, "Calvin's Digest," *Pittsburgh Courier*, 20 February 1932. Calvin, who followed Schuyler as editor of the *Illustrated Feature Section*, said that Schuyler had written

many ten-part serials and "True Confessions" between 1929 and 1930 without signing his name. During these years Schuyler also maintained a satirical column in his own name in the *Interstate Tattler*. BC, 159.

33. Michael Peplow, *George S. Schuyler* (Boston: Twayne, 1980), 117, note 24. To the consternation of white America, Jack Johnson held the heavyweight title between 1908 and 1915. As flamboyant and defiant outside of the ring as he was within it, Johnson flaunted both his wealth and his romantic relationships with white women. In 1912 he was convicted under the Mann Act for transporting his white wife across state lines.

34. Talalay, *Composition*, 11, 46. In naming their daughter, the Schuylers had in mind the Revolutionary War figure General Philip Schuyler, under whom George's great-great-grandfather fought; BC, 251–252.

35. When Schuyler met Josephine, he lived in a neat little apartment on St. Nicholas Avenue. Shortly after they were married, they moved to Chicago for a brief period while Schuyler edited the *Illustrated Feature Section*. After he quit this job, he and Josephine moved back to New York to the apartment on Edgecombe Avenue that they would occupy from that point forward; "and W. E. B. Du Bois": Anderson, *A. Philip Randolph*, 77; "faithfulness": Talalay, *Composition*, 113.

36. The series "Aframerica Today" began on 19 December 1925 and ended on 17 April 1926.

37. "Liberia": BC, 186; and George S. Schuyler, *Slaves Today: A Story of Liberia* (New York: Brewer, Warren and Putnam, 1931). *Slaves Today* tells the tragic story of two lovers: Zo, a member of the Gola tribe, and Pameta, the daughter of a village chief. The day after they are married, David Jackson, a Liberian government official, demands larger payments of rice and palm oil. In the fight that follows, the village chief is killed and Jackson takes Pameta as a concubine. When Zo attempts to rescue his bride, he is captured and sold into slavery on the island of Fernando Po. Two years later Zo returns only to find his wife discarded in the jungle and riddled with disease. As she dies in his arms, Zo vows to avenge her. After sneaking into Jackson's compound and cutting the villain's throat, he is shot by a guard. While *Slaves Today* is in one sense a simple formulaic melodrama, it deserves credit for promoting a realistic attitude toward African politics sorely lacking in the popular black mind-set of the 1920s. BC, 173–186; Williams, "When Black Is Right," 212–239; and George S. Schuyler, "Uncle Sam's Black Stepchild," *American Mercury* 29 (1933): 147–156, and "Monrovia Mooches On," *Globe* 1 (1937): 10–16.

38. Williams, "When Black Is Right," 133, 231–232. Schuyler defended his position on Liberia throughout the early 1930s. See, for example, VR, 21 October 1934. Later in Schuyler's career the idea of a benevolent American presence in Africa combined with his anticommunism. See Schuyler, "Khrushchev's African Foothold," *American Mercury* 88 (1959): 57–59. Schuyler's series on Liberia led to many other investigative assignments all over the world. From 1932 to 1933 he investigated the Mississippi Flood Control Project for the

NAACP; in 1937 he investigated labor unionism in forty industrial centers nationwide; in 1948 he visited Latin America, producing the series "Racial Democracy in Latin America"; in 1949 he conducted a similar tour of the West Indies; in 1958 he was special correspondent for the *Courier* in West Africa and the Dominican Republic; and in 1960 he represented the *Courier* in Nigeria. In addition to these major tours Schuyler made yearly speaking trips around the country from 1927 until World War II, and he used each trip as an opportunity to report on conditions around the country for his audience.

39. VR, 23 November 1935. Hill, introduction to *Ethiopian Stories*, 1–50; Williams, "When Black Is Right," 317–318.

40. *Black Empire* appeared originally in the *Courier* as two stories: "Black Internationale: Story of Black Genius against the World" (21 November 1936 to 3 July 1937) and "Black Empire: An Imaginative Story of a Great New Civilization in Modern Africa" (2 October 1937 to 16 April 1938); George Schuyler to P. L. Prattis, 4 April 1937, P. L. Prattis Papers, Moreland-Spingarn Research Center, Howard University Library, Washington, D.C., quoted in Hill, afterword to *Black Empire*, 260.

41. Schuyler worked for the *Crisis* from 1934 to 1935 as a special publicity assistant and from 1937 to 1944 as its business manager. In 1932 he left the *Courier* briefly to edit the ill-fated *National News*. After its demise in the same year he returned to the *Courier* staff. Because Robert Vann could not pay him very much, Schuyler had to increase his workload during this period to maintain his income. Still, he made fewer than sixty dollars a week for all of his weekly columns, editorials, promotional work, and fiction combined. Hill, afterword to *Black Empire*, 265; BC, 167; and Hill, introduction to *Ethiopia Stories*, 41, note 6.

42. BC, 204–222. Schuyler's main attacks on the Scottsboro defense appear in VR, 22 April 1933, 29 April 1933, and 6 May 1933. Also, he clashes with a former friend and admirer, Eugene Gordon, over the issue of communism. See "Gordon Attacks Schuyler," *Pittsburgh Courier*, 29 April 1933; "controversial trial": Williams, "When Black Is Right," 292–300. As an extension of his anticommunist activities in the early 1930s, Schuyler joined the Committee for Cultural Freedom in 1939. This conservative organization was organized to counteract the threat to intellectual freedom presented by totalitarianism. On this see BC, 317–322; Williams, "When Black Is Right," 339; Christopher Lasch, "The Cultural Cold War: A Short History of the Congress for Cultural Freedom," *The Agony of the American Left* (New York: Vintage, 1969); and Michael Harrington, "The Committee for Cultural Freedom," *Dissent* (Spring 1955): 113–122. Angelo Herndon, a black organizer for the Communist Party, was arrested for incitement to insurrection while leading a biracial demonstration for the unemployed in Atlanta in 1932. The campaign to free him was one of the major efforts by the Communist Party to gain popular support among black workers in the 1930s. "Gun on his desk": Ishmael Reed and Steve Cannon, "George S. Schuyler, Writer," *Shrovetide in Old New Orleans* (New York: Doubleday, 1978), 213.

43. "realism": VR, 29 March 1930; "Cooperative League": Schuyler's interest in cooperatives dates back to the beginning of his career. See, for example, "Shafts and Darts," *Messenger* 7 (1925): 396. His first article on the Young Negroes' Cooperative League was in VR, 25 October 1930. See also George S. Schuyler, "The Young Negroes' Co-operative League," *Crisis* 39 (January 1932): 456, 472; "protests might do": VR, 6 January 1934, and BC, 215–216.

44. Buni, *Robert L. Vann*, 203–221. See, for example, "The Roosevelts," *Pittsburgh Courier*, 26 May 1934; "A New Deal for Bankers," *Pittsburgh Courier*, 10 June 1934; and "Organizing for the New Deal," *Pittsburgh Courier*, 12 August 1933.

45. "job": Ingersol, "Reminiscences," 275–277; "editorials diminished": Buni, *Robert L. Vann*, 221.

46. "1936": Harvard Sitcoff, *A New Deal for Blacks, The Emergence of Civil Rights as a National Issue: The Depression* (New York: Oxford University Press, 1978), 58–83. Schuyler summed up his view of Roosevelt upon the president's death in 1945: see VR, 28 April 1945.

47. George S. Schuyler, "Schuyler Warns U.S. Negroes of Future Danger," *Pittsburgh Courier*, 22 July 1933.

48. "imperialist British": Williams, "When Black Is Right," 319; "gang wins": VR, 30 August 1941.

49. "imperialists": In his "The World Today" column, *Pittsburgh Courier*, 10 January 1942, Schuyler expressed glee at the fall of Manila: "The United States has been defeated. It has been defeated by a foe it despised because of his color"; "strategic isolationism": during the war he joined the isolationist America First Committee. He also wrote a pamphlet called *Why We Are against the War* for the Negroes against the War Committee. Williams, "When Black Is Right," 319; James O. Young, *Black Writers of the Thirties* (Baton Rouge: Louisiana State University Press, 1973), 92, note 85. To address racial tensions during the war, in 1942 Schuyler started the Association for Tolerance in America, which attempted to use advertising to brainwash whites into a more benevolent view of blacks. See George S. Schuyler, "Educating the White Folks," *Interracial Review* 16 (1943): 106–108.

50. "sympathies": VR, 20 December 1941. Also see VR, 6 June 1942, and BC, 256. In "The World Today," *Pittsburgh Courier*, 25 April 1942, Schuyler wrote that the act of putting the Japanese into camps has "placed our democracy on a par with dictatorial European and Asiatic countries. . . . This may be a prelude to our own fate. Who knows?" Also see VR, 29 May 1943.

51. "World War II": Patrick S. Washburn, *A Question of Sedition: The Federal Government's Investigation of the Black Press during World War II* (New York: Oxford University Press, 1986); and Lee Finkle, *Forum for Protest: The Black Press during World War II* (Cranbury, N.J.: Associated University Presses, 1975); "pro-Japanese views": Federal Bureau of Investigation file numbers 100-3671, 100-2498, and 100-35770. All of these files are titled "Pittsburgh Courier; Dissemination of Japanese Propaganda Among Negroes," and all

of them quote Schuyler's editorials extensively and single him out as the only *Courier* reporter who has published pro-Japanese material without also publishing anti-Japanese articles.

52. George S. Schuyler, "More Race Riots Are Coming," *American Mercury* 59 (1944): 686.

CHAPTER 2: THE TEN COMMANDMENTS

1. VR, 16 October 1926.
2. Thomas Nelson Page, *The Negro: The Southerner's Problem* (New York: Charles Scribner's Sons, 1904). The New Negroes of the 1920s were actually the second generation of New Negroes. For more on the first group of New Negroes, see Leon F. Litwack, *Trouble in Mind: Black Southerners in the Age of Jim Crow* (New York: Knopf, 1998), 197–216.
3. "separation": Litwack, *Trouble in Mind,* 216, 291–292; Booker T. Washington, "The Atlanta Exposition Address," in *The Booker T. Washington Papers,* ed. Louis R. Harlan, vol. 5 (Urbana: University of Illinois Press, 1974), 583–587.
4. This theme is most prominent in the third chapter, "Of Mr. Booker T. Washington and Others," in W. E. B. Du Bois, *The Souls of Black Folk: The Writings of W. E. B. Du Bois* (New York: Library of America, 1986), 392–404. See also "Of the Sorrow Songs," in Du Bois, *Souls,* 536–546, and 424–438. For "second sight," see "After the Egyptian," in Du Bois, *Souls,* 364.
5. VR, 16 October 1926.
6. George S. Schuyler and Theophilus Lewis, "Shafts and Darts," *Messenger* 6 (1924): 289.
7. George Hutchinson, *The Harlem Renaissance in Black and White* (Cambridge, Mass.: Belknap Press of Harvard University Press, 1995), 33–61. Richard Rorty, *Consequences of Pragmatism (Essays, 1972–1980)* (Minneapolis: University of Minnesota Press, 1982), xiii–xlviii; and Cornel West, *The American Evasion of Philosophy: A Genealogy of Pragmatism* (Madison: University of Wisconsin Press, 1989).
8. Alain Locke, "The New Negro," in *The New Negro,* ed. Alain Locke (New York: Simon and Schuster, 1997), 6.
9. "As with the Jew," Locke writes, "persecution is making the Negro international," ibid., 7, 14–15.
10. David Levering Lewis, *When Harlem Was in Vogue* (New York: Knopf, 1979; reprint, New York: Penguin, 1997), 25–26, 103–113, and 219–220.
11. "internal problems": Lewis, *When Harlem Was in Vogue,* 3–24; "as usual": Litwack, *Trouble in Mind,* 331; Schuyler was imprisoned on Governor's Island in the fall of 1918 and remained in prison for nine months, well into 1919.
12. "tragic understanding": *The Souls of Black Folk* stands at the origin of this way of understanding black history, which has always provided a sobering corrective to a more optimistic strand of progressive history best exemplified by the title of John Hope Franklin and Alfred A. Moss's popular textbook, *From Slavery to Freedom: A History of African Americans* (New York: Knopf, 2000). For examples of segregationist excesses, see Litwack, *Trouble in Mind,*

229–240, 246, and 335–336. During the 1920s many states around the country, especially southern states, attempted to define race more carefully in the law: Pauli Murray, ed., *State's Laws on Race and Color* (Cincinnati, Ohio: Women's Division of Christian Service of the Methodist Church, 1950), and F. James Davis, *Who Is Black? One Nation's Definition* (University Park: Pennsylvania State University Press, 1991), 51–80.

13. Litwack, *Trouble in Mind*, 258–260 and 328.

14. Litwack, *Trouble in Mind*, 261, 240, and 364. The second joke also appears in Lawrence W. Levine, *Black Culture and Black Consciousness: Afro-American Folk Thought from Slavery to Freedom* (New York: Oxford University Press, 1977), 319.

15. Levine, *Black Culture*, 330.

16. James Weldon Johnson, *Along This Way: The Autobiography of James Weldon Johnson* (New York: Penguin, 1990), 120.

17. Levine, *Black Culture*, 298–366. See also Mel Watkins, *On the Real Side, Laughing, Lying, and Signifying: The Underground Tradition of African American Humor That Transformed American Culture from Slavery to Richard Pryor* (New York: Simon and Schuster, 1994), 16–41.

18. Levine, *Black Culture*, 343–344.

19. Ibid., 359–366. In *Rabelais and His World* (Bloomington: Indiana University Press, 1984), author Mikhail Bakhtin makes perhaps the most famous and powerful case for the radical qualities of laughter.

20. For examples, see VR, 19 December 1929, and 18 May 1929.

21. Litwack, *Trouble in Mind*, 196.

22. Fred Kaplan, *Sacred Tears: Sentimentality in Victorian Literature* (Princeton, N.J.: Princeton University Press, 1987), 16–20.

23. One good example of this mentality is Thomas Nelson Page's defense of lynching; see Page, *Negro*, 76–119.

24. Peter Brooks, *The Melodramatic Imagination: Balzac, Henry James, Melodrama, and the Mode of Excess* (New Haven: Yale University Press, 1976), 11.

25. Northrop Frye names the lynch mob as the most extreme example of the melodramatic mentality: "In the melodrama of the brutal thriller we come as close as it is normally possible for art to come to the pure self-righteousness of the lynching mob." Frye, *Anatomy of Criticism: Four Essays* (1957; reprint, Princeton, N.J.: Princeton University Press, 1970), 47.

26. Following Stowe's *Uncle Tom's Cabin*, Linda Williams uses the term "anti-Tom" to describe this type and "Tom" to indicate his opposite. Williams, *Playing the Race Card: Melodramas of Black and White from Uncle Tom to O. J. Simpson* (Princeton, N.J.: Princeton University Press, 2001), 8.

27. Brooks, *Melodramatic Imagination*, xi and 20–23. Williams describes melodrama as a "perpetually modernizing form that can neither be clearly opposed to the norms of the 'classical' nor the norms of realism." Williams, *Playing the Race Card*, 12.

28. Dustin Griffin, *Satire: A Critical Reintroduction* (Lexington: University of Kentucky Press, 1994), 1–2 and 33–34. See also Stephen Weisenberger, *Fables*

of Subversion: Satire and the American Novel (Athens: University of Georgia Press, 1995).

29. Griffin, *Satire*, 141–149.

30. Alistair Fowler, *Kinds of Literature: An Introduction to the Theory of Genres and Modes* (Cambridge: Harvard University Press, 1982), 110; "inquiry": the works of Derrida, Foucault, and Nietzsche could all be considered satirical.

31. Frye, *Anatomy of Criticism*, 223.

32. Edward A. Martin, *H. L. Mencken and the Debunkers* (Athens: University of Georgia Press, 1984), 6.

33. Ibid., 26–29.

34. For a classic treatment of this rebellion, see Henry F. May, *The End of American Innocence: A Study of the First Years of Our Time* (New York: Knopf, 1959). See also Ann Douglas, *Terrible Honesty: Mongrel Manhattan in the 1920s* (New York: Farrar, Straus, and Giroux, 1995). All through this book Douglas returns to the significance of World War I in shaping what she sees as the manic-depressive personality of the rebellious 1920s.

35. "race relations": For one example of this, see W. E. B. Du Bois, "A Mild Suggestion," *Crisis* 5 (1912): 115–116; James Weldon Johnson, "Views and Reviews," *New York Age*, 20 July 1918.

36. Michael Seidel, *Satiric Inheritance: Rabelais to Sterne* (Princeton, N.J.: Princeton University Press, 1979), 4–5.

37. Ibid., 14–15. Seidel's argument in *Satiric Inheritance* maintains a close relationship with René Girard's theories of the scapegoat and mimetic desire. See Girard, *Violence and the Sacred*, trans. Patrick Gregory (Baltimore: Johns Hopkins University Press, 1977), and *The Scapegoat*, trans. Yvonne Freccero (Baltimore: Johns Hopkins University Press, 1986).

38. Seidel, *Satiric Inheritance*, 26–59.

CHAPTER 3: "THE RIGHT TO LAUGH"

1. "style": Jervis Anderson, *A. Philip Randolph: A Biographical Portrait* (New York: Harcourt, Brace Jovanovich, 1973), 144; "1930s": Schuyler expressed particularly negative opinions about Randolph during the March on Washington movement. See also VR, 1 August 1943, and Anderson, *A. Philip Randolph*, 265–266.

2. BC, 97.

3. Schuyler wrote "Shafts and Darts" alone between September 1923 and April 1924 and between August 1925 and 1928, when the magazine went under. Because neither author signed his own work, it is difficult to decide what Lewis wrote and, more important for our purposes, what Schuyler was responsible for. Because the Schuyler-Lewis collaboration did not change the character of "Shafts and Darts," I have chosen to regard what they wrote together almost as if Schuyler wrote it alone. I do indicate, however, the dual authorship of these passages in my notes and in the text. "Magazine": George S. Schuyler and Theophilus Lewis, "Shafts and Darts," *Messenger* 6 (1924): 101.

4. Both quotes are from Schuyler and Lewis, "Shafts and Darts," *Messenger* 7 (1925): 263.
5. Ibid.
6. William Ingersol, "The Reminiscences of George S. Schuyler," Oral History Collection of Columbia University, New York, 1960, 99.
7. BC, 135.
8. "Russia": For more on the origins of the *Messenger*, see Anderson, *A. Philip Randolph*, 53–82; "working class": in these early days of the *Messenger*, Owen and Randolph went on speaking tours around the country to promote their magazine and took many chances denouncing the war. Anderson, *A. Philip Randolph*, 105–107. For these editorials, see *Messenger* 1 (1917): 6–9.
9. *Messenger* 2 (1919): 16–17.
10. "The Open Forum," letter from W. T. Hornaday, ibid., 29–30; Victor R. Daley, "The Response," ibid., 30–31.
11. "idealists": "The Editor's Statement," *Messenger* 1 (1917): 20. In his account of the cultural politics of the *Messenger*, George Hutchinson emphasizes this irony as the main viewpoint of the magazine: Hutchinson, *The Harlem Renaissance in Black and White* (Cambridge: Harvard University Press, 1995), 289–312.
12. A. Philip Randolph, "A New Crowd—A New Negro," *Messenger* 2 (1919): 26–27. The editors of the *Messenger* devoted themselves especially to criticizing Du Bois in these years. See "W. E. B. Du Bois," *Messenger* 2 (1918): 27–28; "The Crisis of the Crisis," *Messenger* 2 (1919): 10–12; and "Du Bois Fails as a Theorist," ibid., 7–8.
13. Chandler Owen, "The Failure of Negro Leaders," *Messenger* 1 (1918): 24.
14. "Marcus Garvey," *Messenger* 4 (1922): 437. For more on Garvey and the Ku Klux Klan, see Judith Stein, *The World of Marcus Garvey: Race and Class in Modern Society* (Baton Rouge: Louisiana State University Press, 1986), 155–158.
15. "mail fraud": The letter, dated 15 January 1923, was signed by Robert S. Abbot, owner-editor of the *Chicago Defender;* Robert Bagnall and William Pickens of the NAACP; Chandler Owen of the *Messenger;* John Nail, a leading Harlem realtor and James Weldon Johnson's brother-in-law; Harry H. Pace, president of the Black Swan Phonograph Corporation; Julia P. Coleman, president of a black cosmetics firm; and George Harris, New York alderman and editor of the *New York News*. David Levering Lewis, *When Harlem Was in Vogue* (New York: Oxford University Press, 1981), 44–45; and Theodore Kornweibel, *No Crystal Stair: Black Life and the "Messenger," 1917–1928* (Westport, Conn.: Greenwood Press, 1975), 142. "Foreigners": for denunciations of the "Red Scare," see "The Foreigner and the American," *Messenger* 2 (1918): 11, and "A. Mitchell Palmer," *Messenger* 2 (1920): 10–11. The anti–West Indian tone of the "Garvey Must Go Campaign" eventually led to a dispute between Owen and West Indian radical W. A. Domingo. Kornweibel, *No Crystal Stair*, 143–144; see also "The Policy of the *Messenger* on West Indians and American Negroes," *Messenger* 5 (1923): 639–645.

16. In "The World as It Is," *Messenger* 5 (1923): 622, an unprecedented tone of resignation enters the *Messenger* editorial page: "The conscious improvement of society by society is yet a distant dream only 'devoutly to be wished.'"

17. "including Randolph": Ingersol, "Reminiscences," 100; "corroding": BC, 137; "masses": Ingersol, "Reminiscences," 101; "wealthy": Anderson, *A. Philip Randolph*, 138.

18. "infidelity": Chandler Owen, "The Passing of Novelty," *Messenger* 1 (November 1917): 22; "1923": Chandler Owen, "Love: A Type of Truth Found Chiefly in Works of Fiction," *Messenger* 5 (1923): 571–572; "Love—Once More!" *Messenger* 5 (1923): 601–602 and 607; "Marriage and Divorce," *Messenger* 5 (1923): 629–631; "sex": Owen, "Love," 571.

19. Chandler Owen, "The Black and Tan Cabaret—America's Most Democratic Institution," *Messenger* 7 (1925): 97 and 100.

20. "group": George S. Schuyler, "Politics and the Negro," *Messenger* 5 (1923): 658; "lead the way": ibid., 659.

21. George S. Schuyler, "Hobohemia I: The World of the Migratory Worker," ibid., 741; see also Schuyler, "Lights and Shadows of the Underworld II: The Folk Farthest Down," ibid., 787–788 and 796–799.

22. Schuyler, "Hobohemia I," 742, 744.

23. George S. Schuyler, "Shafts and Darts," *Messenger* 5 (1923): 808.

24. Ibid., 808 and 819.

25. "warrants": Schuyler, "Shafts and Darts," *Messenger* 5 (1923): 922. Robert Russa Moton followed Booker T. Washington as president of Tuskegee Institute. Harvard graduate and well-known New York black Democrat Ferdinand Q. Morton was the chair of the Municipal Civil Service Commission and head of Harlem's Colored United Democracy. Lewis, *When Harlem Was in Vogue*, 217. "Rubles": Schuyler, "Shafts and Darts," *Messenger* 6 (1924): 8. Here Schuyler referred to the unusual patience shown to Garvey in his trial by the judge, who put up with his embarrassing attempt to act as his own lawyer in his trial for mail fraud. See Edmund David Cronon, *Black Moses: The Story of Marcus Garvey and the Universal Negro Improvement Association* (Madison: University of Wisconsin Press, 1987), 113–118. Schuyler's longest and in many ways most vicious attack on Garvey occurred in "A Tribute to Caesar," *Messenger* 6 (1924): 225–226 and 231.

26. "democracy": George S. Schuyler, "Shafts and Darts," *Messenger* 5 (1923): 923. By the time Schuyler wrote this, the *Messenger* had already repudiated communism: see "The Menace of Negro Communists," *Messenger* 5 (1923): 785.

27. "Heavens": George S. Schuyler, "Shafts and Darts," *Messenger* 5 (1923): 923; "conferences": a *Messenger* editorial probably written by Schuyler panned Du Bois's 1923 Pan-African Conference as "just about as useful as the Versailles Conference is to chaos-ridden Europe": see Schuyler, "Pan-African Conference," *Messenger* 6 (1924): 5.

28. "Locke": In awarding a dill pickle to Locke, Schuyler and Lewis called him the "high priest of the intellectual snobocracy," in "Shafts and Darts," *Messenger* 6 (1924): 183; "citizen": Schuyler and Lewis, "Shafts and Darts,"

Messenger 6 (1924): 108. This was also the first prize that Lewis and Schuyler awarded together.

29. "beliefs": George S. Schuyler, "Shafts and Darts," *Messenger* 6 (1924): 41; "stock": ibid.

30. Ibid., 42.

31. Ingersol, "Reminiscences," 128.

32. "truth about it": See also Schuyler and Lewis's opening column together, "Shafts and Darts," *Messenger* 6 (1924): 101; "proverbs": Schuyler and Lewis, "Shafts and Darts," *Messenger* 7 (1925): 35–36.

33. "science" and "marching on": Ibid., 36.

34. Ibid., 90–91.

35. Schuyler and Lewis, "Shafts and Darts," *Messenger* 6 (1924): 138.

36. Ibid., 183.

37. For a good statement expressing the main sentiment of many *Messenger* articles and editorials on this issue, see A. Philip Randolph, "American Politics," *Messenger* 5 (1923): 595–598.

38. "animals" and "U.N.I.A.": Schuyler and Lewis, "Shafts and Darts," *Messenger* 6 (1924): 288.

39. Ibid.

40. George S. Schuyler, "At the Darktown Charity Ball," *Messenger* 6 (1924): 377.

41. Schuyler and Lewis, "Shafts and Darts," *Messenger* 7 (1925): 295. Caspar Holstein, a black nationalist numbers runner and native of the Danish Virgin Islands known as the "Bolito King," is probably the best example of this trend. See also Lewis, *When Harlem Was in Vogue*, 129–130.

42. "pickles": In 1924, Schuyler published three long articles boosting business figures in 1924: "Mortimer M. Harris: A Far-Sighted Man Rises to Meet a Need," *Messenger* 6 (1924): 140–144; "John A. Lankford": ibid., 192–93; and "Madam C. J. Walker": ibid., 251–58, 264, and 266. Three years later, in September 1927, he began "Business and Industry," a column featuring news on black businesses and their owners. The column ran until the *Messenger* published its last edition in 1928; Schuyler, "Mortimer M. Harris," 144. One need not search far among Schuyler's writings to find statements directly contradicting this one. For example, in VR, 6 April 1929, he complained about an *Interstate Tattler* article that lavished undue praise on realtors.

43. "bills": The Thurman comment comes from a paraphrase of a conversation he had with Langston Hughes. Hughes, *The Big Sea* (New York: Alfred A. Knopf, 1940), 233–234. "Principles": in "Shafts and Darts," *Messenger* 5 (1923): 342, Schuyler responds to an article in the *New York Age* to this effect concerning Chandler Owen's role as president of the California Development Company.

44. The names on the *Messenger*'s masthead over the years tell its story in miniature: "A Message of Democracy" on the cover of the first issue quickly gave way to "The Only Radical Negro Magazine in America" in July 1918. In Feb-

ruary 1920 this changed to "A Journal of Scientific Socialism." In January 1923, at a crucial ideological turning point for the *Messenger*, the name changed to "New Opinion of the New Negro." Finally in January 1924 the magazine became "The World's Greatest Negro Monthly."

CHAPTER 4: DEBUNKING BLACKNESS

1. George S. Schuyler, *Racial Intermarriage in the United States: One of the Most Interesting Phenomena of Our National Life*, Little Blue Book series (Girard, Kans.: Haldeman-Julius, 1929); "forth": E. Haldeman-Julius, *The Outline of Bunk, Including the Admirations of a Debunker* (Boston: Stratford Company, 1929), 3.

2. A positive anonymous review of *The Outline of Bunk* in the *Illustrated Feature Section* ("Is Civilization Bunk?" [6 April 1929]: 4) was probably penned by Schuyler. "Greatest": Haldeman-Julius, *Outline of Bunk*, 382–383.

3. "lackey": quoted in Andrew Buni, *Robert L. Vann of "The Pittsburgh Courier": Politics and Black Journalism* (Pittsburgh: University of Pittsburgh Press, 1974), 163–164; "government": ibid., 98–112. In fairness to Vann, he did complain about the actions of Attorney General A. Mitchell Palmer when they started to hurt blacks.

4. Ibid., 109.

5. Vann decided to pursue his pragmatic courtship of the left with even more vigor in the late 1920s by becoming the loudest advocate of A. Philip Randolph's Brotherhood of Sleeping Car Porters Union in its battle against the Pullman Company.

6. "1920s": In these years Vann also hired artist Wilbert Holloway, columnist Floyd Calvin, feature writer J. A. Rogers, and sportswriter W. Rollo Wilson; Buni, *Robert L. Vann*, 42–54 and 136–144; "readers": an advertisement on the *Courier* editorial page on 9 October 1926 with the headline "CON-SERVATISM!" clearly indicates Vann's desire to sell the paper as a more "respectable" alternative to his major competitors. Still, the stories and headlines in the *Courier* in this period did not differ very much from those in other major newspapers.

7. In his yearly review of the black press for 1927, Eugene Gordon noted the marked improvement of the *Courier*: see Gordon, "Outstanding Negro Newspapers, 1927," *Opportunity* 5 (1927): 358–362.

8. Theophilus Lewis, "The Harlem Sketch Book," *New York Amsterdam News*, 30 April 1930, SS, GSSP/SU, vol. 2.

9. Ibid.

10. Gunnar Myrdal uses the term "fighting press" in *An American Dilemma: The Negro Problem and American Democracy*, vol. 2 (New York: Harper and Brothers, 1944), 908.

11. Frederick G. Detweiler, *The Negro Press in the United States* (College Park, Md.: McGrath Publishing, 1968), 54–68.

12. Myrdal, *American Dilemma*, 914–915.

13. Ibid., 917. This statement is true of the larger papers vying for national

circulation. Smaller and less-ambitious papers generally employed less sensationalism.

14. "happening": Ibid., 917–918; "violence": this kind of story had a recurring life in the black press because it "played up" white violence against blacks dramatically. Implicitly, such articles stood as counterstatements to the tendency of the mainstream press to exaggerate black violence and crime. For an example, see "Policeman Wantonly Kills Man," *Pittsburgh Courier,* 25 November 1925.

15. Many of the articles of this type featured murder, sex, or a combination of the two. For example, next to news of the Sweet trial in Detroit, the front page of the *Courier* on 5 December 1925 announced in headlines: "Irate Man Slays Wife and Father," "Woman Admits That She Has Two Husbands," and "Sermon Is Cause of Attack." On 21 November 1925 the front page declared: "Poison Candy Used by Woman," "Shoots His Wife for Bobbing Hair," and "Teacher Is Painted as Love Pirate."

16. "press directly": Schuyler made fun of the sensationalism in black news-papers in a humorous article written anonymously for the *Interstate Tattler,* 10 June 1927, called "Pity the City Editor," SS, GSSP/SU, vol. 2. Through the late 1920s Schuyler also occasionally registered direct complaints against the "Yellow Press"; see TL, 15 August 1925. For a more triumphant account of the black press, see Schuyler's pamphlet *Fifty Years of Progress in Negro Journalism* (Pittsburgh: Pittsburgh Publishing Company, 1950). "Directly": for more on the relationship between Adler and Schuyler, see Jeffrey B. Ferguson, "The Newest Negro: George S. Schuyler's Intellectual Quest in the 1920s and Beyond" (Ph.D. diss., Harvard University, 1998), 156–161.

17. Everett Dean Martin, *The Behavior of Crowds: A Psychological Study* (New York: Harper and Brothers, 1920). For more on Schuyler's use of the inferi-ority complex as an explanation for white racism, see Ferguson, "Newest Negro," 161–170.

18. George S. Schuyler, "This Simian World," *Pittsburgh Courier,* 16 December 1924. Schuyler went on to cite the examples of Billy Sunday and Scott Near-ing. Sunday was the premier evangelist in the United States in the 1920s; he urged Americans to return to the "old time religion" and complained of the "excesses" of blacks and immigrants. This earned him the endorsement of the Ku Klux Klan and made him one of Schuyler's favorite whipping boys. Nearing was a socialist public intellectual whom Schuyler often referred to in his columns.

19. VR, 7 September 1926.

20. "similarly" and "face": Ibid.

21. "two thousand": He also visited Delaware and Pennsylvania. In BC, 152–157, Schuyler wrote that he toured Georgia and Florida on his 1926 trip, but there are no articles in the "Aframerica Today" series on cities in these states. Dur-ing his 1930 lecture tour Schuyler visited North Carolina, South Carolina, Georgia, Florida, and Alabama; see VR, 20 December 1930, 1 February 1930, 8 February 1930, and 1 March 1930. "Urbanity": SS, GSSP/SU, vol. 2.

22. Schuyler discusses the details concerning his various trips to the South and the special interview techniques he developed in William Ingersol, "The Reminiscences of George S. Schuyler," Oral History Collection of Columbia University, New York, 1960, 142–189.

23. "economic progress": George S. Schuyler, "Aframerica Today," *Pittsburgh Courier,* 3 April 1926; "grass": the series "Aframerica Today" began in November 1925 and ended in July 1926. The article on Morganstown, West Virginia, appeared in "Aframerica Today," *Pittsburgh Courier,* 9 January 1926, and those on Paris, Winchester, and Richmond, Virginia, appeared in the *Pittsburgh Courier* on 6 February 1926.

24. Schuyler, "Aframerica Today," *Pittsburgh Courier,* 19 December 1925.

25. "South": Schuyler kept Calvin's article in his scrapbook, SS, GSSP/SU, vol. 2; "faults": VR, 20 December 1930.

26. "situations": This aspect of his view comes out best in "A Negro Looks Ahead," *American Mercury* 19 (1930): 220; "schooling": VR, 20 December 1930.

27. TL, 3 May 1925.

28. VR, 3 July 1926.

29. TL, 3 January 1925. See also VR, 15 March 1930.

30. "one of" and "dish washing": VR, 16 February 1929.

31. "ever before": TL, 21 February 1925; "mirth": VR, 3 December 1927.

32. "Garvey": VR, 1 September 1929; Mary Jackson's letter appears on the editorial page of the *Courier* under "Letters to the Editor," 7 September 1929.

33. VR, 5 July 1930. The description of Hancock's editorial follows Schuyler's account of it.

34. VR, 12 July 1930.

35. "myths" and "most of it": TL, 13 June 1925.

36. "relative" and "adjustment": VR, 29 September 1928.

37. VR, 28 November 1925; "intelligently directed": VR, 12 January 1929.

38. "the eyeball" and "overboard": TL, 13 June 1925.

39. Ann Douglas, *Terrible Honesty: Mongrel Manhattan in the 1920s* (New York: Farrar, Straus and Giroux, 1995), 3–28.

40. "blow of the hand": VR, 15 October 1927; "the morrow": VR, 20 September 1930.

41. "necessity": VR, 7 July 1928; "buildings": Schuyler commented often on the Black Church. See, for example, TL, 7 March 1925, 20 June 1925, and 19 September 1925; and VR, 15 October 1927 and 1 September 1928. For a more expansive discussion of Schuyler's views on religion, see Ferguson, "Newest Negro," 340–368. "Black America": VR, 15 October 1927. Often Schuyler would mention fraternal societies in the course of criticizing the wasteful economic practices of the Black Church. His standard criticism accused them of wasting money with unnecessary conventions and gaudy uniforms, which did little more than compensate members for feelings of inferiority. For a typical statement, see VR, 27 February 1926; "to believe": Schuyler's main complaint against the NAACP followed along similar lines. See VR,

6 June 1925, 15 August 1925, 16 October 1926, and 28 September 1929. In 1929, Schuyler began an active effort to improve the NAACP. He wrote a series of nine open letters in favor of the NAACP, published in many black newspapers around the country. He also began sharing his ideas for improving the organization with James Weldon Johnson and Walter White. See George S. Schuyler to James Weldon Johnson, 4 September 1929, and George S. Schuyler to Walter White, 7 July 1930, 4 September 1930, and 31 October 1930, the NAACP Papers, Part I, 1909–1950, reel 23, George S. Schuyler Correspondence, 1929–1937.

42. "cooperative business": See, for example, VR, 17 December 1927, 2 February 1929, and 29 March 1930; "white people": VR, 13 December 1930.

43. VR, 25 October 1930.

44. "needs": The origin of this idea in Schuyler's mind goes back to his reading of the works of Dr. James Peter Warbasse. One of Warbasse's many books, *Cooperative Democracy* (New York: Macmillan, 1923), provided the main information source for Schuyler's "Views and Reviews" columns on cooperative societies: see VR, 28 April 1928; see also BC, 165, 73; and Harry McKinley Williams, "When Black Is Right: The Life of George S. Schuyler" (Ph.D. diss., Brown University, 1988), 150–151. "Five Year Plan": VR, 11 October 1930. Schuyler's plan inspired wide and mostly positive response in the black press. His colleague Floyd Calvin struck the most notable negative blow in his column "Calvin's Digest," *Pittsburgh Courier*, 28 February 1931. Dismissing Schuyler as "young and inexperienced," Calvin wrote that Schuyler would find it much harder to build an organization than to tear down existing ones with criticism. Calvin's statement led to a torrent of letters between March and June 1931, mostly from members and supporters of the YNCL; SS, GSSP/SU, vol. 4.

45. VR, 28 February 1931.

46. For more on Schuyler's views concerning black leadership, see Ferguson, "Newest Negro," 173–210; "District of Columbia": George S. Schuyler, "Consumers' Cooperation, the American Negro's Salvation," *Cooperation* 17 (1931): 144–145; "Officers and Members": Williams, "When Black Is Right," 151–153.

CHAPTER 5: "THE RISING TIDE OF COLOR"

1. This is from an article in the *Pittsburgh Guard*, 28 January 1928, SS, GSSP/SU, vol. 2.

2. "Out-Menckening Mencken," *New York Age*, 10 December 1927, SS, GSSP/SU, vol. 2; "kind": "Read the *American Mercury* for December," *California Voice*, 9 December 1927, and "Schuyler Analyzes the Nordics," *Chicago Bee*, 2 December 1927, SS, GSSP/SU, vol. 2; "jazz literature": "Jazz in Literature," *Baltimore Afro-American*, 3 December 1927, SS, GSSP/SU, vol. 2; "morons": George S. Schuyler, "Our White Folks," *American Mercury* 12 (1927): 391.

3. "Competitor": Schuyler, "Our White Folks," 389.

4. Ibid., 390–391.

5. Ibid., 391.

6. George S. Schuyler, "A Negro Looks Ahead," *American Mercury* 19 (1930): 220.

7. For an account of these theories, see George Fredrickson, *The Black Image in the White Mind: The Debate on Afro-American Character and Destiny, 1817–1914* (New York: Harper and Row, 1972), and Thomas Gossett, *Race: The History of an Idea in America* (New York: Oxford University Press, 1997).

8. Madison Grant, *The Passing of the Great Race: Or the Racial Basis of European History* (New York: Charles Scribner's Sons, 1916).

9. Lothrop Stoddard, *The Rising Tide of Color against White-World Supremacy* (New York: Charles Scribner's Sons, 1920), 3–16 and 87–103.

10. "gassed": George S. Schuyler, "The Negro and Nordic Civilization," *Messenger* 7 (1925): 198; "Grant": ibid., 199.

11. "pseudo-science": Gossett, *Race*, 373–374; "horses": VR, 16 April 1927.

12. VR, 24 March 1928.

13. "coop": See, for example, VR, 22 January 1927, and 19 November 1927; "Hogg": VR, 14 September 1927.

14. "England," "roost," and "everywhere": VR, 20 November 1928.

15. George S. Schuyler, review of *The Twilight of the White Races*, by Maurice Muret, *Messenger* 9 (1927): 126.

16. "Yellow race": See Stoddard, *Rising Tide of Color*, 17–53; "Cantonese": VR, 26 March 1927; "side": VR, 9 April 1927.

17. VR, 7 September 1929.

18. VR, 23 May 1926.

19. VR, 12 December 1925.

20. "tropical conditions": VR, 25 May 1929; Charles Woodruff, *The Effects of Tropical Light on White Men* (New York: Rebman Company, 1905): 190–320; "colors": VR, 25 May 1929. In "Will the White Race Turn Brown? All Races Were Once Black," an article Schuyler published anonymously in the *Illustrated Feature Section*, 18 May 1929, 2 (SS, GSSP/SU, vol. 2), he cited the research done by Charles Woodruff and others to argue for an inevitable browning of the white race. Also see Danton Smith [George S. Schuyler], "Will Negroes Rule Manhattan in 1940?" *Illustrated Feature Section*, 5 October 1929.

21. J. A. Rogers, "Europe's Sun Tan Fad," SS, GSSP/SU, vol. 2.

22. "least attractive": See, for example, VR, 26 October 1929; "mutual attraction": Joel A. Rogers, *Sex and Race: Negro-Caucasian Mixing in All Ages and Lands* (New York: J. A. Rogers Publications, 1940); "lower race": Joel A. Rogers, *As Nature Leads: An Informal Discussion of the Reason Why Negro and Caucasian Are Mixing in Spite of Opposition* (Baltimore: Black Classic Press, 1987), 28–30. Also see Lester Ward, *Pure Sociology*, 2nd ed. (New York: Macmillan Company, 1909), 359–360.

23. "nature": Rogers quotes Ward to support this in *As Nature Leads*, 29. Ward, *Pure Sociology*, 359. "Origin": note that this is quite different from desiring the men who are in fact superior. Rogers's scheme assumes

that women's perceptions would be culturally conditioned and often in-accurate, but that in the long run the general tendency toward progress would prevail.

24. For an excellent summary of Ward's race theory, see Gossett, *Race*, 160–167.

25. Ward, *Pure Sociology*, 359; and Gossett, *Race*, 160–161.

26. "fortune": Ward, *Pure Sociology*, 202–215; "soon": ibid., 220.

27. VR, 21 July 1928.

28. "color line": VR, 13 July 1929. Schuyler got many of his statistics on these matters from Melville Herskovits, *The American Negro* (New York: Alfred A. Knopf, 1928), and Edward Byron Reuter, *The American Race Problem* (New York: Thomas Y. Crowell, 1927). "Struggle": VR, 21 July 1928.

29. "marrying them": VR, 13 July 1929; "frequency": these were the main ele-ments of his argument in *Racial Intermarriage in the United States: One of the Most Interesting Phenomena of Our National Life*, Little Blue Book series (Girard, Kans.: Haldeman-Julius, 1929). "Used to be": VR, 6 November 1926.

30. "attention": He remembered years later that she was on that occasion "beau-tiful, charming, vivacious, fashionably dressed, sharp, witty and well-read," in BC, 163; "magazine": Josephine Schuyler, "An Interracial Marriage," *American Mercury* 62 (1946): 273. Up to this point Josephine had submitted two short articles to the *Messenger*, "Truth in Art in America," *Messenger* 5 (1923): 634–636, and "Those Inimitable Avatars—The Negro and the Jews!" *Messenger* 7 (1925): 302. She had also published a review of *Outline of History*, by H. G. Wells, in *Messenger* 5 (1923): 706 and 723, and three poems: "Irony," *Messenger* 6 (1924): 363, "My Sorrow Song," *Messenger* 6 (1924): 388, and "Spring," *Messenger* 7 (1925): 178. Just after the love affair with Schuyler be-gan, Josephine published three anonymous poems. The first, a testament to the white woman's desire for the black man, called "Temptation" by "A Cer-tain Young Southern White Lady," appeared in *Messenger* 9 (1927): 303. The other two, "Raggetybag" and "The Circle" by "A Young Nordic Southerner," appeared in *Messenger* 9 (1927): 324. In the last days of the *Messenger*, Jose-phine published several articles and poems, both under her own name and as Heba Janath. "Her eyes": Kathryn Talalay, *Composition in Black and White: The Life of Philippa Schuyler* (New York: Oxford University Press, 1995): 17; "raven": ibid.

31. Talalay, *Composition*, 32–37. Josephine writes in her anonymous article "The Fall of a Fair Confederate," *Modern Quarterly* 5 (1930–1931): 528–529, that the shooting of her male nurse, a tall black man named Jim who taught her as a girl to ride horses and to shoot, shocked her and made her begin to question her racist values.

32. "Dream: First Night Home," in JSD, n.d.; see also Josephine Schuyler, "Fall of a Fair Confederate," 531.

33. "World War I": Josephine Schuyler, "Fall of a Fair Confederate," 530. Here she describes briefly her early activities as a "Red" in San Francisco; "advances": Talalay, *Composition*, 20; "diabolical": JSD, 1 January 1928.

34. JSD, 30 December 1927.
35. "pruned," "lamb," and "I'll try": JSD, 30 December 1927.
36. "life": Quoted in Talalay, *Composition,* 19; "civilization": JSD, 1 January 1928.
37. "reasons": George S. Schuyler, "Emancipated Woman and the Negro," *Modern Quarterly* 5 (Fall 1929): 363; "people": George S. Schuyler, "Some Unsweet Truths about Race Prejudice," in *Behold America!* ed. Samuel D. Schmalhausen (New York: Farrar and Reinhart, 1931): 96. "Ellis": in his study of human sexuality, Havelock Ellis builds on racist theories concerning the more developed nervous systems of the "higher" races to speculate that the comparatively blunt nervous system of the African male allows him to have sex for extended periods. This, he wrote, makes him the great favorite of prostitutes everywhere. Ellis, *Studies in the Psychology of Sex,* vol. 2 (New York: Random House, 1942), 234 note; see also appendix A. "anatomy": JSD, 24 September 1927.
38. Talalay, *Composition,* 36.
39. JSD, 22 September 1927.
40. Ibid.
41. JSD, 6 January 1928.
42. "pointing at them" and "the whites": Ibid; "frigidity": "Schuyler Marriage Shocks Elite," *New York News,* SS, GSSP/SU, vol. 2; "opinion": Josephine Schuyler, "Fall of a Fair Confederate," 536. Dabney's poem appeared in the *Cincinnati Union,* 16 October 1930, SS, GSSP/SU, vol. 4.
43. "Taboo," SS, GSSP/SU, vol. 4.
44. Josephine Schuyler to George S. Schuyler, 5 August 1930, SS, GSSP/SU, vol. 4.
45. Ibid.
46. "me" and "dwarfs": George S. Schuyler to Josephine Schuyler, 13 October 1935, Correspondence, 1916–1936, GSSP/SU.
47. "birthday": The first article appeared on 8 February 1934 and the second on 3 August 1934. Talalay, *Composition,* 46; "*Houston Informer*": ibid., 50.
48. Ibid., 56.
49. "attention": Talalay, *Composition,* 55–61; "morning": John and Rosalie Watson, *Psychological Care of Infant and Child* (New York: W. W. Norton, 1928); "poisons": through his wife's influence Schuyler wrote many articles on proper diet in "Views and Reviews" (see, for example, VR, 5 April 1930). Josephine also published many articles on the subject, especially in the *Illustrated Feature Section,* where she gave domestic advice under the name Heba Janath and romantic counsel as Julia Jerome.

CHAPTER 6: THE BLACK MENCKEN
1. Originally Schuyler chose this name for his column in honor of Clarence Day's satire *This Simian World* (New York: Alfred A. Knopf, 1920); George S. Schuyler, "This Simian World," *Pittsburgh Courier,* 24 November 1924.
2. Schuyler, "This Simian World."

3. "Owen": Chandler Owen, "William Jennings Bryan," *Messenger* 7 (1925): 392. Although this article occurs a year later than Schuyler's, it conveys well the general attitude toward Bryan in the *Messenger* group in the mid-1920s; "jabs" and "open": Charles A. Fechner, *Mencken: A Study of His Thought* (New York: Alfred A. Knopf, 1978), footnote 162–163.

4. "flies" and "found there": H. L. Mencken, "In Memoriam: W. J. B.," in *Prejudices: Fifth Series* (New York: Alfred A. Knopf, 1926), 64; "sort": ibid., 66; "rabble": ibid., 69.

5. "Bozart": Richard Wright, *Black Boy: A Record of Childhood and Youth* (Cleveland, Ohio: World Publishing, 1945), 214–218; "gentry" and "superiority": H. L. Mencken, "The Sahara of the Bozart," in *Prejudices: First Series* (New York: Alfred A. Knopf, 1920), 149.

6. "who is": H. L. Mencken, "The Curse of Prejudice," *American Mercury* 23 (1931): 125; "Klan": see, for example, Franz Boas, "The Question of Racial Purity," *American Mercury* 3 (1924): 163–169, and Melville Herskovits, "What Is a Race?" *American Mercury* 2 (1924): 207–210; "contempt": for more on Mencken's racism, see Fechner, *Mencken*, 214–217, and Arnold Rampersad, "Mencken, Race, and America," *Menckeniana* 115 (1990): 1–11.

7. H. L. Mencken, "The American Tradition," in *Prejudices: Second Series* (New York: Alfred A. Knopf, 1924), 32.

8. "cravenly," "third rate," and "experiment": Ibid., 40; "axioms": ibid., 41.

9. Stuart P. Sherman, "Beautifying American Literature," *Nation* 105 (1917): 593–594; and Douglas R. Stenerson, introduction to *Critical Essays on H. L. Mencken*, ed. Douglas Stenerson (Boston: G. K. Hall, 1987), 4.

10. H. L. Mencken, "The Curse of Prejudice," *American Mercury* 23 (1931): 125.

11. "mountebanks": Ibid; "too much": ibid., 126.

12. "decency": H. L. Mencken, "The Burden of Credulity," *Opportunity* 9 (1931): 40–41; "here": H. L. Mencken, *Minority Report* (New York: Alfred A. Knopf, 1956), 234–235.

13. Mencken, "Burden of Credulity," 41.

14. H. L. Mencken, "Hiring a Hall," *New York World*, 17 July 1927.

15. Ibid.

16. "promoting": Charles Scruggs, *The Sage in Harlem: H. L. Mencken and the Black Writers of the Harlem Renaissance* (Baltimore: Johns Hopkins University Press, 1984), 118–122; "mountebanks": H. L. Mencken, "Hiring a Hall," *New York World*, 25 September 1927.

17. "tone": Shortly before this article appeared, Mencken had written to Schuyler asking if he could write something for the *American Mercury*. Mencken to Schuyler, 25 August 1927, HLMP. Mencken had also by this time rejected Schuyler's "Southern Idyll," an article on Okaluna, Mississippi; "loves": VR, 30 July 1927.

18. Ibid.

19. "Menckenese": Jayex, "He Would Have to Work," *Washington Eagle*, 4 November 1927, SS, GSSP/SU, vol. 2; "readers": "The Weekly Diary," *Chicago Defender*, 27 July 1928, SS, GSSP/SU, vol. 2; "God": "Schuyler-Mencken,"

Heebie Jeebies, 17 October 1926, SS, GSSP/SU, vol. 2; "thinkers": Allison Davis, "Our Negro Intellectuals," *Crisis* 35 (1928): 284.

20. Fechner, *Mencken*, 160–161.

21. "whites": See H. L. Mencken and George Jean Nathan, "Clinical Notes," *American Mercury* 1 (1924): 329–330; "Forty": Schuyler's "Reflections of a Bachelor at Thirty" appeared in "This Simian World," 29 November 1924. For Mencken's "Reflections of a Bachelor at Forty," see *American Mercury* 1 (1924): 329.

22. "New Books," *Messenger* 7 (1925): 366.

23. H. L. Mencken, "The Library," "Novels Good and Bad," *American Mercury* 5 (1925): 507–508.

24. George S. Schuyler, "Who Owns the Colleges—and Why?" "New Books," *Messenger* 6 (1924): 322.

25. H. L. Mencken, "The Little Red Schoolhouse," *American Mercury* 1 (1924): 504.

26. Ibid.

27. Quoted in Fechner, *Mencken*, 186.

28. "politeness": H. L. Mencken to George S. Schuyler, 25 August 1927, JWJP. Also in *The New Mencken Letters*, ed. Carl Bode (New York: Dial Press, 1977), 213–214; "without": H. L. Mencken to George S. Schuyler, 30 August 1927, JWJP; "traditions": George S. Schuyler to H. L. Mencken, 10 September 1927, HLMP; "article": H. L. Mencken to George S. Schuyler, 9 September 1927, JWJP.

29. H. L. Mencken to George S. Schuyler, 19 October 1927, JWJP. For more background on this ill-fated article, see H. L. Mencken to George S. Schuyler, 11 October, 8 October, and 4 October 1927, JWJP. Also see George S. Schuyler to H. L. Mencken, 8 October and 20 October 1927, HLMP.

30. "libel": H. L. Mencken to George S. Schuyler, 8 June 1927, HLMP; "moralism": in rejecting "Fair Flower," Mencken called it "somewhat too moral for our great family paper"; H. L. Mencken to George S. Schuyler, 25 March 1930, HLMP; "essays": H. L. Mencken to George S. Schuyler, 5 October 1932, JWJP; "knew already anyway": H. L. Mencken to George S. Schuyler, 5 June, 15 August, and 21 August 1928, JWJP.

31. "extensively": H. L. Mencken to George S. Schuyler, 10 December 1931 and 26 January 1932, JWJP; "Doubt": H. L. Mencken to George S. Schuyler, 26 January 1932, JWJP; "Crow": H. L. Mencken to George S. Schuyler, 18 May 1929 and 2 June 1930, JWJP. Also Harry McKinley Williams, "When Black Is Right: The Life of George S. Schuyler" (Ph.D. diss., Brown University, 1988), 256.

32. "topics": H. L. Mencken to George S. Schuyler, 4 May 1929, JWJP; "competition": Schuyler saved this letter in his scrapbook: H. L. Mencken to George S. Schuyler, 3 October 1930, SS, GSSP/SU, vol. 2; "local": George S. Schuyler to H. L. Mencken, 1 September and 28 October 1930, HLMP; "Zenith": H. L. Mencken to George S. Schuyler, 24 October 1930, JWJP.

33. "clodhopper": George S. Schuyler to H. L. Mencken, 31 December 1936,

HLMP; "constantly": H. L. Mencken to George S. Schuyler, 5 January 1937, HLMP.

34. George S. Schuyler to H. L. Mencken, 12 January 1937, HLMP. "Salvarsan" is a brand name for arsphenamine, a light-yellow powder formerly used in the treatment of syphilis and yaws.

35. H. L. Mencken to George S. Schuyler, 23 January 1937, HLMP.

36. "State": George S. Schuyler to Josephine Schuyler, 7 September 1935, Correspondence, 1916–1936, GSSP/SU; H. L. Mencken to George S. Schuyler, 15 January 1941, HLMP. In his response Schuyler admits to never having heard of the myth. He comments that despite his visits to the South, he still remains alien to the region: George S. Schuyler to H. L. Mencken, 18 January 1941, HLMP; "cents": George S. Schuyler to H. L. Mencken, 26 September 1937, HLMP. Schuyler reported such discoveries to aid Mencken in compiling information for *The American Language*.

37. This note, which comes from Mencken's diary, appears among Mencken's letters to Schuyler, HMLP. It is dated 14 October 1940.

38. Roselind C. Lohrfinick to George S. Schuyler, 1 October 1955, HLMP.

39. Ralph Matthews, "Watching the Big Parade," *Baltimore Afro-American*, 9 April 1932, SS, vol. 6.

CHAPTER 7: HOKUM AND BEYOND

1. George Hutchinson, *The Harlem Renaissance in Black and White* (Cambridge: Harvard University Press, 1995), 14–26.

2. Quoted in Arnold Rampersad, *The Life of Langston Hughes*, vol. 1 (New York: Oxford University Press, 1986), 130. In her letter to Schuyler, Kirchwey explained that his "extreme," "exaggerated," and "cocksure" tone had caused the editors of the *Nation* to go beyond the customary ten-day waiting period in deciding whether to publish "The Negro-Art Hokum." Although she admitted that Schuyler had made an interesting point that would "stir up considerable controversy," she also asked him if he would allow her to edit out of the article "a little of its violence." In any case, she wrote, the editors of the *Nation* wanted to wait for a response from James Weldon Johnson "or someone who holds a more race-conscious perspective." Freda Kirchwey to George S. Schuyler, 15 October 1925, GSSP/NY, Box 7, File 10.

3. "foolishness": George S. Schuyler, "The Negro Art-Hokum," *Nation* 122 (1926): 662; "people": ibid., 663.

4. "cartoonists" and "Goldberg": Ibid., 662. Florian Slappey was the main character of several racist comedies of black life written by Octavus Roy Cohen, whom Schuyler often mentioned in his editorials as the comic counterpart to Lothrop Stoddard and Madison Grant.

5. Ibid.

6. Ibid.

7. Langston Hughes, "The Negro Artist and the Racial Mountain," *Nation* 122 (1926): 694.

8. "issue": William Ingersol, "The Reminiscences of George S. Schuyler,"

Columbia University Oral History Office, Columbia University, New York, 1960, 78; "mountain": George S. Schuyler, "Negroes and Artists," *Nation* 123 (1926): 36.

9. Hughes, "Negro Artist and the Racial Mountain," 694.

10. "own" and "environment": Langston Hughes, "American Art or Negro Art?" *Nation* 123 (1926): 151.

11. "favor": This did not reflect the view of the *Nation*'s editors, whose position on the question of Negro art resembled Hughes's more than Schuyler's. Still, they did not close their pages to Schuyler's position. In June 1929 they published, under the pseudonym George W. Jacobs, Schuyler's "Negro Authors Must Eat," *Nation* 128 (1929): 710–711, which reiterated his contention that needy and greedy black authors served the white publishing industry by promoting stereotypes. The *Nation* also published Schuyler's acerbic "Blessed Are the Sons of Ham," *Nation* 124 (1927): 313–315. In addition, they published "Segregation *de Luxe*" by Augustus Adolphus Steward, *Nation* 131 (1930): 295–296, which repeated many aspects of the position Schuyler took in "The Negro-Art Hokum." "Depth": Morgan Mayo, "The 'Old Negro' as Artist," *Nation* 122 (1926): 724; "possible": Dorothy Fox, "Escaping Seventh Street," *Nation* 122 (1926): 36–37.

12. "develops": Headley E. Bailey, "Brown-Skinned Nordics," *Nation* 122 (1926): 37; "struggle": Michael Gold, "Where the Battle Is Fought," *Nation* 122 (1926): 37.

13. "roots": Fenton Johnson, "Literature Is a Mass Affair," *Amsterdam News*, 7 July 1926. This was Johnson's answer to J. A. Rogers's defense of Schuyler's position a week earlier. Johnson emphasized the peasant origins of great literature in order to refute Rogers's claim that Langston Hughes sentimentalizes the folk. See J. A. Rogers, "J. A. Rogers Discusses the Schuyler and Hughes Articles," *Amsterdam News*, 30 June 1926; "write": William N. Jones, "Day by Day," *Baltimore Afro-American*, 26 June 1926.

14. "American Negro Art," editorial in *Opportunity* 4 (1926): 238–239.

15. "*Messenger*": Between 1926 and 1928, the years when Schuyler had editorial control, Hughes published several poems and two short stories in the *Messenger*. His poetry included "Nocturne for the Drums," *Messenger* 9 (1927): 225, as well as "For Salome" and "Success," *Messenger* 9 (1927): 236. Hughes's short stories were "Bodies in the Moonlight," *Messenger* 9 (1927): 105–106, and "The Little Virgin," *Messenger* 9 (1927): 327–328. "Race": Hughes, "Negro Artist and the Racial Mountain," 693.

16. "bricks," "blank," and "yelp": VR, 12 February 1927. This review essentially repeated what Schuyler said in a letter to Hughes about his previous book of poetry, *The Weary Blues*. George S. Schuyler to Langston Hughes, 24 September 1925, LHP. See also George S. Schuyler to Langston Hughes, 27 January 1927, LHP. Although it started well, the relationship between Schuyler and Hughes eventually went downhill, mostly because of the diametrically opposed political development of each author. During the 1930s, just when Schuyler started to criticize communism more vocally, Hughes became more

devoted to it. In his 1934 review of Hughes's short-story collection *The Ways of White Folk*, Schuyler described Hughes as both a "devotee of the Communist Cult" and a "lampblacked Thomas Dixon." Despite his communist leanings, Schuyler said, Hughes played the role of race cheerleader in *The Ways of White Folk* with his narrow and unbelievable sketches of whites. VR, 30 June 1934.

17. Schuyler's one-act play "At the Coffee House," *Messenger* 7 (1925): 236–237, reveals well his bias against the aesthetes of Greenwich Village.

18. "Art and Propaganda," editorial in *Pittsburgh Courier*, 28 August 1926.

19. David Levering Lewis uses the phrase "civil rights by copyright" to suggest an alternate title for his *When Harlem Was in Vogue* (New York: Oxford University Press, 1981), xv–xvi; "toward him": VR, 3 April 1926. Also see James Weldon Johnson, preface to *The Book of American Negro Poetry* (New York: Harcourt Brace, 1931), 9.

20. VR, 3 April 1926.

21. VR, 14 January 1928.

22. In comparing blacks to the inmates of an insane asylum struggling to produce *The Mikado*, Schuyler comments implicitly on the low quality of plays produced for Harlem audiences in the 1920s. For more on this, see VR, 25 June 1927. Schuyler's friend Theophilus Lewis greatly influenced his ideas on this subject. For a good account of Lewis's ideas about the black theater, see Theodore Kornweibel, *No Crystal Stair: Black Life and the Messenger, 1917–1928* (Westport, Conn.: Greenwood Press, 1975), 107–118, and Hutchinson, *Harlem Renaissance*, 304–312.

23. George S. Schuyler, "Our Greatest Gift to America," in *Ebony and Topaz: A Colectanea*, ed. Charles S. Johnson (New York: Opportunity, 1929), 124.

24. "purchase" and "down": Ibid., 122.

25. "insight": W. E. B. Du Bois, *The Souls of Black Folk: The Writings of W. E. B. Du Bois* (New York: Library of America, 1986), 363–364; "understand it": George S. Schuyler, review of *The Gift of Black Folk*, by W. E. B. Du Bois, *Messenger* 6 (1924): 328 and 331; "*Illustrated Feature Section*": Schuyler showed this tendency especially in his promotion of J. A. Rogers, whom he encouraged during his term as editor of the *Messenger* to write a long series of articles on "black firsts" and great black figures in history. See, for example, J. A. Rogers, "Alexandre Dumas—The Immortal," *Messenger* 9 (1927): 185–186, and "Bilal Ibn Rahab—Warrior Priest," *Messenger* 9 (1927): 213–214.

26. The tensions between Du Bois and Fauset had strong personal connections, both romantic and financial. David Levering Lewis, *W. E. B. Du Bois: The Fight for Equality and the American Century* (New York: Henry Holt, 2000), 187–190.

27. "painted": Du Bois announced the symposium, which ran in the *Crisis* throughout 1926, in "A Questionnaire," *Crisis* 33 (1926): 165; "them": Hutchinson, *Harlem Renaissance*, 166.

28. W. E. B. Du Bois, "Criteria of Negro Art," *Crisis* 33 (1926): 297; and ibid., 290–297.

29. "Harlem": Rudolph Fisher, "The Caucasian Storms Harlem," *American Mercury* 11 (1927): 393–398; "playground": Lewis, *When Harlem Was in Vogue*, 162–165; "life": W. E. B. Du Bois, "Books," review of *Nigger Heaven*, by Carl Van Vechten, *Crisis* 33 (1926): 81–82. For a good account of the issues and debates surrounding the publication of *Nigger Heaven*, see Kathleen Pfeiffer, introduction to *Nigger Heaven*, by Carl Van Vechten (Chicago: University of Illinois Press, 2000), ix–xxxix.

30. In his announcement for the Krigwa Little Theater movement, Du Bois pronounced that the plays of a "real Negro theater" must be "about us," "by us," "for us," and "near us" (W. E. B. Du Bois, "Krigwa Players Little Negro Theatre," *Crisis* 31 [1926]: 134). If Du Bois's troupe had been able to follow this plan, Schuyler would have offered only praise. But when Du Bois's movement failed to live up to its ideals, Schuyler leaped at the chance to criticize it. Schuyler derided the Krigwa Players in VR, 14 May 1927, for portraying the Negro as a "praying, hymn-singing . . . half-wit . . . up to the ears in religiosity, voo-doo buncombe and the filth of the underworld."

31. It is important to note that Schuyler conducted much of his 1926 assault on the Harlem Renaissance while traveling through the South on his tour for the *Pittsburgh Courier*.

32. George S. Schuyler, "Shafts and Darts," *Messenger* 8 (1926): 9.

33. "pulpits": Ibid., 113; "spirituals": VR, 12 June 1926.

34. VR, 12 June 1926.

35. George S. Schuyler, "Shafts and Darts," *Messenger* 8 (1926): 259. Schuyler recalled in 1960 that he did not know Van Vechten very well during the 1920s because he did not associate with the artistic crowd much and was too busy "enjoying Harlem to be bothered about the Village." Ingersol, "Reminiscences," 115. Schuyler's published opinions on Van Vechten became much more appreciative over the years. Much later in his career Schuyler wrote a tribute to Van Vechten portraying him as a member of the "civilized minority" that helped to improve racial tolerance over the years. Also, Schuyler and his wife, Josephine, carried on a personal friendship with Van Vechten and his wife, Fania Marinoff, in the 1950s and 1960s. This included naming Van Vechten the godfather of their daughter, Philippa. See Schuyler, "The Van Vechten Revolution," *Phylon* 11 (1950): 362–368.

36. George S. Schuyler, "Shafts and Darts," *Messenger* 8 (1926): 259.

37. "Locke": Although he commented on art often in the late 1920s, Schuyler did not have much to say about Alain Locke. In his most substantial statement on Locke in the 1920s, Schuyler dismissed the Howard professor for "mourning about African art and the soulfulness of the spirituals" rather than focusing on the larger economic problems facing the black masses (VR, 19 May 1928). "Benefactors": George S. Schuyler, "Shafts and Darts," *Messenger* 8 (1926): 307.

38. VR, 6 November 1926.

39. Ibid.

40. "our people": Quoted in Herbert Aptheker, ed., *The Correspondence of W. E. B.*

Du Bois, vol. 1 (Amherst: University of Massachusetts Press, 1973), 382; "*Section*": this review appears in Schuyler's scrapbook, SS, GSSP/SU, vol. 4.

41. "Negro," "produced," and "everyday": VR, 2 March 1929.

42. Ibid.

43. VR, 14 April 1928.

44. VR, 25 December 1937; "early work": Hurston published several times in the *Messenger* between 1925 and 1926. "The Hue and Cry about Howard University," *Messenger* 7 (1925): 315–319, 338. She also published "The Eatonville Anthology" in three successive issues: *Messenger* 8 (1926): 261–262, 297, and 332. "Writing style": VR, 25 December 1937. Schuyler always had kind words for Hurston. In VR, 10 September 1938, he hailed her as the only black writer ever to make him laugh. He also remembered Hurston in complimentary terms late in his career. See Ingersol, "Reminiscences," 117.

45. VR, 24 March 1928. McKay's West Indian identity and strong connections with white intellectual circles in Greenwich Village figures heavily in the "blacker than thou" implication of Schuyler's review.

46. Ibid.

47. VR, 18 May 1929. Despite Schuyler's disparaging remarks concerning McKay's fiction, he did like the poem "If We Must Die." He led off VR, 19 July 1930, by quoting it in full. The contention between Schuyler and McKay resurfaced in 1937, when the two held a widely publicized radio debate on the question of black nationalism (see "Must the Negro Lose Himself Racially?" *Amsterdam News*, 5 June 1937). Following earlier statements in "The Separate State Hokum," *Crisis* 42 (1935): 135 and 148–49, Schuyler argued for the importance of interracial cooperation, while McKay asserted the necessity of group integrity and cooperation. Schuyler included all of the articles relevant to this debate in his scrapbook, GSSP/SU, vol. 14.

CHAPTER 8: "BLACK NO MORE"

1. For a good account of the satirical devices in the novel, see two articles by Michael W. Peplow: "George S. Schuyler, Satirist: Rhetorical Devices in 'Black No More,'" *CLA Journal* 18 (1974): 242–257, and "The Black 'Picaro' in Schuyler's 'Black No More,'" *Crisis* 83 (1976): 7–10.

2. The name "Disher" may refer to Schuyler's early days as a dishwasher. The character Santop Licorice (Marcus Garvey) of the Back-to-Africa Society (UNIA) is conspicuously absent from this meeting, which recalls the united effort of black leaders against Garvey in the early 1920s. Eventually Licorice, a black nationalist trickster, turns white and becomes a lackey for Matthew Fisher who, along with Joseph Bonds, gladly burns down Henry Givens's house, thus causing Matthew's wife, Helen, to miscarry. This act, both for and against the Knights of Nordica, comments implicitly on Garvey's antagonistic cooperation with the Ku Klux Klan, which set the majority of black leadership against him in the early 1920s. The name "Santop" also associates Garvey with the baseball player Louis Santop. See Jeffrey B. Ferguson, "The Newest Negro: George S. Schuyler's Intellectual Quest in the 1920s

and Beyond" (Ph.D. diss., Harvard University, 1998), 501–503. The name "Henry Givens" strikes a linguistic compromise between the last names of Colonel William Joseph Simmons, the itinerant preacher and rabble-rouser who reawakened the Ku Klux Klan in 1915, and Hiram Wesley Evans, the Imperial Wizard of the organization at the time Schuyler was writing. Matthew Fisher's role in the Knights of Nordica in part reflects that of Edward Y. Clarke of the Southern Publicity Association, who transformed the Klan of the 1920s into big business. Ferguson, "Newest Negro," 553.

3. "novel": Robert Bone, *The Negro Novel in America* (1958; reprint, New Haven: Yale University Press, 1965), 91. For a detailed review of the scholarly literature on *Black No More* from the 1930s until the 1980s, see Ferguson, "Newest Negro," 89–109, 485–492. "Category": Stacy Morgan, "'The Strange and Wonderful Workings of Science': Race, Science, and Essentialism in George S. Schuyler's 'Black No More,'" *CLA Journal* 42 (1999): 331–352; "science": Jeffrey A. Tucker, "Can Science Succeed Where the Civil War Failed? George S. Schuyler and Race," in *Race Consciousness*, ed. Judith Jackson Fossett and Jeffrey A. Tucker (New York: New York University Press, 1997), 136–151; "grace": Jane Kuenz, "American Racial Discourse, 1900–1930: Schuyler's 'Black No More,'" *Novel: A Forum on Fiction* 30 (1997): 169–192. For another version of this argument, see James A. Miller, foreword to *Black No More*, by George S. Schuyler (Boston: Northeastern University Press, 1989), 1–11. "Literature": J. Martin Favor, *Authentic Blackness: The Folk in the New Negro Renaissance* (Durham, N.C.: Duke University Press, 1999), 111–136, stands out for avoiding this pattern; "editions": currently, Northeastern University Press (Boston, 1989), Modern Library (New York, 1999), and the X Press (London, 1998) all publish editions of the novel.

4. H. L. Mencken, "Check List of New Books," *American Mercury* 22 (1931): xxxvi.

5. Lewis Gannett's review appeared in many places, including his column "Books and Other Things" in the *New York Herald Tribune*, 22 January 1931. See also Lewis Gannett to George S. Schuyler, GSSP/SU, vol. 4. "Revulsive": Roger Diddier, "Schuyler Tries Himself Out," SS, GSSP/SU, vol. 4; "opinion": Rudolph Fisher, "A Novel That Makes Faces," *New York Herald Tribune*, 1 February 1931. A full account of the extensive contemporary criticism of *Black No More* appears in the SS, GSSP/SU, vol. 4.

6. Dorothy Van Doren, "Black, Alas, No More!" *Nation* 132 (1931): 210–219.

7. "terms": Josephine Schuyler, "Black No More," ibid., 382; "live" and "levity": this letter appeared in Harry Hansen's column "The First Reader," *New York World*, 20 January 1931, in response to Hansen's favorable review of *Black No More* in the same column: "A Negro Satirist," *New York World*, 16 January 1931. All of this appears in SS, GSSP/SU, vol. 4.

8. "whales": James Ivy to the editor of the *New Republic*, 26 February 1931. See also James Ivy to the editor of the New York *Herald Tribune*, 25 January 1931, SS, GSSP/SU, vol. 4; "problem": James W. Ivy, "Paradise: Model 1940," *Norfolk Journal and Guide*, 24 January 1931, SS, GSSP/SU, vol. 4.

9. "Ivy": These reviews appear in SS, GSSP/SU, vol. 4; "increase": Alain Locke, "We Turn to Prose: A Retrospective Review of the Literature of the Negro for 1931," *Opportunity* 10 (1932): 43; "hurts": Arthur P. Davis, "Black Satire," *Opportunity* 9 (1931): 89–90; "New York Public Library": Theophilus Lewis, "Mr. Cullen Protests," *Amsterdam News,* 4 April 1931. This appears in SS, GSSP/SU, vol. 4. Countee Cullen also attended the meeting. In the article Lewis offers a humorous apology for accusing Cullen of not having read Schuyler's book. "Many others": all of these letters appear in SS, GSSP/SU, vol. 4.

10. The name of the character was actually Shakespeare Agamemnon Beard. Du Bois mistakenly reversed the first two names. W. E. B. Du Bois, "The Browsing Reader," *Crisis* 38 (1931): 100.

11. "Henry Lee Moon": George Goodman Jr., "George S. Schuyler, Black Author," *New York Times,* 7 September 1977; "professor": the first name "Shakespeare" also recalls in a humorous fashion the famous passage that begins "I walk with Shakespeare and he winces not" in W. E. B. Du Bois, *The Souls of Black Folk* (New York: Dover, 1994), 67.

12. "affairs": Schuyler gets most of the biographical detail from "The Shadow of Years," Du Bois's autobiographical essay in *Darkwater: Voices from within the Veil* (New York: Harcourt, Brace, 1920). The portrait of Beard implicitly satirizes this essay, where the author speaks of his past in elevated mythic tones; "Mars": BNM, 90.

13. "hand": BNM, 92; "announcement": Ibid. 218–219; "Von Beerde": ibid., 220. Beard's new name refers both to Du Bois's adoration for Germany and to his Harlem Renaissance nemesis Carl Van Vechten, whose role as the supreme white opponent of prejudice Beard exaggerates in his new identity. Also, the reference combines a mild suggestion of drunkenness (beer) with the idea that Beard had reached his "Nigger Heaven" in becoming white.

14. Ralph Ellison, "An Extravagance of Laughter," in *Going to the Territory* (New York: Vintage Books, 1995), 145–197.

15. Du Bois's biographer David Levering Lewis emphasizes the leader's effort to negate everything having to do with his own rather common background in the first two chapters of his *W. E. B. Du Bois: Biography of a Race, 1868–1919* (New York: Henry Holt, 1993).

16. "Chuck Foster": Hank Johnson seems partially modeled after Caspar Holstein, the Harlem numbers man and patron of the arts. Foster appears to represent the realtor Phillip A. Payton, who was known as "the father of Harlem." *Black No More* refers to famous popular culture and stage figures throughout. The character Siseretta Blandish, who in one of her guises represents both the millionaire queen of hair straightening, Mme. C. J. Walker, and her physically imposing daughter Alelia, also refers to Siseretta Jones, a black opera singer of the period whom racism forced to limit her talents to the minstrel stage. Also, legend has it that Jones's husband employed arsenic to lighten his wife's skin. Following a more comic version of this trajectory, Blandish moves from her marginal hair-straightening salon to

a bonanza business selling her Egyptienne Stain as the white woman Sari Blandine. For more on Blandish, see Ferguson, "Newest Negro," 532–536.

17. "psychology": BNM, 54; "investors": ibid., 55; "Sandol": one might interpret this as a light jab at Du Bois's romantic interest in Africa.

18. In an interview with Michael Peplow, Schuyler said that he had an actual Harlem surgeon in mind in fashioning the character of Dr. Crookman, but he declined to say who it was. Given his prominence and connection with the NAACP, Wright is the likely candidate. Peplow, *George S. Schuyler*, 126 note 42.

19. "vitiligo": BNM, 34 and 219; "period": see, for example, John Pfeiffer, "Black American Speculative Literature: A Checklist," *Extrapolation: A Journal of Science Fiction and Fantasy* 17 (1975): 35–43. Also Benjamin S. Lawson, "George S. Schuyler and the Fate of Early African-American Science Fiction," in *Impossibility Fiction: Alternativity—Extrapolation—Speculation*, ed. Derek Littlewood and Peter Stockwell (Amsterdam: Rodopi, 1996), 87–105. Many stories in science fiction journals of the period contain plots similar to that in *Black No More*. Schuyler may have read one or more of them. See R. D. Mullen, "The Black Mencken (and Black David H. Keller)," review of *Black No More* and *Black Empire*, by George S. Schuyler, *Science-Fiction Studies* 57 (1992): 267–269. For more on the connection between science fiction and *Black No More*, see Ferguson, "Newest Negro," 518–525.

20. BNM, 222.

21. "yellow women": BNM, 19; "Minnie": ibid., 17; "rejection": this scene also satirizes the many nightclub scenes in Harlem Renaissance literature. *Black No More* also satirizes other conventions of the race literature of the period, including the fascination with passing, primitivism, the fetishization of black folk culture, and sentimentalism, and implicitly questions the general goal of producing a separate black artistic tradition. "Resorts": BNM, 23.

22. "sinister" and "skin": BNM, 35.

23. BNM, 37–40.

24. "thorough": This also appears to be the suggestion in the name of Sybil's newspaper, *The Scimitar,* which carries with it a broad association with ancient warfare and castration; "die": Petronius, *The Satyricon,* trans. J. M. Mitchell (New York: E. P. Dutton, 1940), 100–101. The Cumean Sybil was one of the ten women prophets or witches of ancient legend. She wrote her prophecies on leaves that she afterward allowed the wind to scatter unheeded. As a general matter, the centrality of slavery in *The Satyricon* makes it a perfect way for Schuyler to declare by way of allusion his membership in the satirical tradition.

25. "despise": BNM, 70–71; "mother": BNM, 65–67, 79.

26. "feet": BNM, 24; "Matthew": BNM, 107.

27. "ancestry": For more on Schuyler's colorful grandmother, see Schuyler, "Black Art," *American Mercury* 27 (1932): 335–342. The reference to Helen of Troy brings with it a general association with the Trojan Horse as an ironic

metaphor for winning freedom through surreptitious race mixing. It is also worth noting that Schuyler refers to his own family background throughout the satire. Bunny Brown has the same last name as Schuyler's stepfather, Joseph Eugene Brown, whom he describes in his autobiography as a good but somewhat ridiculous man. This may associate the minor character Madeline Scranton, the wise and race-proud "sweet Georgia brown" who becomes Bunny's girlfriend at the end of the satire, with Schuyler's mother. Also, Matthew's marriage to Helen reflects and exaggerates some of the circumstances of Schuyler's relationship with Josephine, including the element of irresistible raw sexual attraction. "Now": BNM, 193; "individual": Matthew's choice to love his wife and his newborn also comes with a decision to turn away from ambition: "An angel of frankness beckoned him to be done with his life of pretense; to flee with his wife and son far away from everything." BNM, 188.

28. "pay": BNM, 120–131; "threatened": ibid., 131.

29. "parts" and "heels": BNM, 128.

30. BNM, 99–101.

31. See VR, 11 August 1928 and 3 November 1928 for typical examples of Schuyler's election analysis. For more on Black No More's political satire, see Ferguson, "Newest Negro," 541–547.

32. Schuyler began writing Black No More too early to gauge the larger impact of the election of 1928. While Smith was trounced, the new constituency he established proved a long-term gain for the Democrats, who would dominate the White House until the 1950s.

33. "Mississippi": BNM, 162. Schuyler most likely depicts Kretin as a senator from Georgia to honor Tom Watson. For more on his thoughts concerning the pragmatic trickery of race-baiting southern politicians, see his unsigned editorial "Senator Blease as a Gauge," Pittsburgh Courier, 19 July 1930; "and so on": BNM, 163.

34. "ignorant": BNM, 149; "Artillery Café": BNM, 146–147. It is also important to note that the "Bert" in "Albert" refers to the black minstrel Bert Williams. Bogalusa is a small town in Louisiana; it indicates the geographic origins of many of the black and white jazz musicians based in Chicago. At this time radio networks would only broadcast black bands locally; they never hired them for national shows. "Entertainers": see Paul Whiteman and Mary Margaret McBride, Jazz (New York: J. H. Sears, 1923). Here Schuyler appears to poke fun at his counterpart, H. L. Mencken, who claimed pontifically that whites produced the best jazz.

35. See "Sammy Stewart's Orchestra," Messenger 7 (1925): 44–45.

36. Here an implicit commentary on Amos 'n' Andy, the most popular radio show of the day, comes into play. Because the predominantly white audience could not see the actors, Schuyler reasoned, they could easily believe that the black stereotypes portrayed on the show represented actual black people, whom they typically regarded as invisible. For Schuyler's ideas on Amos 'n Andy, see VR, 24 May 1930.

37. "say": BNM, 117; "bear": BNM, 148.

38. "1930s": at this time Plecker was registrar of the Virginia Bureau of Vital Statistics, a job he held until 1946. Together with Ernest Sevier Cox, who published several eugenicist texts, including *White America* (Richmond, 1923) and *The South's Part in Mongrelizing the Nation* (Richmond, 1926), and the suspiciously dark John Powell (Arthur Snobbcraft), Plecker helped to organize and head the Anglo-Saxon clubs. This group proved instrumental in pressuring the Virginia legislature to pass three laws between 1924 and 1932 intended to enforce social separation of the races. For more on this see Richard B. Sherman, "'The Last Stand': The Fight for Racial Integrity in Virginia in the 1920s," *Journal of Southern History* 54 (1988): 69–92; Joel A. Rogers, *Sex and Race*, vol. 3 (New York: Helga M. Rogers, 1944), 19–20. For Schuyler's humorous reflections on the Virginia racial-integrity legislation, see "Hooray For Virginia," *Pittsburgh Courier*, 8 February 1930. George S. Schuyler to Walter White, 30 September 1929, George S. Schuyler Correspondence 1929–1937, the NAACP Papers, reel 23. "Aggression": although Plecker provides the main model for Samuel Buggerie, Schuyler probably had other researchers in mind in crafting this character, most notably Frederick L. Hoffman, author of *Race Traits and Tendencies of the American Negro* (1896) and statistician for the Prudential Insurance Company in New York. Also, more tangentially, he probably had in mind Ivan E. Mcdougal and Arthur H. Estabrook, who used data provided by Plecker to "prove" the inferiority of mixed-race people in *Mongrel Virginians* (Baltimore: Williams and Wilkins, 1926). J. A. Rogers appears to make the call for *Black No More* in his scathing review of this book in "Wanted: A Satirist," *Amsterdam News*, 21 July 1926. "Spectacles": BNM, 156; "notes": in this description Schuyler connects Buggerie obliquely to Robert Ferris, editor of the Garveyite publication *Negro World*, whom he described in similar terms in VR, 1 March 1930; "Revolutionary War": BNM, 179–180.

39. In one of his gestures toward Rabelaisian humor, Schuyler depicts Buggerie and Snobbcraft defecating in their pants after their narrow escape from the murderous crowd at the airport (BNM, 200). The connection here between homosexuality and fear combines with excrement in a way that indicates Schuyler's disapproval of more than the racial opinions of these characters.

40. "family trees": BNM, iv; "Work": BNM, 155, 156, and 197. One of Arthur Estabrook's books was called *The Nam Family: A Study in Cacogenics* (1912). The titles of Buggerie's books satirize the pseudoscientific quality of such research and the laughably obsessive obscurity of their interest.

41. "race": BNM, 215; "congregation": BNM, 216–217. This scene bears some resemblance to the lynching scene in Walter F. White, *The Fire in the Flint* (New York: Alfred Knopf, 1924), 236–237.

42. "flames" and "nostrils": BNM, 217. In Schuyler's exact words the flames "crackled merrily." "Americans": ibid., 217–218. The reluctant blacks in whiteface who cast stones at the charred remains of Snobbcraft and Buggerie exaggerate the position Walter White took many times in gathering data on

lynching for the NAACP by passing as a white man in the South. See also Walter White, "I Investigate Lynchings," *American Mercury* 16 (1929): 77–84. The implicit jab Schuyler gives White in the Happy Hill scene and in his depiction as the "voluntary Negro" Walter Williams grants some irony to White's role as a literary adviser to Schuyler during the production of *Black No More*. See George S. Schuyler to Walter White, 4 September, 10 September, and 17 September 1930, George S. Schuyler Correspondence, 1920– 1937, the NAACP Papers, reel 23. The fearful former blacks in the Happy Hill scene also bear a striking similarity to the nameless and confused light-skinned protagonist of James Weldon Johnson's *The Autobiography of an Ex-Colored Man* (New York: Random House, 1989), 187–188, who decides to pass for white permanently when the sight of a lynching makes him realize the ultimate futility and shame of being black. As reluctant participants in the lynch mob, Schuyler's nameless former blacks discover something similar about being white.

EPILOGUE: SINCERITY, AUTHENTICITY, AND RACE

1. "self": Lionel Trilling, *Sincerity and Authenticity* (Cambridge: Harvard University Press, 1972), 2; "like it": ibid., 1–6.
2. "surrounding it": Ibid., 15–16; "identity": ibid., 13–25.
3. "Abraham": Ibid., 99–100 and 120–122; "moments": ibid., 2, 92, and 99–100.
4. It is important to note that both of these critical positions stand against another influential position that sincerely celebrates the Harlem Renaissance for its expression of black cultural essence.

CREDITS

INDEX